PHILANTHROPIC FOUNDATIONS IN CANADA

LANDSCAPES, INDIGENOUS PERSPECTIVES AND PATHWAYS TO CHANGE

Edited by
Peter R. Elson
Sylvain A. Lefèvre
Jean-Marc Fontan

Philanthropic Foundations in Canada
Copyright © 2020 PhiLab

This research was supported by the Social Sciences and Humanities Research Council of Canada.

This work is licensed under the Creative Commons Attribution 3.0 Unported License. To view a copy of this license, visit http://creativecommons.org/licenses/by/3.0/ or send a letter to Creative Commons, PO Box 1866, Mountain View, CA 94042, USA.

Tellwell Talent
www.tellwell.ca

ISBN
978-0-2288-3004-7 (Hardcover)
978-0-2288-3003-0 (Paperback)
978-0-2288-3005-4 (eBook)

 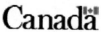

Dedicated to our dear
friend and colleague
Jack Quarter

1942–2019

Table of Contents

Introduction — 6
Peter R. Elson, Sylvain A. Lefèvre and Jean-Marc Fontan

Historical and contemporary landscapes of foundations in Canada — 11

→ A contextual history of foundations in Canada
Sylvain A. Lefèvre and Peter R. Elson — 13

→ Philanthropic Foundations Canada: Building a community and a voice for philanthropy
Hilary Pearson — 33

→ Financial accountability and reporting of foundations in Canada
François Brouard and Marc Pilon — 54

→ Donor-advised funds and charitable foundations in Canada
Carla Funk — 83

→ Corporate foundations: Cases and causes
Cathy Glover and Kelli Stevens — 108

Indigenous perspectives on philanthropy — 128

→ All My Relations: A journey of reciprocity
Stephen Couchman, Marilyn Struthers and Justin Wiebe — 130

→ Decolonizing philanthropy: Building new relations
Roberta Jamieson — 157

→ Relationship, reciprocity and respect: Reflecting on our journey at The Winnipeg Boldness Project
Gladys Rowe and Diane Roussin — 173

Pathways to change 189

→ The cost of social inequalities: Philanthropic field-building in Québec through the creation of the *Collectif des fondations* 191
Annabelle Berthiaume and Sylvain A. Lefèvre

→ Community foundations at work: Mobilizing and connecting place-based philanthropy 216
Laurel Carlton and Sara Lyons

→ Vancouver Foundation: Fostering meaningful engagement with youth 239
Natalie Ord

→ Centraide's Collective Impact Project: Poverty reduction in Montréal 262
Nancy Pole and Myriam Bérubé

→ Foundation House: More than just sharing space 287
Jehad Aliweiwi, Marcel Lauzière and Bruce Lawson

Reflections and conclusions 314

Tim Brodhead

→ Contributors 324

Introduction

Peter R. Elson,
Sylvain A. Lefèvre
and Jean-Marc Fontan

An understanding of the history, role, activities and impact of grantmaking foundations in Canada has never been more important. With media attention on the policy influence of foundations, the growing number of mega-foundations and the recent release (in 2018) of the shackles on non-partisan political activities, observers are starting to ask some very important and pertinent questions about grantmaking foundations. The story of these foundations, as profiled in this book, reflects, in our view, a turning point in the life-cycle of Canada's philanthropic landscape. There is still much to learn about grantmaking foundations in Canada, but there is now a considerable amount that is known, and this book is a testament to the new and ground-breaking knowledge that reflects a distinct Canadian foundation sector.

Within these pages you will hear the fresh voice of younger people who are part of the foundation ecosystem as well as the seasoned voice of experience. Although this book has been nurtured in an academic context, it is dominated by authors who are active, engaged and thoughtful practitioners. As such, they have much to share, and do so with enthusiasm and skill, and with the desire to share what they have learned with their fellow foundation leaders, academics and grant recipients. We are delighted to have contributions from foundation leaders and community-focused academics who bring an openness, candour and reflexivity to their writing – some of the most challenging questions come from within the sector itself. Grant recipient partners and other contributors provide an in-depth analysis of some recent trends in the foundation sector which are as interesting as they are challenging.

The contributors to this book speak from different academic disciplines and worldviews, a variety of foundation experiences, very distinct practitioner experiences and with important and diverse perspectives. Their concerns and questions about the role and relationship of philanthropy in general and foundations in particular are wide ranging, and they include probing questions about the democratic nature of the role of foundations in public policy and society at large (Reich *et al.*, 2016). Carla Funk, for example, through her profile of donor-advised funds (Chapter 4), explores the extent to which the assets of foundations are a means of private tax avoidance or enhanced public benefit. Roberta Jamieson (Chapter 7) challenges the very source of this wealth, its cost, and the exploitive practices that underlie the creation of foundations. The Circle (Chapter 6) and Berthiaume and Lefèvre (Chapter 9) also explore the role of foundations, and their founders, and the generative nature of social inequities and environmental degradation, both as exploiter and mitigator. These issues are directly connected, in our view, to the opportunity Canada currently faces to take responsibility and make reparation for its historic and on-going position as a settler–colonial state. These are also some of the issues authors in this book raise, and thus challenge foundation leaders and policy makers alike to ask themselves. Each chapter ends with three key takeaways the authors want readers to apply to their philanthropic or foundation policies and practice.

This book will appeal to policy makers and foundation leaders who want to understand the history of foundations in Canada and how that legacy continues to influence foundation formation and practice today. For foundation staff, this book provides new insights into the nature and growth of donor-advised funds, corporate foundation funding models and the complex nature of accountability and reporting. For students of philanthropy, there are inspirational examples of foundation collaboration and cooperation, locally, regionally and nationally. Instructors and researchers will find not only insights through case studies but also inspiration for future research founded in community practice. There is not just a nominal nod to, but what we hope is a substantive profile of, the relationship between foundations and Indigenous people and communities in Canada. Each of the three chapters written by Indigenous authors, in their own way, challenges foundations to re-examine their colonial and exploitative history (and its current manifestation in Indigenous relations) and operational and funding policies.

Climate change, social and economic inequalities, and a chronic disconnect between resource and land exploitation and economic growth are all issues that Canada is not alone in finding both divisive and connecting. There are no "correct" solutions for these typically complex issues or "messy problems", all of which require the exercise of significant judgment and involve multiple stakeholders with conflicting goals (Hester & Adams, 2017). Can foundations play a role in addressing some of these issues? In one context it would be easy to think that they can, and are. Foundations, after all, are uniquely placed to make a difference: they may be sanctioned and regulated by the federal government, but they operate with considerable autonomy. Foundations, by definition, are registered charities with independent (non-market) resources and a mandate to provide quasi-public goods affiliated with education, health, poverty reduction and other state-designated public benefits (Anheier, 2005).

At the same time most, although certainly not all, foundations are place-based, providing a range of supports to a particular location or region. Most foundations are not large operations with full-time staff and ambitious mandates. We note this because the expectations of foundations in general are often projected from the activities of a few, large and ambitious foundations. Foundations can, however, and should, be part of the solution whenever action is taken with respect to the environment, the restitution of First Nation, Inuit and Métis lands and sovereignty, and social and economic inequalities. Part 3 of this edited book is dedicated to providing profiles of foundations that are doing just this.

To date, the story of foundations in Canada, with very few exceptions, has been told by the foundations themselves, through media profiles of gift award events, or by organizations linked or associated with them. The history of foundations and their founders has largely been theirs to tell, and the dominant narrative has been one of benevolence and good works, particularly in the areas of education, health and social services (Philanthropic Foundations Canada, 2017). As the number, and particularly the size, of foundations increases, as the potential transfer of massive wealth from aging baby boomers looms, and as foundations take a more active role in non-partisan political activities, different questions start to emerge. Yet only recently have a number of researchers and writers started to move beyond profiling the nature and size of foundations grants to ask significantly different questions about the role of foundations in society.

In Part One the emphasis is on profiling the foundation landscape in Canada: its history, the emergence of a voice for the philanthropic sector, the growing importance of transparency and accountability, the complex and mercurial world of donor-advised funds, and the underpinnings of corporate philanthropy. In Part Two, Indigenous voices speak to their own history and the challenges and opportunities associated with foundation–Indigenous relations, particularly in connection with the calls for action by the Truth and Reconciliation Commission (Truth and Reconciliation Commission of Canada, 2015). Roberta Jamieson provides a poignant and pointed challenge to build new relations by decolonizing philanthropy. The Winnipeg Boldness Project profile provides an insight into balancing Indigenous ways of being, feeling and doing in relationship with foundation partners.

Part Three, Pathways to Change, highlights the innovative and empowering ways foundations engage with youth, poverty, local communities, public policy – and each other. Community foundations provide insights into the complex web of mobilizing place-based foundations within a federally funded mandate. The Vancouver Foundation reveals the implications of making intimate connections with youth. The Collective Impact Project investigates the inside story behind a five-year collaborative partnership; and the Foundation House profile walks us through the principles and practical operational issues in a place-based foundation-to-foundation relationship.

The focus of this book is on foundations, but it has been written within the broader context of philanthropy. Philanthropy is not just an individual choice and a moral commitment. Philanthropy is also a collective issue, because the actions of foundations affect all spheres of society (e.g. health, poverty, culture, education, environment). Foundation resources come from the accumulation of private resources but, critically, also from public contributions – through tax credits – and thus these philanthropic resources constitute a collective venture capital that society as a whole has built.

The core need for all sectors of society to address the ecological crisis and growing inequalities requires philanthropists to critically examine their motives and priorities. The exponential accumulation of private capital and its placement in a financial market that feeds a productivist and extractivist economic system are simply not compatible with the need for a socio-ecological transition. This is the societal context, and the social licence that is a fundamental challenge for foundations. Foundations, in our view, are destined to profoundly change their donation practices, their use of their economic capital, the scale and impact of their actions, and the collaborations they weave. This book is intended to feed that reflection and support the practices of a philanthropic sector in full transformation. We hope that the diversity of insights and voices in this book will foster a deeper and more connected relationship with, and between, foundations, grantees, communities and Canadian society.

References

Anheier, HK (2005) *Nonprofit Organizations: Theory, management, policy*. New York: Routledge

Hester, PT & KM Adams (2017) *Systemic Decision Making: Fundamentals for addressing problems and messes* (2nd ed.). Cham, Switzerland: Springer

Philanthropic Foundations Canada (2017) 'Snapshot of foundation giving in 2015'. Montreal. Retrieved from: https://pfc.ca/wp-content/uploads/2018/05/pfc-snapshot-giving-2015.pdf

Reich, R, Cordelli, C & L Bernholz (2016) *Philanthropy in Democratic Societies: History, institutions, values*. Chicago: University of Chicago Press

Truth and Reconciliation Commission of Canada (2015) 'Truth and Reconciliation Commission: Calls to action'. Winnipeg. Retrieved from: http://trc.ca/assets/pdf/Calls_to_Action_English2.pdf

Part One

Historical and contemporary landscapes of foundations in Canada

11   Philanthropic foundations in Canada

Part One, Historical and contemporary landscapes, gathers together the first five chapters of the book, which provide an overview of the following key elements in the foundation ecosystem in Canada:

- The early history of foundations in Canada
- A detailed profile of the evolution of foundations in Quebec
- The evolution of Philanthropic Foundations Canada (PFC) as a leading voice for private foundations
- How PFC reaches across Canada and leads, connects, educates and supports the whole private foundation community
- The connection between accountability and the ecosystem in which foundations operate
- The increased need for transparency and standardization
- Insights into the nature and role of designated funds and the massive multi-billion-dollar baby boomer wealth transfer
- Corporate philanthropy – where it has come from, how it works and where it is going

Part One
Chapter One

A contextual history of foundations in Canada

Sylvain A. Lefèvre and Peter R. Elson

Philanthropy in general speaks to the altruistic act of giving with thankfulness and the act of reciprocity and selfless generosity. Foundations, as part of the philanthropic ecosystem, are an institutionalized, state-recognized and supported public or private means to redistribute public goods. The history of foundations – from the Middle Ages, through the Age of Enlightenment, global colonialism, the industrial revolution and the modern age – is also the history of resource extraction, wealth creation and accumulation, and the subsequent private redistribution of public goods. What makes these private goods public in Canada is that the purpose of all charities (which all foundations are) must focus on one of four state-sanctioned "pillars of charity". These four "pillars" are: relief of poverty, advancement of education, advancement of religion, and other purposes beneficial to the community in a way the law regards as charitable (Canada Revenue Agency, 2018). Our intention here is to briefly outline some of the historical influences on the nature of foundations in Europe and the USA, before turning our attention to Canada.

Europe: The genesis of local and charitable foundations

In Europe, since the Middle Ages, religious foundations, especially those of certain monastic orders such as the Benedictines and Franciscans, collected bequests and donations, in kind or in cash, to establish asylums and hospitals for the poor, the homeless and the sick. These religious foundations were tolerated provided they remained local and had a charitable mandate. Their expansion, particularly through mortmain properties (which are inalienable possessions that are exempted from taxes and death duties), was seen as a potential threat by the political powers of the day. In France, for example, the holding of such resources by the Catholic Church generated a rivalry with a centralized state in the making. For these two reasons, foundations were ostracized by a state that saw itself as having a monopoly over public interest missions, and deliberately kept intermediary, community and religious bodies at bay.

In the 19th century, foundations regained a certain status primarily as secular foundations and with the aim of reconciling the expansion of a nation state with the diversification of interests of civil society (Anheier, 2001). In an age characterized by flourishing industry and commerce, and an emerging urban proletariat, foundations were formed by the new market elites in England, the Netherlands, Germany and Austria. Overall, foundations across Europe in the 19th century tended to have local and specific mandates and to remain at the municipal or parish level. This market elitism was fueled, in no small way, by imperial expansion, colonial dispossession of Indigenous peoples and resource exploitation around the world, including the USA and Canada.

Philanthropists and the foundations they created not only embody economic capital (e.g. Ford – car industry; Rockefeller – oil industry; and most recently Gates – computer technology) but also social capital. This relationship is synergistic. Branding of philanthropic foundation activities enhances reputation, prestige, and recognition, which are equally valuable to business interests (Morvaridi, 2015). While altruistically "giving back" is a noted motivation for establishing a foundation, it's certainly not the only reason; others are the importance of establishing a positive legacy, an attempt at reparation, penance, and relief of guilt from engaging in exploitative capitalistic practices that are sometimes contrary to religious or moral norms (Whitaker, 1974). As we will see, the role foundations undertake continues to reflect not only the very corporate business strategies that generated wealth in the first place, but also the political context that shaped them, especially the role given to philanthropy by the State.

Table 1 – Historical timeline

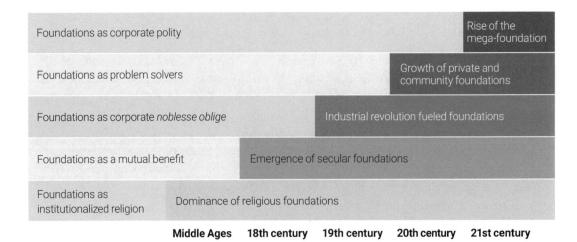

United States: The birth of modern foundations

Compared with Europe, the United States is often presented as a philanthropic paradise with regard to foundations, reflecting an other-than-government role and considerable public recognition. It should be noted, however, that what is now being denoted as a "foundation" has little to do with the religious and charitable heritage from medieval Europe; the foundation, as an institution, was reinvented in the United States at the end of the 19th century. In this case the foundation was built around a particular institutional form, the *trust*, which survives beyond its founder and is recognized as a distinct corporate entity by the legal, fiscal and political system (Zunz, 2012, p. 12, our translation).

During the American industrial revolution, the unparalleled creation of wealth – compared to other continents – together with the pace of wealth accumulation within one generation – did not take place without raising significant challenges. This growth was accompanied by a strong rise in inequalities,[1] dispossession of traditional native territories, and the emergence of an urban

---

[1] The wealthiest percentile of the population owned approximately 30% of assets in the United States in 1860; it owned more than 45% in 1910 (Piketty, 2013, p. 555).

proletariat, often living under deplorable conditions. The image of these captains of industry, dubbed "robber barons", cast a dark shadow on the foundations they created. These entrepreneurs – such as Cornelius Venderbilt, John Rockefeller and Andrew Carnegie – made fortunes during the second industrial revolution (steel, oil, mining, automotive, railway, finance) using methods severely condemned by the press, unions and government. The press, for example, penned articles by "muckrakers" against Standard Oil of Rockefeller;[2] trade unions protested against appalling working conditions and repressive violence; and the government changed corporations under antitrust laws.

The foundation thus became a "problem-solving machine". Problems invariably change with time, though, and these changing problems forced the foundation to adapt, for example by changing the allocation of its funds, the type of projects funded, or the terms of its support, rather than insisting on the strict adherence to the mandate of its founder (Anheier & Hammack, 2013). This institutional innovation was the result of a political and legal compromise in relation to a number of complex issues in the early 20th century in the United States. American foundations can be described as "a hybrid capitalist creation, at the intersection of philanthropy and state: not being subject to taxes insofar as its profits are reinvested in the common good, it nevertheless operates under the same principles as businesses" (Zunz, 2012, p. 12, our translation).

In this regard, Andrew Carnegie's essay *The Gospel of Wealth*, written in 1889, was like a bible for American founders such as Rockefeller and Mellon. Carnegie, "the richest man in the world" at the time, was the founder of one of the first American foundations in 1911. He affirmed his responsibility to give back to society a part of what he had gained, but did so using the same business principles with which he had made his fortune in steel. In other words, philanthropy was no longer seen as a gift but as an investment.

Whereas traditional charity bore the hallmarks of being altruistic and gratuitous, organized philanthropy was now managed with the rigour and method of a capitalist enterprise. At the turn of the century, the captains of industry who created their own foundations – Russell Sage (1907), Rockefeller (1913) and, later, Kellogg (1930) and Ford (1936) – shared common motives and ambitions in this regard. First, their activities no longer addressed only the poorest, but the whole of humanity, or, to use a then fashionable phrase, "the progress of mankind". Second, their aim was to reform society without going through government bodies. Third, this reform was to be undertaken through an alliance with like-minded reformist networks and the support of a science that promised to solve social issues with technological means. Their mantra was not to deal with the consequences of social problems, but with their roots, *through* entrepreneurial and scientific approaches (Sealander, 2003). This philosophy may have funded the eugenics-related research, but it also led to the construction of public institutions.

---

2   Reverend Washington Gladden, figurehead of the Social Gospel movement in the United States, in 1905 censured churches and universities that accepted "tainted money" from Rockefeller, declaring such money to have been acquired by unethical and monopolistic practices.

This explains the flourishing of libraries, museums, hospitals and universities (such as those created by Johns Hopkins in Baltimore, Ezra Cornell in Ithaca, Leland Stanford in Palo Alto, Rockefeller in Chicago, and Vanderbilt in Nashville, for example) that were funded by foundations in the early 20th century, new institutions that produced and disseminated knowledge (O'Connor, 2001).

The First World War changed public opinion about the "robber barons", insofar as their fortunes contributed to the war effort and relief abroad. In the United States, philanthropy in its elitist form (large foundations) and in its more common form (small donations) became an expression of patriotism (Zunz, 2012). A second change was the institutionalization of foundations, within which the founders gradually had to give way (if they hadn't already passed away) to professional management, fund allocation committees, and program officers who ensured a liaison with the funded organizations.

Similarly, during the Second World War and the Cold War, American foundations operating abroad identified closely with the political, cultural, diplomatic and economic objectives of their government – from the "Green Revolution" financed by the Rockefeller Foundation, to the recruitment of intellectuals from Western Europe by the Ford Foundation – and were soon blamed for breaking the limits of their mandate and "playing politics". During McCarthyism in the 1950s, for example, the Carnegie Endowment was accused of being infiltrated by communists; and, during the civil rights riots of the 1960s, the Ford Foundation was accused of supporting unruly social movements (O'Connor, 2011).

Overall, the 20th century was characterized by an oscillation between support for, and disapproval of, tax exemptions for foundations, alternating between a virtuous incentive and an exorbitant expense and loss of tax revenue. This oscillation was essentially determined by economic conditions, problems of state budgets, and a political debate about the legitimacy of philanthropic foundations.

In line with these concerns, in the 1960s and 1970s American foundations engaged in a period of questioning and role reflection. The Patman Commission in 1963 condemned the lack of transparency of foundations, and the political influence and tax privileges they enjoyed. It also identified a number of financial abuses and serious cases of maladministration among foundations (Riecker, 1964). The pressure was so strong that Congress considered ordering all foundations to spend their funds within the next forty years, and then to cease operations. Although this recourse was rejected, a strict regulation on foundations was enacted that required minimum expenditures of 6% of the endowment each year and which prohibited the owning of more than 20% of a company, among other stipulations (see *Tax Reform Act* of 1969).

Canada: From American and British influence to the development of its own approach to philanthropy

There are strong similarities in the genesis of the American and Canadian foundations. In many cases it is not always possible to identify whether a given feature resulted from the influence of American foundations on Canadian foundations or vice versa; both, after all, emerged under similar structural and economic conditions and, in both countries, the *British Charitable Trust Act* (1853) served as the first legal guideline. In Canada, as in England, the definition of charity was determined by the judicial interpretation given to the Pemsel case (1891). There are four legitimate purposes to an organization's establishment for it to be recognized as a charity, and to obtain the related fiscal and legal recognition: poverty relief, advancement of education, advancement of religion, and other activities beneficial to the community. Despite interpretative and legal wrangling, and calls for change (Chan, 2007), these are still the same criteria used by the Canada Revenue Agency to determine charitable purposes.[3]

In addition, the chronologies, founder profiles, and charitable purposes supported in Canada have striking similarities to those of American foundations. For example, the first Canadian foundation, the Massey Foundation, was established in 1918. The Masseys, a Methodist Protestant family that was both Canadian and American, had made its fortune in agricultural equipment manufacturing. Its Foundation, in which the family members sat, and still sit as trustees, financed the creation of a number of cultural and educational institutions in Toronto (Hart House Theatre, Massey Hall, Massey College at the University of Toronto). Vincent Massey, who quickly took lead of the foundation, was strongly influenced by George E Vincent, his mother's half-brother and none other than the president of the Rockefeller Foundation in the United States (Fong, 2008, p. 514).

Studying the evolution of the legal and fiscal frameworks for foundations in Canada and the United States, Iryna Kryvoruchko (2013) also identified many similarities. With little state interference in both Canada and the United States, a form of trust was initially used to create foundations. These foundations were created by wealthy entrepreneurs who had made their fortune rapidly during the industrial revolution, as a means of sheltering their wealth. Over time, the state developed a twofold position with regard to foundations. First, it wanted to avoid the situation in which a financial power takes root that is exempt from any public obligations or temporal limitations; to prevent this, the federal governments instituted laws requiring foundations to transfer a share of their annual profits to the government. Second, at certain times,

---

3 https://www.canada.ca/en/revenue-agency/services/charities-giving/charities/policies-guidance/guidance-017-general-requirements-charitable-registration.html

especially during the two world wars, the state implemented tax incentives allowing it to benefit from the philanthropic resources of foundations.

When comparing more precisely the chronology of transformations in the legal and fiscal framework with regard to these philanthropic issues, Canada was often found to copy and tag along after its southern neighbour. For example, the first tax deductions to encourage philanthropy emerged during the First World War.[4] In the United States, tax deductions for donations from individuals to foundations were first granted in 1917, and tax exemptions for foundations followed in 1921. In Canada, approved registered charitable institutions were exempt from taxes from 1917. Charitable donations, of up to 10% of one's income, were first rendered deductible from taxes for individuals and businesses in 1932. The regulation on foundations followed a similar course. After the Second World War, foundations had to register with the fiscal authority (1943 in the United States and 1967 in Canada) and comply with the *Tax Reform Act* (1969 in the United States and 1977 in Canada), which requires them to make annual transfer payments of a portion of their capital. Starting with the 1980s, the level of that disbursement was gradually lowered.[5]

Despite the parallel timelines, foundations in Canada remained relatively weaker than those of the United States.[6] For example, in the United States, the between-war period gave rise to many powerful foundations (including the Ford Foundation in 1936), whereas only two foundations were created in Canada in the three decades following the establishment of the Massey Foundation: the Winnipeg Foundation and the McConnell Foundation. The Winnipeg Foundation (1921) was the first community foundation in Canada and was created with an initial endowment of $100,000 Canadian dollars from William Forbes Alloway. The amazing journey of this veterinarian-cum-trader-banker-investor, and one of the first millionaires of Winnipeg, is reminiscent of the profiles of the American robber barons, if the practicing of controversial business methods, the building of a notable status (seat in the Winnipeg City Council, governor of the Winnipeg General Hospital) and the creation of a sustainable philanthropic institution are anything to go by (Hanlon, 2003). Nearly a century later, the Community Foundation of Winnipeg

---

[4] It was also the First World War that saw the introduction, in several European countries, of the first laws on income tax and on tax deductions for philanthropic donations. Both types of law had the same objective: to finance, first, the war effort and then the reconstruction. The first law, however, established the pillars of the welfare state, both as financial resources to invest and as a redistributive tool by progressive taxation; the second law laid the basis for philanthropic solicitation ... and the associated lost tax gain!

[5] For a political-economic analysis of the context and the motivations for these policy decisions in Canada, see Charbonneau, 2012.

[6] Although we cannot focus here on the many factors that explain the differences in the paths taken by the United States and Canada on these issues, one point is worth emphasizing: in Canada, a major share of the domestic capital – one quarter in the early 20th century – is owned by foreign (in particular, British) investors, while this share has never exceeded 5% in the United States (Piketty 2013, p. 247).

is still a very large organization that, through its housing of 2,700 capitalized funds, allocated $411 million Canadian dollars to more than 900 charities for the year 2018.[7]

The McConnell Foundation was created in 1937 following the donation of J W McConnell. The biography of this person also mirrors that of some of the American "robber barons". McConnell was revered by some as the self-made man who started with nothing and became one of the richest Canadians, making a fortune in multiple sectors (mining, insurance, transport, sugar refinery, finance), and distributing it massively, anonymously or through his foundation, to the point of being considered one of the greatest philanthropists in 20th-century Canada. He was also a devout Protestant, from the Methodist Church, as was the Massey family, to whom he was close. But he was also criticized by some who "reviled [him] as the symbol of English oppression of French Canada, an anti-Semite, an unbending big business Tory, an exploiter of the working class, and enemy of academic and press freedom" (Fong, 2008). The diverging analyses of his personality aside, he stood out for having achieved significant positions of power within the Canadian elite, in addition to his dominance in the economic sector. McConnell enjoyed close ties to prime ministers: Mackenzie King at the federal level, and both Taschereau and Duplessis at the provincial level (*ibid.*).

These connections were both cross-border and mutually beneficial. Mackenzie King was close friends with both John W McConnell and John D Rockefeller. Mackenzie King also worked at the Rockefeller Foundation from 1914 to 1918, as head of the new Department of Industrial Relations, and advised Rockefeller following the fatal Ludlow Massacre of 1914. He was also approached to head the management of the Carnegie Foundation in 1918 (he declined) before he went on to become Canada's tenth Prime Minister in 1921.

McConnell was publisher and owner of the *Montreal Star* newspaper, governor (for thirty years) of McGill University and of the Royal Victoria Hospital, and he demonstrated his patriotism by making generous donations during the two world wars. Modelled after the three pillars (health, education and arts) of the US-American foundations which inspired him,[8] McConnell's foundation financed McGill University, the Montreal Neurological Institute, the Salvation Army, the United Church, the YMCAs, the Old Brewery Mission, the Royal Victoria Hospital and the Montreal General Hospital. Today, the McConnell Foundation remains very important in the Canadian philanthropic landscape, not only because of the amount of funding it allocates, but also because of its role as guide and steward for various pan-Canadian projects and charitable sector issues (Brodhead, 2011; Pearson, 2007).

This brief portrait of Canadian foundations reveals a sector which is gradually asserting its independence from the economic, political and religious domains from which it originates,

---

7 https://www.wpgfdn.org/Portals/0/Uploads/Documents/Publications/WpgFdn_2018_Annual_Report_Summary.pdf
8 His two main inspirations were the Rockefeller Foundation and the Millbank Foundation (Fong, 2008, pp 515–16).

yet to which it nevertheless maintains a preferential relationship. For example, in the Massey family, whose foundation did so much for the arts and culture in Toronto, one of the founder's grandsons, Vincent, became the first governor general born in Canada (1952–59). Vincent Massey also occupied other important positions, including chairmanships of the Arts and Letters Club (1920–21), and of the Royal Commission on National Development in the Arts, Letters and Sciences of Canada (1949–51), called the Massey Commission. The latter advocated funding of cultural activities by the federal government and thus gave rise to the establishment of public institutions such as the National Library of Canada (now Library and Archives Canada) and the Canada Council for the Arts.

Sometimes, the foundations were directly involved in the structuring of a public service, as was the case, for example, with the Rockefeller Foundation, which, in line with its commitment to support education in the medical field in Canada, from the 1920s financed the leading Canadian universities, such as McGill University, to launch a medical school (Fedunkiw, 2005).

Foundations, having to support designated grantees (i.e. other registered charities), are a significant source of financial support for community organizations and the third sector, particularly in areas where there is mission alignment. The complementary role that foundations play in this regard is most often influenced by the chronic shortage of full-service government funding and the absence of viable private market activity. For example, when there was a period of generous Welfare State growth, core funding and experimental programming in the 1960s, philanthropic support to social agencies was seen as less crucial. Since the mid-1990s, however, with the onset of budget cuts and short-term contract funding, support from foundations has become very valuable for community organizations (Elson, 2011). Foundations have thus become one of the few sources of genuine social sector program and policy research and development.

In the context of the current public funding paradigm, built on the principles of New Public Management and the subsequence increase in competitive, short-term contract funding (Smith & Lipsky, 1993), foundations find themselves again assuming the role of alternative fundraiser. In the 1990s, a group of national organizations, the Voluntary Sector Roundtable, formed and met to reflect on the relationship of the voluntary sector with the federal government, particularly on funding issues and best practices. This roundtable was chaired by former New Democratic Party leader Ed Broadbent and funded, not by the government, but by major foundations, including the McConnell Foundation (Elson, 2007). Foundations have also taken the lead in advocating for the most recent dramatic change to the *Income Tax Act*, namely eliminating any constraints on non-partisan political activities and, as profiled in Chapter 9, in speaking out against government austerity programs.

Before discussing these more recent transformations of the role of foundations, we present an overview of the foundation sector in Quebec, which differs from the one previously outlined for the rest of Canada.

Quebec: A philanthropic history that beats to a different rhythm

In many ways, the evolution of Quebec philanthropy is the exact opposite of what was observed for the rest of Canada. On the one hand, Quebec is hardly a model for philanthropy, the average donation in Quebec in 2013 being less than half (C$213) of the rest of Canada (C$437) (Devlin & Zhao, 2017). The volunteer rate, likewise, is lower in Quebec (32% against 44%), as is the average number of volunteer hours provided annually (123 against 154, 2013 figures). On the other hand, the province is home to the McConnell Foundation, for decades the largest private foundation in Canada, and to the Lucie and André Chagnon Foundation, one of the best endowed and most active foundations today.

Quebec has stronger mechanisms fostering social solidarity than the rest of Canada. For example, 40% of all cooperatives in Canada are in Quebec, although the province has less than a quarter of the country's inhabitants.[9] Moreover, the level of public spending, as a percentage of the GDP, especially on social programs, is greater here than in the rest of Canada, and is borne by a higher tax rate. Finally, the rate of unionization in Quebec is the second highest in Canada, with a rate of 36.3% in 2011 against 29.7% in the rest of Canada. We can conclude that Quebec has a weaker level of philanthropic engagement than the rest of Canada, yet at the same time its low-income brackets and structural income inequality are also less pronounced (Lefèvre et al., 2011, pp. 117–49).

This situation results from the unique history of this province within Canada and from its features. These features tend to solicit a number of simplistic conclusions, be it with regard to language (i.e. the drawback of French in trade between Canada and the United States), the weight of the Catholic Church (compared with Protestantism) or the centrality and verticality of the state, perceived as a legacy of French Jacobinism.

When the Industrial Revolution was in full swing and the first foundations were being set up in North America, Quebec was moving to a different rhythm. There were, certainly, social patrons and bourgeois philanthropists, who generally associated themselves with the hygienist movement. And there was a strong mutualist movement that provided members with services that were covered by neither the market nor the state (e.g. financial compensation in the case of disability, pensions to widows and orphans) by pooling resources and establishing mutual support networks. In the early 20th century, more than one in three men were members of such fraternal benefit societies in major Quebec cities (Petitclerc, 2008, p. 400).

---

9 The definition of "third sector", as used in Canada, excludes social economy organizations (including cooperatives and mutuals), an essential component in the Quebec economy.

The ideal of mutual support values the collective and not the individual, and the egalitarian rather than the paternalistic compassion of elites. The mutualist movement, which began in the 1910s, was subsequently supplanted by the rise of trade unionism, the slow emergence of social welfare programs and the commodification of insurance services. Yet, another collective practice took shape at the time with the development of savings and credit cooperatives, starting with the creation in 1900 of the first credit union by Alphonse Desjardins, whose history is well known.

At the end of the First World War, the economic crisis and the Spanish flu hit hard in Quebec, prompting the provincial government to implement the *Public Assistance Act* (1921). With this pioneering Act, the government and municipalities were required to finance two-thirds of the support to the sick, poor senior citizens, babies and orphans cared for and placed in hospitals, hospices and orphanages. In fact, this measure served primarily to compensate for the lack of structured philanthropy in the French Catholic setting, at a time when the Jewish and Protestant communities had already organized their own charities in Montreal (Ferretti, 2013).

When the great economic crisis of 1929 had exhausted this new social model, the municipalities set up direct distribution systems (donations of food, clothing and household heating fuel) to mitigate the poverty created by endemic unemployment. Such systems were conceived of as auxiliary measures only, however, with the state and municipalities assuming that this responsibility essentially lay with the Church and the family. Then, in the 1930s and 1940s the first social programs were gradually implemented by the federal and Quebec governments, including old age pensions, allowances for needy mothers, unemployment insurance, family allowances, and other types of support. But it was especially after the Second World War that the welfare state developed a strong structure at the federal level, with the implementation of the Marsh Report, discussed earlier, and the establishment of a public and collective social security system. Yet here as well Quebec took a different route.

Back in power, Maurice Duplessis (1944–59) fought at the province-wide level against the strengthening of the welfare state, which he saw as a precursor of socialism and ultimately communism. In particular, he sealed an alliance with the Catholic Church and the dioceses, thereby strengthening the power of the latter. In that context, the religious institutions, becoming ever larger, began taking charge of multiple mandates in the field of health, education and even entertainment. Conventional philanthropy was stymied through incessant collections organized at the level of the dioceses as well as in the cities through fraternal benefit organizations such as the Chevaliers de Colomb, the Richelieu and the Voyageurs du commerce (*ibid.*). During this post-war period, while in the United States and Europe solidarity and social policies were increasingly regulated by government policies and fiscal measures, older forms of local, charitable and religious philanthropy thus still dominated in Quebec.

This period of time was rather slow for foundations elsewhere in Canada,[10] but Quebec engaged in the creation of very large foundations such as the Bronfman Family Foundation (1952), the J Armand Bombardier Foundation (1965), the R Howard Webster Foundation (1967) and the Macdonald Stewart Foundation (1967). The largest foundation of the time, the McConnell Foundation, for its part, benefited from a very close relationship between its founder and Maurice Duplessis, who dubbed the former 'Big Heart'. James W McConnell provided strong support for the Premier in his fight against the 'specter of communism', which was seen to threaten Canada (Fong, 2008, pp. 400–10). Through his foundation, or through direct donations, he funded a number of initiatives in Trois-Rivières (home city of Duplessis), which included the reconstruction of a damaged bridge, support to a Carmelite monastery and the near-complete financing of a recreational centre (Mrg-St-Arnaud Pavilion).

The new wind that blew in with the Quiet Revolution in the 1960s thus marked the decline of a certain form of philanthropy in Quebec. With the establishment of the Ministry of Social Affairs (1966) and the pension plan (1964), family allowance plan (1967), health insurance (1970) and *Act Respecting Health Services and Social Services* (1971), Quebec became a welfare state in only a few years. In addition, with the creation of the CEGEPs (collèges d'enseignement général et professionnel) and the network of University of Quebec universities (1969), the dioceses lost ground in the field of education as well. The sudden secularization accompanying this political and cultural transformation had powerful effects.

The decline of religiosity in Quebec goes a long way to explaining its bad "philanthropic results" compared with the rest of Canada (Devlin & Zhao, 2017), but the history of Quebec philanthropy has always been at variance with that of the rest of Canada. For example, in the decades following the Second World War, religion played a central role in Quebec, while the welfare state was developing in the other provinces. And today, when the Catholic religion has lost its institutional power and its following in Quebec, the Church and state appear to be more politically connected in the rest of Canada and in the United States, especially among particular segments of the Protestant faith.

Another long-lasting consequence of the Quiet Revolution, with repercussions on the decreasing role of foundations even today, was the institutionalization of strong relations between the government of Quebec and the community sector (Laforest, 2011). In the context of increasing government involvement in the domains of health care, social services and education in the 1960s,

---

10 This is obviously the case in Europe, where the welfare state is stronger, but also in the United States, where the Second World War led to a considerable strengthening of the federal government. The amounts which the United States now injects into health care, social services and scientific research render the influence of foundations much smaller. For example, in 1938, the federal government invested $42 million dollars in scientific and technological research. With the approach of war in 1940, that amount rose to $770 million. This situation was summarized by a foundation director in 1949: "We collect $3 million for research against cancer, and then we read that the government proposes to allocate $30 million to the same cause; it's very discouraging" (Zunz, 2012, p. 191).

a number of community networks and projects were coopted. This led to the creation of the local community service centres (CLSCs, centres locaux de services communautaires) in the 1970s, the early childhood centres (CPEs, centres pour la petite enfance) in the 1990s, and the *Act to Combat Poverty and Social Exclusion (Loi visant à lutter contre la pauvreté et l'exclusion sociale)* in 2002 (Dufour, 2004). The creation of a secretariat for independent community action and social initiatives in 1995, the SACAIS (Secrétariat à l'action communautaire autonome et aux initiatives sociales), also illustrates this dynamic.

When observing today's funding structure of community organizations in Quebec, we note the prominence of provincial funding, the very low level of federal funding, and the provision, even if this is a downward trend, of mission-based funding rather than service agreements or funding on a per-project basis. In Quebec, charitable revenues are almost 75% funded by public funds, while philanthropy (both individual and by foundations) accounts for 4% (Gagné & Martineau, 2017).

In contrast, the federal government has significantly withdrawn from its core funding commitments, engaging, if at all, in financing on the basis of a project or service agreements (Phillips *et al.*, 2010), a trend that many community networks denounce and fear. This funding configuration in Quebec helps to explain the unique contribution of the Chagnon Foundation in Quebec. The Chagnon Foundation, created in 2000 with a then-unrivalled endowment, chose to establish an unusual, so-called public-philanthropic, partnership between the Quebec government and the foundation in order to implement large-scale projects (Lefèvre & Berthiaume, 2017) (see also Chapter 9).

Rise of the mega-foundation

As noted by Anheier and Leat (2013), there were never so many foundations in the world, endowed with so much capital, as at the beginning of the 21st century. The figures Anheier and Leat give for the year 2010 indicate orders of a striking magnitude. In the United States, some 75,500 foundations together own assets of $565 billion US dollars. The increase in the number of foundations was considerable over the last three decades. For example, nearly half of the US-American foundations active in 2004 did not exist before 1989[11] (Prewitt, 2007, p. 20).

In Canada, much of the increase in total assets has been driven by a significant number of new foundations founded since 2002. Today, nearly 10,000 foundations hold assets of more than

---

11 Moreover, compared to other more fragile types of NPOs experiencing a very strong revival, and with the incessant new creations and dissolutions, it can be assumed that foundations, by their very structure, are less prone to disappear. This is only an assumption, however, since we do not have statistics on these dissolutions, or about the distinctions between active organizations and dormant organizations.

$69.7 billion Canadian dollars. Here as well, the increase is striking. In 1992, 5,400 public and private foundations gave $1 billion Canadian dollars to other organizations. In 2008, 9,300 public and private foundations gave $3 billion Canadian dollars. By comparison, in 2015, 10,743 public and private foundations gave $5.6 billion Canadian dollars and, in 2017, grants by private and public foundations amounted to $6.7 billion (Philanthropic Foundations Canada, 2016, 2019).

Just over a fifth of current top assets foundations (32 of 150) fall into the mega-foundation category (i.e. assets in excess of $100 million). Collectively, they account for 41% of total assets currently held by the top asset foundations (Imagine Canada & Philanthropic Foundations Canada, 2014). In 2000, for example, the Lucie and André Chagnon Foundation was the richest in Canada, with assets of $1.4 billion. In 2014, there were six foundations in Canada with assets in excess of $500 million (*ibid.*). In 2018, the foundation with the largest asset base was the MasterCard Foundation, with assets of more than $23.7 billion.

Of these mega-foundations, the Mastercard Foundation stands out. Founded in 2006 by MasterCard International, the MasterCard Foundation has assets in excess of $20 billion Canadian dollars and an endowment of more than $23 trillion, almost 25% of all philanthropic capital of Canadian foundations. The assets of the foundation are comprised of MasterCard shares and, while the foundation is autonomous from a governance perspective, relations between the parent company and the foundation are synchronous from the point of view of philanthropic foci, philosophy and how and where resources are mobilized. For example. the self-declared mission of the foundation is to "tackle the youth employment challenge in Africa" for the next decade. To fulfil its mission, the Foundation focuses on advancing financial inclusion and education to economically disadvantaged young people in developing countries to improve their lives (MasterCard Foundation, 2017). In other words, MasterCard is bringing the gospel of capitalism to developing countries and profiling its benefits to those who aspire to improve their lives. To date, the focus of the MasterCard Foundation has been on Africa, although other regions, including charities in Canada, have also benefited from their funding.

The primary strategy of MasterCard is to generate new consumers and thus increase the volume of transactions, the source of MasterCard's wealth. Thus, there is a clear supposition between the firm's strategic interests and the Foundation's mission, which is manifested in the structure of its programs. Its programs focus on creating markets for education, employment, finance and agriculture, sectors which experience high transaction volume.

Yet the vast majority of foundations today in Canada today still reflect their historical legacy: religious foundations, those that are a tool of *noblesse oblige*, the economic elite, foundations designed to solve problems by supporting or complementing state priorities, and place-based community foundations (see Table 1, page 16). But what increases the size and reach of global philanthropic capital, mirroring the size and reach of global capitalism, is the foundation as a distinct corporate polity.

We wish to emphasize, or re-emphasize, one point: despite their growth, philanthropic foundations today have less influence than they did a century ago, at least in rich Western countries. Their financial spread has increased, but not as rapidly as that of the portions of the state budgets allocated to social services, education and health care, or the purchasing power of citizens for these services. In the US-American context, David Hammack (2011) describes this phenomenon as follows:

> This lesser influence of the foundations went hand in hand with the growth of the state, and also that of incomes. Before the Second World War, the federal government spent about 3% of the country's gross domestic product on various aspects of health care, education and welfare. In 1950, that number had jumped to 8% and has remained at over 12% since the 1960s. Meanwhile, the GDP per capita was progressing even faster, doubling between 1939 and the early 1960s, and then doubling again in the early 1990s. And, the richer people get, they more they spend on services. As their incomes rose, Americans spent much more on health care, education and family services. Foundations, too, have continued to grow, but at a much slower rate, and the proportion of money they give away, as grants, rose only from about 0.1% of the GDP in 1944 to just over 0.2% in the early 2000s.[12]
>
> **Hammack, 2011, our translation**

The golden age of the foundations in the early 20th century took place in a context in which the welfare state was either very weak (Europe) or nearly non-existent (North America). In these environments, the first major foundations were not merely providing financial support to other organizations or initiating projects. They built, often from scratch, real institutions: libraries, universities, public baths, museums, hospitals (Anheier & Hammack, 2013, pp. 43–74). They did this mainly in the countries in which they were based, but sometimes abroad, as in the case of the American foundations that were active in Canada and Europe (Tournès, 2010).

Paradoxically, it was the loss of this relative power that required foundations to reinvent themselves after the Second World War. Foundations today are transitioning from the role of institution builder to one of a catalyst that aggregates, with a precise vision, the strengths of

---

[12] In Quebec, private and public foundations have distributed about $685 million Canadian dollars to charities in 2010. For a comparison of scale, the Quebec government invests $29 billion Canadian dollars in the domains of social needs and health care; $15 billion in education, leisure and sports; $4 billion in employment and social security; and $2.4 billion in families and seniors, for a total amount exceeding $50 billion in 2011–12 (Government of Quebec, 2012, p. 12).

28   A contextual history of foundations in Canada

other actors (e.g. governments, social movements, community and business). While there is reason to argue that the emergence of the mega-foundation skews the overall picture of the work of foundations, there are two features that are as old as foundations themselves. First, there is an on-going synergistic relationship between the instruments of wealth creation and their foundation by-product, which is disposed to act in the underlying best interests of their asset creators. Second, the institutionalization of foundations can, with the arrival of professionalized staff and bureaucratization, lead to a focus on internal predictability on the one hand and a push for external systemic change on the other.

At a time of growing social inequality and ecological urgency, these two features have the potential to create either powerful conflicts or complementary dynamics within and between foundations.

Three key takeaways

1 The history of foundations provides a contextual landscape that both defines and constrains their role in society.

2 Foundations are a mirror of tensions that exist between capitalist ideologies, individual benefit and the public good.

3 Foundations will continue to reinvent themselves in relation to the context in which they are formed and operate.

References

Anheier, HK (2001) *'Foundations in Europe: A comparative perspective'*, Civil Society Working Paper 18 (abridged version of chapter in Schülter, A, Then, V & P Walkenhorst (eds.) *Foundations in Europe: Society, management and law*. London: Directory of Social Change

Anheier, H & D Hammack (2013) *A Versatile American Institution: The changing ideals and realities of philanthropic foundations*. Washington, DC: Brookings Institution Press

Anheier, H & D Leat (2013) 'Philanthropic foundations: What rationales?', *Social Research*, 80(2), 449–72

Brodhead, T (2011) *Réflexions sur la philanthropie et la société: discours de Tim Brodhead*. Montréal: La Fondation de la famille JW MMcConnell

Canada Revenue Agency (2018) 'Charities and giving glossary'. Retrieved April 30, 2018, from: https://www.canada.ca/en/revenue-agency/services/charities-giving/charities/charities-giving-glossary.html

Chan, K (2007) 'Taxing charities: Harmonization and dissonance in Canadian charity law', *Canadian Tax Journal*, 55(3), 481–556

Charbonneau, M (2012) *Le Régime de régulation des organisations de bienfaisance et les fondations philanthropiques au Canada et au Québec: un essai d'économie politique historique*. Montréal: Cahier du CRISES, Collection Études théoriques – no ET1202

Devlin, RA & W Zhao (2017) 'Philanthropic behaviour of Quebecers: An empirical analysis of philanthropy in Canada and how Québec compares to other provinces', *ANSER* 8(1), 20–39

Dufour, P (2004) 'L'Adoption du projet de loi 112 au Québec: le produit d'une mobilisation ou une simple question de conjoncture politique?', *Politique et Sociétés*, 23, (2–3), 159–82

Elson, PR (2007) 'A short history of voluntary sector–government relations in Canada', *The Philanthropist* 21 (1), 36–74

Elson, PR (2011) *High Ideals and Noble Intentions: Voluntary sector–government relations in Canada*. Toronto: University of Toronto Press

Fedunkiw, M (2005) *Rockefeller Foundation Funding and Medical Education in Toronto, Montreal, and Halifax*. Montréal: McGill-Queen's University Press

Ferretti, L (2013) 'La philanthropie en français au Québec: une histoire à redécouvrir' in *Culture philanthropique: visages et transformations. Éléments de synthèse et perspectives d'avenir*, Actes du Sommet sur la culture philanthropique tenu à l'Université Laval, les 12 et 13 novembre 2013

Fong, W (2008) *J.W. McConnell: Financier, philanthropist, patriot*. Montreal and Kingston: McGill-Queen's University Press

Gagné E & V Martineau (2017) *Le système philanthropique des fondations et organismes sans but lucratif de la Province de Québec*. Québec: rapport de l'Institut Mallet, Retrieved from: http://institutmallet.org/wp-content/uploads/RAPPORT-PROV-QUÉBEC.pdf

Government of Quebec (2012) *Un plan pour le Québec. Budget 2011–12*. Québec, Ministère des finances

Hammack, D (2011) 'Considérations sur les fondations philanthropiques américaines', *Lien social et Politiques* 65, 271–74

Hanlon, P (2003) 'Alloway, William Forbes' in *Dictionary of Canadian Biography*, Toronto & Laval: University of Toronto/Université Laval. Retrieved from: http://www.biographi.ca/en/bio/alloway_william_forbes_15E.html

Imagine Canada & Philanthropic Foundations Canada (2014) *'Assets and giving trends of Canada's grantmaking foundations'*. Retrieved from: http://sectorsource.ca/sites/default/files/resources/files/trends-canadas-grantmaking-foundations-sept2014.pdf

Kryvoruchko, I (2013) 'Three essays in public economics: Flat taxes, foundation operations and giving'. Thesis submitted to the School of Graduate Studies in partial fulfilment of the requirements for the degree Doctor of Philosophy, McMaster University

Laforest, R (2011) 'L'étude du tiers secteur au Québec: comment saisir la spécificité québécoise?' *Politique et Sociétés*. 30(1), 43–55

Lefèvre, S & A Berthiaume (2017) 'Les partenariats entre secteur public et fondations philanthropiques au Québec: genèse, contestation et épilogue d'une réforme de l'action publique'. *Revue française d'administration publique*, 163(3), 491–506

Lefèvre, S, Boismenu, G & P Dufour (2011) *La pauvreté: quatre modèles sociaux en perspective*. Montréal: Presses de l'Université de Montréal

MasterCard Foundation (2017) 'Doing Well by Doing Good', Corporate Sustainability Report, *2017*. Retrieved from: https://www.mastercard.us/content/dam/mccom/global/aboutus/Sustainability/mastercard-sustainability-report-2017.pdf

Morvaridi, B (2015) 'Introduction' in Morvaridi, B (ed.) *New Philanthropy and Social Justice: Debating the conceptual and policy discourse*. Bristol, UK: Policy Press

O'Connor, A (2001) *Poverty Knowledge: Social science, social policy, and the poor in the twentieth-century US history*. Princeton: Princeton University Press

O'Connor, A (2011) 'Contradictions de la philanthropie libérale face aux mouvements sociaux', *Lien social et Politiques*. 65, 19–42

Pearson, KA (2007) *Accélérer notre impact: philanthropie, innovation et changement social*. Montréal: La Fondation de la famille JW McConnell

Petitclerc, M (2008) 'Compassion, association, utopie. La mutualité ouvrière à Montréal au milieu du XIXe siècle', *Revue du MAUSS*, 32(2), 399–409

Philanthropic Foundations Canada (2016) *Snapshot of Foundation Giving in 2014*. Montréal, Québec, Canada: PFC

Philanthropic Foundations Canada (2019) 'Canadian foundation facts'. Retrieved from: https://pfc.ca/resources/canadian-foundation-facts/

Phillips, S, Laforest, R & A Graham (2010) 'From shopping to social innovation: Getting public financing right in Canada', *Policy and Society* 29 (2010), 189–99

Piketty, T (2013) *Le capital au XXIe siècle*. Paris: Seuil

Prewitt, K (2007) 'Les grandes fondations philanthropiques américaines: comment justifier leur pouvoir?' in Dogan M & K Prewitt (eds.) *Fondations philanthropiques en Europe & aux Etats-Unis* (pp. 19–41). Paris: Éditions de la Maison des sciences de l'homme

Riecker, JE (1964) 'Foundations and the Patman Committee Report', *Michigan Law Review*. 63 (1), 95–140

Sealander, J (2003) 'Curing Evils at Their Source: The arrival of scientific giving' in Friedman, LJ & M McGarvie (eds.) *Charity, Philanthropy and Civility in American History*. Cambridge: Cambridge University Press, pp. 217–40

Smith, SR & M Lipsky (1993) *Nonprofits For Hire: The welfare state in an age of contracting*. Cambridge, Massachusetts and London: Harvard University Press

Tournès, L (ed.) (2010) *L'argent de l'influence. Les fondations américaines et leurs réseaux européens*. Paris: Autrement

Whitaker, B (1974) *The Foundations: An anatomy of philanthropy and society*. London: Eyre Methuen

Zunz, O (2012) *La philanthropie en Amérique: Argent privé, affaires d'État*. Paris: Fayard

Part one
Chapter two

Philanthropic Foundations Canada: Building a community and a voice for philanthropy

Hilary Pearson

Twenty years ago, a small group of private foundations in Canada created a new association to act as a collective voice for organized private philanthropy.[1]

Since that time, the context for organized philanthropy has changed enormously, in line with major changes in our economy and society. What has a dedicated voice achieved for private philanthropy since 1999? How has it evolved in response to social change and emerging digital and generational shifts? These questions are addressed in this chapter, which reflects on two decades of work to build a pan-Canadian association for grantmaking foundations. In it I describe the creation of Philanthropic Foundations Canada (PFC), the evolution of the association and its changing strategic role, the impact of a collective voice and the creation of a philanthropic community, the lessons learned and the challenges for funder networks in a digital age.

---

[1] Thanks, and acknowledgement for their input and comments on this chapter go to the following individuals, who were early leaders or board members of the association: Tim Brodhead, David Elton, David Windeyer, Peter Warrian, Patrick Johnston.

Acquiring a voice: the launch of PFC (1999–2008)

PFC was formally established as Private Foundations Canada in mid-1999, when the leaders of a group of 18 private foundations agreed to incorporate a new nonprofit member association. Many of these leaders, such as Alan Broadbent of Maytree Foundation and David Windeyer of the J P Bickell Foundation,[2] were based in Toronto. There were also individuals in Montreal and in Calgary who played an important part in this initial group, notably, from Calgary, Jim Hume and Shira Herzog of the Kahanoff Foundation and David Elton of the Max Bell Foundation and, from Montreal, Tim Brodhead of the J W McConnell Family Foundation. Many of these were non-family staff leaders of their foundations. Hume, Brodhead and Elton served as the first Board Chairs of the organization. Thus, from the beginning, PFC had leadership and input from foundations outside Toronto itself.

A small group of private foundations had talked for some years previously about creating a dedicated association. Art Bond, a Toronto accountant, took a first step towards this goal almost three decades earlier in 1974, when he launched the Association of Canadian Foundations (ACF) as an informal group, possibly inspired by the US Council on Foundations, a collective advocacy voice for US foundations that had existed since the 1950s.[3] Art Bond and Preston Sewell[4] together created the ACF as a "watchdog" on federal legal and taxation issues affecting foundations.[5] This development happened in sync with the launch of the first comprehensive review of the nonprofit sector by the federal government (National Advisory Council on Voluntary Action, 1977). The goal of the ACF was to contribute an informed perspective on the federal government's development of tax law and regulations shaping the governance and activity of charities and charitable foundations, although there were still very few Canadian private foundations with staff before the 1990s, and thus relatively little contact among them. Foundation trustees tended to see their philanthropy as a discretionary and private affair.

In the early 1980s, Art Bond also co-founded the Canadian Centre for Philanthropy, which took over some of the private foundation sector's efforts to advocate and intervene in the public policy debates and federal government policy decisions about charities and foundations. Although

---

2   David Windeyer was also involved with other private foundations administered by the National Trust and later by Scotia Trust.

3   Art Bond, who was Executive Director of the Physicians' Services Incorporated Foundation at the time was one of the attendees at the Council's annual conference in 1971.

4   Preston Sewell headed National Trust's Private Trusts Division and was very active with Canadian trusts and foundations in the 1970s and 80s.

5   For more on the history of the ACF, see 'The Founding of the Canadian Centre for Philanthropy', The Philanthropist, January 1, 2000, https://thephilanthropist.ca/2000/01/the-founding-of-the-canadian-centre-for-philanthropy/

the ACF continued to be active through the mid-1980s, the growth of the Canadian Centre for Philanthropy made the separate role of the ACF less important, and it became largely inactive in the 1990s.

In the late 1990s, another public policy decision, this time about tax incentives for giving, set the stage for the formal creation of a second association of private foundations, Private Foundations Canada (PFC). This new association was created, at least in part, in frustration at the federal tax changes of 1997, which made it clear that the federal government did not want to foster more charitable giving through private foundations. The 1997 tax change called for the removal of half the capital gains tax payable on donations of listed securities. This incentive was to be available if the donor gave to a public charity but not if the gift went to a private foundation. No advocate for private foundations other than the Canadian Centre for Philanthropy was present to protest against this policy announcement. Discussions within the organized networks of the voluntary sector at the time (specifically the Voluntary Sector Roundtable (VSR))[6] excluded private foundations, although the VSR did include another organized foundation group, Community Foundations of Canada. Tim Brodhead of the J W McConnell Foundation participated in these sector conversations because the McConnell Foundation was an early funder of the Canadian Centre for Philanthropy and the VSR – but there was no collective participation from private foundations. Some sector leaders felt that funders should not be considered as part of the core voluntary sector.

Private foundations realized that they lacked an active forum for discussion of policy issues that specifically affected private foundations. The US Council on Foundations probably served once more as an inspiration for a renewed push to create a dedicated association. Shira Herzog of the Kahanoff Foundation (one of the founders of PFC) served on the board of the Council in the US for several years and brought her knowledge of the mission and work of the Council to PFC. The American organization also held its Annual Conference in Toronto in 1989 and was probably at the peak of its membership and influence through the 1990s.

From the beginning, the founders envisaged PFC as a national association. The founding group of larger private foundations wanted to reach out quickly to the "top 100" foundations for membership and build from there, focusing on "independent" foundations – foundations without links to specific communities, institutions or governments. There was even the brief consideration that the association should be named Independent Foundations Canada, but "independent foundation" was not a widely understood term and the idea was not pursued. From the outset, the founders intended PFC to be a bilingual association, relevant and accessible to francophone and anglophone members (internal communication, 1999). Francophone directors were welcomed on the founding board.

---

6 See: Accountability and Governance in the Voluntary Sector: http://www.ontla.on.ca/library/repository/mon/1000/10280196.htm

The initial board discussions on goals for PFC revealed a difference of opinion at the heart of the new organization over whether it should focus primarily on government relations and public policy (e.g. policy affecting the creation and growth of private foundations) or concentrate on professional development and educational programs and activities for members. The choice between these two goals had implications for how the organization would be resourced. The former suggested an evolution in the direction of government relations and advocacy work, some of which could be contracted out. The latter implied an organization that would need to grow and quickly develop more internal capacity for planning and delivering education and convening opportunities. In the end, the organization chose to do both, much as the US Council on Foundations had done. This was an important decision which shaped PFC's focus over the next two decades; it also created a tension in the organization that endures to this day: the tension between members who value advocacy and policy work above all and those who value the organization as a provider of educational and member-focused services.

The launch of PFC was a success. By mid-January 2000, it had 25 members, funds provided by the leading foundations (each agreed to make a significant grant to finance the organization), a three-person staff and a draft Strategic Plan for 2000 to 2003. The mission of the organization was confirmed:

→ Private Foundations Canada encourages the growth and development of independent, effective and responsible foundations, and fosters a social and regulatory environment that encourages philanthropic contribution.

Internal communication, 2000

To accomplish its mission, the board decided that PFC would:

- work to improve the social, policy and regulatory landscape contributing to philanthropy and the development of private foundations
- create opportunities for private foundations to increase their effectiveness

Operationally, the board decided that the association would focus on "strengthening and building PFC's internal capacity and membership development, government relations, opportunities for sharing and learning from each other, and increasing public awareness of the value of private philanthropy" (internal communication, 2000). PFC set an ambitious target of reaching over 100 members by 2003, particularly given the relatively small number of interested private foundations.

By 2001, PFC had established its presence in the Canadian foundation sector. With over 50 members, it had more than doubled its initial membership and it had developed a website and a corporate brand and positioned itself in Ottawa as a voice for private foundations through briefs to parliamentary committees and meetings with officials. As part of this positioning, PFC had begun to collect and publish important data on the assets and grants of members, and it had held its first member seminar in June 2001 in Toronto, with the explicit goal of educating foundation trustees in good foundation practice. In the same year, PFC staff conducted the first survey on the compensation practices of the foundation members, an important source of benchmarking information and a tool for fostering responsible management practice. In effect, PFC was functioning as an industry association, working on behalf of the private foundation sector. The isolation of private grantmakers was being replaced with the opportunity to be part of an organized "industry", with the potential to gain strength from that perspective.

Early in this period the board decided to pursue registered charitable status, although opinions were divided among board members about doing so. Some had concerns about both the effort and cost required and also the possible limitations on the role of the organization as an advocate for public policy changes. Others believed that charitable tax status would be a way to increase revenue – once the organization was a qualified donee, members could contribute grants to it directly – as, indeed, proved to be the case.

In the fall of 2001, the board decided to relocate PFC from Toronto to Montreal. With Julie White, PFC's first CEO, deciding to move to another leadership role, the board took the opportunity to rethink the question of location, especially considering the commitment of the founders to a bilingual organization with the capacity to represent and provide services to members in both official languages. Hilary Pearson was appointed president in November 2001 and restarted the association in Montreal. At the Annual General Meeting in June 2002, members voted to change the name of the association from Private Foundations Canada to Philanthropic Foundations Canada. This name change put philanthropy at the centre of the association's identity, removed the term "private", which could be seen as elitist, and allowed the association to be more inclusive (e.g. not private foundations only). At the end of 2002, PFC achieved registered charitable status, which aligned it with other umbrella charities such as Community Foundations of Canada and the Canadian Centre for Philanthropy.

In late 2003, aware of media and political discussions in the United States on foundation conduct, and their potential impact on opinion and policy makers in Canada, the PFC board decided to adopt a standard of ethics and principles governing grantmaking behaviour that was "clear, comprehensive and of the highest quality" (internal communication, 2003). After a year of extensive member consultation, the board approved a new aspirational *Statement of Values and Principles*,[7] which existing and new PFC members were asked to sign individually as a way of confirming their agreement. Beginning in 2006, this statement has been at the core of the member relations within the organization. Members are asked to review and re-sign the statement each year as they renew their membership, while new member must sign the statement before they are accepted as a member.

---

7   https://pfc.ca/wp-content/uploads/2018/02/statement-of-values-2018-en.pdf

In 2005, after close to six years of growth, the 82-member organization took stock of the changing environment and of the goals it had set itself at the outset. The founders agreed that the organization had facilitated networking and collaboration among Canadian foundations. PFC had created an "address" for foundations, charities and government policy makers to find out more about this field. But an outstanding question remained: what role could the organization play in mediating the tension between private funders and the public charities they supported?

PFC's members thus asked themselves: are foundations simply extensions of private individual philanthropy, or should they behave as public trusts with an obligation to work for the public good? How did foundations respect the autonomy of charities to do their work, while seeking accountability for impact? The tension revealed by these questions was as long as the relationship between charities and foundations. Indeed, the 2003–04 debate on the Statement of Values and Principles was contentious for this very reason. PFC's commitment to make it a core part of members' relations with the association was an effort to highlight and make more substantial the commitment of PFC members to public accountability and to a respectful approach to community partners. This was a key moment.

Coming out of this period of reflection, PFC took on a more activist stance, deciding to collaborate more closely with the other organizations in the philanthropic and voluntary sectors (e.g. Community Foundations of Canada, Imagine Canada[8]). The aim was broadened to position private foundations as supporters and defenders of the interests of the charitable sector as a whole. The board agreed that PFC should "move over time to a more active brokering role in building national philanthropic infrastructure across the country among and across regional grantmaker networks and affinity groups" (internal communication, 2005).

PFC's first national conference, held in 2005 in Toronto, was an indicator of PFC's growing maturity and capacity. Significantly, the theme of the conference was philanthropic leadership. This successful gathering, which attracted about 175 participants, positioned PFC in a new role as a convenor around key issues and themes in Canadian philanthropy. Subsequent conferences, held every two years and rotating between different locations in eastern and western Canada, confirmed PFC's unique value in convening private funders in Canada, within and beyond its membership. Many of the themes featured in these early conference programs have re-appeared through the years: leadership, accountability, collaboration, impact, innovation.

---

8   Imagine Canada was created in 2002 as the result of the union of the Canadian Centre for Philanthropy and the Coalition of National Voluntary Organization.

While PFC engaged proactively in doing more knowledge brokering and convening, it also remained focused through its first decade on the original objective of its founders, namely advocating for removal of the disincentive for private foundation donors that had resulted from the federal government's charitable tax incentives policy. After years of sustained and increasingly intensive government relations work by PFC, including enlisting support from the other infrastructure organizations in the sector, the federal government agreed to eliminate the capital gains tax on donations of listed securities to private foundations. The federal budget of March 19, 2007 announced this change ten years after the original policy decision had triggered the frustrations of private foundations and led to the creation of PFC. Unfortunately, at the same time, the government announced a new regime for restricting the investment holdings of private foundations ("the excess business holdings rules"). As one commentator noted, this regime, borrowed from the United States, was an indication of a continuing policymaker bias against private foundations: "Rather than implement a regulatory regime that emphasizes charitable benefit, the tax system assumed that non-arm's length transactions were in conflict with charitable giving and that the donors who engaged in such transactions were suspect" (Burrows, 2009, p. 11). The focus of the government on preventing self-dealing, restricting any possibility of private benefit and constraining the operations of private foundations, meant that PFC has had to continue its advocacy efforts with the government to foster a more enabling regulatory environment.

Becoming a member-focused platform (2008–14)

In 2008, PFC's board reviewed the mission statement adopted in 2000 and decided, in the context of a maturing field, that it should revise and expand PFC's role. New vision and mission statements were drafted, focusing on a description of PFC's role as a member-serving organization, and defining the PFC constituency more broadly to include "organized philanthropy" operating for community benefit. The new statements were:

- Vision (what we want to accomplish): "PFC is a *pan-Canadian* advocate and resource for *effective organized philanthropy* that benefits Canadians and their communities"
- Mission (what we do): "We promote the growth and development of effective and responsible foundations and of organized philanthropy through the provision of membership services, resources and advocacy."

From this point on, PFC began a gradual expansion of its membership criteria. While making it clear that the focus was still on grantmakers not fundraisers, and organizations not individuals, the board added to the membership categories over time including corporate giving programs as well as corporate foundations, arms-length government-funded foundations (such as Ontario Trillium Foundation), charities functioning primarily as grantmakers, and nonprofits functioning as grantmakers (such as the Law Foundation of Ontario). In this way PFC was creating a bigger tent for the organized philanthropy "community" as it grew in Canada.

From 2008 to 2011, PFC engaged more staff for both communications and convening activities on behalf of members. In this period, the organization was working on an action plan that included the development of tools for better practice, building learning networks, communicating the work and value-added of organized philanthropy to external audiences, and building membership. The organization grew to four full-time staff; contract staff helped to develop communications platforms such as the website and to build a database on the grantmaking sector. The staff researched and wrote three important resource guides on the basics of grantmaking and governance, targeted to both emerging foundations and to foundations seeking to professionalize their practices.[9] By 2010 the organization had met and exceeded its original goal of 100 members.

In 2011, the board of PFC took time for another strategic reflection. This led to a subtle but important shift in PFC's role: rather than a "one-stop resource shop", PFC began to move towards functioning more like a resource node existing in a broader network of philanthropy. This role

---

9 PFC Guides: Starting A Foundation (4th edition 2019), Good Governance: A Guide for Directors of Canadian Foundations (2010,2014) and Good Grantmaking: A Guide for Canadian Foundations (2012, 2015) https://pfc.ca/resources/pfc-publications/

implied a greater level of interactivity, connection, aggregation and intermediation. PFC, as an organization representing grantmakers, needed to pay attention to the realities that faced grantmakers themselves: the need for collaboration, continuous learning and the adaptability and skill to address complex problems. PFC had a role to play in helping members acquire new skills in grantee communication and partnership management, in developing learning loops, in managing complexity, in working in a network and understanding the components of grantmaking effectiveness. PFC could play a convening role, "pulling" in constituencies of various kinds and initiating alignments of the existing players around key projects. For example, PFC could work with others in the philanthropic community to enhance and amplify a collective voice, and to promote collaboration and connection.

After extended discussions through 2011, PFC adopted a new strategic plan for 2011–14, with four key goals:

- To strengthen PFC as a platform to connect organized philanthropy
- To grow the field for organized philanthropy
- To represent and advocate
- To ensure the sustainability of PFC and its network

For each of these four goals, PFC developed strategies, and articulated the results or indicators that would indicate that the goals were being achieved. For the organization, this represented a new level of maturity and discipline around definition of goals and measurable results.

To implement its strategic plan, PFC realized that it needed to grow once again. A more ambitious plan meant that it had to take a more ambitious approach to investing in growth. Approaching some of the leading members of the organization for sustained multi-year funding support, PFC outlined its case for support:

> To have its greatest impact, organized philanthropy needs a network, tools, contacts and strategies. A strong infrastructure organization that acts as an effective knowledge aggregator, collaborator and catalyst for its members, for other private funders and for other organizations in the philanthropic field, will meet that need. Investing in the capacity of PFC is an investment in the capacity of the whole philanthropic sector
>
> Internal communication, 2012

With the vision of making PFC into a connector and platform for knowledge exchange within organized philanthropy in Canada, PFC's members provided funding support to develop an infrastructure to make it easier for members and other grantmakers to exchange and share knowledge for greater effectiveness and impact, deepen the range of available tools and skills, and provide opportunities for collaboration and building of relationships with other leaders in the funder community. By 2015, the association had added a permanent senior communications staff member and developed a strategic communications plan, created an internal hub for sharing member information, redeveloped its website to add content and facilitate interactivity and, in collaboration with Imagine Canada, produced new research reports on the top grantmakers in Canada.

By 2014, membership in PFC had climbed to 120 members. While family foundations were still the predominant type of member in the association (up to 75%), the mix was changing, with more members from corporations, donor-advised-fund public foundations and other public grantmaking foundations. Significantly, the membership included half of the top 20 grantmaking foundations by assets, representing close to half of the assets held by private foundations in Canada.[10] Remarkably, after 15 years, 13 of the original group of 18 foundations were still members (two had dissolved themselves).

PFC still had one class of membership. Over the years, the board and staff had discussed whether to add associate members, or to differentiate in some way between leading or sustaining members and other members. PFC decided to hold to the principle of equal treatment for all members, regardless of size or type. While the criteria had expanded, different members were not treated differently in terms of their benefits. Thus PFC stayed true to the idea of connecting and bringing together funders of various types to sit at the same big funders table.

From 2010 on, after the short-term negative effects of the 2008 financial crisis, the number of private foundations registered in Canada rose steadily.[11] Various factors account for this growth, the most obvious of which was the favourable state of the US and global economy and financial markets. Secondly, the generational wealth transfer got underway as the generation of the 1930s and 1940s handed over to the baby boom generation. Thirdly, a rising millennial generation began to demonstrate an interest in and a willingness to influence multi-generational philanthropy. Fourthly, government tax incentives for donations of both cash and equities to private foundations were generous. Most importantly, the opportunities for private philanthropy in Canada were becoming better known and more inspiring to would-be foundation creators. From the start, PFC had understood the importance of providing a compelling narrative about the work of foundations. In the early years, PFC put together a story collection, *Foundations Seeing the World Differently*, about individual private foundations and the unique and innovative grants they were making to bring about long-term results beyond the capability of either government or corporate funders. From creating digital music libraries to recycling technological waste, from connecting

---

10 https://pfc.ca/wp-content/uploads/2018/01/assets_giving_trends_sept2014_web.pdf

11 From 2010 to early 2018, registered private foundations grew by over 700 foundations according to PFC internal data drawn from CRA registrations : https://pfc.ca/resources/canadian-foundation-facts/

the dots on global disease transmission to addressing the burnout stresses of caregivers, the stories supported the case made during the early 2000s to the federal government about the importance of recognizing the unique value of private foundation activity.

Storytelling about the work of private foundations continued to be a priority for PFC in its second decade. PFC created a continuing series of *Great Grant Stories*, contributed by members and posted on the PFC website. After 2015, as part of a shift towards more strategic communications, PFC developed another digital platform, *Philanthropy in Action*, designed to be a place to find stories about the impact of organized philanthropy across Canada. While it is not easy to track the direct causal link between storytelling and the more positive impressions of foundations, anecdotal evidence from within the PFC membership indicates that these stories and models have helped foundation leaders and creators aspire to greater possibilities for themselves.

Emerging as a social change network: 2014–18

After 2014, in a recognition that the landscape foundations operate in had shifted significantly, PFC began a major effort to renew its business model and brand. The rapid changes of the digital age were having an impact on PFC's core roles, as they were on similar member associations and funder networks globally. It was no longer possible to believe that PFC would provide all the most relevant data and expertise related to foundation management and grantmaking. Information is accessible everywhere and at any time. The Internet and social media transform organizational roles related to information, and thus, to stay relevant, PFC needed to focus on its unique value. In the information age, issue-specific expertise is not as valuable as knowledge mobilization and convening expertise.

In this digital world PFC's unique value creation is two-fold: playing a leadership role in advocacy for the field, and mobilizing knowledge with and for its members. PFC's ability to connect, to bring people together, to create both virtual and personal spaces for the sharing of member practices and learnings, is also a great vehicle for mobilization. PFC can encourage funders to keep focused, work together, listen to all voices, counter lies/false news, and give ear and voice to the voiceless.

In 2016, the PFC board decided that building an excellent membership organization, a key goal, should be framed around the idea of leading and challenging members to do their best work (internal communication, 2016). The board was clear that PFC served the broader community of organized philanthropy, not just its members. The consistent thread in PFC's evolution since

2008 was the need to serve the whole field of organized grantmakers. Most of its events, learning materials and web content are publicly available. In this way, PFC remained true to its purpose as a charity registered under the heading of education.

In 2017, consistent with this thinking, PFC adopted a new brand identity – **Connecting. Inspiring. Creating Change.** With a more contemporary and assertive message, PFC was moving with the times:

> We seek to support our members and organized philanthropy by encouraging public policies that sustain the sector, by increasing awareness of philanthropy's contribution to the well-being of Canadians, and by providing opportunities for funders to learn from each other. We provide a voice for organized philanthropy, assist in building a professional network for our thought-leaders, and inform on good practice.[12]

Even with the revisions to its core message, PFC's approach remains remarkably consistent: a focus on policies that enable (or discourage) the best work of private philanthropy, the narrative around the contribution of organized philanthropy, and the importance of building connections and learning, all with the goal of having a greater impact on the "well-being of Canadians". The change in the language reflected PFC's realization that it is not only a member service organization but also, with the credibility and the continuity of its relationships, a leadership organization for organized philanthropy.

Building a community: the impact of PFC

PFC's impact on the world of organized philanthropy in Canada over a period of 20 years is best summed up as community building. Before 1999, many private foundations in Canada had known and interacted with each other informally and locally, particularly in anglophone Canada – but there had been little formal collaboration and no capacity for a collective expression of what was important to the effectiveness and impact of this group of private funders. There had also been no formal vehicle that enabled other organizations in the charitable sector to interact with private foundations on a broader policy level.[13] PFC helped foundations to recognize that they were part

---

12 https://pfc.ca/about/

13 The Association of Charitable Foundations, mentioned earlier in the chapter, and which became inactive in the 1990s, is an exception here.

of a professional field, and to show themselves to others outside the field. PFC provided a window into organized philanthropy for everyone: members, other foundations, charities, media and policy makers, and global colleagues.

Another less visible, but no less essential aspect and consequence of the work of PFC has been to link Quebec-based philanthropy to the strategies and actions of organized philanthropy in the rest of Canada. PFC's physical presence in Montreal and its commitment to bilingualism have connected francophone foundations both to each other and also to anglophone foundations beyond Quebec. This has been an important factor in building and sustaining a pan-Canadian community of philanthropy.

How can PFC's impact be measured? I suggest five key indicators:

- The **engagement** of foundations and private grantmakers directly in the opportunities offered by PFC
- The number of new **collaborative events and connections** made through PFC
- The evidence of the growing **professionalization** of the field
- The evidence of the **formalization and deepening** of Canadian foundation **practices**
- The success that PFC has had in influencing **public policy** decisions related to federal regulation of foundations

What do these indicators tell us about PFC's success?

PFC has created multiple opportunities for **engagement** for many foundations. Since 1999, over 60 different foundations have served on the board or committees of PFC. A large number of philanthropic organizations have connected on a regular basis with other foundations and have engaged in collective work for their field. At annual conferences and leadership retreats, the board and staff of foundations have come to know each other and to learn more about the broader field in which they work. The membership of PFC has grown every year since the association was created.

Because of the exposure of foundations to each other through PFC, instances of **collaborative activity** are multiplying: the creation of a shared and collaborative space, Foundation House in Toronto, by three PFC members who connected through their shared membership (see Chapter 13); the creation of the Circle on Philanthropy and Aboriginal Peoples in Canada, which emerged from a table conversation at the 2009 PFC Conference in Calgary (see Chapter 6); the development of other funder affinity groups such as the Mental Health and Wellness Affinity Group, facilitated by introductions made through PFC; and the Collective Impact Project in Montreal, bringing together eight private foundations, many of whom met each other through PFC (see Chapter 12). PFC events and introductions created the trust that allowed many of these activities to be initiated by the members.

The guides, workshops, survey reports and learning events sponsored by PFC over 20 years have led directly to the **professionalization** of the field. A substantial amount of content produced by members or by advisors and experts engaged by PFC has featured Canadian examples, cases and legal frameworks, which makes it more useful to Canadian funders than anything that can be retrieved from US or global sources on the practice of philanthropy. The guides and reports are downloaded regularly from the PFC website, and have been cited in other publications.

PFC has been highly instrumental in providing opportunities for **formal structured learning.** In 2012, PFC began a biannual series of practice-focused gatherings. As an overarching theme, PFC has examined what it takes to "make change" that is wide-ranging, deeper and more effective in addressing some of the complex challenges facing Canadian funders and their partners, such as poverty, homelessness, climate change, mental illness, social exclusion. PFC has approached these gatherings as an opportunity to thoughtfully examine a practice from various perspectives, and to feature examples of Canadian practice in action.

At the first symposium in 2012, PFC looked at the why, how and what of funder collaboration to "make change". Participants told PFC: "It's not the pooling of funds but the pooling of perspectives, ideas, insights – collaboration can be as much about framing a problem as it is about bringing money to the table – it's paying attention to what matters."

- In 2013, PFC examined the practice of thinking systemically about how to bring about change. How can a funder bring creativity, fresh eyes, and boundary-less thinking to the table with community partners?
- At the first symposium in 2012, PFC looked at the *why*, *how* and *what* of funder collaboration to "make change". Participants told PFC: "It's not the pooling of funds but the pooling of perspectives, ideas, insights – collaboration can be as much about framing a problem as it is about bringing money to the table – it's paying attention to what matters."
- In 2015, participants discussed making change in public policy. How do private funders work with public policy makers and systems to bring about deeper and more sustained social changes?
- In 2017, participants explored the practice of listening. How do funders listen better, hold better conversations, reach out to hear those voices that need to be heard?
- In 2019, PFC took on the practice of cross-sectoral collaboration to make change. How do funders engage with community partners, governments and businesses with different motives, accountabilities and indicators of success to tackle community-wide challenges such as mental health and addiction, or social exclusion and poverty?

In all these gatherings, PFC has convened community leaders and practitioners to work with foundations in reflecting on what it takes to be more effective in practice.

PFC has established a credible and well-prepared advocacy presence in Ottawa and among its peers in the sector. PFC has also achieved considerable **public policy success.** Beginning with the campaign to level the playing field of tax incentives for giving, in 2006 PFC pushed the federal government to equalize the treatment of capital gains tax on gifts of public securities to private foundations.

Throughout the first two decades of the 2000s, PFC wrote and presented annual policy briefs and appeared before parliamentary committees every year. Hilary Pearson served on the Canada Revenue Agency (CRA)'s Charities Advisory Committee in the early 2000s and on its Technical Issues Working Group after 2015. PFC successfully lobbied to obtain relieving provisions on the excess business holdings rules for private foundations that had been introduced in 2006, and to allow private foundations to hold units in limited partnerships. PFC encouraged the CRA to create more flexible guidance on program-related investments (or loans to charities and non-charities). More recently, PFC has proactively convened leading sector organizations to promote the modernization of the *Income Tax Act* provisions regarding charities, in order to create more flexibility and reform regulations so that they are less prescriptive and compliance oriented.

PFC has accomplished a good deal in twenty years. But important challenges continue for the association and its members. Funders are faced with more searching questions about their own policies and practices. Do they pay enough attention to diversity and inclusion in a country whose population is changing very quickly from one dominated by the legacy of white European settlers to a mix of global migrants, colonial descendants and Indigenous peoples? Canadian philanthropy must also come to grips with the question of reconciliation with Indigenous history and current-day realities, as other chapters in this book make very clear. Philanthropic practices related to participation, inclusion, power sharing and respect for lived experience must be explored. As a convenor and knowledge broker, PFC can and should work with other philanthropic infrastructure groups to facilitate this exploration.

The issue of the public accountability of private charitable funders is alive and well. Opinion leaders in Canada still don't pay much attention to private foundations, which remain mostly invisible, despite the fact that they control over $40 billion (CDN) in assets and make over $2 billion in grants annually (2018 CRA data) as well as running significant charitable programs. Foundations are privileged institutions, exercising the power of their resources to shape their communities and sometimes the policies of governments. Increasingly, the media, policy makers and other influencers pose the questions: What is the legitimacy of the private foundation in a democracy? Should private foundations receive more scrutiny, or be more publicly accountable? PFC has a responsibility, and a challenge, to create a solid narrative and credible answers to these important questions.

Another challenge to PFC is how best to connect and not compete with other geographic and interest-based funder networks. Since 2010, informal funder networks or affinity groups based on geography or shared areas of funding interest have sprung up. Funders find shared interests in their communities if they are place-based funders, or shared interests in specific issue areas if they are working on broader social challenges. Funder groups in the areas of climate change and carbon emissions, mental health and wellness, food and food security, youth and work, or around specific foundation roles such as grants manager/program officer, are joining existing groups which have been formalized for some time, such as Environment Funders Canada (formerly the Canadian Environmental Grantmakers Network) or the Circle on Philanthropy and Indigenous Peoples in Canada. PFC's challenge is to facilitate, complement and partner with these groups in a way that is most effective for the funders themselves.

PFC has an important relationship with a related pan-Canadian philanthropy infrastructure organization, Community Foundations of Canada (CFC). CFC was formed in the early 1990s and represents almost all of the community foundations across Canada (close to 200 foundations). On the surface the two associations would seem to have different spheres of operation on behalf of their members. The essential nature of community or place-based philanthropies is local, rooted in the issues and concerns of their geographic communities. While not all community foundations are place-based in Canada, the focus of what is self-described as a "movement" tends inevitably to be local or regional. The donors are local and the issues to which they give are often local. PFC's members fund locally but may also (or conversely) have national or international funding interests. They are also in most cases governed not by community members but by families or individuals who are closely connected.

In the late 1990s, when PFC was created, it seemed unlikely that the two associations could collaborate, not least because the members of CFC, working to attract donors, benefited from the tax policy incentive for donors to give public securities to public foundations and charities rather than to private foundations. However, as the two organizations have evolved, and as the public policy framework has created a level playing field for donors, the organizations share an interest in acting as thought leaders and catalysts for their members on charity and purpose-based policy issues and on philanthropic funding practices.

In the policy areas of climate change, migration, reconciliation, recognition of diversity, inequality and social inclusion, public and private funders alike are increasingly engaged in multipartner funding collaborations. In the developing field of impact or mission-related investing, PFC and CFC have worked closely together to provide educational resources and opportunities for funders to share practice and learning with each other. This may well grow. The business models of the two organizations may have developed somewhat differently (PFC being funded largely through membership support and project funding, while CFC is funded both by members and by the partnerships negotiated with governments and corporate sponsors), but more formal collaboration in future may well develop.

Looking ahead: the future of philanthropy networks

No funder network anywhere in the world is secure in its position and role. Most are battling for credibility, funding and attention in an economy and society becoming more individualized and disaggregated by the forces of the digital age. Funder networks have always had difficulty persuading funders to invest in their own support or development. The challenges are common to both geographic networks and also role-based networks (Arundel, 2018). The funding is limited, and the value proposition is hard to articulate. The Worldwide Initiatives for Grantmaker Support (WINGS),[14] the global support organization for funder associations within each country, has been working to create a generic case for support that highlights the value that a solid support system brings to funders, which it has articulated as:

- space for reflection and discussion
- collective action on rules and standards
- thought leadership on key issues
- tools for capacity-building
- an advocacy voice for the system as a whole

In 2018, WINGS surveyed the ways in which the field of institutional or organized philanthropy is changing, and how infrastructure organizations serving philanthropy must change as well (WINGS, 2018). Arguing that there is increasing recognition among philanthropies that they cannot address deep-seated issues or tackle societal change on their own, and that they need to work together, WINGS suggests that support organizations frame their objectives and work programs around the needs of the system, rather than around narrow organizational goals. In this view, the types of organizations that deliver services – whether they are membership bodies, professional agencies, networks, university centres or hybrid entities – matter less than their functions. These functions, broadly speaking, can be grouped as:

- information and intelligence (knowledge)
- convening
- technical support
- advocacy
- education

---

14 https://wingsweb.site-ym.com/

A philanthropy support organization must think strategically about how each of these functions can be performed and by whom within its ecosystem. WINGS neatly summarizes the organizational implications of taking an ecosystem approach to the main functions involved in supporting philanthropy:

> While the main driver of infrastructure growth in the 20th century lay in the principles of organizational development to deliver strong and competent organizations to deliver services, the 21st century model is based on field development that transfers strength and power to the edges of the field based on a networked approach. Organizations at the centre of networks should be nimble, harnessing the power of technology to connect people together, to find joint solutions rather than focusing simply on service delivery.
>
> **WINGS, 2018, p. 19**

This suggests that the future for philanthropic support organizations such as PFC lies in a more fluid concept of organization, one that remains nimble but also porous, able to work in alliance and partnership on various projects which are designed to support the varying needs of philanthropic players. As WINGS puts it: "a successful ecosystem relies less on precise organizational forms and more on relationships – with interstitial action between organizations with porous boundaries through a culture of sharing, experimentation and joint learning" (WINGS, 2018, p. 22). WINGS ticks off succinctly what grantmaking organizations (foundations or other) will need from an infrastructure organization. A funder well supported by a funder network:

- has access to the information, intelligence and research it needs to plan and conduct its core work
- can access one-to-one technical assistance on planning, grantmaking, law, evaluation, technology, finance and other operational matters
- has access to peers at national level for learning, sharing
- can take part in thematic or affinity groups relevant to its work
- can contribute to a joint program of advocacy on issues that affect the sector (WINGS, 2018, p. 22)

This is a roadmap for PFC's future success, increasingly working in partnerships and networks with others in the field to support Canadian private philanthropy in creating value for the long term.

Three key takeaways

1 Funder networks are successful when they build trust. Trust leads to collaboration. Collaboration will be increasingly the most important philanthropic strategy to address Canada's and the world's complex social challenges.

2 To stay relevant, funder networks must focus on where they can bring unique value. In the information age, issue-specific expertise is not as valuable as knowledge mobilization and convening expertise.

3 The future for funder networks lies in a more fluid concept of organization, one both nimble and porous, able to work in alliance and partnership on various projects to meet the varying needs of philanthropic players.

References

Arundel, C (2018) 'A sense of place and the potential for connection: How geographic networks address local challenges and build stronger communities', *The Philanthropist*, August 2018

Burrows, M (2009) 'Charitable tax incentives in Canada: Overview and opportunities for expansion', *The Philanthropist*, vol. 22, p.11

National Advisory Council on Voluntary Action (1977) *People in Action: Report of the National Advisory Council on Voluntary Action to the Government of Canada*. Ottawa: Secretary of State

WINGS (2018) 'What makes a strong ecosystem of support to philanthropy?' Retrieved from: http://wings.issuelab.org/resource/what-makes-a-strong-ecosystem-of-support-to-philanthropy.html

Part one
Chapter three

Financial accountability and reporting of foundations in Canada

François Brouard and Marc Pilon

Foundations operate in a complex and multifaceted environment that creates a number of organizational challenges and increased calls for accountability, among them: perception of secrecy and pursuit of private interests, reputational challenges, increased demands for support, reliance on philanthropy as a substitute of government, demands for transparency, public trust expectations, demonstration of value, increased social needs, and social divides (Johnston, 2012; Pearson, 2010; Pitt, 2018; Ravenscroft, 2017; Rourke, 2014). The general increase in public interest also brings additional accountability pressures on foundations (Dhanani & Connolly, 2015; Gates & Rourke, 2014; Shienfield, 2012).[1] And statutory bodies and the general public alike are demanding information of better quality, particularly in the wake of increased visibility of incidences of mismanagement, tax fraud, and scandals (Cordery et al., 2017).

Of the various forms of accountability foundations must manage, financial accountability constitutes an important part of the overall accountability framework that foundations operate under. This conceptual paper explores the financial accountability of foundations in Canada and the ways in which it is managed through governance mechanisms and reporting. The chapter focuses on the financial accountability dimensions of foundations in Canada and the important financial accountability strategies that Canadian foundations should focus on.

From a financial perspective, financial accountability covers regulatory and legislative requirements, measurement and reporting challenges, ethical dilemmas, transparency demands, information systems, risks management and performance measurement. Financial reporting itself is defined as the "communication of information by an individual or organization to interested parties by way of financial statements and other financial data" (CICA, 1992, p.93).

---

1   See also Chapter 10 by Laurel Carlton and Sara Lyons on accountability.

In Canada, foundations represent an important group of actors in the nonprofit sector and philanthropic ecosystem. Many foundations may have the impression that they are able to operate outside any external scrutiny (Rourke, 2014). However, considering the fiduciary responsibilities associated with charitable foundations, multiple stakeholders are, could or should be involved in the accountability process.

The Canada Revenue Agency (CRA) (2009) describes a registered charity as an organization established and operated exclusively for charitable purposes. Foundations are a subgroup of charities that include both charitable organizations and foundations. Legally, according to the *Income Tax Act* (ITA), "Charitable foundation means a corporation or trust that is constituted and operated exclusively for charitable purposes, no part of the income of which is payable to, or is otherwise available for, the personal benefit of any proprietor, member, shareholder, trustee or settler thereof, and that is not a charitable organization" (*Income Tax Act*, section 149.1(1)).

As funding organizations, charitable foundations do not need to carry out the charitable activities themselves, although an increasing number do so. Charitable foundations are subdivided into public and private foundations. A public foundation means a foundation where more than 50% of its board operates at arm's length and no *de facto* or *de jure* control is exerted by a person who has donated more than 50% of its capital (i.e. a major donor) (ITA 149.1(1)); a "private foundation means a charitable foundation that is not a public foundation" (ITA 149.1(1)). Public foundations tend to be associated with fundraising activities, while private foundations are generally not.

In addition to their legal public and private classification, Chamberland *et al.* (2012) have also classified foundations by their form as family (e.g. Fondation Lucie et André Chagnon, The J W McConnell Family Foundation), corporate (e.g. RBC Foundation, Mastercard Foundation), community (e.g. Winnipeg Foundation, Vancouver Foundation, Community Foundation of Ottawa), governmental (e.g. The Ontario Trillium Foundation, Alberta Innovates – Health Solutions), philanthropic clubs (e.g. Rotary, Lions, Kiwanis) and specific goals foundations (Canadian Wildlife Federation, Fondation Hôpital Montfort, The Hospital for Sick Children Foundation/SickKids Foundation). Imagine Canada and Philanthropic Foundations Canada (2014) categorize foundations according to their activities: as fundraising arms (e.g. hospital foundations), fundraising intermediaries, donor-advised funds, operating foundations, nondiscretionary funders, grantmaking foundations and community foundations. The diversity of foundations, as demonstrated by their multiple classifications, may add to the accountability challenges they face, which requires a different set of potential stakeholders and standards (see also Chapter 4 by Carla Funk on types of foundations).

The remainder of the chapter is organized into six sections. The first section describes the historical context. The second section presents the concept of financial accountability and its dimensions. Governance mechanisms, both internal and external, are then explored in the third section. The fourth section then looks at and examines financial reporting. The fifth section presents possible improvements in financial accountability. And the sixth and concluding section sets out the main implications of the chapter.

The historical context

In Canada, the Voluntary Sector Roundtable commissioned a report on accountability and governance, which resulted in the release of the Broadbent Report in 1999. The Broadbent Report called for standards, best practices and guides to help regulate the sector. Subsequently, the Voluntary Sector Initiative (1999a; 1999b) had three joint tables, drawing on the work of government officials and sector leaders, on building new relationships, strengthening capacity and improving regulatory frameworks. These tables include suggestions for accountability and reporting that cover financial capacity, human resources, knowledge, information management, and legislative, institutional, administrative and funding changes. Even 20 years later, many of these suggestions remain relevant, for example: "a voice of the sector in government policy making", "being transparent, including communicating to members, stakeholders and the public, and responding appropriately to requests for information", "different reporting requirements for large and small organizations", "greater consistency in accounting practices" (Voluntary Sector Initiative, 1999a, pp. iv, vii). Some efforts have been achieved, but improvements are still needed.

The purpose of presenting the historical context is to underline the failures and challenges of accountability – mainly relating to frauds, scandals and the internal and external environment within which foundations operate – and to understand the evolution of issues over the years. The information flow between stakeholders is then presented in order to give some indication of the complexity of relationships.

Accountability failures: frauds and scandals

Recent examples of nonprofit accountability failures such as frauds and scandals – which feature regularly in the press – further highlight the troubles that the sector faces. Frauds could relate to asset misappropriation, corruption, fraudulent financial statements and misrepresentation (Chen et al., 2009).

One such example is the fundraising effort for a non-existent foundation, as in the case of Wish Kids Foundation, rather than the genuine Children's Wish Foundation (Kennedy, 2014). In 2010, a 48-year-old Sudbury woman was convicted of misappropriating funds from her employer, the Northern Cancer Research Foundation, and sentenced to 10 months in prison (Vaillancourt, 2010). The employee, an executive director, defrauded the foundation of more than $50,000 over the course of at least one year, by stealing cash donations and claiming fictitious expenditures.

Such cases, sadly, are not unusual: the Ottawa police estimates that about 20% of Canadians are victims of charity fraud (Kennedy, 2014).

International examples, where a similar fraudulent fundraising scheme, or the apparent proximity fraud perpetrated by an international network, may also have a spill-over effect on Canada (*ibid.*). More recently, the Cancer Fund of America and three of its affiliates (Children's Cancer Fund of America, The Breast Cancer Society and Cancer Support Services) were dissolved in what is possibly the largest international foundation fraud of all time. The organizations were found guilty of stealing virtually all the US$187 million in donations they received over a number of years (Federal Trade Commission, 2016). The same spill-over effect may come from nonprofits in general, not just from other foundations (Chen *et al.*, 2009).

Accountability failures like these are highly visible and, while the foundations may have been victims of fraud, their financial accountability practices were less than ideal. Frauds are clearly illegal, and even the perception of accountability failures can tarnish a reputation (Sarstedt & Schloderer, 2010). Media coverage in recent years of frauds and waste has mired the sector's reputation and overall social capital (Hall *et al.*, 2003). When publicly disclosed, these scandals shine the spotlight on a foundation's management issues and point to a clear problem of accountability (Gibelman & Gelman, 2004). When the events of the fraud become public, donors lose confidence, and donations can drop significantly. These accountability failures raise concerns about the ability of organizations to manage their financial accountability and impede an organization's ability to deliver on its mission (Costa *et al.*, 2011).

Accountability failures have hurt the nonprofit sector and its foundations by reducing its credibility (Gibelman & Gelman, 2004). The accountability failures undermine citizens' trust in the sector and negatively impact its ability to solicit donations, attract members and recruit volunteers effectively. If the lack of accountability were to become so pervasive that citizens reduced their donations and volunteering, it could have serious consequences on the economy and on society. Reputational effects are especially damaging to smaller organizations, because they are more vulnerable and dependent on donations, members and volunteers (Puentes *et al.*, 2012). Therefore, accountability failures have required foundations not only to be more accountable but also to demonstrate greater accountability (Ossewaarde *et al.*, 2008).

Accountability challenges: Internal and external environment

In addition to accountability failures, accountability management is further complicated by internal and external challenges (Salm, 1999). As with many organizations and in any resource-limited sector, foundations face challenges that affect their ability to manage their accountability and achieve their objectives. Hall *et al.* (2003) distinguish between two prominent accountability challenges: internal capacity factors and external environmental factors.

Internal capacity is defined as "the human and financial resources, technology, skills, knowledge and understanding required to permit organizations to do their work and fulfil what is expected of them by stakeholders" (Broadbent Report, 1999, p.118). The external environment consists of relevant factors outside the boundaries of the organization (Duncan, 1972). Pressures on funding are growing for foundations, especially public foundations. On the demand side, an increase for their products and services required more funds to satisfy demand (Hall et al., 2004; Lasby & Barr, 2014), as governments have downloaded many services to the nonprofit sector (Hall et al., 2003; Smith, 2008). On the supply side, there has been a shift from stable, long-term funding to project funding (Barr et al., 2006; Hall et al., 2003). A study by Statistics Canada found that 98% of nonprofit organizations reported an unwillingness of funders to fund core operations (Hall et al., 2004). As a result, funding has become more cyclical and uncertain, which has made it more difficult for nonprofits to do long-term planning *(ibid.)* and for foundations to fundraise. This increase in demand and a shift in revenue sources have created a lack of resources, which prior research has suggested might be a significant potential barrier to nonprofit accountability (Palmer, 2013; Yetman & Yetman, 2012).

The external environment is composed of numerous factors which can affect the organization's capacity by creating or amplifying organizational challenges (Hall et al., 2003). Foundations face a competitive external environment for the attention of donors and funders (Hall et al., 2003, 2004; Salm, 1999). Donations, as a percentage of GDP, continue to decrease (Emmett & Emmett, 2015), and charities are relying on a smaller proportion of taxpayers for donations (Imagine Canada, 2018). Foundations are often volunteer driven and tend to rely on a small number of key personnel, which may affect their accountability.

Imagine Canada standards program

Governance mechanisms may be used as a way to overcome accountability challenges. A practical application to overcome these challenges is an accreditation process that follows certain standards. The standards program for charities and nonprofits by Imagine Canada (*ibid.*, p.1) is a program "designed to strengthen their capacity in five fundamental areas: board governance, financial accountability & transparency, fundraising, staff management, and volunteer involvement". The program presents three levels of standards on the basis of a combination of the size of organization in term of employees (range from 10 to 50 FTE – full-time equivalent – threshold) and annual expenses (from $3 to $10 million) (*ibid.*). In its ethical code, Imagine Canada (2011) distinguishes three main areas: donor policies and public representations, fundraising practices, and financial practice and transparency. Table 1 summarizes the ethical code requirements for financial practice and transparency. Imagine Canada closed the ethical code program on December 31, 2016. Table 2 presents a summary of the standards regarding financial accountability and transparency, which will be discussed later.

Table 1 – Imagine Canada's ethical code on financial practice and transparency

	Extracts from the code on ethical requirements
C1	"The charity's financial affairs shall be conducted in a responsible manner, consistent with the ethical obligations of stewardship and all applicable laws."
C2	"All donations shall be used to support the charity's objects, as registered with CRA."
C3	"The cost-effectiveness of the charity's fundraising programs shall be reviewed regularly by the governing board. No more will be spent on administration and fundraising than is required to ensure effective management and resource development."
C4	"The charity shall accurately disclose all costs associated with its fundraising activity."
C5	"The charity shall make the following information publicly available (e.g. on its website, in its annual report, in its financial statements) within six months of its year-end: • total fundraising revenues • total fundraising expenses • total expenditures on charitable activities/programming"
C6	"Charities with over $1 million in annual revenue must have their financial statements audited by an independent licence public accountant. Charities with annual revenue between $250,000 and $1 million may have a review engagement unless required by their governing legislation to have an audit."
C7	"If the charity's investable assets surpass $1 million, an Investment Policy shall be established setting out asset allocation, procedures for investment decisions, and asset protection issues."

Source: Imagine Canada (2011)

Table 2 – Imagine Canada's standards on financial accountability & transparency

Standards summary for foundations	
Financial accountability	
B1	"Organizations must complete annual financial statement in accordance with an acceptable accounting framework as identified by [...] CPA Canada (Chartered Professional Accountants of Canada)."
B2	"Organizations with over $1 million in annual revenue must have their financial statements audited by an independent licensed public accountant. Other organizations may have a review engagement unless required by their governing legislation to have an audit."
B3	"The organization's financial statements must be received and approved by the board and released within six months of year-end"
B4	"The board has a process to ensure that an accurate Registered Charity Information Return (T3010) is filed with the CRA within six months of year-end, as required by law."
B5	"The board approves the annual budget and has a process to monitor the organization's performance in relation to the annual budget. The board or a board committee reviews actual revenues and expenses versus budget at least twice a year."
B6	"The board or a board committee receives from management, at least twice a year, assurance that all statutory remittances have been made."
B7	"The board regularly reviews the cost-effectiveness of the organization's fundraising activities. No more will be spent on administration and fundraising than is required to ensure effective management and resources development."
B8	"Organizations with investable assets over $1 million must have an investment policy setting out asset allocation, procedures for investments, and asset protection issues."
Transparency	
B10	"The organization's financial statements are publicly available. The organization makes the following information available on its website: annual reports, financial statements with opinion, names of all board members, T3010."
B11	"The organization makes information on compensation accessible to its stakeholders to at least the same level as that required by CRA in the T3010."
B12	"The organization discloses on its website details of the purpose and amount of payments for products or services to board members or companies in which a board member is an owner, partner or senior manager."
B13	"The organization accurately discloses all costs associated with its fundraising activities."

Source: Imagine Canada (2018)
Note: B9 standard on protection in electronic commerce was eliminated in 2018.

Ecosystem of information flows

To prevent failures and challenges, a large component of accountability is the exchange of information between stakeholders.[2] In a philanthropic ecosystem, many stakeholders drive accountability (Fontan & Lévesque, 2017). Among the most important stakeholders of grantmaking foundations are the government, donors, grantees, the public, media and intermediaries (Charity Commission, 2009; CICA, 2011; Connolly et al., 2013).

It is important to identify each of these stakeholders more closely. *Grantmaking private or public foundations* are registered charities and must therefore respond to the reporting requests set out by regulators, most notably the CRA. Directors and employees (including the management team and volunteers) are stakeholders within foundations. *Government*, as a regulator, plays a key role in the aggregation and disclosure of financial and governance reporting information (Hyndman & McMahon, 2010). For the purpose of this chapter, "government" includes all the agencies, ministries and statutory agencies such as CRA, Industry Canada, Finance Canada, and Statistics Canada. *Donors* (for public foundations) and funders (for private foundations) are considered important stakeholders (Hyndman, 2010), because without them there would be no foundation in the first place. *Grantees* are organizations or individuals who receive grants from grantmaking foundations. *The public* includes the general public and beneficiaries. *The media* includes newspapers, television, radio, and various social media. *Intermediaries* present multiple faces, which include rating agencies, the accounting profession and researchers: some are organizations that monitor the charitable sector, disseminate information and provide ratings (Gordon et al., 2009; Phillips, 2013). The accounting profession is another intermediary that plays a role in the development of accounting standards applicable to foundations (Hyndman & McMahon, 2010), and auditors provide assurance on financial statements and financial information (Sinclair et al., 2011). Researchers could be seen as intermediaries as well (Brouard, 2014).

Figure 1 shows the key stakeholders and main information flows connected to grantmaking foundations. The main nexus of information flows are between foundations and donors, foundations and government, foundations and grantees, foundations and the public, governments and the public, and grantees and the public. All these stakeholders operate in a web of information exchanges. Information requests and transfers represent the information inflows and outflows between stakeholders. Information flows are presented with arrows of different colours, depending on whether they are requests or transfers. Some exchanges are mediated by media and/or intermediairies. Requests for information could be mandatory (e.g. T3010) or voluntary (e.g. website content). The disclosure and accessibility of information could be public or private. Informal and private reporting may be restricted to specific foundations or available to peers. Information flows may fall between the continuum of those dimensions (disclosure/accessibility, public/private). Information disclosures could also originate from stakeholders themselves or from

---

2   See also Chapter 2 by Hilary Pearson for the importance of information.

other stakeholders, with or without their consent. For foundations, managing the information flows is, therefore, a critical component of accountability.

Figure 1: Ecosystem, stakeholders and information flows

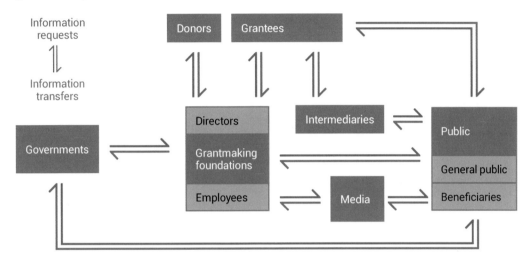

Source: Brouard & Glass (2017)

The framework in Figure 1 includes networks of grantmaking foundations and government institutions because information sharing and collaboration are considered growing trends (Pearson, 2010). Information sharing occurs within a group of grantmaking foundations, especially larger ones – associations such as Community Foundations of Canada (CFC), Philanthropic Foundations Canada (PFC) – or as the result of common interest, with organizations such as the Canadian Environmental Grantmakers Network and the Circle on Philanthropy and Aboriginal Peoples in Canada (*ibid.*).

Financial accountability

A number of dilemmas could be cited to explain some of the general debates regarding accountability. From an institutional perspective, Rourke (2014) cites the distinction between public and private money, the discrepancy between more information and better information, and the difference between being transparent and demonstrating impact.

Definition and dimensions of financial accountability

Financial accountability is imposed and "prioritises formal, coercive, compliance-based forms of accountability [...] using mainly quantitative measures" (O'Dwyer and Boomsma, 2015, p. 38). There are explicit rules (Morrison & Salipante, 2007), often legal requirements to achieve at specified and regular intervals. There are many dimensions of financial accountability: ethics, regulatory and legislative requirements, information systems, transparency, risks management, measurement and reporting challenges, performance measurement, social responsibility.

The role of regulators

In Canada, the federal government regulates the charity sector and plays a key financial accountability role (Cordery & Morgan, 2013; Hyndman & McMahon, 2010). This role is assumed by CRA and the Charities Directorate. Canada is known to have a strong reporting system in comparison with others. All charities, including foundations, are required to comply, and it is possible to find T3010 information from the CRA website or on the charitydata.ca website (Brouard, 2017). With the open data movement, regulators may not control the access to information completely (Phillips, 2013). Any suggestion that the quality of data is becoming insufficient may affect the reputation of these organizations, which could bring about more regulation (Tremblay-Boire *et al.*, 2016). Forthcoming changes within the CRA on-line T3010 reporting requirements for charities are likely to improve data quality and quantity.

As registered charities, grantmaking private or public foundations must respond to the reporting requests set out by CRA and the *Income Tax Act*. The main obligations of a registered charity are to devote its resources (funds, personnel, and property) to its charitable purposes and activities, control and direct the use of all its resources, maintain its status as a legal entity, keep adequate books and records, meet its annual spending requirements (disbursement quota), make sure that official donation receipts are complete and accurate when issued, and file its annual form T3010 within six months of its fiscal year-end (Brouard, 2014).

Governance mechanisms

Governance mechanisms are used to manage the accountability demands of stakeholders and may be divided between internal and external mechanisms (Walsh & Seward, 1990). Harris *et al.* (2017, p.164) describe the importance of both internal and external governance to foundation activities: "Prior research suggests that donors value certain governance mechanisms voluntarily adopted by charities [...]. Our results provide specific reasons why donors should care – good governance reduces the likelihood that their funds will be misappropriated. Moreover, donors may also want to consider the presence of external oversight." Table 3 presents a summary of internal and external governance mechanisms, many of which, while not exclusive to grantmaking foundations, apply to foundations and should provide a helpful checklist for them. Most of these mechanisms are related to financial accountability in some way and examples are provided below. More details will be provided later for mechanisms that are more specific to financial reporting.

There is growing interest about the impact evaluation of the activity of foundations, which will continue to follow the regulations and disclose their financial statements in accordance with accounting standards and to provide an external audit report.

Table 3 – Internal and external governance mechanisms

Internal governance mechanisms	External governance mechanisms
Beliefs and values	Market
Board of directors	Shareholders/Members
Audit committee	Employees
Other board committees	Legal system
Advisory board	Disclosure requirements
Family groups and rules	Accounting profession
Remuneration plans	Results and performance
Management systems	Media pressures
Ownership structure	Societal ethics and morality

Source: Brouard (2016)

Internal governance mechanisms

Internal governance mechanisms can be grouped into the following categories: beliefs and values, board of directors, audit committee, other board committees, advisory board, family groups and rules, remuneration plans, management systems, and ownership structure (see Table 4 for details).

Table 4 – Internal governance mechanisms

Internal governance mechanism	Components
Beliefs and values	beliefs and value systems, code of values, code of conduct, code of ethics, conflict of interest rules, trust, culture, and management philosophy.
Board of directors	statutory and oversight role, size, composition, frequency of meetings per year, proportion of executive directors/non-executive directors on the board, proportion of independent directors on the board, proportion of independent directors with accounting and finance background on the board, proportion of directors external to the family on the board of directors (especially important with a family foundation), mix of inside and outside directors (the Imagine Canada (2018) standard A18 recommends five or more outside directors). Further specific aspects relating to the role of chief executive officer (CEO): e.g. whether their role is combined with or distinct from the chair of the board; their power/influence re board membership selection, terms and length of board membership. Important considerations for board composition include: reputationof executive/non-executive directors on the board, qualification of directors on the board, membership criteria for directors on the board (experience, personal characteristics, gender, independence, core competencies, availability). Criteria relating to board directors' election (age, election term, term limit, mandatory retirement), the number and kind of positions that each board director holds in other organizations, and procedures for evaluating board members.

Audit committee	The *audit committee* (one of the board of directors' committees) has a special role with regard to financial accountability (Ellwood & Garcia-Lacalle, 2016) and may be responsible for performing Imagine Canada (2018) standards B5 on budget approval and B6 on assurance.
	The establishment, role, size and composition of audit committees are matters for consideration, as are the membership criteria for the directors on it (experience, personal characteristics, independence, core competencies, availability, remuneration), the frequency of audit committee meetings per year, and the level of independence of the committee from the board.
	As far as the composition of the audit committee is concerned, some considerations may include a high proportion of independent directors, a high proportion of directors with an accounting and finance background, a high proportion of independent non-executive directors, and CEO and CFO presence.
Other board committees	*Other board committees* cover numerous aspects of organizational governance. Organizations use various names for these committees, such as governance, fundraising, nomination, management, executive, finance, remuneration and benefits, pension, environment and health, human resources, investment, risk, regulatory, compliance and government affairs, public responsibilities, technology and innovation, sustainability and ethics.
	Imagine Canada (2018) standard B8 on investment and asset management may be performed by an investment committee.
	An investment policy (asset allocation, procedures for investments, asset protection issues) is mandatory when an organization's assets are over $1 million. As with the board of directors and the audit committee, there should be clarity for each committee on its mandate; procedures; criteria about roles, size, composition; membership criteria such as experience, personal characteristics, independence, core competencies, availability, diversity; remuneration; proportion of independent directors.
Advisory board	An *advisory board* can complement an existing board of directors when terms of office make it difficult to provide the full scope of representation or long-term experience for prudent decision-making. As above, the terms of reference and scope of activity for an advisory board is important to define and enforce.
Family groups and rules	*Family groups and rules* may be relevant for family foundations. A family foundation may be regulated by family procedures and rules such as the establishment of a family assembly, the number of family assembly meetings a year, the establishment of a family council, the number of family council meetings a year, the number of meetings a year between family members, family business rules and family charter.
	The interconnection between the foundation and the family, especially for private foundations, may be unofficially settled at the family meetings.

Remuneration plans	*Remuneration plans* may be a source of tension between donors and the foundation. The level of remuneration for charitable organizations is often cited in the media. Among the factors to be considered here are the executive compensation structure, executive compensation level, CEO compensation, remuneration systems, and performance incentives. Imagine Canada (2018) standard A5 indicates a requirement for the board or a board committee to approve the total compensation package of the most senior staff person.
Management systems	*Management systems* include a wide variety of mechanisms such as constitution, bylaws, policies and guidelines, vision and mission, strategic plan, accounting systems, budget, business plan, rules and procedures, internal controls, internal auditor, strategic intelligence, balance scorecard, risk management system, systems for conflict resolution, whistleblower policy and tools, crisis management, continuity plan, and insurance. Imagine Canada (2018) standards in section A propose various guidelines on management systems.
Ownership structure	*Ownership structure* of a foundation may include the structure, the ownership by a family and its use for other objectives, namely control of a corporation with a transfer of shares to a foundation (McQuaig, 1987). Corporate foundations act as the philanthropic arm of a for-profit corporation (see Chapter 5).

The Imagine Canada standards program, noted above, is relatively recent, having been launched in 2012. By September 2018 it had accredited more than 200 organizations (not all foundations). Under this program (now Imagine Canada 2018), foundations are able to strengthen their financial accountability through governance and reporting. Establishing formal processes and systems are a continuous challenge, especially for smaller foundations, because they are often volunteer driven and may be unable to acquire or train key personnel to acquire the necessary managerial knowledge and expertise (Barr *et al.*, 2006). Collaboration between foundations may help them share their experience and best practices.

External governance mechanisms

The external governance mechanisms are: market, shareholders/members, employees, legal system, disclosure requirements, accounting profession, results and performance, media pressures, societal ethics and morality (see Table 5 for details).

Table 5 – External governance mechanisms

External governance mechanism	Components
The market	*The market* has fewer implications for foundations than it does for for-profit corporations. The financial market and subsequent transactions may be relevant when considering asset managements or donor transactions by donors (0% inclusion rate for taxable capital gain on gift of publicly traded securities – unless donated to a private foundation). Other market-related facets may include debt/loan market (debt covenant), labour market, managers market, goods and services market, and competition between organizations, especially for attracting donation dollars.
Shareholders/ members	*Shareholders/members* of an organization may be in a position to exercise a right to vote on, and thus influence, a variety of governance issues including board membership, by-laws, budgets and the appointment of auditors.
Employees	*Employees* may exercise a certain control over an organization, which may be increased with the presence of unions, though this is quite rare in foundations. Employees may have a say in the election of directors to the board of directors.
The legal system	*The legal system* includes corporate law, securities legislation, labour law, environmental law, access to information legislation, privacy legislation, disclosure protection legislation (whistleblowing), lobbying legislation, other laws and regulations, governance codes, and codes of best practice. Imagine Canada (2011) ethical code C1 calls for financial affairs to be conducted in a responsible manner, consistent with the ethical obligations of stewardship and all applicable laws.
Disclosure requirements	*Disclosure requirements* are a major component of demonstrating financial accountability, and include financial statements, management and discussion analysis (MD&A), annual reports, governance reports, environmental reports, social responsibility reports, governmental reports (tax return, information return – T3010), disclosures of remuneration, and voluntary disclosures. Imagine Canada (2018) standards B1, B3 and B4 require complete financial statements to be approved by the board and for there to be a process to ensure accurate and timely release of the T3010.
The accounting profession	*The accounting profession* regulates the financial disclosure and the assurance of financial statements according to the accounting standards – Generally Accepted Accounting Principles (GAAP) – and the auditing standards (GAAS). For instance, the accounting profession regulates audit engagements, including auditor independence, the presence of two auditors, and the proportion of services other than auditing offered by an auditor. Imagine Canada (2018) standards B1 and B2 require an acceptable accounting framework, as identified by CPA Canada, accompanied by an audit or review report.

External governance mechanism	Components
Results and performance	*Results and performance* could be measured in various ways beyond net income or the surplus of revenues over expenses – for example, the social impact and reputation of an organization. Imagine Canada (2018) standards A24, D9–D10 and E9 require board performance reviews, staff performance objectives and assessment, and volunteer impact and contributions evaluation. These standards do not focus on the social impact, even if some trends demonstrate a potential evolution toward such measurement.
Media pressures	*Media pressures* could play a role in the flow of information with media enquiries focusing on various aspects of an organization. For foundations, media pressures are probably the most crucial aspect of external governance, and media scrutiny of a foundation's actions continues to increase.
Societal ethics and morality	*Societal ethics and morality* provide a context for what is or is not acceptable in a society. The #metoo movement and its implications is an example of the evolution of societal ethics and morality. Debates around partnerships agreements between the Fondation Lucie et André Chagnon, the Québec government and community actors underline issues about taxation, democracy and autonomy (Fortin, 2018).

Financial reporting

Financial reporting is an important component of demonstrating accountability to external stakeholders. Financial reporting includes definition, measurement, presentation and disclosure. There is a need for reliability and consistency in the way in which charities report their finances, and for enforcement of this reporting (Breen, 2013). For our purpose, reporting is defined as the organization of information flows along a common set of characteristics and objectives.

Financial information types

Information, such as financial information, could lead to knowledge that is also a valuable resource for foundations (Schorr, 2004). Information reporting should have a good fit with the information needs of charities (Hyndman, 1991): in other words, there should be a correspondence between information requests and information transfers. There are four broad categories of financial information reporting (Brouard & Glass, 2017): tax and regulatory, performance, social, and grantmaking. Table 6 presents examples of financial information shared within the philanthropic ecosystem.

Table 6 – Examples of financial information that might be shared

	Tax and regulatory reporting	Performance reporting	Social reporting	Grantmaking reporting
Financial statements	■	■		
Audit or review report	■	■		
T3010 return for CRA – section D & schedule 6	■			
Annual Information Return for Industry Canada or provincial incorporating body	■			
Donations receipts	■			
Annual report		■	■	■
Foundation reports to donors		■	■	■
Foundation website		■	■	■
Policies (e.g. investment)			■	■
Budget information		■	■	■
Input, outputs		■	■	■
Outcomes		■	■	■
Salary scales			■	■
Granting policies and procedures				■
Past and current grants disbursed (amount, recipient, purpose)				■
Grantee application				■
Grantee report				■
Ratios (e.g. ratio of administration costs to total budget)		■		■

Tax and regulatory reporting is influenced by the general requirements imposed on charities by governmental agencies and specific requirements on foundations by the *Income Tax Act*, such as the T3010 Information return, and other regulatory requirements.

Performance reporting refers to financial statements and other financial information which are generally prepared internally and are mostly quantitative. Performance, which may include more than financial information, is often the responsibility of the same group of individuals.

Social reporting refers to information shared about a foundation's activities, non-financial performance and impacts. Such information can be prepared internally or by external stakeholders such as the media, government agencies or other intermediaries and can include both quantitative and qualitative measures.

Grantmaking reporting refers to information requests and disclosure between foundations and grantees and information about grants shared with other stakeholders.

Financial statements

The main vehicle for reporting financial information to internal and external stakeholders is financial statements. The five components of financial statements are the statement of operations/income statement with revenue and expenditures; the statement of financial position/balance sheet with assets, liabilities and net assets; the statement of changes in net assets; the statement of cash flows; and the notes to the financial statements. An auditor's report may accompany the financial statements to provide assurance about their preparation in accordance with generally accepted accounting principles (GAAP) (Sinclair *et al.*, 2011). Imagine Canada (2018) standards B1 and B2 require complete annual financial statements with an audit or review report. Instead of a full set of financial statements, summary or highlights of financial information are sometimes prepared and presented. Such summaries may reduce the level of details available to stakeholders, but simplify the financial information for non-experts. Providing both complete and summary financial statements, however, may present the various audiences of an organization with the level of financial information they need and increase transparency.

In the absence of research here in a Canadian context, international studies provide some guidance. According to a study of the Charity Commission for England and Wales (2017, p. 1), although three-quarters of charities provided information of acceptable quality, a "quarter of charities failed to provide this basic information and fell well short of the standard the public has every right to expect". This basic information required charities to demonstrate how they had used their resources and to provide an audit report. Among the reasons given for charities' failure to do so, the Charity Commission cited: "the accounts as a whole were inconsistent or not transparent", "the accounts did not balance or were incomplete", "a proper independent examination had not been carried out", "the annual report did not cover the charity's objectives and/or its charitable activities", "one or more of the annual report, independent scrutiny report and the accounts were missing" (Charity Commission for England and Wales, 2017, p. 4).

The accounting profession plays a role in the development of accounting and assurance standards (CPA Canada, 2018a; 2018b; 2018c) for nonprofits, charities and foundations (Hyndman and McMahon, 2010). With different types of organization and a wide range of activities, foundations face a different financial reporting and accounting context in Canada. From the CPA Canada handbooks (CPA Canada, 2018a; 2018c), foundations could choose various versions of accounting standards, such as the International Financial Reporting Standards (IFRS) (Part I), the accounting standards for private enterprises (ASPE) (Part II), the accounting standards for not-for-profit organizations (Part III), and the Public Sector Accounting standards. Charitable nonprofit organizations are part of a larger set of organizations (Crawford *et al.*, 2018). However, Imagine Canada (2018) standard B1 requires an acceptable accounting framework as identified by CPA Canada. An audit report will attest to the acceptable accounting framework used. Given the different nature of various types of foundations, those of similar type will be comparable. The development of financial reporting standards is even more complicated at the international level (Crawford *et al.*, 2018; Kilcullen *et al.*, 2007). The various standards may bring a lack of comparability and understandability of financial reporting.

Financial information in T3010 – Information return

Every registered charity in Canada is required to file a T3010 (Registered Charity Information Return) for each taxation year (ITA 149.1(14)) within six months of the year-end; not doing so may incur a revocation by CRA of the charity's charitable status. The T3010 information for all charities is publicly available through the CRA and also through the charitydata.ca websites. Executive summary of T3010 information profile could offer an efficient way to ensure public understanding of a foundation. Donors use that information to address their main concern that donations are being used efficiently and effectively. For instance, a recent survey by Imagine Canada found that 61% of donors reported that they would like charities to explain where or how their donation would be spent, 46% would like to know if too much money is spent on fundraising and 39% want charities to demonstrate the impact on the cause and community they are serving (Lasby & Barr, 2018).

On the T3010, most financial information is found in Section D (1 page) and more detailed financial information is found in Schedule 6 (2 pages). Detailed financial information is required when a charity's revenue exceeds $100,000, the amount of all property not used in charitable activities is more than $25,000, and if the charity has permission to accumulate funds during the fiscal period. Financial information includes assets, liabilities, revenues and expenditures. Schedule 3 of the T3010 requires remuneration details of the ten highest-compensated, permanent, full-time positions. Table 7 presents the content of the 2019 version of the CRA T3010 Information Return. It should be noted that the form T3010 changes regularly, generally every year.

Table 7 – Canada Revenue Agency T3010 content

Section	Description	Additional form
Section A	Identification	Schedule 1 Foundations
Section B	Directors/trustees and like officials	T1235 Directors/Trustees worksheet
Section C	Programs and general information	T1236 Qualified donees worksheet Schedule 2 Activities outside Canada Schedule 3 Compensation Schedule 4 Confidential data Schedule 5 Non-cash gifts Schedule 7 Public policy dialogue and development activities
Section D	Financial information	Schedule 6 Detailed financial information
Section E	Certification	
Section F	Confidential data	
	Privacy statement	
Schedule 1	Foundations	T2081 Excess corporate holdings worksheet for private foundations
Schedule 2	Activities outside Canada	
Schedule 3	Compensation	
Schedule 4	Confidential data	
Schedule 5	Non-cash gifts	
Schedule 6	Detailed financial information	
Schedule 7	Public policy dialogue and development activities	

Source: CRA T3010E (19) version

Annual report

In addition to the quantitative information provided in the financial statements, narrative reporting, which is usually found in the annual report and which places the financial information in the context of the organization's overall story, is considered important (CICA, 2011). Narrative reporting, for example, would include accounts of impact and volunteer contributions, items that are not usually to be found in the financial statements (Shienfield, 2012). The narrative may be helpful for donors to know the impact on the cause and community they are serving (Lasby & Barr, 2018).

According to a CICA (2011) report, key elements of reporting may include: organizational purpose, mission/vision, strategy, goals and performance, risks and opportunities, financial and non-financial highlights, fundraising methods and outcomes, outlook for the future, organizational structure and leadership, and governance. The report also gives some guiding principles of reporting to help organizations in writing their annual report, such as "focus on the mission", "tell the story", "have a strategic perspective", "account for stewardship", "meet stakeholder needs", "be fair and balanced" (*ibid.* p. 6).

Other financial information

Other financial information may include quantitative and qualitative formats (Hyndman, 1991). For example, in addition to previous years' information, future information may be included, such as budget information and service level estimates.

Social reporting may include a variety of content choices such as a statement of an organization's goals and information on problem issues or areas in need of support (Connolly & Hyndman, 2003). Mandatory public benefit reporting may be included as part of social reporting. Measurement of social impact is a developing area. Performance reporting may include the economic performance of an organization, effectiveness and efficiency measures based on input/output, outcomes, volume, quality of service (Connolly & Hyndman, 2003; 2004), and using administration and fundraising cost to total budget as a way of measuring cost-benefit ratios (Connolly & Hyndman, 2013). The content of grantmaking reporting may also include the funding application or grantee reports.

Considering all the content choices, data is a vital organizational resource. Pardy and Fritsch (2017) underline the importance of data literacy to make the most of the data. Various types of data exist, such as administrative data (e.g. accounting transactions, financial statements, T3010), program data (e.g. service level measures, operational data collected about programs) and social data (e.g. demographic trends, well-being of communities) (*ibid.*). The data could be private, shared, simple or highly complex. Big data and analytics may involve multiple datasets and require sophisticated tools and expertise, which may be available only to larger foundations.

Possible improvements in financial accountability

Financial accountability could be improved through additional transparency: relationships and trust are important to accountability (Gates & Rourke, 2014). Vinten (1997, pp. 25–8) suggests thirteen elements "to make accountability a reality" in a charity, namely: fulfilment, formality, periodic reporting, adequate detail, consistent form, accountability to all directly and indirectly responsible or properly interested parties, purposes, principles, procedure, relationships, results and outcomes, efficiency and performance, and incomes and expenditures.

It is also possible to have more transparency by having some open decision-making meetings of the charities and foundations, which will allow questions by interested stakeholders (Fiennes & Masheder, 2016). Foundations are funded by society through the benefits of the tax system on charitable donations, and therefore all stakeholders should be considered in accountability matters. Fiennes and Masheder (*ibid.*, p. 4) suggest specific examples such as "inviting the public to observe discussions and decision-making meetings", "holding open public meetings", "hold an AMA (Ask Me Anything) [...] on physical or social media", "collecting (and publishing) feedback from grantees", "publishing transcripts of all board meetings". At the Hôpital Montfort in Ottawa, for example, holding public meetings for some of the regular board of directors' meetings is a common practice, open to anyone who is interested.

Another way to improve financial accountability is to adopt standards, such as Imagine Canada (2018), sharing best practices and increasing the participation of different stakeholders (The William and Flora Hewlett Foundation, 2015). Open access to information about a foundation's assets, investment policies, and program impact could be examples of sharing best practices. Reinstating national surveys (similar to Statistics Canada (2005, 2009)) should be a key priority (Lalande & Cave, 2017), and having a more unified and strong charitable sector in Canada would enable foundations to cope better with changes and challenges as they occur (*ibid.*).

Conclusion

As the historical context shows, accountability is not a new issue. Reports in the 1990s, the conclusions of which are still relevant today, established a need for improved accountability, by improving collaboration and relationships between the sector and government institutions, by strengthening capacity and by improving the regulatory framework. The increased attention on financial accountability, however, has put additional pressures on foundations and all stakeholders to react and be proactive. The exchange of information between key stakeholders in the philanthropic ecosystem presents various information flows for requests and transfers. A clear set of policies by government and foundations is still a work in progress. In a landscape which is changing and likely to continue evolving, being vigilant is essential.

Financial accountability is a specially important part of accountability, given the need for financial sustainability in response to failures, such as frauds and scandals, and internal and external challenges. The variety of internal and external governance mechanisms offers numerous ways to manage accountability. Even if they may be imperfect and not completely foolproof, governance mechanisms may help to mitigate errors and failures in creating the appropriate accountability system.

Financial reporting is an umbrella term encompassing the financial dimension of tax and regulatory, financial, social and grantmaking reporting. Financial statements, as the primary tool, are a means to communicate the financial position and operations of a foundation. The CRA T3010 form, as a mandatory requirement, is a major driver of information requests. There is a variety of other information reporting which is valued by the different stakeholders.

The implications for foundations of the requirement to tighten accountability include the need to strengthen their accountability role by providing more variety in the content of the information communicated on their finances and their performance, but also on the general context of their actions. Better information quality on the foundations' goals and actions will help those working with foundations to understand the difficulties they are facing with limited financial and human resources. For academics with an interest in accounting, financial accountability is an open area of research with multiple ramifications.

Given the shift towards more accountability, the foundations that will thrive in the future are likely to be those that adopt greater transparency with more and better information and exercise real leadership in managing their stakeholder relationships, governance and financial reporting.

Three key takeaways

1

Financial accountability should be an important part of an organization's overall strategy. Taking financial accountability seriously can help prevent costly frauds and scandals.

2

Annual financial reporting to regulators should not be seen as a burden and a task to be completed as quickly as possible. Financial reporting requires strong attention to detail and regular monitoring throughout the year.

3

Beyond financial reporting, narrative and social reporting is an important means to gain legitimacy with important stakeholders.

References

Barr, CW, Brock, K, Brownlee, B, Frankel, S, Hall, MH, Murray, V & K Scott (2006) *Strengthening the Capacity of Nonprofit and Voluntary Organizations to Serve Canadians*. Imagine Canada. Retrieved from: https://www.yumpu.com/en/document/view/51176027/the-capacity-to-servepdf-imagine-canada/4

Breen, OB (2013) 'The disclosure panacea: A comparative perspective on charity financial reporting', *Voluntas*, 24(3), 852–80

Broadbent Report (1999) *Final Report of the Panel on Accountability and Governance in the Voluntary Sector – Building on Strength: Improving governance and accountability in Canada's voluntary sector*. Ottawa: Government of Canada, February

Brouard, F (2014) 'T3010 Challenges for Research', Sprott Centre for Social Enterprises/Centre Sprott pour les entreprises sociales (SCSE/CSES), May, 51p

Brouard, F (2016) 'Note of Governance Mechanisms', Sprott School of Business, Carleton University, March 20, 8p

Brouard, F (2017) 'L'Information et les outils pour la recherche auprès des fondations subventionnaires' in Fontan, J-M, Elson, PR & S Lefèvre (eds.) *Les fondations philanthropiques: De nouveaux acteurs politiques?* Québec: Presses de l'Université du Québec

Brouard, F & Glass, J (2017) 'Understanding information exchanges and reporting by grantmaking foundations', *ANSERJ – Canadian Journal of Nonprofit and Social Economy Research/Revue canadienne de recherche sur les OSBL et l'économie social*, 8(2), 40–56

Canada Revenue Agency (CRA) (2009) 'Registered charity vs. non-profit organization'. Ottawa: Canada Revenue Agency, April 22. URL: https://www.canada.ca/en/revenue-agency/services/charities-giving/giving-charity-information-donors/about-registered-charities/what-difference-between-a-registered-charity-a-non-profit-organization.html

Chamberland, V, Gazzoli, P, Dumais, L, Jetté, C & Y Vaillancourt (2012) *Fondations et philanthropie au Canada et au Québec: influences, portraits et enjeux*. Laboratoire de recherche sur les pratiques et les politiques sociales (LAREPPS), Université du Québec à Montréal (UQAM), cahier du LAREPPS no 12-02, juillet, 88p

Charity Commission (2009) *Charity Reporting and Accounting – Taking stock and future reform*. Dundee, UK: Charity Commission/Office of the Scottish Charity Regulator

Charity Commission for England and Wales (2017) *Accounts Monitoring Review – Do charity annual reports and accounts meet the reader's needs?* UK: Charity Commission for England and Wales, 7p

Chen, Q, Salterio, S & P Murphy (2009) 'Fraud in Canadian nonprofit organizations as seen through the eyes of Canadian newspapers, 1998–2008', *The Philanthropist/Le Philanthrope*, 22(1), 24–39

CICA (1992) *Terminology for Accountants*, 4th edition. Toronto: The Canadian Institute of Chartered Accountants

CICA (2011) *Improved Annual Reporting by Not-for-Profit Organizations, A Canadian performance reporting board publication*. Toronto: The Canadian Institute of Chartered Accountants, 40p

Connolly, C & N Hyndman (2003) *Performance Reporting by UK charities: Approaches, difficulties and current practice*. Edinburgh, UK: The Institute of Chartered Accountants of Scotland

Connolly, C & N Hyndman (2004) 'Performance reporting: A comparative study of British and Irish charities', *The British Accounting Review*, 36(2), 127–54

Connolly, C & N Hyndman (2013) 'Charity accountability in the UK: Through the eyes of the donor', *Qualitative Research in Accounting & Management*, 10(3/4), 259–278

Connolly, C, Hyndman, N & D McConville (2013) 'UK charity accounting: An exercise in widening stakeholder engagement', *The British Accounting Review*, 45(1), 58–69

Cordery, CJ & GG Morgan (2013) 'Special issue on charity accounting, reporting and regulation', *Voluntas*, 24(3), 757–59

Cordery, CJ, Sim, D & T van Zijl (2017) 'Differentiated regulation: the case of charities', *Accounting & Finance*, 57, 131–64

Costa, E, Ramus, T & M Andreaus (2011) 'Accountability as a managerial tool in non-profit organizations: Evidence from Italian CSVs', *Voluntas*, 22(3), 470–93

CPA Canada (2018a) *CPA Canada Handbook – Accounting*. Chartered Professional Accountants of Canada

CPA Canada (2018b) *CPA Canada Handbook – Assurance*. Chartered Professional Accountants of Canada

CPA Canada (2018c) *CPA Canada Public Sector Accounting Handbook*. Chartered Professional Accountants of Canada

Crawford, L, Morgan, GG & CJ Cordery (2018) 'Accountability and not-for-profit organizations: Implications for developing international financial reporting standards', *Financial Accountability & Management*, 34, 181–205

Dhanani, A & C Connolly (2015) 'Non-governmental organizational accountability: Talking the talk and walking the walk?', *Journal of Business Ethics*, 129(3), 613–37

Duncan, R B (1972) 'Characteristics of organizational environments and perceived environmental uncertainty', *Administrative Science Quarterly*, 17(3), 313–27

Ellwood, S & J Garcia-Lacalle (2016) 'Examining audit committees in the corporate governance of public bodies', *Public Management Review*, 18(8), 1138–62

Emmett, B & G Emmett (2015) *Charities in Canada as an Economic Sector: Discussion paper*. Imagine Canada. Toronto

Federal Trade Commission (2016) 'FTC, states settle claims against two entities claiming to be cancer charities; orders require entities to be dissolved and ban leader from working for non-profits', retrieved January 15, 2018, from https://www.ftc.gov/news-events/press-releases/2016/03/ftc-states-settle-claims-against-two-entities-claiming-be-cancer

Fiennes, C & E Masheder (2016) *Transparency and Accountability of Foundations and Charities: A study of whether large US and UK charities and foundations have open meetings*. Giving Evidence & Feedback Labs.

Fontan, J-M & B Lévesque (2017) 'Conclusion – Penser le secteur philanthropique en termes d'écosystème écologique à visée éthique et à portée esthétique' in J-M Fontan, PR Elson & S Lefèvre (eds.) *Les fondations philanthropiques: De nouveaux acteurs politiques?* Québec: Presses de l'Université du Québec

Fortin, M (2018) *Impact du financement des fondations privées sur l'action communautaire – Le cas de la Fondation Lucie et André Chagnon*. Institut de recherche et d'informations socioéconomiques (IRIS), Note socioéconomique, mars

Gates, C & B Rourke (2014) 'Foundations must rethink their ideas of strategic giving and accountability', *The Chronicle of Philanthropy*, May 18, 4p

Gibelman, M & SR Gelman (2004) 'A loss of credibility: Patterns of wrongdoing among nongovernmental organizations', *Voluntas*, 15(4), 355–81

Gordon, TP, Knock, CL & DG Neely (2009) 'The role of rating agencies in the market for charitable contributions: An empirical test', *Journal of Accounting and Public Policy*, 28(6), 469–84

Hall, MH, Andrukow, A, Barr, CW, Brock, KL, de Wit, M, Embuldeniya, D & Y Vaillancourt (2003) *The Capacity to Serve: A qualitative study of the challenges facing Canada's nonprofit and voluntary organizations*. Toronto

Hall, MH, de Wit, M, Lasby, D, McIver, D, Evers, T, Johnston, C & V Murray (2004). *Cornerstones of Community: Highlights from the National Survey of Nonprofit and Voluntary Organizations*. Statistics Canada. Retrieved from: http://sectorsource.ca/sites/default/files/nsnvo_report_english.pdf

Harris, E, Petrovits, C & MH Yetman (2017) 'Why bad things happen to good organizations: The link between governance and asset diversions in public charities', *Journal of Business Ethics, 146(1)*, 149–66

Hyndman, N (1991) 'Contributors to charities – A comparison of their information needs and the perceptions of such by the providers of information', *Financial Accountability & Management, 7(2)*, 69–82

Hyndman, N (2010) 'Debate: The challenge of calling charities to account', *Public Money & Management, 30(6)*, 328–29

Hyndman, N & D McMahon (2010) 'The evolution of the UK charity Statement of Recommended Practice: The influence of key stakeholders', *European Management Journal*, 28(6), 455–66

Imagine Canada (2011) *Ethical Code Handbook*. Toronto, ON: Imagine Canada. Retrieved from: http://boothuc.ca/wp-content/uploads/2015/08/Imagine-Canada-Ethical-Code-Handbook.pdf

Imagine Canada (2018) *Standards Program for Canada's Charities & Nonprofits*. Toronto, ON: Imagine Canada. Retrieved from: http://www.imaginecanada.ca/sites/default/files/standards_program_handbook.pdf

Imagine Canada and Philanthropic Foundations Canada (2014) *Assets & giving trends of Canada's grantmaking foundations*, September. Montréal, QC & Toronto, ON: Imagine Canada/Philanthropic Foundations Canada. URL: http://sectorsource.ca/sites/default/files/resources/files/trends-canadas-grantmaking-foundations-sept2014.pdf (access May 1, 2015)

Income Tax Act, RSC 1985, c. 1 (5th Supp.), as amended

Johnston, P (2012) *Good Grantmaking: A guide for Canadian foundations*. Montréal & Toronto: Philanthropic Foundations of Canada, September

Kennedy, B (2014) 'When it comes to fraud, how safe are Canada's charities really?' March 24. Retrieved from: https://hilborn-charityenews.ca/articles/When-it-comes-to-fraud-how-safe-are-Canadas-charities-really

Kilcullen, L, Hancock, P & HY Izan (2007) 'User requirements for not-for-profit entity financial reporting: An international comparison', *Australian Accounting Review*, 17(1), 26–37

Lalande, L & J Cave (2017) *Charting a Path Forward – Strengthening and enabling the charitable sector in Canada*. Mowat Centre, Mowat NFP Research #145, April

Lasby, D & CW Barr (2014) *Sector Monitor*. Imagine Canada (Vol. 4). Toronto

Lasby, D & CW Barr (2018) *30 Years of Giving in Canada – The giving behaviour of Canadians: Who gives, how, and why?* Ottawa, ON & Toronto, ON: Fondation Rideau Hall Foundation & Imagine Canada

McQuaig, L (1987) *La part du lion – Comment les riches ont réussi à prendre le contrôle du sytème fiscal canadien*. Montréal: Éditions du Roseau, 406p

Morrison, JB & P Salipante (2007) 'Governance for broadened accountability: Blending deliberate and emergent strategizing', *Nonprofit and Voluntary Sector Quarterly*, 36(2), 195–217

O'Dwyer, B & R Boomsma (2015) 'The co-construction of NGO accountability', *Accounting, Auditing & Accountability Journal*, 28(1), 36–68

Ossewaarde, R, Nijhof, A & L Heyse (2008) 'Dynamics of NGO legitimacy: How organising betrays core missions of INGOs', *Public Administration and Development*, 28(1), 42–53

Palmer, PD (2013) 'Exploring attitudes to financial reporting in the Australian not-for-profit sector', *Accounting & Finance*, 53(1), 217–41

Pardy, A & B Fritsch (2017) *Demystifying Data for the Charitable Sector*. February 21. Retrieved from: https://www.imaginecanada.ca/en/360/demystifying-data-charitable-sector

Pearson, H (2010) 'Funder collaboratives: Trend or tool?', *The Philanthropist/Le Philanthrope*, 23(2), 120–25

Phillips, SD (2013) 'Shining light on charities or looking in the wrong place? Regulation-by-transparency in Canada', *Voluntas*, 24(3), 881–905

Pitt, A (2018) 'What are the biggest challenges facing charities right now?', *Civil Society Voices*, May 16. URL: http://www.civilsociety.co.uk/voices/what-are-the-biggest-challenges-facing-charities-right-now.html (access June 24, 2018)

Puentes, R, Mozas, A, Bernal, E & R Chaves (2012) 'E-corporate social responsibility in small non-profit organisations: The case of Spanish "Non Government Organisations"', *The Service Industries Journal*, 32(15), 2379–98

Ravenscroft, C (2017) *Facing Forward – How small and medium-sized charities can adapt to survive*. London: Lloyds Bank Foundation England & Wales/Evidential Consulting, 29p

Rourke, B (2014) *Philanthropy and the Limits of Accountability: A relationship of respect and clarity*. Kettering Foundations/PACE Philanthropy for Active Civic Engagement, Summer, 20p

Salm, J (1999) 'Coping with globalization: A profile of the Northern NGO sector', *Nonprofit and Voluntary Sector Quarterly*, 28(1_suppl), 87–103

Sarstedt, M & MP Schloderer (2010) 'Developing a measurement approach for reputation of non-profit organizations', *International Journal of Nonprofit and Voluntary Sector Marketing*, 15(3), 276–99

Schorr, LB (2004) 'From knowledge management to knowledge building: An essential foundation journey', *New Directions for Philanthropic Fundraising (45)*, 51–61

Shienfield, R (2012) 'Accountable reporting for nonprofit organizations', *The Philanthropist/Le Philanthrope*, 24(3), 173–9

Sinclair, R, Hooper, K & M Mohiyaddin (2011) 'The quality of charities' audit reports in New Zealand', *New Zealand Journal of Applied Business Research*, 9(2), 23–41

Smith, SR (2008) 'The challenge of strengthening nonprofits and civil society', *Public Administration Review*, 68, S132–S145

Statistics Canada (2005) *Cornerstones of Community: Highlights of the National Survey of Nonprofit and Voluntary Organizations*, catalogue no 61-533-XIE. Statistics Canada Small Business and Special Surveys Division Business and Trade Statistics Field, September 2004 revised June 2005, 79p

Statistics Canada (2009) *Satellite Account of Non-profit Institutions and Volunteering 2007*. Statistics Canada catalogue no 13-015-X, December, 58p

Tremblay-Boire, J, Prakash, A & MK Gugerty (2016) 'Regulation by reputation: Monitoring and sanctioning in nonprofit accountability clubs', *Public Administration Review*, 76(5), 712–22

Vaillancourt, B (2010, October 8) 'Woman gets 10 months for defrauding cancer foundation', *The Northern News*. Kirkland Lake. Retrieved from: https://www.pressreader.com/canada/the-welland-tribune/20101005/281840050016504

Vinten, G (1997) 'Corporate governance in a charity', *Corporate Governance: an international review*, 5(1), 24–8

Voluntary Sector Initiative (1999a) *Building on Strength: Improving governance and accountability in Canada's voluntary sector*, final report of the Panel on Accountability and Governance in the Voluntary Sector. Ottawa, February

Voluntary Sector Initiative (1999b) *Working Together: A government of Canada/Voluntary Sector joint initiative*, report of the Joint Tables. Ottawa, August

Walsh, JP & JK Seward (1990) 'On the efficiency of internal and external corporate control mechanisms', *The Academy of Management Review*, 15(3), 421–58

William and Flora Hewlett Foundation (2015) *Transparency, Participation & Accountability Grantmaking Strategy*. The William and Flora Hewlett Foundation, December

Yetman, MH & RJ Yetman (2012). 'The effects of governance on the accuracy of charitable expenses reported by nonprofit organizations', *Contemporary Accounting Research*, 29(3), 738–67

Part one
Chapter four

Donor-advised funds and charitable foundations in Canada

Carla Funk

The entire Canadian economy faces upheaval as the "baby boomers", that large demographic bubble of people born in the two decades following the Second World War, shift into retirement, old age, end of life – and trigger a massive wealth transfer. This wealth transfer has been estimated to be in the order of $750 billion (Parkinson et al., 2017; Tal, 2016). This paper will explore in some detail the repercussions of this substantial wealth transfer, which has only just started and which is about to accelerate rapidly. It will explore the impact of this wealth transfer on charitable foundations in Canada in general, and on donor-advised funds in particular.

In Canada, end-of-life wealth distributions have two main options: funds can be distributed to individuals, or to a registered charity. A third option, distributing funds to taxes, is not strictly an option, since there is some tax liability on both these options. Making a charitable donation has long been available as an estate-planning tool. Charitable donations support worthy causes and divert monies that might be subject to tax. As Figure 1 illustrates, a direct donation to a charity is the only option that imposes no long-term administrative cost to the donor. This option assumes that the donor is prepared to invest their own time, and is interested in doing so, in selecting a given charity or charities, and is also prepared to pay a transactional fee to a professional advisor, should they be making tax-savvy donations such as gifts of appreciated stock or ecologically sensitive land. Transaction or administrative costs increase in the case of either the donor-advised fund or private foundation option.

Figure 1 – Donation options

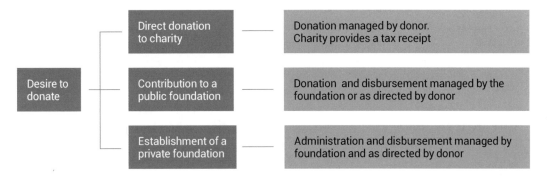

As registered charities, Canadian foundations benefit from the donation of these wealth disbursements from individuals, just as they themselves disburse grants to charitable organizations in the form of grants. Donor-advised funds, a specific sub-set within public foundations, have increasingly become a charitable giving vehicle of choice for donors in the United States (Levine, 2018), and this trend is showing similar signs of growth in Canada (Barhat, 2010; Funk, 2018; Sjogren & Bezaire, 2018).

The use of donor-advised funds has simplified and streamlined the process of giving. Some professional wealth advisors, such as those affiliated with banks, are assisting clients to create these funds under their financial institution's charitable giving foundations, referred to here as "privately sponsored public foundations". Others choose to work with community foundations and other kinds of public foundation. Table 1 provides examples of various types of public foundations in Canada.

The type of foundation advisors work with has implications on their own bottom line. Funds that are directed to a community foundation or other charities leave the "books" of the financial advisors and by doing so have compensation implications for that advisor. Financial advisors are often financially rewarded on the overall size of their investment portfolio; when the portfolio shrinks as a result of charitable giving, the advisor's income shrinks accordingly.

Funds that are directed to a donor-advised fund within their affiliated privately sponsored public foundation, however, reward the advisor with an immediate commission and annual "trailing commissions" on these monies. Trailing commissions are the commission investors pay each year that they own an investment; the fee is paid upon purchase and every year after (Paladin Registry, n.d.).

With financial institutions delving further into the charitable giving arena, this chapter explores financial advisors' use of donor-advised funds as a strategic philanthropic planning tool, and the long-term implications of these funds for the future of foundations.

Table 1 – Canadian public foundations: categories, characteristics and examples

Public foundation type	Characteristics	Example
Community public foundation	Dedicated to philanthropic social improvement primarily in a given place	The Winnipeg Foundation http://www.wpgfdn.org/ also see Community Foundations of Canada http://communityfoundations.ca/
Religious public foundation	Dedicated to the philanthropic guiding principles of particular religious belief	Abundance Canada(formerly The Mennonite Foundation of Canada) https://abundance.ca/
Intermediary public foundation	Promoting giving in Canada generally	Gift Funds Canada https://giftfunds.com/
Single-cause public foundation	Promotion of giving for a single cause	Canadian Breast Cancer Foundation http://www.cbcf.org
Single-purpose public foundation	Promotion of giving for a single cause, and to a particular institution	Hospital for Sick Children's Hospital Foundation https://www.sickkidsfoundation.com/
Privately sponsored dedicated public foundation	Financial institution or private firm's dedicated affiliated charitable giving foundations	Aqueduct Foundation (exclusively offers donor-advised funds, affiliated with Scotia Wealth Management) http://www.aqueductfoundation.ca/
Privately sponsored collective public foundation	Financial institutions collectively sponsor a charitable public foundation	Benefaction Foundation (an independent, non-exclusive foundation that facilitates donor-advised funding for several financial institutions or firms such as CIBC Private Wealth Management, CIBC Wood Gundy, Richardson GMP, and Assante Wealth Management) http://benefaction.ca/

Donor-advised funds

If philanthropic giving were a spectrum, a donor-advised fund would be situated somewhere between a donor writing a cheque directly to a charity and a donor creating a private foundation for philanthropic purposes (Borzykowski, 2011; McCaffery, 2006, p. 25). It is essentially a segregated, or a separately identified, fund within a supporting public foundation, whose purpose is to make grants to other charitable organizations (Barhat, 2010). According to one such supporting foundation, "Once a donor-advised fund is created, the donor's gift is then invested in order to provide perpetual annual funds to the donor's charities of choice from the income of this investment. This allows the donor's selected charities to realize not only immediate benefits, but also annual benefits well into the future" (Canadian Medical Foundation, n.d., para. 6).

Unlike the named fund described above, which is designated to a particular charity, donor-advised funds allow donors to be flexible about which charity or charities the fund supports. After a donor makes a contribution to the supporting public foundation (and gains a charitable tax receipt) that organization has legal control of the contribution. However, the donor maintains advisory privileges for the distribution of funds and, in some cases, for the investment of assets in the account (Blades & Burrows, 2012; Levine, 2018).

Community foundations have been making use of donor-advised funds as a philanthropic giving tool for decades. As of the end of 2017, almost 50 years after the first donor-advised fund was created, about one-third of the individual funds the Vancouver Foundation administered were donor advised. Vancouver Foundation held 1,885 funds: 673 were donor-advised funds and 684 were charitable agency funds. The remaining 528 funds were classified as designated, corporate agency funds and "others" (C Fong, personal communication, June 28, 2018). All of the individual funds are collectively invested in their Consolidated Trust Fund and Socially Responsible Investment Fund and have a market value of $1.1 billion. With a market value of $236 million, donor-advised funds represent approximately 22% of that total market value (C Fong, personal communication, June 28, 2018).

Cindy Lindsay, director of learning at Community Foundations Canada, indicates that, while this percentage varies from community foundation to community foundation, in general donor-advised funds represent approximately 30–35% of the total market value of Canada's community foundations; this percentage has remained consistent for decades (C Lindsay, personal communication, August 10, 2018).

Advantages of donor-advised funds

There are six distinct advantages in using donor-advised funds over creating a private family foundation. First, they are seen as cost-effective, easy to establish and flexible, and enable a donor to "give on (their) own terms" (CanadaGives, n.d., para. 1).

As an example, Vancouver Foundation charges an annual fund administration fee of 0.70%. This recovers the investment management fee charged by the fund managers (on average 0.60% per annum on their Consolidated Trust Fund and 0.30% on their Socially Responsible Investment Fund) (C Fong, personal communication, June 28, 2018). In comparison, private foundations can be costly to initiate, especially if they involve complicated direct charitable activities or if foreign charitable activities are involved. A simple private foundation can be established for a little as $5,000 CDN (Blumberg, 2016), but the ongoing decision-making, administration and governance of a private foundation can carry on for generations and entail a lot of work (Bouw, 2018).

Second, donor-advised funds provide a long-term strategy to coordinate and streamline a client's annual charitable contributions. They are a convenient alternative to having to go through the legal and administrative hassle, and expense, of creating a private foundation. Once given, the donor's money belongs to the administering fund, which then disburses donations or grants on behalf of the donor. This does entail some loss of control. For example, donors cannot make legally binding pledges for future contributions to a charity since the administering foundation now owns the money (Fritz, 2018). Succession and inheritance represent another potential loss of control. While donors can specify whom the account will go to after their death, inheritance can't be prescribed indefinitely and eventually the funds go into a general pool of money at the administering fund (*ibid.*).

A third advantage ascribed to donor-advised funds is that they are a simple and effective tool for investment advisors to use to talk to their clients about philanthropy (McCaffery, 2006, p. 25). In Canada, one of the reasons financial advisors hesitate to speak with their clients about philanthropy has been identified as their lack of comfort and knowledge with the topic. Quite simply, professional advisors are reluctant to raise a topic that they don't know much about (CAGP, 2016, 5:59; Funk, 2018). Presumably, were the donor-advised fund process simple for an advisor to explain to a client, and an efficient way to put a philanthropic plan in place, more financial advisors would be encouraged to speak with their clients about philanthropy.

Fourth, financial advisors have an added incentive to embrace donor-advised funds as a charitable vehicle if their financial institutions or firms have created sponsoring charitable foundations, which, in this paper/article/report, are collectively referred to as "privately sponsored public foundations". These foundations provide a platform for facilitating donor-advised funds for advisors' clients and are either dedicated platforms for a single, specific affiliated financial institution, or are collectively sponsored by a variety of financial institutions. See Table 1 and Table 2 for examples of "privately sponsored" donor-advised fund foundations in Canada.

A further advantage to the use of a donor-advised fund over the establishment of a private foundation is the relatively low threshold for entry. In the United States most programs require a commitment of only $5,000 USD (Fritz, 2018). In Canada the figure tends to be somewhat higher. For example the Toronto Foundation requires $25,000 CDN over two years (Toronto Foundation, 2016), and the SickKids Foundation of Toronto requires a minimum commitment of $100,000 CDN payable over five years (SickKids Foundation, n.d.), while The Winnipeg Foundation requires a minimum of $20,000 CDN to create a donor-advised fund (The Winnipeg Foundation, n.d.). These are still substantial sums, but they are much smaller than the dollar amounts typically invested when establishing a private foundation.

Finally, an advantage implicit in the donor-advised fund arrangement, whether within a community or privately sponsored foundation, is privacy for the donor. Joshua Thorne (manager, philanthropic advisory services, Scotia Private Client Group) notes that "For some clients the number one selling feature of donor-advised funds is the ability to make significant charitable gifts without letting either their family or the rest of the world know that they are the philanthropist behind that [donation]" (Barhat, 2010, para. 13). Privacy provides double-barrelled advantage to the donor by "eliminating pressure from over-solicitation [for donations from charities] and the disclosure of detailed financial information required for a [private] family foundation" (CanadaGives, n.d., para. 3).

Table 2 – Examples of *The Globe and Mail* donor-advised-fund foundations in Canada (2018)

Privately sponsored foundation	Affiliation	Total assets (000)
The Charitable Gift Funds Canada Foundation	RBC Dominion Securities	$384,011
Private Giving Foundation	TD Wealth (Waterhouse)	$297,265
Aqueduct Foundation	Scotia Wealth Management	$196,563
Strategic Charitable Giving Foundation (collectively sponsored)	Investors Group	$221,375
Benefaction	various, including CIBC Private Wealth/Wood Gundy, Richardson GMP, Assante Wealth Management	$31,671

Source: *The Globe and Mail*, 2018

Private Giving Foundation, the first privately sponsored donor-advised fund program in Canada, was created in 2004 by TD Waterhouse (Investment Executive, 2004). In 2006 Mackenzie Investments followed suit, becoming the first mutual fund company in Canada to launch a donor-advised fund (Offman, 2015). Since that time more privately sponsored public foundations have been created. "Canadian commercial financial institutions have eagerly entered the space, providing programs that invest the money with their own managers and sometimes continue to pay the client's advisor a trailing commission" (McCaffery, 2006, p. 29).

Given the advantages of donor-advised funds as a strategic philanthropic tool, the topic of trailing commissions and other financial incentives is worth examining in the context of the influence of financial advisors on foundations in Canada.

Financial incentives for advisors

What kind of incentives are in place to encourage private financial advisors to employ donor-advised funds? At a conference speech in 2016, Brad Offman, then Vice-President Strategic Philanthropy at Mackenzie Financial Corporation, provided an example of a hypothetical client investing $100,000 into a privately sponsored donor-advised fund: as a result of this transaction a financial advisor could expect to earn approximately $5,000 immediately as commission, and to continue earning an annual $1,000 trailing commission thereafter (CAGP, 2016, pp. 4–32). For those advisors with high-net-worth clients exhibiting charitable giving habits and intentions, these commissions could prove highly lucrative. If we were to use these as benchmarks, we could estimate the commission and continued trailing commissions on a $2 million gift as $100,000 (commission) and $20,000 (annual trailing commission) and, on a $5 million gift, as $250,000 and $50,000 respectively. These commissions could place the advisor in a conflicted position; they create a powerful incentive for financial advisors to direct charitably minded clients to create donor-advised funds within privately sponsored public foundations rather than towards any of the various other strategic charitable giving options available, including community foundations. Whether in practice advisors act with bias is difficult to ascertain, but the situation does illustrate the potential for conflict of interest and raises ethical questions that are examined later in this chapter.

Do donor-advised funds spell the end of private foundations?

Given the multiple advantages of the donor-advised fund, is there a danger that their use by public foundations will push out the more costly (and, ironically, less private) private foundations?

So far private foundations are holding their own, in numbers at least. Both public and private foundations increased rapidly from 1994 to 2014: the number of public foundations increased by 69% to 5,100, while in the same period private foundations increased 76% to 5,300 (Imagine Canada & Philanthropic Foundations Canada, 2014). In 2015 Canada was reported to have a total of 10,743 foundations. Of these, 47% were public foundations and 53% were private (Philanthropic Foundations Canada, 2017b). In terms of total assets, public foundations account for $30.4 billion of the total $69.7 billion held by foundations in Canada, with private foundations carrying a greater asset volume at $39.3 billion. A new trend for the Canadian philanthropic sector has been the appearance of a large number of very large private foundations with assets over the billion dollar mark (Philanthropic Foundations Canada, 2017a, p. 3). This data suggests that, for the very wealthy at least, the private foundation is still the philanthropic vehicle of choice.

So, if they are not affecting private foundations, is the increase in use of donor-advised funds having an impact on public foundations in Canada?

Donor-advised funds and public foundations

Donor-advised funds were traditionally offered through community foundations, but this changed in 2004 when TD Waterhouse launched the first commercial donor-advised fund program in Canada. Since that time many Canadian financial institutions have moved into this space with the creation of privately sponsored public foundations offering donor-advised funds (Barhat, 2010; Funk, 2018). Unfortunately, the Canadian Revenue Agency T3010 form for reporting charitable activity does not make a distinction between donor-advised funds and other donations, which makes it difficult to both measure growth in dollar terms and also clearly identify trends in this area. Data for donor-advised funds in the United States are more readily available through their charitable reporting process, and this aids the process of tracking American trends. As donor-advised fund usage increases in this country, we can reasonably expect to foreshadow a similar experience in Canada by examining well-documented trends in the United States.

Because donor-advised funds were so successful in the United States, and because they offer financial advisors powerful financial incentives, it is generally thought that these sponsoring foundations would gain rapid traction in Canada.

A deep dive into murky waters

For the uninitiated, the path of donor-advised funds can be convoluted and murky. Understanding who is responsible for their administration, governance and distribution requires insider knowledge. Here we turn to philanthropy professional Brad Offman, of Spire Philanthropy, for expertise in classifying these funds. Table 3 illustrates Offman's advice to classify donor-advised funds using their distribution channels. The term "distribution" represents the sales, marketing and promotion of donor-advised funds.

While helpful in classifying the organization responsible for distribution, these organizations are not necessarily the same as the governing body, or those responsible for the administration of the fund.

Table 3 – Donor-advised fund distribution channels

Distribution channel	Example
Community foundations	Winnipeg Foundation, Toronto Foundation, Vancouver Foundation
Banks	Royal Bank of Canada, Scotia Trust, Toronto Dominion
Large financial services	Mackenzie, Raymond James, Investors Group
Small financial services	Jarislowski, CGOV
Other	CHiMP, SickKids, United Way

Sub-classification of distribution, governance and administration is necessary in order to follow the funding channels. Offman provides an example: the distribution provided by Investors Group is governed by Strategic Charitable Giving Foundation and administered by its sister company, Mackenzie Investments.

Of the five banks in Canada, all have donor-advised fund distribution programs but only two administer these internally; the remaining three use external firms to manage their programs.

These various pathways from client–donor to a particular implementing charity can be difficult to follow. Donors, financial advisors, and charitable professionals alike may be forgiven for finding the donor-advised fund pathway murkier and less understandable than the actual process of setting up such a fund.

Growth of donor-advised funds

Use of donor-advised funds started earlier in the United States than in Canada. The first donor-advised fund there was created in 1931 by William Barstow at the New York Community Trust (New York Community Trust, n.d.). Trends and growth of the use of this charitable giving vehicle have been rigorously examined for over a decade. The independent public charity, National Philanthropic Trust has produced an annual report on donor-advised funds for the past thirteen years. The numbers show a rate of growth of 12.7% in 2018, growth that was reflected in all key metrics (number of individual donor-advised funds, total grant dollars from them, total contributions to them, and total charitable assets) for seven consecutive years (National Philanthropic Trust, 2019).

The growth in dollar amounts for these funds across the United States has been remarkable. "Contributions to donor-advised funds in 2016 totalled $23.27 billion ... surpassing the 2015 (contributions) of $21.62 billion" and "charitable assets under management in all donor-advised funds totalled $85.15 billion in 2016" (National Philanthropic Trust, 2017, section 6).

Donor-advised funds started in the 1930s, but it was only in the 1990s that the United States witnessed large leaps in their growth. After languishing as the "stepchildren of philanthropy", the sudden success of donor-advised funds is attributed to investor and businessman Edward (Ned) Johnson. Johnson petitioned the IRS to create a charitable vehicle for the mutual fund company Fidelity Investments, and in a landmark ruling in 1991 received approval to create the Fidelity Charitable Gift Fund (Metcalf, 2018; Shakely, 2015). Greater donor control had been successfully advanced, and the advantages at the time were many:

> Now [advisors] could offer clients a philanthropic vehicle that cost nothing to establish and that didn't need IRS approval. They also had the same financial incentive to serve advised-fund donors as they had to serve other clients. What's more because investment fees are quantity-driven, Fidelity Charitable could charge fees that were lower – often much lower – than those of any community foundation.
>
> **Shakely, 2015, para. 13**

Fidelity Charitable Gift Trust, through advertising and direct marketing by their financial advisors, was highly successful. It was not long before Charles Schwab, Vanguard and other financial companies followed suit – by 2012 the top three donor-advised fund foundations were all privately sponsored public foundations: Vanguard Charitable Endowment Program had total assets of $2.3 billion, Schwab Charitable Fund assets of $3.05 billion, and Fidelity Charitable Gift Fund had a total of $5.57 billion, beating long-established religious foundations and community foundations such as the Chicago Community Trust and the New York Community Trusts (Epstein, 2012).

Today, Fidelity Charitable is "one of the country's [USA] largest grantmaking organizations, issuing more than 930,000 individual grants totalling $3.8 billion in fiscal year 2016–17" (Fidelity Charitable, 2017, p. 6). In that same fiscal year, total assets of Fidelity Charitable rose approximately $5.1 billion, from $16.0 billion to a total asset value of $21.2 billion (Fidelity Charitable, 2017, p. 25). In order to appreciate the growth of philanthropy through donor-advised funds, consider this: donor-advised funds currently make up half of America's biggest charities, and four of the top ten charities are privately sponsored public foundations (Metcalf, 2018).

Given the meteoric growth of Fidelity Charitable and other similar foundations in the United States, it is small wonder that Canadian financial institutions and firms have followed suit in creating similar privately sponsored public foundations to facilitate philanthropic donor-advised funds. It is estimated that a total of $3.5 billion is held in donor-advised funds in Canada. This number includes privately sponsored public, community and other public foundations that offer the service of donor-advised funds (Sjogren & Bezaire, 2018).

The total donor-advised-funds assets in Canada is dwarfed by the American counterparts: the $3.5 billion total assets of all donor-advised funds in Canada represents less than the $3.8 billion that was *granted out* to charities by a single privately sponsored public foundation in the United States: Fidelity Charitable. Philanthropy is big business in the American financial industry; with our baby-boomer demographic shift and resultant intergenerational wealth transfer occurring here, Canada is just beginning to show signs of the same.

Competition? Or increased philanthropy?

So, does the rise of philanthropy on the backs of financial advisors constitute an opportunity or a threat? Will donor-advised funds affiliated with financial firms push aside Canadian community foundations in terms of attracting strategic charitable wealth funds? Brad Offman, Founder and Principal of Spire Philanthropy, describes the American experience:

→ In the United States, the relationship between commercial firms and community foundations was not a particularly healthy one. Community foundations mobilized to improve their practices in order to compete in a world where donors had the ability to access instant information disseminated by corporations with considerable resources. Furthermore, commercial firms failed to recognize community foundations as important stakeholders in the philanthropic landscape. The unhealthy tension between commercial and community philanthropy undermined the resources of both sides and created a market characterized not by philanthropic values but by traditional cutthroat competition.

Offman, 2015, para. 6

While some community foundations might have been threatened by the changing landscape, others embraced the attention that philanthropy and donor-advised funds were receiving. Jack Shakely, president emeritus of the California Community Foundation, describes how this foundation used the situation to their benefit:

→ In the mid-1990s, Fidelity launched a huge advertising campaign ... [that] very effectively explained the advantages of donor-advised funds. The Fidelity campaign was so effective, in fact, that I developed a campaign of my own on its coat-tails: I simply extolled the added benefits that come with local management of a donor-advised-fund.

Shakely, 2015, para. 14

In Shakely's experience, the rise in the use by privately sponsored public foundations of donor-advised funds has been of net benefit to philanthropy in general:

→ Entities like Fidelity Charitable have the financial incentive and the marketing might to reach a vast constituency of would-be donors. The growth of such funds represents the greatest marketing phenomenon in the recent history of charitable giving: for the first time ever, philanthropy has a sales force. And philanthropy as a whole has benefited from it.

Shakely, 2015, para. 7

Data is not readily available through the regulatory reporting system in Canada to study the effect advisor compensation has had on the funnelling of funds to community foundations as opposed to privately sponsored public foundations. It is, however, an important question.

There will always be those that gain and those that lose in a changed landscape of this kind, but the American experience indicates that Canadian community foundations and privately sponsored public foundations should find ways to work together, rather than compete, in order to expand philanthropy in general. Donor-advised funds represent the potential for a new and dynamic growth of charitable fund development. This is an opportunity for commercial firms, which are predicted to continue to launch more programs and, by doing so, further penetrate the Canadian philanthropic landscape. Equally, this is potentially an opportunity for community foundations, which are predicted to experience an era of unprecedented growth through donor-advised fund management (Offman, 2015).

Controversy over warehousing charitable funds

In spite of the multiple advantages attributed to the charitable vehicle of donor-advised funds, and despite their consistent growth, not everyone in the United States is equally enamoured of their use. Boston College Law School's Professor, Ray D Madoff, fears that the use of donor-advised funds means a detour of funds away from immediate charitable use (Madoff, 2011). Her concern rests with the rise of activity by large financial institutions such as Fidelity, Schwab and Goldman Sachs, which, through the creation of affiliated privately sponsored public foundations, hold, invest, and distribute dollars for charitable purposes. Madoff is concerned that these funds "generate significant management and investment fees for the institutions that house them, which have little incentive to speed up the distribution of resources to the charitable sector" (*ibid.*, para. 3).

Unlike regulations for donor-advised funds in Canada, donor-advised funds in the United States are under no obligation to make minimum annual distributions. Nonprofit consultant Alan Cantor echoes the general concern about the increased use of donor-advised funds within privately sponsored public foundations, stating that this "accelerating trend of warehousing philanthropic dollars is a deeply troubling trend for American philanthropy" (Cantor, 2014, para. 2).

Despite Madoff and Cantor's fear that donor-advised funders will sit on their philanthropic assets indefinitely, American data to date shows no signs that such warehousing of charitable funds is taking place. In fact, the contrary is true: while there have been large leaps in contributions to donor-advised funds in the past years, the percentage payouts from these funds have been equally generous. National Philanthropy Trust reports that "grants from donor-advised funds to charitable organizations reached a new high at $23.42 billion. This is an 18.9 per cent increase from a revised 2017 total of $19.70 billion" (Heisman, 2019, sec. 5).

Regardless of the data, highly visible exceptions to the aggregate data have recently brought the question of warehousing of charitable funds to the fore. A *New York Times* article on donor-advised funds with the provocative title "How Tech Billionaires Hack Their Taxes With a Philanthropic Loophole" details the increasing lack of transparency of philanthropy (Gelles, 2018). The article focuses on a 2014 donor-advised-fund contribution of GoPro stocks valued at $500 million by GoPro founder and billionaire Nicholas Woodman, thereby creating the Jill and Nicholas Woodman Foundation. Four years later, there is little evidence of pay-out to the community by the Foundation – only a grant to the Bonny Doon Art, Wine and Brew Festival, as a benefit to an elementary school in California (*ibid.*, para. 5). In fact, since this is a donor-advised fund, in the United States, no pay-outs are required.

In this case the benefit of this large donor-advised fund to society is difficult to see, but the benefit to Woodman is clear. Through this donation Woodman avoided paying capital gains on the $500 million (a savings estimated to be in the tens of millions). In addition, Woodman likely saved more millions by claiming a charitable tax deduction, and will probably continue to reduce his personal tax bill in future years. The article sums up the situation: "Mr Woodman achieved this enticing combination of tax efficiency and secrecy by using a donor-advised fund – a sort of charitable checking account with serious tax benefits and little or no accountability" (*ibid.*, para. 8).

Canada has prevented potential "warehousing" of charitable dollars by imposing disbursement quotas (Blumberg, 2010, para.2). In contrast to the American system, the Canadian Revenue Agency regulations stipulate that a foundation must disburse at least 3.5% of the fund's average value of assets in the previous 24 months each year (Canada Revenue Agency, 2017). The "3.5% rate is roughly equal to the historical real rate of return, which is the rate of return after inflation. Prior to 2002, the rate was 4.5%" (Burrows, 2013, para. 7). Perhaps this regulation was imposed in recognition that the US regulation, which allows the receipt of a charitable receipt for donating to a vehicle with no payout requirements, makes little public-policy sense (Cantor, 2014; Gelles, 2018).

The Canadian *minimum regulated rate* of disbursement (3.5%) for all registered charities is much lower than the *actual rate* of disbursement for donor-advised funds (20.4 %) reported in the United States. Critics, however, warn that these numbers can be skewed to give the illusion that meaningful philanthropic activity has taken place where there is none (Gelles, 2018, para. 34). This illusion is created when one privately sponsored public foundation trades donor-advised funds with another – for example, Vanguard Charitable might shift $15 million donor-advised funds to Fidelity Charitable. Privately sponsored public foundation representatives indicate that this is simply a case of wealthy donors adjusting their accounts, but sceptics see a system ripe for abuse: "Donors may wait for years to engage in meaningful philanthropic activity, or decide to simply leave the fund for their children to manage" (*ibid.*, para. 31).

Critics of the American system are alarmed that donors can realize a tax deduction by contributing to a donor-advised fund without actually contributing funds to an operating charity. The Canadian system is not perfect, either: "due to the minimum assets requirement [$100,000], the 3.5% disbursement quota affects only a minority of larger Canadian charities" (Burrows, 2013). Since the disbursement quota is calculated on the basis of a charity's entire annual expenditures for charitable purposes, and is not linked to investment alone, most charities that fundraise may receive and spend much more than the equivalent of 3.5% of its investment assets.

This amount is then added to a disbursement quota surplus, which can be carried forward for up to five years (*ibid.*). In effect, "the 3.5% is not an onerous requirement for charities that have multiple income streams and do not rely on investment payouts alone to support their charitable activities. Most public charities now have disbursement quota surpluses, although there are exceptions" (*ibid.*, p. 2). It is important to note also that, since the 3.5% quota applies to the average value of assets within a foundation, some individual funds within a foundation may not make donations to any registered charities.

This is certainly a cause for concern in the United States, where it is observed that the numbers are deceiving: "While the overall payout rate at an organization that manages DAFs [donor-advised funds] may be substantial, the numbers could be warped by a few donors who give away huge sums, while the majority of donors give away virtually nothing at all" (Gelles, 2018, para. 35).

Given the debate in the United States on this matter, Canadians might wish to consider whether the 3.5% disbursement regulation goes far enough to alleviate concerns of warehousing of charitable dollars in Canada. Canada does not track disbursement of donor-advised funds specifically and so, while it would be interesting to make comparisons, it is difficult to ascertain donor-advised fund disbursements in general, let alone distinguish between disbursements from privately sponsored public foundations and those from other public foundations or track disbursements from one privately sponsored public foundation to another. If the American example holds true for this country, there is increasing cause for vigilance about the warehousing of philanthropic funds in Canada as the use of donor-advised funds becomes an increasingly popular giving vehicle here. However, without Canadian-specific data to examine donor-advised fund activity here, there is little opportunity to accurately address this possibility.

While warehousing may not be deemed cause for immediate concern, the question of "independence of interest" has created considerable controversy in the United States and is worthy of scrutiny in the Canadian context. Detractors fear that the commercialization of philanthropy will be distorted to reflect the financial advisor's self-interest.

Independence of interest in establishing donor-advised funds

Cantor bemoans the "inexorable takeover of the charitable sector by Wall Street", noting that, despite protestations from these sponsoring organizations that they are not commercially interested:

> [n]early all donor-advised fund dollars are invested in the mutual fund of the affiliated financial firm and, given the constant cross-selling between the for-profit and nonprofit entities, that notion of independence is little more than a legal fig leaf

Cantor, 2014, para. 9

A recent qualitative investigation of the value proposition of the inclusion of philanthropy in the business practices of professional advisors in Canada highlights similar implications, noting the potential for conflict of interest in the process of establishing a donor-advised-fund (Funk, 2018). When a client seeks assistance with strategic charitable giving, some advice is laden with self-interest. An ethical advisor looking out for the best interests of their client will present various options, which might include creating a private foundation, donating directly to charity, or donating to a community foundation *in addition* to the option of creating a donor-advised fund within a privately sponsored public foundation.

Clients need to be aware – should an advisor recommend establishing a donor-advised fund within privately sponsored public foundations – that this is not a completely unbiased conversation. Monies that otherwise would be lost from the client's managed portfolio to a charity or to a community foundation are maintained within the advisor's "books" if the client chooses to create a donor-advised fund under the auspices of an affiliated sponsoring firm. In this case the advisor is likely to be compensated through "trailing commissions", as noted earlier, at a rate of approximately 1% annually. One financial advisor candidly described donor-advised funds as "the ultimate revenue generator" for the financial advisor (*ibid.*).

Alternatively, when a client expresses interest in dedicating part of their portfolio to be donated directly to a charity, it is not in the immediate best interest of the advisor, since in this case those funds would leave their "books"; the managed fund portfolio for that client would be depleted by this move, which would represent a decline in an advisor's income. It is in the best interest of the financial advisor to keep the funds under their management to ensure that they would be compensated. Dissuading clients from making any charitable contributions at all is certainly one option, and the use of donor-advised funds is certainly preferably to that kind of client–advisor conversation.

Not all client–advisor situations constitute self-interest. In some cases, such as when a client has sought out a values-based firm with a strong commitment to ethical investing, the client-as-donor might find comfort in the knowledge that their advisor's long-term commitment to a particular investing model will continue on in their philanthropic portfolio, with the understanding that the advisor will be using the same ethical and value-based approach (*ibid.*).

In other cases, an advisor may have a strong relationship of trust with a client, built over decades of effective investment advice and wealth management. Donor-advised funds provide that client with a comfortable belief that their charitable contributions will be similarly dealt with should they commit donations to an in-house foundation under that same investment management. This client would naturally expect to rely on the same level of effectiveness from their professional advisor in dealing with their philanthropic goals – for this reason financial advisors are advised to gain a solid understanding of the philanthropic sector, in order to speak comfortably on the topic of philanthropy and be equipped to offer clients a full suite of financial advice that includes strategic charitable giving (Funk, 2018; Sjogren & Bezaire, 2018).

Ultimately, "donor(s) should be wary of the financial advisor that insists that strategic charitable giving plans be directed exclusively to [privately sponsored public] foundations, since this is clearly the option most beneficial to that advisor, and is not necessarily in the best interest to the charity or to the donor's charitable intent" (Funk, 2018, p. 17). Ethics come into play when a client's advisor does not clearly inform them of possible self-interest, when an advisor does not inform the client of options that might not provide the advisor with compensation but which more clearly represent the client's charitable interests (such as giving directly to a charity), or when an advisor refuses to execute their client's charitable strategies unless funds are directed to the sponsoring foundation.

The potential for unscrupulous financial advisors acting in self-interest rather than in the best interests of their clients is very real and can only be combated by ensuring transparent transfer of funds in the sector, through the provision of clear information to and by all advisors, and through the education of donors. In Canada, are donors explicitly aware of the affiliation between the privately sponsored public charitable foundation and the commercial financial institution providing their financial management services? There are likely to be requirements of disclosure to this effect when committing funds to a charitable foundation, but this fact is not easily discernible to anyone outside the financial sector seeking to unravel the tangled web of charitable fund options.

Are privately sponsored foundations the right choice?

Another important question when considering donor-advised funds is whether privately sponsored charitable foundations are as well-equipped as community foundations to disburse funds. Grant-giving requires specialized and sophisticated skill sets that might not immediately be apparent to either donors or financial advisors. This harks back to the concerns of Ostrander (2007) that, when donors increased control, recipients' control was diminished and in the process valuable on-the-ground knowledge would be ignored or lost.

Community foundations in Canada have been honing those skills for nearly one hundred years – establishing the philanthropic networks and relationships required to build, support and develop resilient communities. Community Foundations of Canada describes some of the activities that are required to disburse funds in a meaningful manner: "We connect people with causes that inspire them. We animate civic engagement and dialogue. And we invest in talent, impact and innovation with a focus on tackling some of the most persistent social challenges facing our communities, our country and the world" (Community Foundations of Canada, n.d.). Kate McCaffery of Advisor's Edge agrees that community foundations possess worthy qualities: "Those running the (community foundation) have specialized knowledge of their given charitable sectors, which can sometimes be leveraged to provide very personalized service to donor clients" (McCaffery, 2006, p. 31).

If financial institutions with privately sponsored public foundations for the purpose of facilitating donor-advised funds are primarily motivated by maintaining management of client portfolios and providing personal tax planning for their clients, how well do they perform in these specialized, community development tasks? Why would a donor not simply choose to gain the same tax benefits and create a donor-advised fund directly within their local community foundation? Concerns about values-based and ethical investing, or continuing with the management of a trusted advisor might be good reasons; yet these are being addressed in some larger community foundations through increased flexibility and responsiveness on the management of those donor-advised funds.

Cindy Lindsay (personal communication, 2018), learning director of Community Foundations Canada, indicates that, depending on the size of the community foundation and the size of the gift, there are options for what they call a "third party advisor", which would enable the creation of a donor-advised fund within the auspices of a community foundation and yet be managed by the donor's professional advisor of choice. These arrangements are made cautiously, however, and they are reserved for large donations that start at $500,000 or $1 million minimum, depending on the community foundation in question.

Lindsay notes that some community foundations in Canada are concerned about donor-advised funds that are housed at privately sponsored public foundations; they are worried that these are enabling the wealthy to gain tax advantages without following through on their philanthropic commitment. Others, though, are not at all concerned, and she explains that variability in reactions is a result of how "savvy" local professional advisors are about philanthropy. Advisors may realize that in certain cases a client shows little charitable intent and has a greater focus on the tax break donor-advised funds bring to the table. These clients might be better served by the privately sponsored public foundation; yet they sometimes approach the community foundations seeking the competitive rate of fees that a large commercial financial institution is offering. "Donors that seek tax loopholes are not necessarily about philanthropic intent. However, 'charitable intent' is what community foundations do: we gather as many dollars as we possibly can in order to funnel funds back into the community. We are not particularly hoping to attract a client that has no interest in creating community good, and is only focused on personal gain" (C Lindsay, personal communication, 2018).

An added concern about privately sponsored public foundations is in the case of "orphan funds", when a donor dies without leaving direction for the complete distribution of the fund. For those public foundations with a clear purpose or cause, this does not pose a problem – monies are easily disbursed in alignment with donor intent. However, "when funds are left to organizations whose only business is operating these funds, like those with financial firms, it seems more problematic. Charity is not their focus, and how these 'orphan' funds will eventually be used is less clear" (Levine, 2018).

More data on donor-advised funds in Canada is required

In Canada, is financial advisor influence directing more funds to sponsoring foundations? If privately sponsored public foundations have no intention of developing community development skills, have we simply created a well-paid intermediary within this institutional entity?

Is this a positive influence, generating more aggregate dollars to charity that might not otherwise have been donated – is the philanthropic pie getting bigger as a result of the influence of financial advisors? Or is the pie perhaps unchanged: are philanthropic funds simply being diverted from community foundations and towards privately sponsored public foundations? Or are community foundations holding their own in the unchanged pie – are direct donations to charities the losers in this drive for philanthropic dollars?

The implication of these questions is that much about the use of donor-advised funds remains obscure. Canada lacks the data required to critically examine the impact of this charitable giving vehicle in the philanthropic sector. In the United States, some say community foundations have been losing market share to privately sponsored public foundations (Levine, 2018) while others argue that aggressive marketing by these foundations has "encouraged a new set of donors to enter the field" (Shakely, 2015, para. 19).

In private conversation, financial advisors suggest that without personal incentives the majority of advisors would not consider engaging their clients in a conversation about philanthropy, and so the privately sponsored public foundations are indeed encouraging conversations about philanthropy and promoting the concept of Canadians' giving. Better sources of data and further study are required in both countries in order to verify these assertions (Funk, 2018; Heist & Vance-McMullen, 2019).

Expect upheaval

Privately sponsored public foundations and the use of donor-advised funds have seismically shifted philanthropic giving in the United States over the past three decades. Given the demographic shift occurring in Canada, and the intergenerational wealth transfer that is obliged to occur as the baby boomer demographic bubble ages out, we can expect a similar shift in Canada as well.

If the American example is an accurate foreshadow of the Canadian experience, not everyone is going to come out of this upheaval unscathed. Advisors have access to channels of capital that charities don't have. Donors rely on good advice, and it is perhaps inevitable that they would rely on the advice of the individuals and institutions that carried them through the period of their wealth accumulation for their philanthropic advice. Financial advisors have the potential to drive more philanthropic dollars into the charitable system, to enlarge the philanthropic pie to benefit more Canadians. Community foundations are at risk of losing charitable funds to privately sponsored public foundations unless they embrace the concept and find ways to accommodate both donors and advisors.

Community foundations are still the experts on charity, community development, and the community's needs. Religious foundations will always attract donors who share common values and concepts of generosity. Foundations with specific causes will attract those donors passionate about the impact of their dollar in a very specific manner. All of these foundations can offer the donor the same tax benefits, flexibility, ease of donor experience, and privacy afforded by the in-house foundations.

In Canada, with the added benefit of hindsight through examination of the American experience of these charitable vehicles, and by learning from those experiences, it would be prudent to put in place measures for ensuring that the Canadian philanthropic system remains proactive about disclosure and transparency. The vast wealth this philanthropic vehicle represents, the unanswered questions raised about increased donor control, and the vested interest of a highly organized and professional financial machinery focused on the creation and growth of donor-advised funds all point to an urgency for their rigorous review.

As Canada's wealthy baby-boomers approach the two inevitable occurrences in life, death and taxes, there is an opportunity to embrace the best of the American experience, and to learn from the worst of philanthropy in that country. In Canada we embrace the generosity and philanthropic intent of our citizens, and encourage those acts through significant tax incentives. At the same time, it is critical to ensure that the tax benefits accrued by the wealthy are legitimized through benefit to those that are actively engaged in helping Canadians towards building a stronger and more resilient Canada.

Three key takeaways

1 With an impending massive transfer of wealth from baby boomers to the next generation, donor-advised funds are poised to radically alter the face of philanthropy in Canada.

2 Philanthropic resources are increasingly shifting into the hands of commercial financial institutions through the brokerage of donor-advised funds, spelling potential opportunities and threats for foundations.

3 Donors gain greater control through the use of donor-advised funds on the one hand, and lose it in the long term on the other. While it is clear that financial professionals stand to gain, it is not clear whether there is a net benefit to Canadian society.

References

Barhat, VB (2010, December 9) 'Donor advised funds: Flexible philanthropy'. Advisor.ca Retrieved from: https://www.advisor.ca/news/industry-news/donor-advised-funds-flexible-philanthropy/

Blades, E & MD Burrows (2012, September 17) 'Giving through donor-advised funds'. Advisor.ca. Retrieved from: https://www.advisor.ca/tax/estate-planning/flexible-certainty/

Blumberg, M (2010, March 4) 'Canadian Budget 2010 announces disbursement quota reform for Canadian charities', *Global Philanthropy*. Retrieved from: https://www.canadiancharitylaw.ca/blog/canadian_budget_2010_announces_disbursement_quota_reform/

Blumberg, M (2016, April 19) 'Top fallacies about private foundations in Canada – Part one'. Retrieved from: https://www.canadiancharitylaw.ca/uploads/Fallacies_about_Canadian_Private_foundations.pdf

Borzykowski, B (2011, October 25) 'How donor-advised funds work and help you give', *Canadian Living*. Retrieved from: http://www.canadianliving.com/life-and-relationships/money-and-career/article/how-donor-advised-funds-work-and-help-you-give

Bouw, B (2018, April 13) 'Private foundations: Giving away money is harder than you think', *The Globe and Mail*

Burrows, M (2013) 'Legal, governance and accountability issues'. Retrieved from https://www.scotiabank.com/ca/en/about/storytelling/legal-governance-and-accountability-issues.html

CAGP (2016) 'FRANK Talks 2016: Brad Offman, can we break the silos between gift planners and PAs?' Retrieved from: https://www.youtube.com/watch?v=j73oxIzt5Xc&feature=youtu.be&list=PLYE9TVHA93iPnkpgw2kJGrPCJSrsoR5l-

Canada Revenue Agency (2017) 'Disbursement quota calculation'. Retrieved: https://www.canada.ca/en/revenue-agency/services/charities-giving/charities/operating-a-registered-charity/annual-spending-requirement-disbursement-quota/disbursement-quota-calculation.html

CanadaGives (n.d.) 'Donor advised funds'. Retrieved from: http://www.canadagives.ca/donor-advised-funds/

Canadian Medical Foundation (n.d.) 'Donor advised funds', Retrieved from: http://medicalfoundation.ca/en/what-you-can-do/donor-advised-funds/

Cantor, A (2014, October 28) 'Donor-advised funds let Wall Street steer charitable donations', *The Chronicle of Philanthropy*. Retrieved from: https://www.philanthropy.com/article/Donor-advised-Funds-Let-Wall/152337/

Community Foundations of Canada (n.d.) 'Canada's community foundation movement'. Retrieved from: http://communityfoundations.ca/network-benefits/

Epstein, E (2012, June 8) 'Wealthy Americans are donating tons of money to these funds – and reaping huge tax breaks', *Business Insider*. Retrieved from: http://www.businessinsider.com/the-biggest-donor-advised-funds-2012-6

Fidelity Charitable (2017) *Fidelity Charitable 2017 Annual Report* (p. 28). Retrieved from: https://www.fidelitycharitable.org/content/dam/fc-public/docs/annual-reports/2017-annual-report.pdf

Fritz, J (2018, March 14) 'What is best? Donor-advised fund or a foundation?' Retrieved July 27, 2018, from The Balance Small Business website: https://www.thebalancesmb.com/donor-advised-funds-vs-private-foundations-4160358

Funk, C (2018) 'Doing good for business—The inclusion of philanthropy in the Canadian professional advisor's business practice'.

Gelles, D (2018, August 5) 'How tech billionaires hack their taxes with a philanthropic loophole', *The New York Times*. Retrieved from: https://www.nytimes.com/2018/08/03/business/donor-advised-funds-tech-tax.html

Globe and Mail (2018, March 6) 'Canada's top 100 non-profit organizations (registered charities)', *The Globe and Mail*. Retrieved from: https://www.theglobeandmail.com/report-on-business/top-100-non-profit-organizations-registered-charities/article34067186/

Heisman, E (2019) *2019 Donor-advised-fund Report*. Retrieved from: https://www.nptrust.org/reports/daf-report/

Heist, DH & D Vance-McMullen (2019) 'Understanding donor-advised funds: How grants flow during recessions', *Non Profit and Voluntary Sector Quarterly*, 48(5), 1066–93

Imagine Canada & Philanthropic Foundations Canada (2014) *Giving Trends of Canada's Grantmaking Foundations*, Toronto and Montreal

Investment Executive (2004, October 6) 'TD Waterhouse launches new private giving foundation' *Investment Executive*. Retrieved from: https://www.investmentexecutive.com/building-your-business/financial-planning/td-waterhouse-launches-new-private-giving-foundation/

Levine, M (2018, January 2) 'Growth in donor advised funds: How nonprofits can adapt', *Nonprofit Quarterly*. Retrieved from: https://nonprofitquarterly.org/2018/01/02/growth-donor-advised-funds/

Madoff, RD (2011, November 21) 'Opinion | Tax write-off now, charity later', *The New York Times*. Retrieved from: https://www.nytimes.com/2011/11/22/opinion/tax-write-off-now-charity-later.html

McCaffery, K (2006, August) 'Simplified philanthropy – Donor funds make it easier for advisors to talk to clients about leaving a legacy', *Advisor's Edge*, 25–31

Metcalf, T (2018, March 14) 'A peek Into Goldman's black box charity reveals tech billionaires', *Bloomberg.Com*. Retrieved from: https://www.bloomberg.com/news/articles/2018-03-14/peek-into-goldman-s-black-box-charity-reveals-tech-billionaires

National Philanthropic Trust (2019) 'The 2019 Annual report'. Retrieved from: https://www.nptrust.org/reports/annual-report/#contributions

New York Community Trust (n.d.) 'About'. Retrieved from: https://www.nycommunitytrust.org/about/

Offman, B (2015) 'Impact of donor advised funds'. Retrieved from: http://spirephilanthropy.com/impact-of-donor-advised-funds/

Ostrander, SA (2007) 'The growth of donor control: Revisiting the social relations of philanthropy', *Non Profit and Voluntary Sector Quarterly*, 36(2), 356–72.

Paladin Registry (n.d.) 'Trailing commission definition'. Retrieved from: https://www.paladinregistry.com/financial-dictionary/trailing-commission?letter=T

Parkinson, D, McFarland, J & B McKenna (2017, November 12) 'The boomer shift: How Canada's economy is headed for major change', *The Globe and Mail*. Retrieved from: https://www.theglobeandmail.com/globe-investor/retirement/the-boomer-shift-how-canadas-economy-is-headed-for-majorchange/article27159892/

Philanthropic Foundations Canada (2017a) *A Portrait of Canadian Foundation Philanthropy* (p. 23). Retrieved from: https://pfc.ca/wp-content/uploads/2018/01/portrait-cdn-philanthropy-sept2017-en.pdf

Philanthropic Foundations Canada (2017b, November) *Snapshot of Foundation Giving in 2015*. Retrieved from: https://pfc.ca/wp-content/uploads/2018/01/pfc-snapshot-giving-2015-en.pdf

Shakely, J (2015, May 21) 'Who's afraid of DAFs?'. Retrieved: http://philanthropynewsdigest.org/columns/ssir-pnd/who-s-afraid-of-dafs

SickKids Foundation (n.d.) 'Donor advised funds'. Retrieved July 27, 2018, from: https://www.sickkidsfoundation.com/waystodonate/majorgiftsendowmentsandfoundations/donoradvisedfunds

Sjogren, K & C Bezaire (2018) *Help Canadians Give: Donor-advised funds as a philanthropic strategy*. Retrieved from: https://www.mackenzieinvestments.com/en/services/mackenzie-charitable-giving-program/help-canadians-give-donor-advised-funds-as-a-philanthropic-strategy

Tal, B (2016, June 6) 'Canadian baby boomers stand to inherit $750 billion in the next 10 years', CIBC. Retrieved from: http://cibc.mediaroom.com/2016-06-06-Canadian-baby-boomers-stand-to-inherit-750-billion-in-the-next-10-years-CIBC

Winnipeg Foundation (n.d.) 'Give your way – Giving'. Retrieved from: https://www.wpgfdn.org/Portals/0/Uploads/Documents/Giving/Giving_-_Ways_to_Give.pdf

Part one
Chapter five

Corporate foundations: Cases and causes

Cathy Glover and Kelli Stevens

Any business leader who has created a corporate foundation has probably been challenged to explain why they would choose to operate the majority of their community investments through this particular structure. It's not uncommon, after all, for people to question whether the limitations and reporting requirements of the Canada Revenue Agency (CRA) constrain or facilitate a corporate foundation's ability to respond to business objectives. People perceive that it must be much more expensive to operate through this format than it would be to operate within a regular business structure. They also wonder if a corporate foundation is limiting rather than freeing, imposing hurdles rather than offering opportunities.

Our response has been that, while it is challenging to operate *solely* through this model, a corporate foundation works extremely well for most types of business. Increased expenses are not significant and are usually attributable to financial audits and the rigour of regular meetings. These requirements, however, result in a much more formal program that can add significant value to a company. We have also witnessed benefits to a foundation being arm's-length from the company: for example, a foundation allows for centralized funds and the creation of a strategic national program across multiple business lines and provides leadership development opportunities for executives and other senior management. A foundation also allows for clear governance of granting decisions, and is a powerful vehicle to support the overall corporate social responsibility efforts of the business's, and society's, evolving expectations.

We will expand on these points – first by exploring a brief history of corporate foundations in Canada, and the influence of corporate social responsibility. We will also discuss how the challenges of a foundation model can be addressed with a blended model of philanthropy, before going on to describe the various sources of revenue that can be used to structure corporate foundations. Using an example of the Suncor Energy Foundation, we will also explore the emerging role of corporate social innovation. Throughout the chapter, we will discuss the pros and cons of using a foundation model, and attempt to show how corporate foundations can help support businesses by finding new ways for them to engage with society.

A short history of corporate foundations in Canada

Chapter One identified a number of Canadian foundations that were created by business leaders with gifts of cash or stock to create an initial endowment. In fact, early Canadian corporations had one factor in common: they were owned, controlled and managed by a single, dominant personality who influenced the values and attitudes of the company.

> Our [Canadian] great retail chains – Eaton's, Simpsons and Woodward's – were founded by men who exhibited a generous public spirit themselves, and instilled the same tradition of service and duty in the succeeding generations … In early years, gifts by the Molson family and the corporation were indistinguishable as to their source.
>
> Martin, 1985, p. 225

Examples of such philanthropists were emerging because of their ability to amass surplus wealth in the management of business ventures, rather than from inherited family wealth. Liverant shares the story of Edmund Walker, president of the Canadian Bank of Commerce from 1907 to 1924: Walker's legacy was to use his position "to create a new relationship between the banking profession and the community at large", and his many voluntary board positions enabled him to "zealously promote the legitimate interests" of the bank in a variety of social settings (Liverant, 2009, p. 196). In other words, Walker was able to leverage the opportunities and connections he made within the Bank of Commerce to raise money for causes he was committed to, and also used the network of contacts forged in building these associations and institutions to the benefit of the bank.

> Walker was unique in his ability to integrate business and philanthropy in the support of common causes. The corporate business model began to saturate the organizations of civil society, with new leaders transferring their knowledge and expertise, as well as their wealth, to organized philanthropic endeavors. In time, corporations also began to donate money directly to philanthropic causes.
>
> ibid., p. 196

This history is distinct from the emergence of family foundations such as the Massey Foundation, founded in 1918, and the J W McConnell Family Foundation, formed in 1937, that operated independently of corporate interests.

Even as company money began to be directed toward philanthropic causes, however, it was not until well into the 20th century that corporations and businesses began to create foundations to manage their donations. According to the CRA database, the earliest corporate foundations were reported in 1967, which is also the first year that charitable registration was required nationally. It appears that the earliest corporate foundations either were trusts to collect and grant employee payroll contributions, or were based on Canadian affiliates of US parent companies.[1] Foundations from this time included the Imperial Oil Charitable Foundation, Canada Safeway Employees Fund, Algoma Steel Ltd. Employees' Charity Trust, and CBC Employees Charity Trust. Other foundations followed in the 1970s and 1980s (e.g. Ronald McDonald House Charities, KPMG Foundation) and the 1990s (e.g. RBC Foundation, Suncor Energy Foundation, Canadian Tire Jumpstart Charities, Maiwa Foundation, Intact Foundation), and, more recently, in the 2000s (e.g. Trico Foundation, PWC Foundation, Montreal Canadiens Children's Foundation, Home Depot Canada Foundation, Canadian Online Giving).

Currently, corporate foundations in Canada can be registered with Revenue Canada as public or private charitable foundations. The difference between the two is how they receive their income and the composition of their boards of directors. Foundations that solicit funds from customers to support their work (e.g. Ronald McDonald House Charities) and receive more than half their funding from arm's-length supporters must be registered as public foundations. Public foundations must also have more than half of their directors work with one another at arm's-length, and they must disburse the equivalent of more than half their annual income on gifts to qualified donees. On the other hand, organizations in which half or more of the foundation's directors do *not* deal with each other at arm's-length and/or 50% or more of the foundation's funding comes from a person or group of persons that control the charity in some way, must be registered as a private foundation. These foundations include the many employee-based foundations or trusts, as well as those owned by companies such as RBC or Suncor Energy, that receive funds annually from a parent company. In these (private) corporate foundations, the boards of directors are often made up entirely of internal employees or leaders.

The influence of corporate social responsibility

As multiple facets of a company's business are regulated and affected by a variety of actors, it has become fairly well-established that corporate community investment could function as a way of mitigating reputational risk and helping to ensure a company maintains its licence to

---

[1] It is likely that employee trusts preceded the 1967 federal registration requirement, but the regulatory data provide the only consistent way of verifying companies that were operating in this sphere.

operate – either socially or literally. There is a case to be made, however, that this view has been expanding as companies and their foundations move beyond traditional (donor) philanthropy and into more socially innovative and impact-oriented partnerships with community members (Glover et al., 2018).

Today there are increasing pressures on businesses and corporations to address environmental, social and economic issues. In turn, companies are responding by using many different strategies to enact and demonstrate their corporate social responsibility or sustainability strategies and goals. Some companies focus their strategy on being "purpose-driven" or "values-based". Even without directly initiating a business in this way, some companies develop products that focus on addressing a social issue, like the relationship between poverty and payday loans. Others use their position and marketing power to extend research, encourage awareness, and foster behaviour change about an issue. Indeed, it is possible for companies to connect business risks with social and environment issues, and to use risk mitigation efforts to turn these issues into opportunities – for business development – and new ways to become part of solutions.

In doing so, it is possible – and even fruitful – for companies to engage customers and suppliers in these efforts. There is a growing realization that, to address today's complex issues, all sectors of society will need to work together collaboratively. For example, by reviewing the Truth and Reconciliation Commission recommendations, the United Nations Sustainable Development Goals, or by understanding concerns within their own operating communities and/or employee base, Canadian businesses can discover better ways to structure their community investment strategies in support of these initiatives and their relationships with community members, customers, and other stakeholders.

Addressing challenges through a blended model

Corporate foundations are one of the ways that businesses can engage with community members. In some cases, a foundation is the primary vehicle for this engagement. In other cases, a foundation is part of a suite of programs that include direct business contributions, marketing sponsorships, product innovation, supply chain management, and employee engagement.
A foundation model works for businesses of all sizes, geographic scope, management structures and industries.

It is also true that CRA regulations for charitable foundations can create some barriers and additional expenses These barriers are not necessarily prohibitive – most of them are primarily related to requirements for separate audits and financial reporting. The more difficult challenges, however, come when a foundation is offered, or is looking for, extensive brand recognition or sponsorship opportunities. This restriction comes with the CRA's definition of a charitable gift as a "voluntary transfer of property without valuable consideration to the donor" (Government of Canada, 2018, p. 58) – or, put more simply, the transfer of an asset (usually cash) without expecting anything in return. By these rules, a company cannot expect promotion of its brand, which is a significant challenge for consumer-facing businesses.

In situations where companies feel recognition is necessary, they can either partially or fully support the initiative through a corporate community investment budget (i.e. not the foundation's budget). Similarly, corporate budgets can be used to fund any contributions to non-qualified donees, including many non-profit organizations that do not have charitable status,[2] Indigenous or stakeholder communities.

This possibility of pursuing a two-pronged or "both/and" approach (through *both* a corporate foundation *and* a community investment or sponsorship/marketing program) may be the most appropriate choice for some businesses. At Suncor Energy, for example, if a donation was expected to provide company benefit, then the community investment was paid by the company directly (instead of the foundation). In this case, Suncor split budgets by directing 70% of the company's overall community investment funds to the Suncor Energy Foundation, and allocated the other 30% to corporate community investment budgets.

Sources of revenue for corporate foundations

Every company will have to make its own decisions about these types of fund allocations. With this point in mind, let us turn to the various ways that corporate foundations are funded. Factors affecting the funding structure can include the type of business – whether it is regional or national; consumer-facing or business-to-business; public, private or co-op; product or service-focused. This section will discuss a number of ways that funds can be provided to foundations with these considerations in mind, and examples for each.

---

2 Many community initiatives are managed through non-profit organizations, rather than registered charities. Foundations are only permitted to donate funds to the latter.

Employee giving

As mentioned earlier, the earliest registered corporate foundations emerged as trusts for employee giving. These initial foundations or trusts would have been structural mechanisms to hold payroll deductions made by employees, with funds then disbursed to charitable organizations on behalf of the employees. In some cases, payroll contributions were pooled, and a group of employee volunteers served as a granting committee. In other cases, payroll deductions were first pooled with other retail fundraising activities before the employees decided which organizations would receive the grants. These approaches are still viable.

The Canada Post Community Foundation, for example, continues to operate in this manner. Funds raised through in-store campaigns, sales of special stamps and employee support are consolidated. Then employees review applications (almost 1,800 in 2017), and provide funding recommendations to a board of trustees. The board of trustees is chaired by the president and CEO for the organization. The board conducts the final evaluation of applications and ensures grants are awarded across Canada to support education, community projects, and health initiatives (Canada Post, 2018). From 2011 to 2017, the foundation has used this method to contribute over $6 million (CDN) to organizations across Canada.

In terms of employees deciding where to direct their donated funds, employee grants often go to organizations and programs that employees are actively volunteering with or are personally associated with. As employee-giving programs have matured and expanded to include multiple ways of supporting employee engagement, the programs have also become more complex and costlier to manage. As a result, companies and their foundations have looked for more effective ways to support employee giving. One increasingly popular option is the use of online intermediary platforms such as Benevity. This Canadian B Corporation, established in 2008, provides a software platform for businesses to manage employee programs such as volunteer involvement, grant processing and incentive programs. Benevity takes on the cheque-processing function, and streamlines the deposit of funds to the bank accounts of charitable organizations. Benevity's first clients included American and multinational companies such as Google, Microsoft, Apple, Coca-Cola, and Nike.

One of many Canadian businesses using this service is Meridian, a financial co-op that is based in Ontario. Meridian launched a Benevity employee engagement portal in 2015 to support their employee community investment programming. Using Benevity instead of their previous reliance on manual processes led to increased employee engagement, reaching more than 24% of the employee base. The Benevity system also offered Meridian benefits related to effectiveness and efficiency, because the platform consolidates all donations, offers multiple payment options for employees, and automatically issues tax receipts. The portal also incorporates standard metrics for the company's community investment staff, such as participation rates and up-to-date snapshots of employee giving and volunteering trends (Volunteer Canada, 2016).

The company is not the only one to benefit from this approach. By consolidating all donations from corporate clients into their own foundation (called the Canadian Online Giving Foundation), Benevity is also able to effectively and efficiently transfer gifts to Canadian charities. The scale of this benefit is sizeable: in 2015, the Canadian Online Giving Foundation made donations of over $26.9 million (CDN)[3] to qualified Canadian donees in 2017 (CRA). The consolidation of donations into Benevity's foundation can result in significant cost savings (De Lottinville, 2016). Consider: Benevity estimates that the cost to a charity for processing a donor cheque is as high as $30. If one assumes it costs as much (if not more) to get a cheque prepared within a corporation, the cost for each donation is in excess of $60 per gift. With most employee-matching gifts in the $100–$150 range, this math suggests that as much as 60% of a gift can be lost to processing.

Conversely, the Association for Financial Professionals (2015) estimates that the median internal cost for sending and receiving electronic direct deposit payments is $0.29, and the median external cost for sending and receiving these payments is $0.27, for a total cost of $0.56. In other words, the significant savings here should benefit both sides of the transaction by reducing operational expenses for both the corporate/foundation donor and the donee. Ideally, this result will increase the funds available for charitable work.

Customers and supplier engagement

Several foundations have been established to raise funds from both their employees and their customers. These foundations can be further sub-categorized into those that use funds to direct grants to other qualified charities, and those that use funds toward their own charitable purposes (which may also include contributions to qualified donees). Examples are described below.

The TD Friends of the Environment Foundation was founded in 1990 by the Toronto Dominion Bank and funds environmental projects across the country. With more than 180,000 donors, the Foundation has provided approximately $89 million to over 26,000 environmental programs and projects. Since the administrative costs of the foundation are covered by the TD Bank Group, 100% of every donated dollar is directed to environmental projects in local communities. In addition, the bank itself donates $1 million annually to TD Friends of the Environment. As customers become clients of TD Bank, they are asked if they wish to make a monthly contribution directly from their account to the TD Friends of the Environment (TD Friends of the Environment Foundation, 2018).

Another example is the Ronald McDonald House Charities, also registered as a public foundation. This foundation manages all the coinbox collections in restaurant sites across the country. They also receive funds from McHappy Day meal promotions and direct gifts. In 2016, these promotions

---

3   Funds are expressed in Canadian (CDN) dollars unless otherwise specified.

collected more than $9.7 million in unreceipted donations. The foundation provides operational support to the 15 Ronald McDonald Houses across Canada, 16 Ronald McDonald Family Room programs within hospitals, and the Ronald McDonald Care Mobile program. In this case, funds are collected from customers and the donations are managed by the foundation and directed to specific programs.

Next in our list of examples, the Montreal Canadiens Children's Foundation is a public foundation that raises its funds from 50/50 draws and other activities at professional hockey games, golf tournaments, and third-party fundraising efforts that seek contributions from fans. The foundation provides financial support to organizations in Quebec that work with young people living in underprivileged areas. The foundation has joined with the Canadian Tire Jumpstart Charities (Jumpstart) to present the Bleu Blanc Bouge programs that enable children to learn how to skate and handle a stick and which facilitate the construction of outdoor multisport rinks.

Jumpstart is an example of a private foundation that operates its own charitable programs and is therefore different from most granting foundations. Jumpstart's history dates back to 1992 when Canadian Tire created the Child Protection Foundation – which became the Canadian Tire Foundation for Families in 1999, and the Canadian Tire Jumpstart Charities in 2005 – to address the issue of inactivity among children across Canada (Jumpstart, n.d.).The program provides financial aid to children who otherwise might not be able to participate in organized sports and other physical activities. Funds help to cover registration, equipment and/ or transportation expenses. Canadian Tire is the foundation's largest supporter and donor, and covers administrative costs.

As with McDonald's, therefore, 100% of customer donations go towards programming expenses. If funds are transferred directly to the corporate foundation or another charity, the business is eligible to receive a charitable tax receipt for these collected funds. In addition to donations from the company and customers, Jumpstart also receives funding from all levels of government, the company's dealers, employees, and vendors, and from third-party fundraising events. In 2017, Jumpstart used these multiple approaches to raise more than $24 million . With 14 different brands ranging from Canadian Tire, to Sport Chek, to Part Source, to L'Équipeur, Jumpstart is able to work with a core group of companies to help develop different fundraising strategies that support the work of each brand. The foundation has also been able to leverage the support of vendors in the companies' supply chain to assist in fundraising efforts – ranging from SC Johnson and 3M, to Dyson and Clorox. This integration of the company's charitable activities with its various brands is a leading-edge model of new corporate citizenship. Jumpstart is able to make a greater impact than might have occurred by simply providing grants to other charitable organizations.

Home Depot is operating in a similar way by engaging employees and suppliers to help them address youth homelessness. The Home Depot Canada Foundation started the Orange Door Project in 2009 by commissioning a white paper entitled *Social Purpose through Thought Leadership – Homeless in Canada: A Context for Action*. Since the paper's publication, they have invested more than $10 million in housing and community improvement projects across Canada, and currently collaborate with leading charities focused on youth homelessness, and directly with young people. Home Depot also engages their suppliers as advisory council members, which helps expand the program's impact. Employee and customer engagement programs have been aligned with the Orange Door Project, and the initiative is beginning to see positive outcomes, such as rising rates of employment for at-risk youth. Ultimately, the foundation has established a group of charitable partners to work closely with – not only by providing funds, but also by continuing to engage in research, impact assessments, and collaborative efforts that ultimately work to end youth homelessness (Home Depot Canada Foundation, 2013).

Maiwa is an example of customer and supplier engagement on a much smaller scale. This artisan textile company has retail offerings on Vancouver's Granville Island, and formed the Maiwa Foundation 20 years ago. Long before terms like "social purpose" described businesses that create both economic and social returns, Charllotte Kwon used her role as Maiwa's founder to re-invest profits to support the artists in India who were providing their products for Maiwa to sell. Maiwa offers access to suppliers and markets, but also works to further develop the artists' skills through education. When Kwon established the Maiwa Foundation in 1998, it was partly because customers were asking to join with Maiwa in supporting the artisans and their communities. Customers trusted that Maiwa would be able to invest the funds ethically, and that the funds could directly benefit communities in a way that would not be possible via larger aid organizations. The foundation typically raises $80,000 per year, with most funds coming directly from Maiwa's auctions of the artists' work. Funds then are used to provide small grants and no-interest, long-term loans to these artists and their communities.

Corporately funded foundations

A major source of funding for a corporate foundation is the corporation itself. By directing funds for community investment to a foundation, corporations are typically the biggest funders of their own foundations. This approach provides a unique benefit: once the money has been donated to a foundation, the gift has been made and the assets are retained by the foundation. This model allows for more stable financial management and charitable giving – including multi-year giving – regardless of economic conditions that might otherwise cause fluctuation in community investment budgets. As noted earlier, some companies will choose to split their community investment budget between their foundation and corporate budget. Examples of each are discussed below.

Founded in 2007, the PwC Charitable Foundation is relatively new and was created to help support the culture of PwC employees, partners and stakeholders in addressing issues that are important to them. By providing a centralized granting process and applying consistency to some investments, while also allowing partners to manage their own community investments within local communities, the foundation is able to support initiatives that their key stakeholders are interested in while supporting an overarching strategic issue or issues.[4] While the foundation is funded by PwC, it is also held at arm's-length from the company and can therefore increase both trust and transparency among those who might be skeptical about the role of business in society. At the same time, this approach allows PwC to address business drivers like recruitment and retention through their engagement with local communities.

The "both/and" solution of operating community investment through a foundation and through the corporation is also how RBC (Royal Bank of Canada) works. The RBC Foundation is consistently one of Canada's top granting foundations, and they also invest a significant amount annually from within their business operations. In 2017, RBC contributed over $98 million globally to more than 6,700 organizations, and this amount included $70.1 million contributed by the RBC Foundation. As is the case with PwC and others, both categories of donated funds are provided annually by RBC's annual earnings and disbursed to qualified donees. President and CEO Dave McKay states:

> At RBC, we think of corporate citizenship as an approach to business in which we work to make a positive impact on society, the environment and the economy. A good company is purpose driven, principles-led, and performance focused. That's how we think a good company can help build a better world.
>
> RBC, 2018, p. 11

With these "better world" objectives in mind, the RBC Foundation is guided to focus on specific initiatives. In 2017, the foundation celebrated the achievement of its target to invest $50 million in the RBC Blue Water Project. This 10-year initiative focuses on providing clean water (for drinking, swimming, fishing, etc.) and demonstrates how a corporate foundation can achieve outcomes within the environmental, social, and economic spheres. It also demonstrates that they were able to support cross-sector innovation and capacity building by creating 2,549 partnerships involving 319,336 volunteers. The initiative created 445 paid jobs, increased the protection and

---

4 PwC has chosen to invest in the issue of youth unemployment in Canada because "being young and unemployed is at the core of many societal issues such as: increases in the risk of poverty, low self-esteem, de-skilling, social exclusion and mental health issues. Data also shows that there is increased risk of loss of talent and skills to support Canada's advancing skilled labour force – especially within the digital and information technology sectors. This is a real issue for our clients and for our firm. That is why we are focusing our efforts on finding a solution to this important societal problem" (PwC, 2018, p. 8).

remediation of urban waterways, supported more efficient water usage, and increased knowledge about conservation.

To ensure the outputs and outcomes from the RBC Foundation are also linked to a bigger picture, the foundation has developed an "impact measurement framework" that allows them to measure and communicate how they are performing, and how their outcomes relate to the United Nations Sustainable Development Goals. In addition to the work that is facilitated by donations and grants provided through the foundation and RBC's wider business, the bank evaluates whether the creation of new business products can drive social benefit. Such products include social impact bonds, impact investments, and ways to support social entrepreneurs – further strengthening the depth and breadth of the overall community investment support that RBC provides.

Trico Homes, privately held, offers a different blended model of philanthropy. Based in Calgary, this business was founded by Wayne and Eleanor Chui. Trico uses company resources when a donation is a sponsorship or naming opportunity (e.g., the Trico Centre for Family Wellness, the Chui School of Business at Bow Valley College, or the Chinatown Street Festival). In 2008, they also created the Trico Charitable Foundation to give other types of donation – those that come with less brand recognition – and they decided to focus the foundation on social entrepreneurship and creative solutions to the sustainability of the non-profit sector. Wayne, upon being named to the Order of Canada in 2015, shared that "We are in business, but we have to make sure that we are able to marry the business to a positive impact in social society ... In our business, we are looking at affordable housing, looking to house people who need a hand up" (Smith, 2015, p. 3). Further to the foundation's focus on social entrepreneurship, their website profiles what they refer to as their Big Hairy Ultimate Goals (BHUGS), which envision "a unique contribution to the advancement of social entrepreneurship", in which the "financial becomes more social, [and the] social becomes more financial", as "social entrepreneurship goes mainstream" and "gaps in society are closed" (Trico Charitable Foundation, n.d., p. 5).

Suncor Energy also makes use of both a foundation and business line contributions. The company established the Suncor Energy Foundation in 1998 to centralize and focus its community investment efforts. In the 20 years since, the majority of the company's community investment has been managed through the foundation. The foundation's ability to work at arm's length and to build a "rainy day" or "reserve" fund has been a positive aspect – as suggested by Martin (1985), foundation models are a good fit for companies operating in highly cyclical industries (e.g. mining, agriculture, energy, forestry). Managing community investments from a foundation can help smooth the ups and downs of the business cycles that affect these types of industries; large gifts can be transferred by the company to the foundation in good years, and then those funds can provide a stable base for donations in leaner years.

There are obvious benefits of this approach to both the company and to the charitable sector (which is otherwise held at the mercy of an industry's ups and downs). The Suncor Energy

Foundation saw the truth in this philosophy as the price of oil dropped in 2015, sending Alberta into a recession. Through its use of the foundation model, Suncor was able to maintain donations to almost all community partners, even while other companies in the industry were making drastic cuts to community contributions. This enabled the Suncor Energy Foundation to continue as one of the top 20 grantmaking foundations in the country, measured by disbursement (Philanthropic Foundations Canada, 2015).

Business associations and member donations

Beyond corporate donations, foundations have also been funded through the operations of business associations or by contribution from members of those associations. While the following examples are not the largest foundations, they demonstrate the possibilities that can be realized through the creation of foundations that rely on receipt of local, place-based contributions. These foundations are often able to provide much-needed unallocated/unrestricted funding to local charities.

The Alberta Real Estate Foundation, for example, was established in 1991 under the *Real Estate Act*. The foundation is funded by real estate transactions across the province: "When a home buyer deposits money in trust through a real estate broker, the interest that's earned on the deposit is accumulated and forwarded to the Foundation for reinvestment in Alberta's communities" (Alberta Real Estate Foundation, 2014, p. 8). In turn, the foundation makes grants/donations that promote education of professionals and the public in relation to real estate, undertakes law reform and research related to the real estate sector, and/or funds other projects or activities that advance the sector and benefit the people of Alberta. Such goals are set out according to Section 64 of the *Real Estate Act,* and the foundation has worked within the Act to refine its scope so that it supports five key areas of funding (Alberta Real Estate Foundation, 2014). The foundation has contributed more than $18.5 million since being established, benefiting more than 550 projects in Alberta (Alberta Real Estate Foundation, 2018).

Chartered accountants present another type of profession that can work through a professional, regulated body to form a charitable foundation. The Chartered Professional Accountants Manitoba Foundation pools contributions from members, through both direct donations and event fundraising (e.g. golf tournaments). The foundation then turns these contributions into grants such as scholarships, bursaries, university programming, and awards, all of which ultimately "support the pursuit of quality business and accounting education" (CPA Manitoba, 2015).

Funding via asset transfers

A final category of corporate foundation revenue to consider is the asset transfer mechanism. Foundations in this case are initially funded by corporate assets, such as stock or cash transfers, and may not technically be considered corporate foundations. Once they are formed and an endowment is created, they become independent of the original funding source. These foundations may nevertheless be subject to restrictions on how assets can be used (e.g. restrictions put in place by the original donor).

The Mastercard Foundation is a recent example of this type of organization. A strategic business decision in 2006 to donate shares on the day of Mastercard Incorporated's initial public offering created Canada's largest foundation by assets. As part of that donation, there were a number of financial restrictions established that will be in effect until 2027 and beyond. These limitations will control the way in which the foundation can dispose of the original shares and convert them to cash (Mastercard Foundation, 2018). Philanthropic Foundations Canada (2015) reported that total assets of the Mastercard Foundation were $12.7 billion in 2015, with disbursements of $66 million – making it the largest foundation in Canada.

Another example here is the Medavie Health Foundation. In 2006, as the non-profit Medavie EMS Group of Companies was being formed to become the largest private provider of Emergency Medical Services in Canada, funds were contributed to create a charitable foundation. Today, the Medavie Health Foundation has a capital asset base of $50 million and the business is committed to contribute 10% of its annual net income to the foundation. Like many examples of foundations that have been highlighted here, this centralized model allows for more rigour in foundation governance and clear parameters for charitable contributions, greater innovation, and the ability to take risks and engage with more flexibility than government funders (Medavie Health Foundation, 2018).

A different model is the Shorefast Foundation, which is structured as a charitable organization but operates like a foundation. The mission of the Shorefast Foundation is to "build cultural and economic resilience on Fogo Island. [They] believe in a world where all business is social business" (Shorefast, 2018, p. 1). The organization's activities include: an internationally renowned artist-in-residence program; multiple academic-in-residence programs spanning the disciplines of geology, marine sciences, business, and the arts; the operation of a luxury inn to serve as a catalyst for local economic activity; a micro-lending fund; and other spin-off social enterprise activities to help improve the community's socio-economic conditions. Proceeds from the organization's three businesses (Fogo Island Inn, Fogo Island Shop, and Fogo Island Fish) go toward supporting social programs that range from boat building, to arts and culture, to geotourism. Ultimately, these initiatives help to build both cultural and economic resilience on Fogo Island, and demonstrate what businesses (and associated foundations) can do when it comes to creating both social and economic impacts.

Moving toward corporate social innovation

There is increasing pressure to create these kinds of shared-value partnerships between business and community to address complex societal and environmental issues – this approach is also referred to as corporate social innovation. The influence of corporate social responsibility and changing societal expectations have increased the stakes for corporate philanthropy. It is no longer enough to donate money alone; relationships and active participation are becoming more critical. The norms that have been in place for the last 20 years are beginning to shift in favour of finding new ways of working – in the community and within the corporations. Like the Shorefast Foundation, other corporate foundations are becoming better-positioned to step into this new space.

In 2010, Suncor Energy had established five-year targets related to environmental sustainability and the company was working towards those goals. As the company began planning for the next iteration of its goals beyond 2015, however, it identified a need to articulate a target for social performance in addition to environmental sustainability. With the involvement of staff from the Suncor Energy Foundation and the broader company, a process was undertaken to create a socially sustainability goal for Suncor – a goal that ultimately became focused on Indigenous Peoples. The Foundation became a key player in this process, as it had been investing and working with several Indigenous organizations for many years, and already held trusted relationships from which staff could ask difficult (and often very poorly worded and embarrassing!) questions that led to the goal's creation and later refinement.

The fact that these relationships were initially with the foundation and not the business meant that there were organizations and people who were prepared to engage with Suncor. In turn, foundation and company staff were also prepared to listen and think carefully about what they were told. Cathy Glover, one of the authors of this chapter, who worked at the foundation at this time, reflects: "We talked to Elders, and to youth. We took the opportunity to bring these people and their organizations together with Suncor employees and executives. Through a series of facilitated processes and multiple gatherings, we told stories; we cried; we came up with words for a goal; and then we re-worked the goal ... over and over."

This iterative process, though frustrating for many, enabled the foundation to co-create a social goal that addresses the need to change the way its staff think and act, so they can strengthen relationships with Indigenous Peoples and communities. Ultimately it identified that, if it wanted to effect a change, then its staff needed to change themselves. Once this conclusion had been arrived at, an action plan fell into place quite quickly, and the work transferred into the business as metrics and targets were established to measure progress. Throughout this process, the community partners and foundation staff played a unique role in helping to inform and design the goal, as well as the process leading to the goal. Moreover, the foundation's relationships played a role in keeping the social and community issues integral to the process.

Providing this example at Suncor is intended to briefly describe what can happen when a company and its foundation begin to explore shared values and complex social issues; it is not to suggest that Suncor has all the answers – the company and foundation continue to find ways to learn and improve their approach and their relationships. Putting relationship at the centre, however, has certainly helped support their work.

→ "Our collaborative approach allows us to work in partnership with communities to understand the needs that impact both society and Suncor," says Lori Hewson, director, community investment and social innovation. "Going forward, we're being more deliberate about focusing on the systems connected to three areas: Indigenous Peoples, energy futures, and community resilience. When we have a clear understanding of all the elements of a system – including who's involved, the roles they play, and how impacts are felt – we can be more strategic with our investments and better ensure they support transformative and lasting change."

Suncor Energy, 2017, para. 6

Innovation opportunities

Part of being strategic for a corporate foundation – and in thinking about corporate social innovation – is maintaining a connection to the purposes and drivers of the founding company. Unlike some other types of foundation, corporate foundations are unlikely to be completely free to choose their areas of focused giving. That said, corporate foundations can often take greater risks than companies whose community investment programs are limited solely to a business budget. Because foundations are still independent charitable entities, their governance boards can be proactive (as opposed to reactive to business needs) and also support initiatives that involve taking risks in funding provision – including initiatives with less certainty in outcomes (but greater certainty about the possibility of learning something more about an issue or system). Foundations are able to exercise greater flexibility in considering the full extent of a challenge – and its range of potential solutions – rather than feeling pressured to find and fund quicker fixes to directly involved organizations or groups. In other words, they are able to consider the types of program like the Home Depot Canada Foundation's Orange Door program, or RBC's Blue Water project. These programs are in support of the corporations' business, but not directly tied to business issues.

These examples demonstrate that a corporate foundation's opportunity to explore and innovate can lead to work that is complementary to the company's business activities and associated community engagement needs. In fact, a foundation's collaborative efforts with other social partners can help build trusting relationships externally, while simultaneously helping internal stakeholders to better identify and understand risks and challenges for the business and the community. In this way, the individuals staffing the corporate foundations can play important translator roles by bringing the outside in, and the inside out. All these benefits make it a wise move for organizations to consider the creation of a foundation that can extend a company's existing efforts and reputation.

As a company begins to examine its community investment program, or corporate social responsibility strategy, a foundation should be considered as a serious and viable option for innovation and for furthering the mission of the business. We believe that the corporate foundation model can work successfully in many types of businesses. It is possible for a business, and in many cases advantageous to it, to effectively manage its community investments in this manner. If the investment strategy is aligned with the mission of the organization and able to focus on issues and opportunities that the business might not be able to do directly, a foundation could provide a competitive advantage. The examples highlighted above demonstrate different business models and methods of providing funding to a foundation that can ultimately offer a long-term investment and source of ongoing strategic and social advantage.

It takes time and resources to go through the regulatory process to attain charitable status – and it requires the business's commitment to ongoing funding and other support – but the foundation model can be a powerful option for business leaders who want to make meaningful investments in community organizations while still maintaining alignment with business mission and strategy.

Charitable organizations need to understand the shifts that are occurring with corporate community investment and corporate foundations. As expectations shift and as foundations learn to be more proactive, they will begin to change the focus of their investments. We predict that there will be more focused investments like those found within the Home Depot or RBC foundations. If charities want to work with foundations that want take a big-picture perspective, or systemic approach to their activities, this may also require a different (e.g. more co-creative) relationship between the charity and corporate funder.

Over the next ten years we believe that individuals working in corporate foundations will play a critical role in helping business understand its current and potential position in society. Foundation staff and management will need to become innovators, facilitators, incubators, and internal advocates for the purposes of exploring new ways of working together across sectoral boundaries. Foundations will become a go-to place for those beginning to forge relationships, create trust, and develop solutions between businesses and community organizations.

Conclusion

The way we think about business and its role in society is changing. With more and more pressure for businesses to think about social value, social purpose, shared value or any of the other emerging terms, the connections between community organizations and business will grow in importance. A move toward new ways of engaging and working with corporate foundations is one way to begin the shift for businesses to engage differently with society. A corporate foundation model allows for unique relationships to develop that will inform, engage, and co-create strategies.

The role that corporate foundations play within a community and within a business will differ depending on the revenue stream – as will their methods for engaging employees, customers, stakeholders, vendors, and others. By utilizing a "both/and" approach (through *both* a corporate foundation *and* a community investment or sponsorship/marketing program), a business is able to mitigate the challenges of operating a foundation while adhering to CRA regulations. A foundation can provide benefits by centralizing programs, creating greater transparency, allowing for greater risk taking, building trust, planning for cyclical financial futures, and entering into difficult conversations and relationships. The foundation model is not the solution for every business, but this chapter has provided a glimpse of how the model can be used to benefit businesses both large and small. Foundations can work for cooperatives, non-profits, companies that focus on sales to other businesses, and companies that sell directly to consumers. Corporate foundations offer benefits to both the community and the business. As some foundations begin to focus on specific social issues (e.g. homelessness and affordable housing, water sanitation and conservation, youth employment, healthcare, sport and recreation), and others on processes and capacity building (e.g. in social innovation, economic and community development, and social enterprise), they are demonstrating the important impact they are likely to have on the Canadian foundation landscape.

Three key takeaways

1
A foundation can provide benefits by centralizing programs, creating greater transparency, allowing for greater risk-taking, building trust, planning for cyclical financial futures, and entering into difficult conversations and relationships.

2
To address both charitable and non-charitable investment, a two-pronged approach of *both* a foundation *and* a corporate budget is recommended.

3
Foundations can have clear governance and strong fiscal management and yet still be innovative and take risks that may result in longer-term positive change within both the corporation and the community.

References

Alberta Real Estate Foundation (2014) 'Two decades of impacting our community'. Retrieved from: http://aref.ab.ca/our-story/

Alberta Real Estate Foundation (2018) 'March 2018 community investment'. Retrieved from: http://aref.ab.ca/march-2018-community-investment/

Association for Financial Professionals (2015) '2015 AFP payments cost benchmarking survey: Report of survey results'. Retrieved from: https://www.bottomline.com/application/files/faster-cost-effective-afp-payments-cost-benchmark-survey-gen-us-srr-1510.pdf

Canada Post (2018) 'About Canada Post Community Foundation'. Retrieved from: https://www.canadapost.ca/web/en/pages/aboutus/communityfoundation/about.page

Chartered Professional Accountants Manitoba (2015) 'CPA Manitoba Foundation'. Retrieved from: https://cpamb.ca/foundation

De Lottinville, B (2016, May 11) 'Electronic payments allow charities to focus on the things that matter'. Retrieved from: https://insights.benevity.com/blog/electronic-payments-allow-charities-to-focus-on-the-things-that-matter

Glover, C, Stauch, J & K Stevens (2018) 'The business-community interface: From "giving back" to "sharing value"'. Manuscript submitted for publication.

Government of Canada (2018) 'Charities and giving glossary'. Retrieved from: https://www.canada.ca/en/revenue-agency/services/charities-giving/charities/charities-giving-glossary.html

Home Depot Canada Foundation (2013) 'Social purpose through thought leadership – Homeless in Canada: A context for action'. Retrieved from: http://impaktcorp.com/wp-content/uploads/2015/10/Foundation-White-Paper-Sept-2013_FINAL.pdf

Jumpstart (n.d.) 'About Jumpstart'. Retrieved from: http://jumpstart.canadiantire.ca/content/microsites/jumpstart/en/about-jumpstart.html

Liverant, B (2009) 'The incorporation of philanthropy: Negotiating tensions between capitalism and altruism in twentieth century Canada', *Journal of the Canadian Historical Association*, 20(1), 191–220: doi:10.7202/039787ar

Martin, SA (1985) *An Essential Grace – Funding Canada's health care, education, welfare, religion and culture.* Toronto, Ontario: McClelland and Stewart

Mastercard Foundation (2018) '2018 Financial Statement Note #4'. Retrieved from: http://mastercardfdn.org/financials/

Medavie Health Foundation (2018) 'Improving the health of Canadians'. *Retrieved from:* http://medaviehealthfoundation.ca/

Philanthropic Foundations Canada (2015) 'Snapshot of foundation giving in 2015'. Retrieved from: https://pfc.ca/resources/

PwC (2018) 'PwC's young people project'. Retrieved from: https://www.pwc.com/ca/en/about-us/corporate-responsibility/empowering-young-people-for-the-future.html

RBC (2018) 'Citizenship'. Retrieved from: https://www.rbcits.com/en/citizenship.page

Shorefast (2018) 'Integrity of place'. Retrieved from: http://shorefast.org

Smith, M (2015, July 1) 'Speaking with some of the 2015 Order of Canada honourees', *The Globe and Mail*. Retrieved from: https://www.theglobeandmail.com/news/national/speaking-with-some-of-the-2015-order-of-canada-honourees/article25213961/

Suncor Energy (2017) 'Community investment'. Retrieved from: https://www.suncor.com/en-ca/community-investment

TD Friends of the Environment Foundation (2018) 'Greening communities across Canada'. Retrieved from: https://www.td.com/ca/en/about-td/documents/pdf/TD-FEF-2019-Year-in-Review.pdf

Trico Charitable Foundation (n.d.) 'Our story'. Retrieved from: https://tricofoundation.ca/about-us/

Volunteer Canada (2016) 'Leading with intention: Employer supported volunteering in Canada'. Retrieved from: https://volunteer.ca/index.php?MenuItemID=359

Part Two

Indigenous perspectives on philanthropy

In this part of the book, Indigenous voices tell their story in their way and provide critical insights into ways in which foundations can address their own history and a relation-based future. Some of the areas covered include:

- the history of colonization and its impact on Indigenous ways of giving
- walking the fine line between colonial structures and Indigenous pathways
- building trusting relationships in a good way
- how foundations can be held accountable to Indigenous communities
- how Indigenous communities have learned to work with foundations in a spirit of reconciliation
- opportunities to engage with Indigenous people in a way that is based on reciprocity, respect, relationship and responsibility

Part two
Chapter six

All My Relations:
A journey of reciprocity

The first ten years of the Circle on Philanthropy and Aboriginal Peoples in Canada

Stephen Couchman, Marilyn Struthers and Justin Wiebe

For Indigenous people, philanthropic practices were, and continue to be, deeply engrained in Indigenous ways of being and doing. First Nations, Inuit and Métis (FNMI) peoples across what is currently called Canada have complex legal, social and political systems that include philanthropic practices. For example, the Nehiyaw (Cree) concepts of *wicihitowin* (helping each other or sharing) and *kanawayhitowin* (taking care of each other's spirit) demonstrate how integral philanthropic ideas are to Nehiyawak (Cree People). These concepts, and many others, guide the ways in which Indigenous peoples live, engage with other Nations, and govern. Juxtaposed with western philanthropy, Indigenous philanthropic practices aren't merely about extending "goodwill", but, rather, simply the ways things are done in relationships.

Differences between Indigenous and settler worldviews of helping were evident from the moment of first contact. Although Indigenous Nations have long histories of giving and receiving aid, the first written record of an act of philanthropy in what was to become Canada occurred in the winter of 1535–6. Jacques Cartier and his men were overwintering in Wendat territory at Kébec or "where the river narrows", near current-day Quebec City. They had no idea of the severity of winter in this part of the world. They constructed a fort to protect themselves from the local peoples who, they feared, would attack at any time, and hunkered down. Not long into the winter, the crew's health began to deteriorate badly. They became so sick with what, in all probability, was scurvy that they did not have the strength to bury their own dead:

→ [T]heir mouth became stincking, their gummes so rotten, that all the flesh did fall off, even to the rootes of the teeth, which did also almost all fall out. With such infection did this sicknesse spread itselfe in our three ships, that about the middle of February, of a hundred and tenne persons that we were, there were not ten whole, so that one could not help the other, a most horrible and pitifull case.

Hakluyt, 2008

Journals from the time tell of how they received a gift of medicine prepared by Indigenous women from a nearby community:

→ Domagaia straight sent two women to fetch some of it, which brought ten or twelve branches of it, and therewithall shewed the way how to use it, and that is thus, to take the barke and leaues of the sayd tree, and boile them togither, then to drinke of the sayd decoction every other day, and to put the dregs of it upon his legs that is sicke: moreouer, they told us, that the vertue of that tree was, to heale any other disease: the tree is in their language called Ameda or Hanneda, this is thought to be the Sassafras tree. Our Captaine presently caused some of that drink to be made for his men to drink of it, but there was none durst tast of it, except one or two, who ventured the drinking of it, only to tast and prove it: the other seeing that did the like, and presently recovered their health, and were delivered of that sickenes, and what other disease soever, in such sorte, that there were some had bene diseased and troubled with the French Pockes foure or five yeres, and with this drinke were cleane healed.

ibid.

The journals also describe how the recovered sailors repaid the gift by locating and stripping the limbs and bark from the medicine tree:

→ After this medicine was found and proved to be true, there was such strife about it, who should be first to take it, that they were ready to kill one another, so that a tree as big as any Oake in France was spoiled and lopped bare, and occupied all in five or six daies.
ibid.

This early story demonstrates the tension between Indigenous and Western worldviews. For Indigenous peoples, offering support to keep the settlers alive was grounded in their philanthropic practices. The response from settlers was one of betrayal, and so began the complex and tension-filled modern story of settler philanthropy in relation to Indigenous peoples.

Later, terrible suffering began for Indigenous people as a result of illegal occupation, fur trade rivalries, land dispossession and treaty violations. Altruistic intentions, acts of "philanthropy" for the most part, did great harm. Sponsored by the church and wealthy patrons, the first wave of European philanthropy and religious imperialism came in the form of missionaries' campaigns to convert Indigenous peoples. This was followed by the outlawing of Indigenous traditions of sharing such as the potlatch societies (discussed further by Roberta Jamieson in Chapter 7), and the assimilation, dispossession and reserve policies established by the Canadian government of Sir John A MacDonald. The Indian Residential Schools System, developed through a collaboration between government, church and private donors, would be one of the next forms of European-style colonial "philanthropy" experienced by Indigenous communities, with devastating consequences that continue across generations in families today. The intention, which has since been documented and acknowledged, was cultural genocide aimed at "taking the Indian out of the child" (Chief Justice Beverly McLauchlin in Fine, 2015).

Philanthropy also "supported" programs for Indigenous peoples in recent Canadian history: contributions to child welfare supported the "60s Scoop", an active program of adopting Indigenous children out of their home communities to non-Indigenous families across Canada and beyond. By 1977, an estimated 15,500 Indigenous children in Canada were living in the care of child welfare officials. In Canada, Indigenous children represented 20% of all children in care, even though they made up less than 5% of the total child population. Unfortunately, not much has changed in the nearly 50 years since: 90% of the 11,000 children currently in care in Manitoba are Indigenous (Johnston, 2016). These sorts of philanthropic endeavours, ones often filled with pain and hurt for Indigenous peoples, have continued from the arrival of settlers to today.

In a nation that likes to see itself as an advocate of justice, diversity, and peace, failing to recognize and act on the national crisis of poverty, exclusion, and dislocation of Indigenous peoples by Canadian philanthropic organizations is unacceptable. The complexity of the historic relationships, lack of trust and repeated failures to uphold treaty and other obligations mean that old patterns must now be challenged and replaced with new approaches.

Philanthropy, the gifting and sharing traditions of communities, is an expression of care and solution-seeking, and its practices can be found in almost every culture. In Canada, dominant settler traditions of charity are deeply rooted in the Christian churches of colonial England and France. Generally, they refer to the redistribution of accumulated wealth with the intention of goodwill, an act or gift made for humanitarian purposes. What seldom comes into that account are the ways in which that wealth was accumulated on and through stolen land and resources.

Less recognized, and much older, are the different traditions of First Nations, Métis and Inuit communities such as potlatches and gifting, giveaways and sharing traditions. These traditions are rooted in worldviews of relationship – not only between each other, but also between the generations who came before and after – and with spirit and non-human relations: the land, waterways, plants and animals that share the land. This broad view of an ecosystem based in relationship and stewardship of resources contains many lessons for philanthropists seeking social change. It is in these variations in view and the way they shape the application of philanthropy that the conflict co-exists with the opportunity to develop a uniquely Canadian approach to philanthropy based on reciprocity. It is out of this complexity that the Circle began to emerge. This paper tracks the first 10 years of a rich and complicated conversation between Canadian philanthropists and Indigenous peoples.

Creation of the Circle

→ "Where do you begin telling someone
  their world is not the only one?"

Lee Maracle (1993) *Ravensong – A Novel*, p. 61

The Circle on Philanthropy and Aboriginal Peoples in Canada, known as the Circle, strives to build a community of good dialogue among First Nations, Métis, Inuit communities and private, public and community foundations, corporate philanthropy programs, charitable organizations, and United Ways. It is the only Canadian organization representing this diversity of funding organizations. In the same way that a canoeist seeks a clear path down a set of rapids, the Circle focuses on opportunities that present a clear opening for relationship-building, education, policy development, and philanthropy within values of reciprocity. The journey has not always been a smooth one and the work continues to evolve and grow. New people have continually joined us, and there have been many lessons along the way.

Winston Churchill famously said, paraphrasing George Santayana, that "those who fail to learn their history, are condemned to repeat it" (1948). It is unlikely at the time that he was reflecting on relationships between Indigenous and non-Indigenous peoples in Canada, or that he was thinking in terms of Seven Generations before and after. We have learned to see concepts of "philanthropy" and "charity" as evolving over time, with a history before and after colonization (Struthers, 2018). The unique meaning of notions of "sharing" and "community" in an Indigenous context are profiled by Roberta Jamieson in Chapter 7.

This chapter tells some of the stories of the Circle and some of the lessons learned along the way. Like any organization working at the cusp of change, our wisdom is often held in our stories, and we seldom have time to stop the work long enough to sit together and mine for the learning. Because "we" are, by definition, not a homogenous group, the selection of stories and the interpretations will reflect those doing the writing. This piece has been written primarily by two non-Indigenous long-time funders who were there at the beginning. We are joined by two younger Indigenous people who have joined more recently and carry the vision of the future. One is the executive director of the Circle and the other works at a major global foundation based in Canada. Writing together across difference is one of the practices the Circle has developed to create voice, and it often brings surprises – and so learning.

How the Circle began

→ "The lack of philanthropic involvement in Aboriginal community development does not reflect a lack of need."

Bruce Miller, *The Circle* (2010)

In 2006, a small group of non-Indigenous funders from the McConnell Foundation, the Ontario Trillium Foundation, Gordon Foundation and an anonymous private foundation began a series of conference-call conversations, all wondering how to better support Indigenous communities. We could see the need, had access to funds and had the will, but "fundable" opportunities (in foundations' terms) were hard to come by and seldom an unqualified success.

Too often the "best" funding opportunities were to non-Indigenous organizations interested in supporting Indigenous communities. Our bureaucratic processes were often a poor fit for Indigenous community-led efforts. Our decision-making processes were missing cultural context and often asking the wrong questions. Non-Indigenous applicants often lacked genuine relationships with the communities they applied to work in and seldom had working partnerships or a good grasp of issues at the community level. The projects that did receive funding often shifted in unexpected ways. Our monitoring and evaluation processes were not equipped for the hairpin turns of emergent work necessary to address long-standing problems with no recognized solutions.

The scope of the problems Indigenous applicants were trying to solve required a much more sensitive and engaged kind of philanthropy than our organizations knew how to perform. Philanthropy, and the charitable organizations it funds, is the structural product of the same colonial processes that generated the social upheaval Indigenous peoples have experienced. Worse, we now recognize that charities such as the church-run residential schools have been instruments of terrible oppression and violence.

These conversations began in 2006, before the Prime Minister's statement of apology to survivors of residential schools and the establishment of the Truth and Reconciliation Commission, and before news of murdered and missing Indigenous women had hit the mainstream. Even then it was clear, however, that to replicate non-Indigenous solutions to community problems, or to assume we, as non-Indigenous people, had any idea of the best projects to invest in, was to simply reproduce the same colonial attitudes that had also built our organizations and frameworks for social investment. These were new ideas, not necessarily shared across our organizations. We also began to notice, then, that we had no Indigenous funder colleagues to turn to for advice. Not one.

Yet within our own networks, non-Indigenous people and funders were beginning to recognize ongoing practices of Indigenous philanthropy within communities. For example, have you ever sat with an Indigenous Elder and experienced that deep commitment to reciprocity and sharing? The group of non-Indigenous funders soon learned that Indigenous-led philanthropy was new only to us: Indigenous peoples and communities had, and continue to have, unique forms of giving and receiving grounded in each Nation's unique social, spiritual, legal and cultural practices.

At the same time, Indigenous communities had begun to adapt cultural values to familiar corporate forms: community trust funds to support youth and community-led healing projects, fundraising walks and events and, eventually, community foundations.[1] Indigenous communities were establishing the networks of nonprofits and charities that other Canadian communities use to provide service, seek solution and acquire funding – but there were few bridges between philanthropists and Indigenous communities. Funders were learning mostly through the trial and error experience of investment, in and around power imbalances of granter and grantee, and mostly alone.

Something new was needed. As a funding community we needed to enter into conversations with Indigenous peoples, not funder to applicant, but community to community. As non-Indigenous funders, we felt strongly that our foundations were meeting neither the challenge of investing in Indigenous community-led social change nor our mandates to support innovative community solutions. The process of grantors talking to grantees about funding dilemmas was isolating us from the very people we needed to learn from.

And so this small group of foundations began, without knowing where we were going, to generate conversations that attempted not "us and them" but "we". Along the way there have been many lessons, and the learning is far from over.

Some Circle practices include: bi-annual All My Relations gatherings; deliberate conversations of learning and trust-building across difference; working in ceremony; research that begins to shed light on the realities of Indigenous charities – and some of what funders need to know to fund well; experimental new funding calls and processes to Indigenous communities; and the Philanthropic Community's Declaration of Action, a journey into formalizing the commitment to reconciliation and accountability by Canadian foundations.

The mission of the Circle has changed a little over time. Now, the Circle works to "transform philanthropy and contribute to positive change with Indigenous communities by creating spaces of learning, innovation, relationship-building, co-creation and activation." We describe ourselves as "an open network to promote giving, sharing, and philanthropy in Indigenous communities across the country. We connect with and support the empowerment of First Nations, Inuit and Métis nations, communities, and individuals in building a stronger, healthier future." The Circle continues to provide a public platform that seeks to challenge existing funder–recipient relationships, a task that requires listening, trust, sacrifice and a lot of effort. We are committed to our effort being Indigenous-led and collaborative, one that tries to model right relations.

---

[1] Community Foundations of Canada now includes three Indigenous community foundation members, and a fourth is in the process of being included.

The work begins

→ "If the mission of a foundation is to address social inequity, health, poverty, hunger, child welfare, seniors or education in Canada, and they do not support any Indigenous-led or -focused organizations, there is a massive disconnect."

Circle member

The language of our work, terms such as "charity" and "philanthropy", reflects the earliest relationships of colonization and betrayal. It is understandable that these terms are not always understood by First Nations, Métis and Inuit peoples to denote benevolence and sharing. At one of the early Circle gatherings, a First Nation leader spoke following a presentation by the head of a foundation who had just explained that his organization had resources which they wished to share with his community. There was a long pause, and the First Nation leader said, "You're welcome."

This was a jarring moment for many in the room who had come to learn how to support Indigenous communities better and who held familiar assumptions of gratitude for gift-giving. As profiled by Lefèvre and Elson in Chapter 1, by the early 1900s, the consolidation of wealth by Canadian industrialists, largely the result of resource extraction, led to the emergence of some of the private and public foundations that now make up the philanthropic sector. This wealth was gained through exploitation of Indigenous lands and resources. From this perspective we can see the essential betrayal in the value chain from land to business to charitable gifts that has helped to build and sustain many of the health, social, and cultural institutions of settler culture that improve the quality of life for mostly non-Indigenous Canadians.

Philanthropy is seen by many Indigenous communities as a return of value – in a somewhat diminished form – of what was previously taken. Understandably, entering into a relationship by accepting funds can raise feelings of lack of trust and belief that what is offered is truly intended for the betterment of Indigenous children, families and communities. One of the important lessons for philanthropic members of the Circle is to understand how Indigenous peoples may view western philanthropy and that successful granting must rely on fundamentally different kinds of relationship.

Long before the sharing of medicine with the Cartier expedition, the treaty between the Anishinaabe and Haudenosaunee created an agreement on sharing of resources in the Great Lakes Basin called the Dish with One Spoon Wampum. This wampum is a sacred treaty and outlines the protocols and obligations of sharing resources and lands in ways that benefited everyone and everything. Conversations in the Circle meetings are often peppered with stories of traditional sharing: wood gathered first for an Elder, moose shared with the community.

Settler actors are much more likely to hold more paternalistic views of giver and beneficiary. Traditions of philanthropy have a long history which predates European arrival in North America, deeply connected with church and faith. Because settler philanthropists may have little access to Indigenous oral history and cultural practices, the Circle offers a potent space to learn and shift understanding.

For the most part, it is only in the last thirty years that the philanthropic sector can be seen as beginning to contribute positively to the well-being of Indigenous peoples. However, it is important to recognize that most non-Indigenous people working in philanthropy have little sense of Indigenous history, including resistance and resilience, as the result of a Canadian education system that has omitted or white-washed Indigenous history. This can make foundations impatient to see change happen, but also confused when "best intentions" are met with scepticism. If handled with respect and care, this dynamic can be fertile soil for careful conversation and learning.

Telling our stories: Where the learning begins[2]

→ "Origin stories are important. They remind us where we were and who we were with, what the weather was like and where we came from."

Circle member

The birth of the Circle took place on a spring day on Treaty 1 and Métis territory north of Winnipeg, Manitoba. Although the Circle was formally incorporated in 2012, its story really begins on that day in June of 2008. The group had no name then, but the series of teleconferences had grown to a gathering called All My Relations. This phrase is often used by Indigenous peoples at the end of a prayer or public statement to indicate their inclusion of ancestors, non-human relations, people in the room, and those yet to be born. It is spoken with humility.

It had been raining all week and the Red River was cresting. The land was soggy with spring runoff. About forty people from philanthropic organizations and First Nations, Métis and Inuit communities gathered to spend two days together to explore what deeper relationships between Indigenous and non-Indigenous people could mean for the work of philanthropy and social change.

---

2 The following section draws from 'Journey of Reciprocity: The First Eight Years of the Circle on Philanthropy and Aboriginal Peoples in Canada', *The Philanthropist*. March 14, 2016.

The first day took place on land that was then the Grandmother Moon Lodge, an hour away from Winnipeg, and was hosted by Elder Mae Louise Campbell. Most of the forty participants arrived not knowing more than two or three others. Many were afraid of being devoured by mosquitos or washed downstream into Lake Winnipeg by the torrential rains of the previous week. Despite dire weather forecasts, it was a perfect day – sunny and spring warm and dry, because organizers bought every pair of rubber boots in Winnipeg and had laid plywood over the muddy meeting space.

The day began with everyone sitting around a fire, making introductions. It ended pretty much the same way. Elder Mae Louise began in prayer and created a space that was unlike the usual meetings of philanthropists. She encouraged us to take our time and when participants had finished saying who we were and why we were there, the day was nearly done. For those focused on process and agenda, this was the first lesson of this newly forming group: the bedrock of any solution to the challenges is taking the time to build relationships, trust and mutual understanding. To do this, you must start with listening. There is no shortcut.

The next day, June 11, 2008, has since become an historic moment. For most participants it seemed a profound coincidence. Organizers had no idea that the meeting would coincide with the federal apology to residential school survivors and their communities. We were together on such an important moment, and yet many of the non-Indigenous participants were taken completely by surprise. After lunch, with still much of the formal agenda to cover, the Indigenous participants called for an early end to the gathering. The hotel, owned at the time by the Tribal Councils Investment Group of Manitoba, was opened to the public for a video viewing of the Prime Minister. People, mostly Indigenous, packed every ballroom, meeting room, and gathering place in the building. Volunteers distributed tissues and together we watched big TV monitors as Stephen Harper apologized on behalf of the Canadian people for the atrocities of the residential school system. It was an emotional, cathartic experience for everyone present and, looking back, a critical juncture in the relationship between Indigenous and non-Indigenous peoples in Canada and also for the Circle.

The first All My Relations gathering didn't go at all as planned in terms of "desired outcomes and goals". Or, rather, because our ancestors were invited into this circle and allowed interactions to take place in a good way, perhaps it played out exactly as it should have. The result was that an unlikely group achieved a remarkably quick alignment around a common vision.

In the 480 years since the first written account of a philanthropic act in what would become Canada, the history has become painfully clear. "Cultural genocide" was the term used by the Truth and Reconciliation Commission (TRC, 2015) to describe systematic attempts to absorb Indigenous peoples into "Canadian" culture. Some would argue that what has taken place is much worse. These attempts have not only failed but have led to social, political, cultural and environmental degradation with a significant human toll. This is tough terrain on which to create a new vision of relationship.

140   All My Relations: A journey of reciprocity

There were many lessons for the group who gathered just outside Winnipeg. The first was an idea that has become more commonplace in the subsequent decade, that Indigenous peoples and non-Indigenous Canadians are all in some relationship with how this land was settled and with each other, and thus have obligations to the lands and to one another. Reconciliation is inevitably a shared proposition. Secondly, we recognized that philanthropy is a way for communities to innovate, share, learn and build resilience in a process of self-determination that is separate from government. Finally, when we recognize how the wealth held in foundations was accumulated, often through business exploitation of Indigenous lands and resources, it forces us to think differently about how and why foundations "do" philanthropy and on whose terms. "You are welcome" becomes a play on words, a subtle rebuke and an invitation to historical lesson all in one.

There are also important lessons about how the work is done. Very different ways of meeting create very different outcomes. Settler philanthropy too has a culture and way of meeting, around board tables and in suits and ties. Disruption of how we meet allows new possibilities for relationship and ways of thinking.

The All My Relations strategy

→ "'All My Relations' is an encouragement for us to accept the responsibilities we have within the universal family by living our lives in a harmonious and moral manner (a common admonishment is to say of someone that they act as if they had no relations)."

Thomas King, in Nelson Education Ltd (2004)

The first All My Relations gathering (AMR) at Grandmother Lodge provided the template for future Circle convening activities. Held every second year, the intent of the AMR gatherings is to create space for a broad range of individuals from Indigenous communities, philanthropy and beyond to come together to share perspectives, problem-solve, examine and share best practices and innovations and learn together in community. Some of the principles the AMR has developed over time and in constant regeneration are to:

- host in different territories across Canada, and in some relationship to the land and Indigenous peoples
- embrace Indigenous traditions of dialogue where possible, including the long view of seven generations forward and back, listening and sharing, working in ceremonial space
- seek out diverse and sometimes challenging participation

- recognize the critical role of Elders and young people in creating and holding conversational space
- design and facilitate well to create space for hard, sometimes disruptive and creative conversations
- encourage connection and relationship building
- focus on the possibility and potential
- invite others in to continually build a community of practice which energizes the work

Over the past decade the Circle has hosted four AMR gatherings, along with several smaller regional or issue-specific meetings and many webinars. The Circle has become somewhat known for the ability to host these kinds of dialogue across difference. By convening in conjunction with partner organizations such as Canadian Environment Grantmakers' Network, Philanthropic Foundations of Canada (PFC) (now Environment Funders Canada), International Funders for Indigenous Peoples (IFIP) and Community Foundations of Canada (CFC), the Circle has often helped to bring issues to the surface and to raise awareness in good, positive learning environments. In describing how the Circle helps, we say: "The Circle develops programs and spaces that cultivate better conversations, connections and relationships among Indigenous peoples and philanthropic organizations to create awareness, through education and engaging communities and organizations, [in order] to create alliances on the path to true reconciliation."

Stepping into the deep end: The Ashoka Changemakers Competition

→ Funders said: "It was amazing for us, as a non-Aboriginal organization, to hear directly from such a diversity of First Nations, Inuit and Métis educators and social change agents about what is working and needed in their communities. It reinforced our approaches but gave excellent ideas of how we could strengthen as well."

→ Participants said: "This type of initiative is critical for ongoing learning. The simple act of conversation, learning [and] sharing has value notwithstanding what will result after the Summit ends."

The Ashoka Changemakers Competition in Indigenous Education

The growing group of non-Indigenous funders had begun to imagine how philanthropic dollars and Indigenous participation might come together to support unique ways to explore, test and scale social solutions in Indigenous communities. The Ashoka Changemakers Competition in Indigenous Education was an early and bold experiment for the fledgling Circle. It was a way for some of the philanthropic community to "try out" the idea that many foundations working together in relationship with people in Indigenous communities could create impact beyond what each might do alone. It was a venture that we would now characterize as "engaged philanthropy" (Alberg-Seberich, 2016) and "collective impact" (Kania & Kramer, 2011). When the adventure began, these terms were not widely used, there was little of the guidance the philanthropic body of literature offers today, and the group was largely unaware of Indigenous literature that could have guided the work.

The Circle convened its second AMR gathering in Treaty 7 Territory in 2009. Part of that event was a long bus ride from Calgary to Blackfoot Crossing on Sisika First Nation. The intention for that day was to focus on building understanding of the twin themes important to both Indigenous communities and to philanthropic granting: the wellbeing of Indigenous youth and their community's relationships to the land. Imagine Indigenous leaders, many of the heads of Canada's largest foundations, young emerging leaders and others, on a long-curated bus ride. We began with a simple exercise: "Tell us the story of your name." There were traditional names and English names, names from adoption, names of Portuguese and Somali origin, funny nicknames and complex histories.

Celia Cruz, a consummate networker and the new director of Ashoka Canada, had been a last-minute addition to the gathering. Seizing the opportunity, she worked the bus, pitching the idea of a Changemakers Competition. By the time the bus returned to Calgary, the idea had set. Cindy Blackstock, Ashoka's first Indigenous fellow, became part of the organizing group.

Philanthropists from the Circle created the financial means to launch the Competition, with Ashoka Canada acting as the secretariat. The Ashoka model provided the vehicle to reach across Canada and attract entries to both see the work that was emerging in communities and try to map the range of outcomes these initiatives were reaching for. The goal was a national online competition and final summit where innovators in Indigenous education and philanthropists could share ideas, learn from each other, and explore the potential for funding relationships.

Nine foundation partners – including Martin Aboriginal Education Initiative (now the Martin Family Initiative), the McConnell Family Foundation, the Counselling Foundation of Canada, the Ontario Trillium Foundation and the RBC, Donner, Chagnon and Vancouver foundations – entered into a partnership with Ashoka Canada and eleven other participating organizations, ranging from the Assembly of First Nations, Congress of Aboriginal Peoples, Indspire, Métis National Council, Inuit Tapiriit Kanatami and the Native Women's Association of Canada, along with the Canadian Teachers Federation and Mamow Sha-way-gi-kay-win, and The North South

Partnership for Children. Some partners came to the table with funds, others with participation and still others as contributors toward cash awards. Some 266 educational initiatives entered the competition, more than anyone had imagined, and almost one hundred thousand dollars was awarded to support the activities of thirty "winning" organizations in the three-day summit.

The event was a stunning success. The competition enabled the cash awards, and the presentations were opportunities for shared learning. Perhaps most important were the number of quiet meetings that created relationship between funders and potential grantees who didn't usually have access to philanthropists. We will never know the actual amount of investment that resulted from those conversations, but it was an important lesson that access to funding is often more about who knows whom and that potentially impactful Indigenous initiatives were often unnoticed until those relationships were established.

The back story of getting to the Summit was of course much more complex, and few in the room for those sparkling three days knew that the event had come together in an eleventh-hour effort to salvage the entire venture from conflict and power struggles among steering organizations. The story is recounted in a developmental evaluation document created by a team of evaluators, one Indigenous and one not, called *The Road to the Summit* (Wilson & Coates, n.d.). Job changes had upended the relational balance between organizers. Goals had become uncertain. Power struggles emerged everywhere – between seasoned funders, new ones and non-funders; between powerful and less powerful foundations; between different Indigenous representatives; between staff and the steering group and even between evaluators. The evaluators made an intervention, but tension was already running high.

Although as organizers we set out with the best intensions and an explicit desire to be aware and wary of power dynamics, we relied too heavily on relational organizing. Both Indigenous communities and philanthropists tend to work in highly relational ways with people they know well. In a diverse collaboration without structural agreement on process and roles, the discriminating use of power and privilege thwarted our efforts. Confusion reigned even within Ashoka about whether the project "lived" inside Ashoka Canada or Ashoka Global, and over who would own the knowledge development. The partnership templates didn't account for the rather fluid orientation of new partners through relational invitation. The confusion ultimately manifested in a showdown about who actually held decision-making power.

While, the deeply relational process brought well-meaning people together to commit to the enterprise, it couldn't limit the circumvention of the process and power plays that emerged. The evaluators set out six important lessons for foundations entering into complex collective solution finding:

- Don't underestimate the power of personal relationship in the work and the importance of weaving people in
- Be mindful of multiple aspects of individual and collective wellbeing in the group
- Don't underestimate the complexity of power and difference
- Focus on the important outcomes and the conditions needed for collective success
- Deliver well on what you can deliver, scale your results to your capacity
- Balance flexibility and adaptability with the efficiency and predictability needed to actually get the work done

So in the midst of this jumble, how did the group use the lessons to align our efforts and pull off a highly successful summit? First, all players were motivated not to lose the work done and concerned about loss of reputation and accountability for investment – so the will was there. Second, a project charter was developed using a template from the Counselling Foundation of Canada which articulated three clear goals. Finally, the group appointed a small working group with a single staff person and chairperson with solid process skills, who took pains to reach clarity and consensus on each direction forward.

How do we know it was a success? Apart from the number of participants and the clear engagement of funder and organizational participants, the evaluators created two composite evaluative narratives suggesting impact for both Indigenous educators and non-Indigenous foundations. Each of the philanthropic players continued to build relationship and deepen investment in Indigenous solutions to educational challenges. As for the Circle, for years, in moments of uncertainty, we would look at each other and say "Remember Ashoka", a touchstone reminder of the importance of building genuine working relationships across power difference.

Holding tension: becoming a registered charity

→ "Charity implies the opposite of self-determining, community-based ways of being and knowing. In particular, spiritually and culturally based relationships based on reciprocity of giving and receiving among one another, are viewed by Indigenous Elders and Traditional Knowledge Holders as outside the parameters of 'charities' which carry with them confining methods and rules."

The Circle, 2017a, p. 25

Formally, the Circle registered as a charity in 2012. There are similar organizations around the world, such as Native Americans in Philanthropy and International Funders for Indigenous Peoples, which are focused on building understanding about systemic racism and increasing the philanthropic resources to support Indigenous solutions to the problems facing Indigenous communities. Systemic racism creates invisible barriers inside large systems such as philanthropy in ways that limit access often invisibly though the nature of processes and relationships:

→ "When I fought to protect my land and my home, I was called a savage. When I neither understood nor welcomed his way of life, I was called lazy. When I tried to rule my people, I was stripped of my authority."

Chief Dan George, 'A Lament for Confederation', July 1, 1967

Over the ensuing years, there was much discussion about the formal/informal relationship structure of the Circle. When the name was still the Canadian Aboriginal Grant-making Circle, the group had begun to expand membership to include other foundations and Indigenous people with connections and interest in the work. The Circle had begun to take on projects that required receipt and administration of funding – the first research, publication and a website. The workload began to increase and funders, on top of their day jobs, supported the more complex work sometimes with administrative contributions of their organizations. We rotated our chair about every ten months and began to think about attracting an intern to provide some support. By 2011, an Ontario Trillium Foundation application was made to provide initial funding for the Circle.

Working as an ad hoc committee of representatives of foundations, with several Indigenous people with connection to the work, had gone well when the work was focused on attracting participation from foundations and creating new conversations on funding Indigenous communities. But the work had begun to expand – and become more political.

In June 2010, the Circle convened the core group in Toronto for a first planning day. David Paul Achneepineskum, a committee member from Metawa First Nation, pointed out that we could not just invite Indigenous people to the gatherings for funders' learning, but needed to answer the question Indigenous participants had asked at the Blackfoot Crossing AMR gathering: "When will we be asked to get involved?" It was time to structure in Indigenous participation and not just rely on relationships. Of course, that also raised the necessity of seeking new relationships to include both Métis and Inuit representation. Once again, the lesson was how easily a purely relational approach can exclude, even with the best of intentions. We learned to continually ask ourselves: "Who needs to be here? Who is missing?"

So what sort of structure did the Circle need to steward the burgeoning interest? Form follows function – but any structure also begins to shape the work and the relationships within. The group wrestled with ideas of whether the Circle should remain a network with fluid relational ways of working, or find a sponsoring organization or become a charity with a government-regulated structure with the ability to receive funds directly and issue tax receipts for donations. The Circle had, until this point, quietly avoided any relationship with government. We had not accepted government funds or courted government funders for participation, and members had simply "managed out" any requests from government funders to attend events.

That day the group set priorities for what the Circle's new structure must accomplish: create the ability to receive and spend money; support a staff person; include significant influence from First Nations, Métis and Inuit people; create a flexible adaptive structure that would enable changing partnerships; be administration-light and not costly to operate; maintain a relational capacity but also have a reporting structure and the capacity to communicate – to listen and be responsive.

The options for a more permanent structure were weighed carefully or, as one member put it, "agonizingly". In the end, with the advice of a prominent charity lawyer, the Circle sought charitable status, which would help ensure its presence over the long term. The permanence and accountable structure made us "players" in the nonprofit scene. But tension can still be felt between the charitable structure and a network's more relational style of organizing – flexible, and well suited to a mobile agenda in a fast-changing social issue. The Circle preserves the language of a network in our description of the work, but has also "structured in" Indigenous and regional engagement on the governance circle and recently moved to a new model with Indigenous and non-Indigenous co-chairs along with the commitment to hire Indigenous staff.

The first official board of the Circle was sworn in on Toronto Island around a picnic table in 2012. Five Indigenous people representing First Nations and Métis communities (including a representative of Canada's then only First Nations Indigenous-engaged Community Foundation)

and four non-Indigenous funders from as many philanthropic organizations were on the roster. The name was changed slightly, but significantly, to fit the shift in our thinking and goals, from the Circle on Aboriginal Grantmaking in Canada to the Circle on Philanthropy and Aboriginal Peoples in Canada. The organization was no longer just about grant makers' learning, but on a shared journey in which First Nations, Métis and Inuit people would participate more fully in a conversation about access to non-governmental funds to seek community solutions.

Once registered, the governance circle began to put the governance systems in place to ensure national and balanced representation and build the usual policy pieces to ensure accountability. One of the key pieces was to identifying key partners and core offerings.

To date, the Circle has had three executive directors and one acting director. Each has been an Indigenous woman. They have brought very different skills and perspectives to the organization. The path has not always been smooth, as the Circle has struggled along on a shoe-string budget and the usual project-based patchwork of funding, and a tremendous demand for representation and partnership with other organizations seeking to engage with Indigenous communities. All the original foundation partners remain as members and many new ones have signed on. For the Circle – born as it was at the moment of the Apology in 2008, and then engaged through the release of the Truth and Reconciliation Commission Report in 2015, the effort involved in both not missing opportunities and not burning out our people has sometimes felt overwhelming. This has not always been successful, but the amount of activity the Circle has generated on the national stage belies the small staff complement it has been able to fund. It has also managed to remain independent of both government and any particular philanthropic agenda – two small but important measures of success.

More recently, the idea of adaptive and emergent strategies for social change organizations has begun to appear in the social sector literature. A recent paper (Darling *et al.*, 2018) compares the strategy options in playing a game of chess with those of playing a team sport. The chess game requires an adaptive strategy: strategy that limits play to a set of rules and outcomes, in this case driven by a funder. The latter requires emergent strategy, one that shifts constantly in the huddle of community as the ecosystem both emerges and also becomes visible through the work. The Circle has done a little of both but, as the organization has matured, we have become much more effective at engaging in the more emergent work.[3]

Today, the Circle's board includes Indigenous funders and change makers. Many of the original members have retired into positions as volunteers or on the Ambassadors' Circle, others remain actively engaged on the governance circle. As the understanding of the change we desire becomes deeper, the Circle's goals have become a little broader.

---

[3] For more thinking on this topic, see *Emergent Strategy: Shaping change, changing worlds* by Adrienne Maree-Brown, AK Press. https://www.akpress.org/emergentstrategy.html

The 2018 strategic plan recognizes six key goals:

- Increase capacity of Indigenous organizations
- Increase capacity of philanthropic organizations
- Increase organizations' commitment to and engagement in reconciliation
- Foster investment in Indigenous communities and Indigenous-led initiatives
- Increase accessible information about Indigenous philanthropy
- Become a nimble, professional, credible, efficient and self-sufficient organization

Circle Strategic Plan, 2018

Part of the core offering decided on in those early formation days was the inclusion of a research agenda. In 2010, the Circle began to research projects that would develop and share learning at the juncture of philanthropic practice and Indigenous community efforts for change. The first project, *Aboriginal Philanthropy in Canada: A Foundation for Understanding* (The Circle, 2010), was written by Bruce Miller, an Indigenous partner in the United Way of Winnipeg. One of the most striking findings was the degree to which the Indigenous organizations he interviewed lacked access to fundraising training, a finding that led to training development.

The next project was in partnership with AJAH, a social sector data firm that has developed "big data" methodology and access to the CRA database. Called Measuring the Circle, it was an early attempt to ask ourselves who the philanthropists were who were funding Indigenous projects and who and how they were funding. AJAH's methodology develops a 1,200 keyword list used to scan CRA charity data to pull out charities whose name or description contains one or more of the keywords. From here, they could to begin to sketch the outline of Indigenous-focused charitable activity and the funders who support the work.

The first report of this work, *Measuring the Circle: Emerging Trends in Philanthropy for First Nations, Métis and Inuit Communities in Canada* (2014), included a data report and case study stories of philanthropic investment. The second, an infographic, set out an early framework to tracking indicators of the organizational health of the Indigenous-focused charities compared with the Canadian "core"[4] charitable sector (The Circle, 2017b).

The data provided only the broadest snapshots at the time the data was gathered. About 1% of the core charitable sector in Canada could be considered Indigenous-focused, in that they provide some form of service to Indigenous peoples. But the data told us nothing about whether their governance included or was led by Indigenous peoples. Generally, these organizations received smaller grants than the average core sector organizations, had less fundraising and were growing more rapidly in numbers than the core sector as a whole. More Canadian foundations than were

---

4   In Canada the "core" charitable sector refers to organizations that are not municipal, universities, schools or hospitals.

Circle members were making grants, outsiders to the conversations that had started the Circle – and potential members (The Circle, 2014).

The Measuring the Circle research was conducted mostly by settler philanthropists, and the reports started to raise more questions than the data could answer. What was an Indigenous charity anyway? How could a set of key words developed by a non-Indigenous company capture the right charities (this was compounded by the occasional Sikh temple that appeared in the results as the word "Indian" was in the name)? What about the work being done by organizations that would never be charities, didn't want to be charities, and found the whole concept of charity oppressive? Further, the data varied dramatically from one region to another across Canada.

CRA can offer nothing reliable to determine "how Indigenous" an Indigenous-focused charity actually is. Lumped together as "Indigenous-focused", we might find a church-run meal program that serves Indigenous people, picked up in the data scrape along with an Indigenous-operated healing lodge. Some programs may be governed entirely by Indigenous people – or have none at all on the board; they may take a traditional approach or eschew tradition altogether. The research brought us back to the same dilemma that engaged the original group of funders in conversation.

In 2017, the Circle released *Measuring the Circle – Emerging Trends in Philanthropy for First Nations, Métis and Inuit Communities in Canada: A focus on Manitoba* (The Circle, 2017b). This research was undertaken under the direction of Indigenous leaders at United Way of Winnipeg. The project looked in depth at what the data meant for one region and then interviewed and listened to story after story of charitable work from an Indigenous perspective. The report creates an articulate message about the conflicts inherent in making change in colonially produced social issues from within a colonial structure of organization and regulation still based in Canada on 15th-century British laws. The focus groups in the Manitoba study asked people – from Indigenous executive directors to Elders – what they thought an Indigenous charity was. Many participants felt the words "charity" and "charities" connote a deficit model of helping that is not culturally relevant and does not fit within the Indigenous concept of reciprocity. The term has connotations of one group acting out of benevolence to assist others who may be incapable of acting for themselves. The respondents' answers created a much more complex view than that of the data research.

It has been a strong theme in the Circle's work that language matters – a lot. Reconciling difference in understanding is just not possible when we are speaking without agreement on what our words mean. The Circle's commitment has been that a "good" definition is one that makes sense in Indigenous communities. This commitment often creates new perspectives for philanthropy, and the Measuring the Circle study offers three distinct categories of "Indigenous-focused" charity (*ibid.*, pp. 48, 49):

- **Indigenous charities** are led by, operated by and dedicated to Indigenous peoples and historically rooted and contemporarily grounded in Indigenous culture and self-determining ways
- **Indigenous-led charities** are organizations where the majority of board members and management are Indigenous people
- **Charities that have Indigenous beneficiaries** include other non-Indigenous-led charities that serve Indigenous peoples, nations, communities, organizations and individuals who benefit from charitable donations

Two further definitions help us to clarify the philanthropic side of the discussion. These originated in the broader data work of the Measuring the Circle project, but their endorsement by the Manitoba project helps us to move more confidently in our future work (*ibid.*, p. 5):

- **Indigenous philanthropy** refers to activities of both donors and recipients that are directed to the benefit of Indigenous peoples. The term encompasses charitable foundations, charities, non-profit organizations and qualified donees.[5]
- **Charitable funders** are registered Canadians charities that make grants or gifts to other charities. **"Charitable funders of Indigenous charities"** have made one or more grants to an Indigenous-focused charity and **"active funders"** have made 23 or more gifts or grants in 2013 – a list that included 100 foundations.

There is a movement taking hold in Manitoba, and other parts of the country, which advocates for a "new" – or, more accurately, "old" – model for "charity" seen through Indigenous lenses. This focuses on the exchange of gifts, roles for caring in multi-generational communities, and resilience. There is a tension in the disconnect between these approaches and the charitable structures required for CRA charitable status, but there is also opportunity. As reforms begin to creep into the regulation of charities, there is hope that, in a spirit of reconciliation, traditional practices will eventually be better understood to be a "fit" with charity regulations.

In the near term, these definitions help philanthropists to better target grant-making. Many well-intentioned philanthropists invest significant resources in charities with Indigenous beneficiaries, rather than seeing Indigenous communities and people as experts in what their communities need and investing directly in Indigenous or Indigenous-led charities. If we believe that settler solutions have largely failed to alleviate the social issues produced by settler practice, it makes sense to put a priority on strengthening Indigenous-led organizations and funding the solutions developed close to the ground and in Indigenous communities. This must be where the innovation lies: recognizing and funding Indigenous expertise and solutions rather than setting a funding agenda. This will bring us closer to a practice of reconciliation.

---

5 In 2011, First Nations could register with CRA as "qualified donees", with the capacity to receive charitable donations under the provision that recognizes "a registered municipal or public body performing a function of government in Canada" (CRA, 2011).

Learning forward together: A declaration of commitment

→ "[U]ntil people show that they have learned from this, we will never forget, and we should never forget, even once they have learned from it, because this is part of who we are. It's not just a part of who we are as survivors and children of survivors and relatives of survivors; it's part of who we are as a nation. And this nation must never forget what it once did to its most vulnerable people."

Senator Murray Sinclair

Eight years after the agenda for the first AMR in Winnipeg was shelved for the Prime Minister's Apology, the Circle joined the march and held a gathering to coincide with the release of the report of the Truth and Reconciliation Commission (TRC, 2015) in Ottawa. During the TRC's final sessions, members of the Circle and allies presented the Commission with the Philanthropic Community's Declaration of Action, committing signatories to act on the 94 TRC recommendations through their funding programs.

At the point of inception, thirty of Canada's major foundations signed the declaration. Signatories to the declaration committed to learning, truth-telling, engagement, measurement and action. Over the years since the original document was presented to commissioners, many additional organizations and individuals have signed on and joined the learning journey.

The signing of the declaration is largely a symbolic gesture, a statement of commitment made by foundations to act as allies to do more in supporting Indigenous Nations, communities, and peoples in achieving their goals. It also expresses the belief that self-determination – the real innovation of community-led solutions – can come only from investment directly in Indigenous communities, and Indigenous and Indigenous-led charities. The overarching lesson of the Circle is that supporting meaningful change always comes back to relationships.

Not replicating colonial or settler-centered frameworks in philanthropic practice means seeking out and investing in those organizations that are Indigenous-led to strengthen capacity and support innovative and impactful work that supports self-determination. When faced with competing opportunities to fund, this is often difficult for foundations. The work of review and relationship building is often more time-consuming, the path forward is emergent and the outcomes are less certain. Indigenous charities, despite under-investment from the philanthropic sector, are still working hard to deliver essential programs and services. Often framed as lacking capacity, many Indigenous organizations have not had significant opportunities to work in relationship with foundations and many foundations still use rigid and bureaucratic application forms and evaluation criteria. Furthermore, many Indigenous organizations have more experience with restrictive and sometimes punitive government funding processes than those required by philanthropic organizations. We cannot begin to catalogue the many quiet interventions the Circle and its members have undertaken over the last decade. Some, like the AMR gatherings, have had a significant profile. Others, like coaching foundation staff on how best to support reconciliation with their boards, or travelling to Indigenous communities, may bear fruit in the long run.

Senator Sinclair's words and influence, along with those of fellow TRC commissioners Marie Wilson and Chief Wilton Littlechild, have emboldened members of the Circle to continue to press forward. On many occasions Sinclair has reminded us that reconciliation is not an exercise which is likely to be completed in the lifetime of those currently engaged in this work. It has taken generations to come to where we are now, and it will take generations for balance to be restored.

At the moment of writing, the Circle is shifting again, from the early partners – many of whom were non-Indigenous agents in private philanthropy, leadership and governance – to a new generation of First Nations, Métis and Inuit leaders who are imbedded in the sector and their communities, and are committed to supporting Indigenous philanthropy and building a new type of uniquely Canadian philanthropy.

The Circle will continue to push the philanthropic sector to transform the ways funders think, act, and fund. It is critical for philanthropists to recognize Indigenous leadership, invest in Indigenous-led solutions, and support Indigenous peoples and communities in their pursuits of self-determination. The 2019 All My Relations gathering offered a unique focus on the seasons and how alignment to the seasons connects to governance and operations (winter), emergence and partnerships (spring), relationship-building and celebration (summer), and increasing wisdom and knowledge dissemination (fall). This slowed-down seasonal framework has shaped how the Circle does all our work. Winter is a time for ceremony, the integration of learnings and reflections from the year before, and governance and operational foundation-setting for the year ahead. Each spring, the Circle offers a multi-day facilitation and personal leadership training that increases our shared efforts to design, co-convene and be together in times of change. This growing network of Indigenous and non-Indigenous practitioners is returning to its philanthropic and community settings equipped and eager to make change. Our summer season is dedicated to being on the land and in relationship with our members in shared learning experiences. And finally, each fall, our focus shifts to a collective story harvest to gain more insight and wisdom. During this time, we see the patterns, practices and policies that enable foundations to move forward on the Declaration for Action, their commitments to new ways of thinking and doing, and ultimately what it takes to co-create a new future.

The Circle has thus oriented itself towards a focus on inviting new ways of thinking and doing. Through convening, fee-for-service offerings, research and knowledge mobilization, and the development and use of a unique storytelling methodology focused on people, practice and policy, we continue to influence the sector through unique experiences and resources. As the Circle moves into another year of strategic orientation, aligned to the seasonal approach, we will continue to show up where invited, invite others to join this learning journey alongside us, and continue to amplify solutions led by Indigenous and Indigenous-led organizations. We will continue to enable and expand thinking and doing differently in the space between settler-created philanthropic organizations and Indigenous and Indigenous-led charitable and grassroots organizations. The last ten years have taught us that truly taking action on reconciliation requires asking ourselves the hard questions, naming power and privilege imbalances, owning up to the ways in which non-Indigenous Canadians have benefited (and continue to benefit) from colonization, working tirelessly to eradicate white supremacy, and even questioning the existence of settler-created philanthropy in the future we envisage. If you're excited by the prospect, and challenge, of envisaging and practicing new ways of being and doing, we invite you to join the Circle and our members on that learning journey.

Three key takeaways

1

Philanthropy isn't the solution or the point. The key point is honouring and building partnerships with Indigenous communities and organizations to make their ideas, programs and solutions a reality on their terms.

2

Building relationships takes time and trust, requires an openness to thinking and doing differently, and offers limitless opportunity and learning. Canada will be a better place to live if Indigenous ways of thinking, being, and knowing and caring are embraced, celebrated and adopted.

3

This work is a long journey. There have been tears and mistakes, and there will be more, but there will also be laughter and transformation. You've been invited on the journey. Don't be afraid to join us.

References

Alberg-Seberich, M (2016, Nov. 9) 'Reconciliation as a driver for engaged philanthropy', *Alliance*. Retrieved from: https://www.alliancemagazine.org/blog/reconciliation-driver-engaged-philanthropy/

Canada Revenue Agency (2011) *Qualified Donees*, Aug. 15, 2011, CG-010. Retrieved from: https://www.canada.ca/en/revenue-agency/services/charities-giving/charities/policies-guidance/qualified-donees.html

Churchill, W (1948) Speech to the British House of Commons

Circle (2010) *Aboriginal Philanthropy in Canada: A Foundation for understanding, the Circle on Aboriginal Peoples in Canada*. Toronto. Retrieved from: http://caid.ca/AboPhiCan2010.pdf

Circle (2014) *Measuring the Circle*. Request from: admin@circleonphilanthropy.ca

Circle (2016) 'Journey of reciprocity: The first eight years of the Circle on Philanthropy and Aboriginal Peoples in Canada', *The Philanthropist*. March 14

Circle (2017) *Measuring the Circle: Emerging trends in philanthropy for First Nations Métis and Inuit Communities in Canada: A focus on Manitoba*. Request from: admin@circleonphilanthropy.ca

Darling, MJ, Sparkes Guber, H & GS Smith (2018) *A Whole Greater than Its Parts: Exploring the role of emergence in complex social change*. Washington, DC: Fourth Quadrant Partners

Fine, S (2015, May 28) 'Chief Justice says Canada attempted cultural genocide on aboriginals', *The Globe and Mail*. Toronto

Hakluyt, R (2008) *The Principal Navigations, Voyages, Traffiques, and Discoveries of the English Nation*. Volume 13 (Gutenberg eBook) original ed. Richard, E & G Goldsmidt (1889) *Second Voyage of Jacques Cartier*, Ch. 13–15 Translated from Jacques Cartier, *Voyages de découverte au Canada entre les années 1534 et 1542*, ed. René Maran, Paris, Éditions Anthropos, 1968, éd. Originale 1843

Johnston, P (2016) 'Revisiting the "Sixties Scoop" of Indigenous children', *Policy Options Politiques: The Public Forum for the Public Good*. July 16.

Kania, J & M Kramer (2011) 'Collective impact', *Stanford Social Innovation Review* (Winter)

King, T (2004) 'All My Relations' excerpt in Nelson Education Ltd. (2004) *Aboriginal Perspectives*, Toronto, ON, pp. 71–80

Maracle, L (1993) *Ravensong: A novel*. Vancouver, BC: Press Gang Publishers

Struthers, M (2018) 'At odds or an opportunity? Exploring the tension between social justice and social innovation narratives', *The Philanthropist*, March 19

Truth and Reconciliation Commission of Canada (2015) *Honoring the Truth, Reconciling the Future: A summary of the final report of the Truth and Reconciliation Commission of Canada*. Author, Winnipeg

Wilson, D & T Coates (n.d.) *The Road to the Summit: Inspiring approaches to first Nations, Métis and Inuit Learning Initiative, final report of the developmental evaluation*. Retrieved from: http://www.counselling.net/jnew/index.php?option=com_content&view=article&id=113

Part two
Chapter seven

Decolonizing philanthropy: Building new relations

Roberta Jamieson

→ "All Canadians, as Treaty peoples, share responsibility for establishing and maintaining mutually respectful relationships."

Truth and Reconciliation Commission, 2015

Dozens of Canada's philanthropic organizations have embraced the call to action from the Truth and Reconciliation Commission (TRC) that starts this chapter. A number of them presented a Declaration of Action to the closing session of the Commission on June 1, 2015, promising to engage in the dialogue necessary to ensure the philanthropic community understands the cumulative impact of the unresolved trauma caused by the Residential School System. They also pledged to do this with, and not for, Indigenous communities, in all their diversity (Pearson et al., 2015). Since then, a total of 80 philanthropic organizations have signed on and promised to support the specific elements of the Declaration of Action (Archie, personal communication, June 27, 2018).

As a result, many philanthropic organizations have been working hard to decolonize their attitudes and programs. This is not an easy process. We are not always aware of how our own beliefs and attitudes have been colonized. Organizations such as the Circle on Philanthropy and Aboriginal Peoples in Canada (the Circle) are helping charities and philanthropists understand the cultural differences that could cause well-intended approaches to be misinterpreted as signs of disrespect (the story of the Circle's origins is discussed in Chapter 6). As one of the Circle's recent publications pointed out, the philanthropic sector, like most other parts of Canadian society, has not had a lot of experience engaging with Indigenous communities, and vice versa: "All sectors of Canadian society – government, corporate and philanthropic – have a stake in, and share responsibility for, the wellbeing of Aboriginal peoples and communities. To date, the dominant role played by government has overshadowed and perhaps even excused the comparatively small role of philanthropy" (The Circle, 2012, p. 16).

This paper springs from my life as a Mohawk woman living on the reserved lands of the Six Nations of the Grand River Territory in Ontario, my ten years of work as Ontario's Ombudsman and my work as president and CEO of Indspire. Indspire is a national Indigenous-led charity that provides bursaries to assist First Nation,

Métis and Inuit persons in obtaining post-secondary education or trades, so they can contribute their full potential to their families, communities and Canada. I offer my experience to help philanthropic organizations to contribute better to an historic transformation, a future that includes sustainable Indigenous communities.

Past cannot be prologue

Despite some good intentions, history shows that the efforts of the philanthropic sector have often not been that philanthropic – they have often advanced colonial enterprise at the expense of Indigenous peoples. There was, for example, the Residential School System, the appropriation of cultural artifacts for museums, and the "Sixties Scoop" that saw thousands of Indigenous children torn from their families and communities for adoption elsewhere. This did not happen "historically" but in our own lifetimes (Brascoupé Peters et al., 2016). At the root of this dark and cruel history was a desire to eliminate our Peoples.

I have heard many senior officials in both the public and private sectors ask, "Why don't we just get rid of these reserves? They're wastelands." To which I replied, "Excuse me, you want to blame the victims, the people in communities who you have displaced and disempowered? You want to blame them for being hopeless and helpless? You believe the way to fix them is to have them come into cities and mainstream communities?"

I ask again the key question all Canadians have to answer: "Do we or do we not want sustainable Indigenous communities in Canada?" Some of those who see the problem make great commitments, but by and large they do not see sustainability as the outcome. What these officials want is the inclusion of Indigenous peoples in the broader society. That's not about sustainable Indigenous communities – it's about assimilation and our eventual disappearance. *We* have other plans.

There are three major fault lines running through the history of philanthropic engagement with Indigenous communities: invisibility, benevolence and self-awareness. As the Circle notes, the problems of the country's Indigenous people were long thought to be the responsibility of the federal government. Philanthropic organizations felt there were more worthy efforts for them to undertake. Indigenous peoples wanted, and still want, what is ours, based on our inherent rights, rather than to be objects of charity.

The pressing problems of Indigenous communities are very complex and require long-term solutions. The inflicted trauma of residential schools, addictions and unacceptable living conditions are long-term problems with deep, complex roots, not as easily solved as providing school supplies or a better diet to children or looking for a cure to a disease.

159 Decolonizing philanthropy: Building new relations

The Circle has pointed out the results of this stark and profound indifference and neglect. Its latest figures show that, in 2013, Indigenous-focused "charities" made up approximately 1% of total "charities" in Canada, and their revenues were 1.6% of the core charities identified in the report (The Circle, 2014, p. 5). While there have been some recent increases, they have not negated the Circle's 2012 conclusion that "there is little doubt that foundations are either not known or poorly understood among Aboriginal communities and organizations, and philanthropy has not, overall, played a significant role in Indigenous development in Canada" (The Circle, 2012, p. 16).

When Philanthropic organizations did get involved in Indigenous communities, they often came as providers of benevolence rather than as people willing to engage with people to resolve problems. They came with a "do to" attitude, as opposed to a "working with" commitment. Rebecca Adamson, the founder of the First Nations Development Institute, maintains, "The traditional philanthropic paradigm is a transaction: one gives, the other receives. This is alien to most Indigenous communities whose giving instead stresses reciprocity ... If we want to change outcomes in Indigenous communities, the first step for donors is self-reflection ... Philanthropic organizations need to understand that cash cannot buy relationships – nor can it be a substitute for human involvement – and they need to see that transparency, trust, and compliance are natural components of good relationships" (Adamson, 2011, para. 1).

Rebecca Adamson is right. We can't just use the same old methods and routines. They won't work: the Indigenous history of Canada is proof of that. Indigenous communities have a lot of what is needed to make ourselves much healthier, but we have become so damaged by colonialism that this task is challenging. The wounds and scars and debris of over a century of legalized racism, exclusion, exploitation, domination that came out of the thinking of past generations of Canadians must not be perpetuated by this generation of Canadians.

The answer is simple – the same Canadian values and expectations that settlers have for themselves and their families must also be available to the First Nations, Inuit and Métis people who have such deep roots in this place called Great Turtle Island. The TRC noted that, when Indigenous communities entered into treaty relationships with the Crown, they entered into them as equals, not as inferiors.

Indigenous reciprocity

The second essential change that is required if philanthropic organizations want a constructive relationship with Indigenous communities is a recognition and embrace of reciprocity. Reciprocity is the foundation that underpins all our relationships; it is the lens through which we look at all relationships, both human and non-human. Reciprocity is the essence of how we give and receive. It maintains the cycle of life and the sustainability of our people. Rebecca Adamson describes the core principles of reciprocity this way: "I have the honour of giving, the honour of receiving ... I honour you by giving. You honour me by receiving" (Adamson, as cited in Steinem, 1997).

While the word "reciprocity" is not always used in our daily lives, the concept is still deeply embedded in many aspects of most Indigenous cultures. And while colonialism has seriously eroded our systems of reciprocity, we have a strong philosophical connection to the concept that continues to this day. Indigenous reciprocity is an integral part of a nearly universal Indigenous worldview. The specific protocols and ceremonies that give voice to the concept, though, vary from nation to nation, highlighting the need to enter into any long-term relationships with humility and cultural awareness.

Long before the Spanish came in the 15th century, *compadrazgo* was a belief and cultural cornerstone throughout the Americas. It was made manifest in reciprocity, ritual kinship, and the elaborate festivals and practices of gift-giving and communal work.

- The Zapotecas in Mexico assume reciprocal responsibilities through *guendaliza*, which means "We all are relatives." They say *chux quixely* when they say thank you. The phrase means "I will reciprocate."
- Article 2 of the Bolivian Constitution says, "Bolivia is founded on the principles of unity, solidarity, and reciprocity." Evo Morales, the first Indigenous president of that fundamentally Indigenous country, used reciprocity, solidarity and community as the basis for a new economic system intended to provide a better future for the Bolivian people.
- The potlach provided benefits on the Pacific coast of North America that are essential to sustainable communities, including the redistribution of wealth, the claiming of status, and rights to hunting and fishing territory.

Indigenous reciprocity is sometimes symbolic – a hunter asking permission from an animal before a kill or a healer placing tobacco on the earth before picking leaves from a plant. These are all simple yet profound expressions of reciprocity.

It is far more complex than a simple two-way exchange of favours. There are reciprocities of reciprocities, an involvement of intricate social systems, usually accompanied by protocols and etiquettes that trigger a series of events, which in turn trigger another series of events.

Reciprocity energizes the framework of how we see ourselves in the world. When we get up every morning, we recite a Thanksgiving address that centres ourselves in the world. It addresses and is focused on our relationship with the Creator. You begin with under the earth, then on the earth, then you talk about the plants, the animals, the birds, the clouds, the winds, the sun and the moon. The least we can do is say "Thank you." You identify everything by their relationship to you: my mother the earth, my cousins the animals, my eldest brother the sun.

So, you start every day by seeing yourself as part of a whole, part of a larger picture – I have responsibilities, and my responsibilities are to the whole, to the collective, to keep sustainable communities alive.

Decolonizing philanthropy: Building new relations

At its heart, reciprocity is not about the individual. It is not about "acting" upon the world, or "doing" things to it. It is about a relationship that has to be mutual, holistic and concerned about more than one thing.

Reciprocity rarely stands alone – usually it is one essential aspect of a constellation of positive attributes which are integral to Indigenous societies – and it is very badly needed right now by the rest of the world.

Here at Indspire, we have taken a modern registered national charity, and incorporated the Indigenous value of reciprocity by having student applications commit to giving back to their communities as one of the criteria for awarding bursaries.

Testimony from recent recipients show that Indspire is the spark that starts a transformation. When we survey our students, the vast majority say, "I am working for my people." Recipients like Natu Bearwold told us they have never felt so part of a community; they have never felt such an obligation to return. "I'd like to work in northern BC in Indigenous communities," said Bearwold, "because I know there is a great need for doctors in my home territory and I'd like to contribute to the healing of my people. This award has made all the difference in my life right now" (personal communication, May 2018).

Cheyenne Bisson echoed those feelings: "My future aspiration is to establish a Youth Healing Lodge for the seven First Nations along the North Shore, a place for our youth to come and learn about their culture and language, a place where they can see the possibilities that life has to offer themselves. This award is truly a blessing … It is knowing that there are beautiful people out there that kept me going and encouraged me in fighting the good fight" (personal communication, May 2017).

By giving them support as Indigenous people and not as needy students, Indspire is validating the identity of Indigenous youth. "You valued me for who I am and supported me in strengthening that identity" is not the usual response you get from a recipient of philanthropy. Part of that identity is a responsibility to the whole and to giving back in a reciprocal way.

Decolonizing philanthropy

When our people talk about reconciliation, we are talking about structural and systemic change. We are not talking about wanting a seat at your table. We want to build an entirely new table.

The Circle highlighted this goal back in 2012: "We are not looking for a one-way relationship, from a wealthy benefactor to a deserving cause. We are looking for a collaborative, multilateral relationship where all parties are committed to learning and growing. In return, we offer a deep engagement in growing, thriving communities that goes far beyond a grant application or a project report" (The Circle, 2012, p. 4).

Indigenous communities are now asking charities and philanthropic organizations to deeply question their own intentions when they engage with them, and many find that difficult to do. We are asking them to acknowledge that simply having money does not mean they know best what is needed for Indigenous communities.

Kris Archie, executive director of the Circle, acknowledges that this is more difficult than it appears at first blush and that many organizations have found that good intentions are not enough when they go to sign the Declaration of Action. "Before anyone can sign it now," says Archie, "we have a form they have to fill out. It's intentionally created to provide them with an opportunity to reflect upon the questions we are asking. What we have noted is that it tends to be a very important exercise for people. Many come back to us and say, 'Wow, I saw this document and wanted to sign it, and I started to fill out your form and I realized there's much more we need to do before we can consider ourselves prepared to sign this'" (personal communication, 2018).

If people are asked to think about their own social position and privilege and the ways they are complicit in the ongoing destruction of Indigenous lands and communities, it can be very hard for them to know what to do next.

Archie says these initial difficulties and uncertainties, the fears and fragilities, are generally because people don't have the capacity to confront the reality of their history. "Settlers need to learn their own history and what that process of colonization continues to do here in Canada – not just for Indigenous communities, but for many racialized communities. Canada has a long history of really atrocious behavior towards to all kinds of racialized communities" (personal communication, 2018).

Archie also feels that some philanthropies need to acknowledge that their own organizations were blemished from the very beginning. "When you look at the larger family foundations in this country, they were predominantly built on the wealth created from resources extraction and other settler activities. What would be really amazing would be if one or more of these philanthropic organizations would do some analysis of how their original endowment came off the backs of

Indigenous communities and acknowledge that their organizations contributed to behaviours like the residential schools, the Sixties Scoop and unethical research. They could offer to pay reparations or restitution" (K. Archie, personal communication, 2018).

Nothing for us, without us

If this is our current reality, how are we ever going to get to the future that we have envisaged?

One way for philanthropic organizations to start is by working to support our economic self-sufficiency and development. That is key to ensuring sustainable Indigenous communities, but it is not addressed by most foundations in Canada. We must have a more holistic approach. Although there are specific needs in communities, a transformational change is essential in order to sustain a reciprocal approach to philanthropy.

This is the challenge we bring to philanthropy. The philanthropic sector needs to realize we have the solutions, and the ability to develop new solutions for challenges that may occur in the future. The question we need philanthropists to answer is whether they would like to join us in developing decolonized, reciprocal relationships with Indigenous peoples – not to "help" them because they are "poor and needy", but rather to strengthen our own ability to realize our potential, so that we may then make our full contribution to society and to the future of everyone's children.

If that is to happen, we have to work together to change the rules of engagement. It is my hope that we will be successful in meeting this challenge and that our success will be a proud example that will encourage others to develop reciprocity in their own fields. It would be a tool for decolonizing many of the terribly damaging relationships that continue to prevail in every part of the world.

We need to join together as two parties working jointly toward a shared goal. In those terms, philanthropy's move to reciprocity would mean two cultures building bridges, maturely moving beyond assessing blame and concentrating instead on creating solutions (for more on this, see Rowe and Rousin's discussion of Winnipeg Boldness in Chapter 8).

We need to remember that Indigenous values generally cause us to distrust anyone who refuses to share, and to distrust a person who refuses to accept offers of sharing from others, however humble they may be. That's because reciprocity is intended to maintain a balance, an equilibrium in a relationship. With reciprocity, we feel good about giving, and we feel good about being offered a gift. We feel nourished by the exchange, both as giver-receivers and receiver-givers.

When reciprocity is not practised, things can easily go awry: givers feel unappreciated and resentful, receivers believe their dignity has been diminished, and guilty about not having been able to give back. This loss of balance is felt in our hearts.

Philanthropy is too precious an activity to be limited to people of means. People with limited resources have few chances to be philanthropic. But we can create our own opportunities. I believe philanthropists have an important role to play in creating more opportunities for people of limited means to be philanthropic. Not just by giving to charities, but by allowing them to enjoy the same satisfactions that philanthropists enjoy: opportunities to feel involved; opportunities to be useful contributors, rather than just perpetual recipients of someone else's generosity.

If we are to move into a philanthropy of reciprocity, philanthropists have to build long-term relationships that are built and nourished for the sake of the relationship itself, long before there is any thought of "philanthropy". Enduring relationships have to be developed, even if it turns out that no money is provided. It also means linking any philanthropy program to the strategic goals of Indigenous communities.

The relationships that are formed must be intended to continue even after the "giving" is over – they will cherish opportunities for "giving" and "giving back" many times over. Indigenous reciprocity requires developing an interconnectedness.

As Indigenous peoples we all see ourselves as part of the same whole. There is no room in our way of thinking for "us" and "them". Everyone is "us", members of the same family, children of the same earth, part of the same Creation.

Doing it right

The recent donation by the Slaight Family Foundation of $12 million dollars for Indigenous youth programs is an example of how philanthropic organizations can work with Indigenous communities to achieve Indigenous goals. The foundation was established in 2008 and, until recently, had little experience in Indigenous philanthropy.

Gary Slaight, president of the Slaight Family Foundation, has developed a unique way of giving: he supports several organizations working on a similar concern, at the same time, to really make a difference to a particular sector. The foundation's most notable donation to date has been a gift of $50 million to five Toronto hospitals for major priority areas important to each hospital.

Given the difficulties experienced by our Indigenous communities, Gary wanted to address some of the issues facing our Indigenous population by working with several organizations at the same time.

The foundation's philanthropic advisor, Terry Smith, said they consulted a wide range of Indigenous leaders and experts to determine the focus of the initiative: "Gary very specifically wanted to make sure that whatever funding came from the foundation came because Indigenous communities wanted it and felt it would make a difference" (personal communication, July 3, 2018).

Smith said they didn't have any notion of what the Foundation would support when they started the discussion: "Gary knew he wanted to help and also knew he needed assistance identifying the best way his support could really make a difference. Do we deal with water? Do we deal with housing? Do we deal with youth? Do we deal with suicide prevention?"

Based on what it heard, the foundation decided to focus on programs for Indigenous youth that would produce long-term benefits for the communities. Criteria were developed with guidance and input from Indigenous leaders. Smith said, "This was done with extreme care given our lack of expertise within the foundation, so the feedback and advice provided from the Indigenous community was critical to ensuring a successful initiative" (personal communication, July 3, 2018).

The final criteria are outlined below:

- The proposed programs should be national in scope or have an ability to expand nationally
- They should help indigenous communities build their own capacity
- They should leave a long-term legacy
- The programs must be led or directed by Indigenous people and provide leadership capacity that will stay in the community
- The programs should have measurable impact and produce quantifiable change
- If supported, organizations must have the capacity to deliver on the initiative

As well as ensuring that programs met these criteria, the foundation met and worked closely with each organization to ensure their proposals would be relevant to their communities. In some cases, proposals and budgets had to be rewritten several times to ensure all initiatives were of the calibre to be included as part of the initiative.

In the end, the Slaight Family Foundation committed to giving $12 million over five years to fifteen Indigenous-led programs, including: the Gord Downie and Chanie Wenjack Fund, which supports Indigenous education and culture; the Moosehide Campaign, which develops programs to reduce violence against women; and my own organization, Indspire, to support increased scholarships for Indigenous students to continue their schooling.

One of the unique aspects of this group giving is that the Slaight Family Foundation brought all the recipients together in a meeting to share their initiatives with one another and to ensure the organizations were aware that they were part of a larger initiative that would be monitored and assessed collectively over the term of the grant agreement. Since that time, several of the groups have contacted one another and have created their own partnerships, something the foundation hoped would happen but did not insist on.

Foundations such as the Slaight Family Foundation take huge risks in trying to support a specific sector or deal with a specific social problem. Their nimbleness and ability to get funds out of the door quickly is often the instigator that leverages government or other funders to contribute to a cause. The grants from the Slaight Family Foundation all required successful applicants to make their own commitments, rather than simply disbursing funds from the Foundation.

For example, the Slaight Family Foundation had been supporting an Indigenous coordinator position at the Royal Ontario Museum (ROM) on a project basis for several years to increase awareness of the Indigenous collection and to incorporate Indigenous teachings within ROM programs. As a result of the Slaight Family Foundation's Indigenous initiative, ROM has now created and funded from their own budget a permanent full-time staff position responsible for Indigenous programs. This will now enable ROM to incorporate Indigenous teachings and beliefs fully into their programs on a more permanent basis.

Right to Play is an international organization that uses play and sports as a means to empower children and youth in war-torn and disadvantaged communities.

It has developed a successful model that allows these children to learn new skills, build relationships and establish leadership through play, sport and recreation, while helping youth in the very worst situations. In Canada, Right to Play has extended its program to at-risk youth and, with the support of both the federal and provincial governments, has begun operating play programs in Indigenous communities to help reduce the incidents of suicide and overdosing.

While Right to Play has provided these programs many times in many different situations, their staff were not prepared for what happened when it began to deliver programs in the Indigenous communities. Right to Play found that, once young people really trusted its program leaders, they would come up and say, "I tried to commit suicide last night", or "My brother overdosed". This would give the program leaders critical information that, if they had been trained, they could have used to refer the young people to services and help. But, at that time, they were just the program leaders.

So, Right to Play asked the Slaight Foundation for funding to develop a training program, in cooperation with experts such as the Canadian Mental Health Association and the Centre for Addiction and Mental Health. It developed an entire training program,[1] which, while initially intended for the program leaders on Indigenous communities, is now being used to train all their program leaders. It provides answers to questions such as "What do you say? What do you do? How do you refer them? Who else can they talk to?"

A grant to Right to Play is a good example of how a philanthropic organization cannot just take a successful program and expect the same results in an Indigenous community. This is a hard, but necessary, message for charities to learn.

---

[1] http://www.righttoplay.ca/Learn/ourstory/Pages/PLAY-Program.aspx

The Slaight Family Foundation does not dictate how organizations should report on their accomplishments. Smith says it is more concerned about letting the organizations report back by telling their own story, rather than filling in a bureaucratic form that may be of benefit only to the donor. Instead, organizations are asked to send in a report in whatever manner they choose and to simply tell the Foundation what they did, whether the intended results were achieved and whether they spent the money as they had originally planned. If the Foundation finds the reports lacking in content or requires further details, it then contacts the organization and seeks clarification. Charities seem to appreciate this flexible method of reporting back, as many funders insist on a formalized format that may not truly reflect what the organization has actually achieved in the past year.

"If foundations don't take these kinds of risks," says Terry Smith, "we may never find innovative solutions to many of our social problems nor would we know if such support can really make a difference." The Slaight Family Foundation is one of those funders that are willing to take the risk, try innovative solutions and hope to make a positive difference in the lives of Canadians.

Certainly, there is a time and place for more scientific reporting, but sometimes qualitative and quantitative data is not a key element of the issue that is being supported; it is more valuable that the result of an experience be documented. At the end of the initiative, the Foundation will review with each organization the successes and lessons learned and will use the successful ventures as examples that can be shared with other Indigenous groups across the country.

The criteria for grants set by the Slaight Family Foundation served it well when determining who would get funding. The principles ensured the programs engaged with Indigenous communities and met their needs. But it would be presumptuous to think those six points contain all that is required to have respectful relationships with Indigenous communities. Just as Indigenous communities are diverse, so are their relationships. One size does not fit all.

A number of other organizations have also developed principles and guidelines that would benefit philanthropies in their relationship with Indigenous peoples. The International Funders for Indigenous Peoples talks about the four Rs: reciprocity, respect, responsibility and relationships (International Funders for Indigenous Peoples, 2014, p. 33).

My own organization, Indspire, has a set of Seven Foundational Guiding Principles. These include the recognition that Indigenous knowledges are a valued and foundational aspect of learning, because they convey our responsibilities and relationships to all life; and that the process of decolonization must seek to strengthen, enhance and embrace Indigenous knowledge and experience (Indspire, n.d.).

Indspire's Global Ethics Policy promotes ethical research, data collection and evaluation in Indspire-funded programs involving Indigenous communities. The policy's core principles are:[2]

- Any research program depends on the active involvement, participation and consultation of the Indigenous community
- Any data collected must be considered as the shared ownership of both Indspire and the Indigenous community or organization that supplied the data
- The participating First Nations, Non-status First Nation, Métis and Inuit peoples must have access to the research data, not just the resulting reports
- Meaningful capacity development will be built into all projects
- All community protocols will be respected

I have my own suggestions for what philanthropic organizations should think about when approaching Indigenous organizations. They go a bit further than the criteria I have previously cited and reflect my own experience:

- Anybody who wants to get into the business of working with our people needs to be authentic. Don't pretend. Our people will decide whether or not they want to work with you. But we need to know who you are
- Know the history of the Indigenous community you are involved in, the trauma that was involved and the impact that continues to this day
- We want to establish relationships before we discuss money. We want relationships that continue after the philanthropy ends
- We are looking for ways to offer reciprocity in return. Indigenous reciprocity is dynamic, and constant. It requires on-going renegotiation, arising from a respectful relationship of mutual trust and the assurance of mutual obligations
- Concentrate on outcomes and goals, rather than on the means to achieving the outcomes and goals. Rather than talk about how programs will operate, talk about a future in which our children will feel validated, a future in which First Nations, Inuit and Métis will be economic players and live the kinds of lives that all human beings are entitled to live

If Canada is to surmount its historic and continuing injustices to Indigenous communities, we must encourage exercises in which we work together to develop a new vision; a vision of a future where all communities have conditions worthy of Canada and where we become examples of how people from different cultures and origins can work together to create sustainable communities and futures.

Why should anyone care about this? Why should people contribute to resolving these issues? Because if we do not attend to these situations now, they will fester and worsen and overflow into

---

2 https://indspire.ca/seven-foundational-guiding-principles-2/

169 Decolonizing philanthropy: Building new relations

general society. If we do not deal with these issues now, they will grow beyond our ability to deal with them and poison our entire society, socially, economically and spiritually. Ironically, if left unattended, they will reduce the ability of philanthropists to be philanthropical.

On the other hand, if solutions can be found, designed and implemented by Indigenous communities for Indigenous communities, they will provide new ways of doing and thinking that all Canadians can learn and benefit from. I think that's the biggest invitation with the work we are trying to do.

The truth is that all of us, indigenous and settler, are in a world where more and more communities are living together in smaller and smaller spaces. All of us need to be more inter-culturally fluent, more inter-culturally literate. We need to figure out how to get along better with people who are "different" from ourselves, and to offer reciprocity to the natural world that sustains all of us.

Am I dreaming that the changes I have been talking about can be accomplished? I know from the many examples offered by Indigenous cultures that this way of working does happen. That means it can happen.

I am convinced that cross-cultural philanthropy is achievable, and that philanthropy can be transformed in our generation.

Let's do it.

Three key takeaways

1 Examine your own intentions before engaging with Indigenous communities.

2 Establish authentic relationships. Design programs and decide on funding *together*.

3 Programs must be led or directed by Indigenous leaders and build capacity that stays in the community.

References

Adamson, R (2011) 'Learning to see "invisible" capacity', *Alliance*, vol 16 (2) pp. 22–3

Brascoupé Peters, W, Couchman, S, Hanson, U & M Struthers (March 2016) 'Journey of reciprocity: The first eight years of the Circle on Philanthropy and Aboriginal Peoples in Canada', *The Philanthropist*. Retrieved from: https://thephilanthropist.ca/2016/03/journey-of-reciprocity-the-first-eight-years-of-the-circle-on-philanthropy-and-aboriginal-peoples-in-canada

Circle on Philanthropy and Aboriginal Parties in Canada (2012) *Aboriginal Philanthropy in Canada: A foundation for understanding*. Ottawa, Canada

Circle on Philanthropy and Aboriginal Parties in Canada (2014) *Measuring the Circle: Emerging trends in philanthropy for First Nations, Métis and Intuit communities in Canada*. Ottawa, Canada

Indspire (n.d.) 'Seven Foundational Guiding Principles'. Retrieved from: https://indspire.ca/global-ethics-policy/

International Funders for Indigenous Peoples (2014). *Grantmaker's Guide: Strengthening international Indigenous philanthropy*. San Francisco, USA

Pearson, H, Lawson, B, Nemtin, A, Brascoupé Peters, W, Santoro, L, Lyons, S & V Grant (June 2015) 'The philanthropic community's declaration of action', *The Philanthropist*. Retrieved from: https://thephilanthropist.ca/2015/06/the-philanthropic-communitys-declaration-of-action

Steinem, G (1997) 'Rebecca Adamson: For helping Indigenous people claim their rights and preserve their wisdom', *Ms. Magazine*, Jan–Feb, pp. 48ff

The Truth and Reconciliation Commission of Canada (2015) *Reconciliation, Volume Six, Final report of the Truth and Reconciliation Commission of Canada*. Ottawa, Canada: The Truth and Reconciliation Commission of Canada

Part two
Chapter eight

Relationship, reciprocity and respect: Reflecting on our journey at The Winnipeg Boldness Project

Gladys Rowe and Diane Roussin

Tansi! Aniin! Boozhoo! We are thankful for the opportunity to share what we have learned in working with our philanthropic partners on The Winnipeg Boldness Project.[1]

We are a social innovation project that began in 2014. We have been working in the Point Douglas neighourhood, in Winnipeg, Manitoba, since then to positively impact the health and wellbeing of families through systems change. Social innovation is a field that has emerged with a goal to bring together diverse collaborators to develop solutions that tackle complex challenges (Westley *et al.*, 2016). Labs that use social innovation have also expanded to include approaches such as person-centred design. At The Winnipeg Boldness Project we have combined social innovation with Indigenous ways of knowing, being, feeling, and doing. From this we have created a space where we have the opportunity to learn through emergence and through iteration – taking what is learned and responding to it.

By using principles that honour Indigenous ways of knowing, being, feeling and doing, we have worked to continue to allow for an experiential, deeply reflective process. While this can feel exciting, it also means that *how* we know and have been taught to work in the design and provision of social services can be challenging.

As we sat down to explore these challenges and what we have learned so far, we thought it would be a story to tell through conversation. What follows is a conversation between myself, Gladys Rowe, former research & evaluation manager, and Diane Roussin, project director, as we explored what our learning has meant for the partnerships, and those we have with our philanthropic partners in particular.

---

[1] More information about The work of The Winnipeg Boldness Project can be found at http://www.winnipegboldness.ca

174 Relationship, reciprocity and respect

Gladys: The Project[2] has been really framed as a part of the reconciliation process. I was wondering what you feel the role of our philanthropic partners has been, considering our work as community-driven reconciliation?

Diane: I wanted to take a second and define who I feel our philanthropic partners are. For example, the chair of our board, Gregg Hansen,[3] I include him as one of our philanthropic partners. That is the role he is playing here. He is supporting the Project through his connections, asking the people in his networks to consider making donations. He's really invested in the work of the Project, trying to impact the people in his network, influencing them to support the work happening through the Project. Our other philanthropic partners obviously include the McConnell Foundation, United Way Winnipeg, and an anonymous donor. We have also been supported by the Richardson Foundation and Winnipeg Foundation – those are all considered philanthropic organizations who support our work.

When we say reconciliation, I always have in my mind this equation: reconciliation equals relationships – that's just the bottom line for me. And then everything else flows from there. If we have a relationship, we can talk about anything and we can work through anything. It's the first building block. Boldness has been working to build the necessary relationships for reconciliation through a collaborative process, collective impact, and through the cross-sectoral work. Each of those elements are concerned with fostering relationships and trying to bring together the diverse perspectives. Social innovation brings together diverse people to solve complex problems; it's about the diversity. And because of the diversity – whether it's in the corporate sector or the community sector – everybody speaks a different language, has a different perspective, and a different value set. The only way that we are going to come together is through relationship. The only way we're going to understand one another's perspective, values, and drivers is when we are in relationship with one another. The deeper and fuller this relationship is, the deeper and fuller everything else.

We can have surface relationships, but then we will have surface reconciliation. For example, when someone simply offers a land acknowledgement and then calls it a day, because someone said it's what we're supposed to do. We are looking for a deeper and sustained relationship with reconciliation.

---

2   Project, used throughout this chapter, refers specifically to The Winnipeg Boldness Project.

3   Gregg Hanson (Chair): Former president and CEO of Wawanesa Mutual. Now retired, Gregg remains active in Manitoba's business community on several company boards and has taken an active interest in the well-being of Winnipeg's Indigenous citizens in particular.

Gladys: Do you think the relationships with the philanthropic partners themselves are acts of reconciliation?

Diane: I think so. You think about our relationship with Stephen Huddart (president and CEO of the J W McConnell Family Foundation); that's easy, because he gets so much about why we need to do this work. But as a Project, our relationships with other people don't come so easily sometimes. It can be difficult, because these relationships start from a different place, often with a lack of information, and with a lack of awareness of privilege. As a Project, it is these relationships that have taken more work to foster and build trust. We have had to come to know and appreciate the intent that each of us brings and allow for the leeway to make mistakes. This appreciation also means we are committed to learning how to be in relationship and to become educated on the foundational issues as to why reconciliation is a necessary process to work on together in the first place. We have had to reflect on and assess questions like: What role do the philanthropic partners play? What is the purpose to the relationship? Why do we both need to keep working together towards the end goal?

Gladys: That ties in really well to the next question, which is about reciprocity. The way that I understand reciprocity is that it is a give and take. It is a responsibility to one another as well as a commitment to work together. We talked about reciprocity in terms of our community partners and the guide groups. One of the ways reciprocity worked in these relationships has been through building capacity. Instead of simply asking our partners to give of themselves – to share their experiences, knowledge, skills, and expertise for a finite project (essentially extracting these resources) – we have worked to leave tangible products, skills, and resources behind. One legacy is the building of capacity as a result of the project, where the reciprocal relationships have facilitated this growth.

Thinking about reciprocity as a principle that guides the project – can you share your own understanding of what reciprocity is for you?

Diane: I think it's probably what you laid out there – similar to what you think about reciprocity. It is interdependence – recognizing that we are interdependent and we both have value. Recognizing we both get something out of this relationship and, like it or not, we are linked. Good, bad, or ugly – we are linked. When I think about it specifically at its simplest, it's about give and take. You scratch my back and I scratch yours. That's at the surface level. Then, we can talk about a deeper interconnectedness as being meaningful reciprocity.

When I think about the philanthropic community I think of an interconnected and engaged community of partners. It is about people using philanthropy as influence to affect a social cause. They are in a place in their lives to try to help make it better for others. I feel that our philanthropic partners – and I can't speak of all of them in the same manner – but many are trying to bring more to the table than just their dollars. I think the philanthropic groups are also trying to highlight and make visible other contributions. For Boldness, these contributions are the community wisdom that we are trying to surface through the prototypes – the philanthropic partners recognize that they don't have all the answers, and they want to know what to do to make it better for families. Philanthropic partners are looking to community wisdom to make things better – and so, in our case, there needs to be an understanding of the equal value of contributions to the Project.

Obviously, we are not as far down that recognition road as we could be, as far as valuing what each of us is bringing to the table. But I think there's an awareness and recognition that community wisdom is valuable. And this is felt more by some philanthropic organizations than others. Some are willing to walk with us, and others "just want us to figure it out".

Gladys: There are varying levels of readiness and willingness to take risk – but also varying levels of trust in the relationship. You talked about reconciliation having a grounding in relationship – I'm wondering if you can speak a bit more about the importance of relationship in the Project?

Diane: This is a space where philanthropic groups can come together and collaborate. Often social service organizations are called upon to become coordinated and prevent duplication. This can also be seen in the realm of philanthropy. The Project is a platform for philanthropic collaboration to take place. As a community, community-based organizations in the North End of Winnipeg have worked together for a long time.

When we think about the cross-sectoral role of the Project, this is also an important relationship. We don't often see reaching out across sectors to learn and take the best parts of approaches and frameworks and applying this in a social setting. Experiment, take risks, and develop good products – we are borrowing this from different fields. Boldness is another place where philanthropic organizations can be in relationship with each other. If they weren't already, this is a place for them to be in relationship.

Gladys: So, there's been a different level of commitment with our philanthropic partners in that they have a willingness or openness to participate in the process in a hands-on way?

177   Relationship, reciprocity and respect

Diane: Absolutely. We've always framed our relationships as the difference between transactional versus relational kind of funding. Funders are not sitting disconnected from the Project; they are actively participating each month all along the way. They are helping figure it out as we go. When it is relational, partners get more invested and take more responsibility. This is about responsibility and accountability, and it changes the way the relationship works.

Gladys: At the beginning we didn't explicitly state that we were an Indigenous project – but, truly, because of who we are and how we operate personally and professionally, we have a strong foundation in Indigenous values and principles. How do you think this has impacted the work we have done with the philanthropic organizations? Or the way they work with us?

Diane: I think we are living in the question. We are having the messy conversations about what sharing of knowledge is and what is considered to be appropriation. Really, we need to think about this – do we want every non-Indigenous person out there to adopt our ideas and scale them? There have been really negative experiences where we as Indigenous peoples have shared our knowledge, have had it taken, and then it's even been sold back to us! We get evaluated on it, and then we fail – to be blunt. That kind of appropriation is something we talk about.

In terms of the work that we are doing on the Project, we are talking about who gets to speak, whose voice gets centred, who has the responsibility and accountability, and who has the rights or entitlement. I think there isn't one answer. Within each of our relationships, we have those difficult discussions and then we come to the answer that is right for that relationship.

I am always saying, if you are in that good relationship, you can say the dumbest or silliest thing, and you are going to be given lots of leeway and support and patience. However, if you're in a bad relationship, you are going to get persecuted for blinking wrong or looking sideways. In the end, better relationships make difficult conversations more meaningful and easier to have.

Gladys: In the Project, reconciliation and the Truth and Reconciliation's calls to action have been a point of constant reflection: What are we contributing in response to the calls? With the various philanthropic partners participating at the table, they are also doing their own reflecting on their action in reference to the calls. Do you feel this is strengthened by the relationship they have with Boldness?

Diane: Yes, I believe that. Putting in the work takes a lot of effort and a good relationship. I think that a good relationship is something that transcends all the calls. Actually, it transcends all of the topic areas. There's always a topic area – mental health, education, child welfare. There're always going to be issues to deal with – but a strong foundation of relationships is critical. For example, I have had a relationship with one of the partners over several projects – it transcends the issue areas – when we do our work and wrap on that one, we move to the next one. That's a lifelong commitment. It's a long-term commitment, it may even be intergenerational.

Gladys: I'm thinking about iterative-ness – the idea of think, act, reflect, adjust, and living in the question. This has been a process we have used in the Project from the beginning. I think it has also been a process that we've used with our philanthropic partners as well. Can you think of any examples of where this has come through in how we work with our partners?

Diane: I do feel that the lab process is very conducive to what I would call my Indigenous way and method. That's why I really ended up embracing the lab process, and for all those reasons you just said – the emergence, the iteration, the relationship base, whose voice gets centred in terms of figuring issues out, and how solutions get determined. It fits very much with the child-at-centre model (see Figure 1), that way of working. I think that the philanthropic partners groups we work with have put resources on the table in a way that allowed that way of working to come forward. Without these resources, this Project would have never happened. Being able to really bring forward this lab approach and show how conducive it is to this Indigenous way, this wouldn't have happened had the philanthropic groups not been the catalyst with their dollars. They are really that seed, that catalyst, that initial, short-term, up-front spark kind of money.

Figure 1 – Child-at-centre model

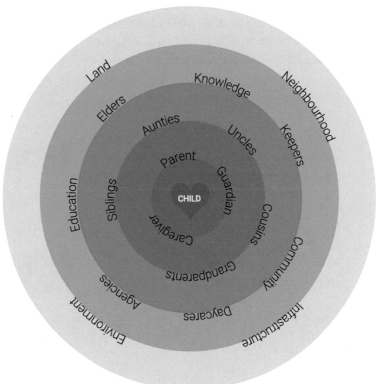

	Also, the philanthropic partners themselves, I feel like they are trying to figure out how they can implement this way of being. They are examining how their frameworks and methods do this work – because the granting process can be very transactional. Instead, they are funding this thing [the Project] that they really believe in, while also turning the mirror back on themselves and asking: "How are we doing this work? How can we be iterative and relational? Whose wisdom gets centred? How can we benefit from living in the question?"
Gladys:	The last question I have is a typical interview wide-open question. Do you have any other insights or "aha" moments that you feel are important to share from our work with the philanthropic partners on the Project?
Diane:	Well, the word "trust" comes to mind. Trust is built on really good, deep, solid relationships, what we just talked about: emergence, iteration, giving space for responsiveness, and turning on a dime and moving in another direction. It's anti-planning and anti-long-term planning to some degree. The things that people have normally put their trust in, such as month-to-month planning, clear activities outlined, clear reporting on those exact activities – that's where people put their trust. And they call that accountability. And with Boldness we are very process driven – people have to look at the process. They judge that the process looks good, but they still don't know where it is going or where it will end up – so people need to fall back on trust. The knowledge mobilization framework (see Figure 2), and the values and principles outlined in the "ways of knowing, being, feeling & doing" ask our partners to participate in a meaningful process where the journey is just as important as the outcome itself.

Figure 2 – Knowledge mobilization framework

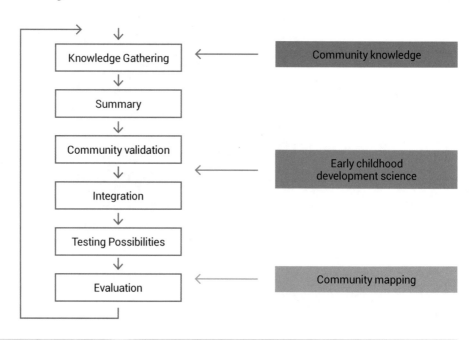

I feel like lots of our funders have given us money because of who is sitting around the table and the trust level. Not so much because of what we're doing. We don't fit the mold, so they can't trust a workplan and reporting on predetermined activities. The leadership at the Guide Group tables have trust. How do you have a trusting relationship? Based on lots of conversation, understanding, respect – all built over time. It's easily lost but hard to get and build up – but once it's there you can really count on it. It's all relational (see Figure 3).

Figure 3 – Winnipeg Boldness accountability framework

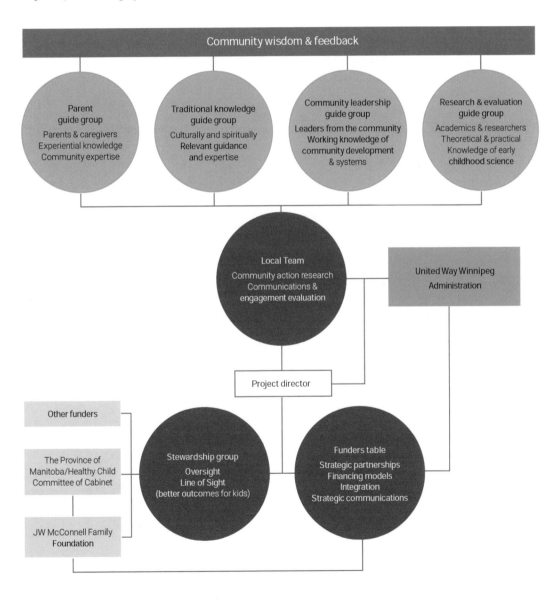

Gladys: The structures that have been built in the Project have supported a way of relating to one another with the underlying goals of respect, understanding, empathy, relationships, and trust. You have touched on trust and relationships, you talked about reciprocity – all of those are really personal and human-focused values. The "ways of knowing, being, feeling, and doing" (see Figure 4) were outlined not only as a guide to the work with families in Point Douglas, but also as a guide to how the Project works itself. These values, however, are very subjective and heart-centred, based on instinct sometimes. This can be very contradictory to what many people have been taught about how you judge value in the world of programming, evaluation, and philanthropy. So, trust and the relationships – all those things that you talk about – are really key. They seem really straightforward – and it is straightforward at Boldness, but it's also not straightforward because it's not really the normal way of operating, judging worth, and measuring progress. You keep going back to the value of relationship: it is so fundamental. Without it nothing else is going to happen.

Figure 4 – Indigenous Ways of Knowing, Being, Feeling, and Doing

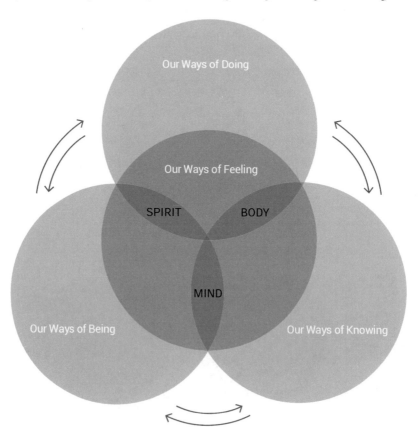

Diane: The other two words I'll throw in there are "risk" and "vulnerability" – because I don't think I say enough about those things. In order to live in the question, in order to experiment, which I think we really need to do, in order to try things out we need to take risk. We hear this in the business community all the time. People take risks and they fail ten times to succeed once. We need to take risks. We don't do that in the social services world. And the only way that we can become comfortable with risk, I think, is if we are in those deep relationships. It is like we say to ourselves, "We will be okay, we are going to venture out here, but we know we have one another's backs. We are going to do it together, and we are going to take this big leap of faith. And even if we fail we will be okay – because we are going to do this together." With that risk is that vulnerability – to go "Uh-oh, we don't know; uh-oh, we can't fail; uh-oh, we did fail." And then "Uh-oh, did we wreck the funding world for everyone else coming after us now, because we failed?" As a Project, to put ourselves out there in that way is about vulnerability.

The other words that were coming to my mind as you were talking, from Peter Senge, are related to value-based decision-making. I can share an example, when I worked in group homes. Many of these kids were considered as being really challenging and this was their last resort. This was the last place on the list where they would be sent. If they didn't make this work, then they are seen as lost causes.

They would come to our centre and, as with any other group home, expect the rule book. The rule book is what governs the relationship. A worker can stand back, stand an arm's-length away or more behind this rule book. And the staff can make all kinds of decisions that affect this kid and not have to be accountable for the decisions because it's the rule book that says so. Not they themselves, they are not the bad person; the rule book is the bad person. I'm imposing this decision on you because the rule book says I have to. Not because I want to. Then the kid freaks out, gets mad – but you can't get mad at the staff, you have to get mad at the rule book. But who makes the rule book? Well, we don't know. Someone made a policy somewhere. Maybe the executive director did, maybe the government did, maybe there's legislation. The rules came from somewhere. Then we have nobody to interact with because someone somewhere made the rule.

In value-based decision-making we didn't have a rule book, we didn't have a book of strict policies that said, when the kid swears at you, you take away their phone. We didn't have a rules-based approach. It was more about the framework that we had. It began with, this is your home, we love you, you are a good person, you are valuable, we want the best for you, and we want to work with you. All these value statements. This is what is important, all the values. What this looks like in practice then is, if a certain kid does a certain thing, then staff have to assess that thing and they have to have a response on this thing based on values. Based on that relationship. In this case staff and kids – a whole bunch of us had a hard time responding when asked about the standardization, and equal treatment. We had to have conversations about customization and equity. Each kid is different and has a whole different set of needs and they need a whole cup of water – you, on the other hand, you only need half a cup of water, but you also need a bun to go with it. Here's you, here's what you need – so let's customize to you and get you what you need, and then let's customize to that kid and get that kid what they need.

I think we do that in the world in general; we stand behind policies and rule books and displace the relationship. Therefore, we don't have to be accountable for our behaviour and our reactions, because the rule book says so. And then no one can ever figure out who made the rule book and how you change the rule book. And how do you create a rule for every scenario anyway? That's rule-based thinking and operating, and I think we are trying to figure that out in Boldness – that's the iteration, the risk, living in the question – we are trying to figure out how to do value-based work.

I think our model is very much about value-based work – but here we have so many systems that are built on a hierarchical model that is all about punching out the same parts of the car, standardization, everyone does the same thing and let's get the end-product the exact same every single time. That's not human reality. When we are doing value-centred work, it's highly customized. The end product looks like a circle, not that triangle, not that bureaucracy. It feels very different – it's not equality; it's equity.

Gladys: Do you think that the philanthropic partners came to the table with an understanding of that values-based decision-making, or was it a learning curve for them?

Diane: The partners had to have had some level of understanding. There is no way they could have come to this Project and stuck with us without understanding it. I do think that some came to us with more of an understanding than others. For those who may not have had a strong understanding, they at least came and were open to something, even if they did not know about values-based decision-making. I think there would have been barriers and an uphill battle for people who had no clue or no awareness. The optimist in me believes that there is not a person who, fully aware of the current realities and understanding the context that has brought us to today, would just dig in and work to maintain the status quo.

Gladys: I think this is great because you have validated the observations I made. I had a list of insights that I had copied down for myself – and you touched on all of them. Here they are:

- You need to be okay being in a space of unknowing, discomfort, and risk
- You need to ensure space to learn is kept open
- You need to have the tolerance, the ability, and the framework to be able to support and take risks
- Reconciliation and innovation are a journey that takes time and strong, trusting relationships
- The voice of those who are directly impacted must lead the process. This is not an opportunity for those who are privileged to continue to hold the microphone – this is important to remember and support.

There is a responsibility to carry the work in a good way. I would include participation in ceremony, but I questioned myself after saying that, as one who is a part of this project and being in relationship – do you necessarily have to participate in ceremony as a part of the project – do you have any thoughts?

Diane: I struggle with that one, I do think it's a sensitive one. You don't want to force anyone to do anything. But then how do you understand Indigenous wisdom if you don't participate in some of that?

Gladys: Yes, and is that key, participation? Or is it in knowing that Indigenous wisdom is important and knowing that it must be centred and then stepping back and letting the space exist?

Diane: Well, that might be the answer – if I know I am not going to be participating in those ceremonies, then I'm not going to be the lead on that. I have to step back and let those people lead the way. I often say that the heart-work – people who can go to the heart of people and tend to people – that is really not me. I'm more of a head-person, an administrative type. I mean, I can lead that kind of process work and I have done ceremonies in the past, but I know that is not my strongest skill. I know when I need to step back and let heart-people lead. Ceremony is the same, there are some people who have deep wisdom because they've put the time in. Knowing your role, maybe it's the clan system – knowing your role and what your responsibilities and gifts are.

Conclusion

The Winnipeg Boldness Project has been built by capitalizing on and respecting the need for diverse partnerships, collaborations and networks. With this comes a necessary commitment to a shared vision. Getting to this point, however, is not an easy task. It requires great skill in relationship-building, the ability to listen to understand rather than to respond, and an awareness of the roots of structural inequities that are faced daily by families in Point Douglas. Finally, and perhaps one of the most critical aspects of this commitment, it requires the time and space to engage people who are directly involved in the work of creating systemic change.

We have had the great opportunity to work alongside families, organizations, community leaders, various helping professionals, policy makers, government representatives, funders, and philanthropic partners to work towards our bold goal. We have learned along the way that this can be bumpy. The stories that we share about these experiences over the last few years have not come easily. We hope that through this chapter you have been able to take something that is meaningful for your experience – something that you can implement in the work that you do in your own community, and in your relationship with Indigenous peoples.

Meanwhile, we continue to learn and grow while remaining committed to the vision of systemic change that is driven by the voices of children and families in Point Douglas.

Three key takeaways

1 It is critical to understand that the people who are directly impacted by an issue must be the ones to lead. We must make space and provide support to ensure this happens.

2 Relationships are necessary for this work. Strong relationships are based on trust, reciprocity, and openness. Reconciliation is about relations. Being committed to working together is one aspect of reconciliation.

3 This is values-based work that requires people to come to, be present in, and contribute to the whole. It is circle work.

References

Westley, F, McGowan, K, Antadze, N, Blacklock, J & O Tjornbo (2016) 'How game changers catalyzed, disrupted, and incentivized social innovation: Three historical cases of nature conservation, assimilation, and women's rights', *Ecology and Society*, 21(4). Retrieved from: http://www.jstor.org/stable/26270034

Part Three

Pathways
to change

The five distinct case studies that feature in this third part of the book, 'Pathways to change', profile innovative practices by foundations that have made a significant impact in communities, networks and Canada as a whole. Across the five cases they demonstrate:

- the movement by Quebec foundations (e.g. the *Collectif* in Chapter 8) to challenge the provincial government's austerity plan

- strategies and dilemmas underlying the engagement of foundations in the public arena

- highlights of the political and organizational dynamics associated with developing and implementing national initiatives

- the importance of respecting local place-based interests and priorities

- insights into large-scale coalition-building and partnerships

- the creation of the Vancouver Foundation's Fostering Change initiative and its lessons for youth engagement

- the Collective Impact Project in Montreal involving ten philanthropic organizations and three municipal and community partners

- the evolving expressions of community leadership by place-based foundations

- the challenge to funders to embrace learning itself as the return on their investment

- a profile of a unique private foundation collaborative that extends beyond projects to embrace a shared working space – and more

Part three
Chapter nine

The cost of social inequalities: Philanthropic field-building in Québec through the creation of the *Collectif des fondations*

Annabelle Berthiaume and Sylvain A. Lefèvre

Only a handful of foundations in Canada have been pursuing advocacy activities and public campaigns geared towards public policy reform over a sustained period of time. More recently, however, foundations are increasingly adopting this approach as a way to increase their leverage and advance their missions (Coffman, 2008; Elson & Hall, 2017). Foundations are therefore increasingly shedding their role of staying on the sidelines and leaving it up to the state and community organizations to take the lead in debating and addressing social issues. This can be seen in Quebec, where, in the spring of 2015, social movements had been mobilizing for months to fight against the austerity policies introduced by the provincial government. Foundations then decided to join the voices of those denouncing the unequal impacts of those stringent budgetary measures.

The publishing of an open letter signed by nine Quebec foundations marked the beginning of a new form of collaboration between these organizations. The letter reiterated calls from international economic organizations urging vigilance about budget stringency measures and inviting the Liberal government to weigh the effects of its public policies on inequalities within Quebec society. Even today, this collective appeal remains an exception to the rule: foundations rarely address the government publicly, much less as a group. The fact that social inequalities were being addressed was also surprising insofar as, historically speaking, philanthropy has tended to focus on poverty issues.

This chapter will analyze the creation of this collective of Quebec foundations in response to social inequalities in the spring of 2015 by revisiting the conditions that gave rise to such an unlikely mobilization. To do this, a series of participant observations and semi-structured interviews were conducted with member foundations of the *Collectif des fondations* – hereafter called the Collectif – and consultants who worked with the Collectif at different stages, and public documents (e.g. websites, newspaper articles, etc.) were analyzed.

We begin with a presentation of the political context and internal questionings that characterized the foundation sector in the months leading up to the issuing of their public statement. This is followed with an examination of some of the issues and challenges involved in the continuation of the foundations' initiatives. We then conclude with an assessment of the real and potential impacts of the creation of this collective.

At first glance, this collective action of foundations seems to be oriented outwards, that is, it appears to be addressing the provincial government. However, we show that this action has above all benefited the philanthropic sector itself (in this case, the philanthropic sector in Quebec). The action also helped to redefine the relationship established with the grantees, which has thus far been characterized by a certain mutual mistrust. In this sense, the intention of this collective and collaborative action to put itself on the map, in the sense of even being publicly discussed (Neveu, 1999), appears to have been able to build bridges within and outside the philanthropic sector.

Context: Increase of inequalities and restructuring in the foundation sector

Quebec's social services sector and the provincial philanthropic landscape have undergone substantive changes over the past 20 years. This transformation had been triggered by the emergence of new philanthropic actors and practices. More generally, it can also be attributed to the reconstitution of the role of the Quebec state in addressing social issues (Lefèvre & Berthiaume, 2017). Indeed, foundations' growing questions about their own role was one of the key factors behind the emergence of the Collectif. Most of these foundations have traditionally sought to fund emerging initiatives, with the idea, or hope, that the state would subsequently institutionalize the initiatives that prove effective and legitimate (e.g. seed money). But what is the role of foundations, the foundations asked themselves, in a context where public funding no longer provides, or even promises to provide, such support? This question provoked nothing short of an identity crisis in some foundations.

Following multiple provincial government austerity budgets involving major cuts to health, social services and education, the Collectif issued its first public statement in 2015. The nine participating foundations were concerned about the organizations they were supporting – which were being financially suffocated by the cuts – and had become acutely aware of their own financial limitations in the face of ever-increasing needs. In the desolate context of austerity, where public services and funding were being cut, foundations thus felt they were shouldering an ever-mounting burden of responsibility. Many community-based organizations had been relying on state subsidies not merely as a supplement to allow for, say, renewal and innovation, but to secure the main funding of their mission and the very survival of their organization.

In this context, foundations, given their financial autonomy and their experience of working with community organizations, had both the expertise and credibility required for engaging meaningfully in public debate. In the words of one interviewee:

> As foundations, we work very closely with organizations in each of our activity sectors, and we see first-hand what's happening on the ground. We can also see how the government might want to outsource to organizations rather than assume its state responsibilities ... At the end of the day, our role is really to keep a watch, and to provide support, because we can speak out freely ... We aren't government funded.[1]

In the interviews for this study, foundations closer to community or rural settings mentioned their empathy with discouraged grantees: "The whole idea [of the Collectif] was sort of to put a foot down, to say 'This is ridiculous; what can we do?'" The austerity measures that prompted the foundations' mobilization could thus be seen as the straw that broke the camel's back. What emerged was a much broader and more acute question about the role of foundations in Quebec.

Several foundations, especially smaller and medium-sized ones, told us that, without government investment, their efforts to combat inequalities would add insult to injury. One interviewee went so far as to say he found himself trapped in an unwanted role: "Organizations are so fragile that funding cuts are like the sword of Damocles hanging over their head; and filling that gap is not the role foundations want to play." He felt as if he had the power of life or death over organizations that are increasingly in need of funding. Moreover, in the absence of the state funding required to institutionalize innovative initiatives within the grantee organizations, some foundations have come to question the niche they had carved out for themselves. In other words, why fund innovation and creation if there is no prospect of it ever becoming institutionalized?

As foundations saw that social inequalities continued increasing despite their efforts, they decided to take a stance in support of the organizations they funded by reminding the state of some of its social responsibilities:

---

[1] Except where otherwise noted, the quotations in this chapter are excerpts from interviews conducted in the context of our research. As verbatim transcriptions which convey the tone and expressions of our respondents, they also contain typical errors of spoken language. All translations of interviewee statements are ours.

→ I don't want to criticize the government, but I do want to speak up, and I think things were expressed pretty clearly in the letter. The fact is that Quebec is one of the most egalitarian societies in America, and that's a good thing ... It gives us a certain quality of life, and it allows a certain percentage of Quebec's population to have a better life. It results in us having what's probably one of the lowest crime rates in America, among all sorts of other things ...

Interview respondent

Further afield, talk about the "cost of inequalities" around the world and within philanthropic networks had intensified in recent years. For example, a 2014 report by the Organization for Economic Co-operation and Development (OECD) showed that the rise in inequality was connected to recent transformations in taxation (income tax in particular) and a systemic decline in the re-distributive role of the state (OECD, 2014). Discussions around the book *The Price of Inequality: How Today's Divided Society Endangers Our Future*, by Nobel-winning economist Joseph Stiglitz (2013), also contributed to mainstreaming the acknowledgment of the growing inequalities and their repercussions on social bonds and wellbeing. Indeed, the issue of social inequalities has rallied many credible international policy actors to its cause and extended into the foundation world.

At the same time, the foundations agreed that their stance should not be a challenge to the state or the government but rather a statement of concern about budget stringency measures and their impact on social inequalities. The chosen tone was more a benevolent warning than criticism, to ensure the foundations' discourse was favourably received by the public: "As long as we're staying neutral and apolitical rather than pressuring, it's alright." The foundations' desire to take a public position was accompanied by the hope, or expectation, that the vast majority of stakeholders would agree with them. Indeed, the negative impacts of budget cuts had increasingly been exposed and denounced in journalistic circles, communities and certain business sectors across Quebec. In that sense, the public debate on inequalities promised to be a debate with few if any opponents, thereby incurring little risk for the foundations.

Some interviewed foundations also saw the position-taking on public policy as an opportunity to improve their visibility and make themselves more widely known. In that context, some even revamped their brand image from the bottom up, so as to reflect, beyond a mere change in their logo and website, their new philanthropic role. At the municipal level, this was the case with Centraide of Greater Montreal when it launched its Collective Impact Project in some neighbourhoods of the city, to which several of the Collectif foundations ended up contributing financially (see Chapter 12 by Nancy Pole and Myriam Bérubé on this subject). Likewise, at the municipal level in Montreal, the first Policy on Children in 2015 solicited the participation of community and philanthropic organizations in providing services.

This new approach was especially appealing to foundations, including the Lucie and André Chagnon Foundation (hereafter, the Chagnon Foundation), who sought ways to mend fraught relationships with community groups who had been levelling harsh criticism against them. For example, with the announcement of the Chagnon Foundation that its three public-philanthropic partnerships with the Quebec government – Québec en forme (2007–17), Avenir d'enfants (2009–19) and Réunir Réussir (2009–15) – would not be renewed, the foundation marked a transition to a new stage.[2]

Some foundations also expressed the desire for a networking space and platform for interacting with the government, to facilitate their engagement in the public debate. At the time of the Collectif's formation, only a few of the Quebec foundations were consistently taking part in Canadian meetings of foundations. Nevertheless, the formation of a new group of foundations was not viewed as competition with any existing networks so much as a way to establish a complementary coalition. In building the Collectif, a number of participating foundations drew on a previous, time-limited collaborative experience with one another.

By taking a position, and above all one that aligns with the latest trend observed in OECD countries, the Collectif seized the important opportunity to demonstrate its loyalty to the funded community groups, either by reaffirming solidarity or by building a relationship of trust – all with next to no risk of making enemies. Indeed, the goal of (re)creating a bond of trust with its members' funded groups was perceived as a more feasible and attainable outcome than that of actually raising concern among politicians. It was only a little later, on the occasion of the Collectif's public meetings and events, that the representatives of the participating foundations grew to appreciate the new dialogue between the foundations which they had contributed to establishing.

---

[2] At the time these partnerships were being established, during the previous decade, the foundation was heavily criticized by unions, community groups and academics for playing an active role in the privatization of public services. The announcement of the end of these partnerships was then an opportunity for the foundation to communicate a change of attitude and an organizational repositioning toward their funded organizations (Lefèvre & Berthiaume, 2017).

Chronology of the Collectif's creation

In the fall of 2014, the Béati Foundation, rooted in Christian and progressive values, contacted other foundations about taking part in collective action on the issue of social inequalities.[3] Although aware that their political vision is not widely shared across the heterogeneous philanthropic field, Béati viewed the mobilization of other foundations around social justice issues as a prerequisite for success. Having a strong reputation within the community sector (at times stronger even than that of foundations with much bigger endowments), Béati's social capital was a strong asset in its capacity to mobilize other foundations around the creation of the Collectif.

To start, the director of the Béati Foundation approached the Chagnon Foundation – one of Canada's largest, in terms of capital – which agreed to team up and to play a leadership role in the Collectif initiative. The interviewees all mentioned the competence of this alliance in successfully rallying large foundations around the same table, without intimidating the smaller ones.

Béati's proximity to funded communities gave it legitimacy to talk about the realities reported by actors on the ground. The Chagnon Foundation, for its part, gave the Collectif credibility, both early on, in the eyes of the other foundation managers, and later on, when launched, in the eyes of the media. Moreover, it enjoyed significant resources, including: existing relationships with consultants; access to organizational know-how; a position at the crossroads of the political, community and economic sectors combined with an ambition to connect with the general public; and expertise on the issue of inequalities, thanks to a recent awareness campaign on this topic.

Having chosen to address the issue of social inequalities, these initiating foundations used their contacts to reach out to other foundations that they thought might be interested in addressing this topic with the government. In spite of a few refusals, several foundations agreed to join discussions on what form the group should take. From the beginning, the organizing model proposed seemed to mesh with the usual working methods in the philanthropic sector (email exchanges, rather brief meetings, etc.). Four meetings were held between the handful of interested foundations, in the course of which the initial decision was made to write the first collective letter setting forth the foundations' official position. During these meetings, with the support of a consultant and a public relations firm, a draft was reworked and the letter's release and course of action were addressed. All aspects were discussed: the tone of the letter, finding common ground

---

3   With an endowment of approximately CAD$12 million, the Béati Foundation ranks among the medium-sized foundations. While there is no direct link between the Béati Foundation and the US-American social change philanthropy that emerged in the 1970s, the Foundation does exhibit characteristics that align with this approach. For example, Béati continues to pursue an in-depth reflection on philanthropy's internal contradictions, and particularly on the intrinsically asymmetrical power structure in the grantor–grantee relationship. Beyond a declaration of principle, this positioning is embodied in a number of practices, from the direct contact between support agents and organizations to the inclusion within the grantee selection committee of representatives belonging to the communities they wish to support.

with one other, and consequently finding the right positioning while avoiding overly accusatory or divisive formulations.

Following the fourth meeting, the foundations sent their letter directly to the Quebec premier, the president of the Treasury Board, the Minister of Finance and the Minister of Labour. A few days later, given that the foundations had not received a reply or an acknowledgement of receipt, they decided to go forward with releasing the letter to the public. The open letter, entitled "Les risques de la rigueur budgétaire" (The risks of budget stringency),[4] was published on March 11, 2015 in the Quebec newspaper *Le Devoir* (the letter is given on pp. 198–9). Widely circulated in the media, the letter essentially reiterated international economic organizations' entreaties to be vigilant about budget stringency measures, and encouraged the Quebec government to weigh the effects of its public policies not only on the most vulnerable populations but also on Quebec society at large.

"The risks of budget austerity"

We are concerned about rising social inequalities, an issue that is leading our most respected economic organizations to issue calls for vigilance.

For the first time, Quebec foundations are coming together to voice their concerns and express the unease felt by the individuals, families, and communities they support. At a time when many government programs are being re-evaluated and the tax system is subject to an in-depth review, we question the potential impacts these changes could have on society.

We are particularly concerned about their impact on social inequality, a growing phenomenon worldwide, which has led to calls for vigilance by the most credible economic organizations and, increasingly, by recognized political leaders.

A criterion for judging the reforms

We would like to constructively participate in the debate by inviting the Quebec government to consider our concerns and to fully measure the impact of its reform plans on citizens and communities.

It is, of course, necessary to manage public finances responsibly. It is equally important to ensure that public services are effective and that they achieve their goals, which is why they must be reviewed periodically.

---

4 All translations of the Collectif's statements are ours.

We urge the government to guide its policy choices by the effects they have on social inequality, while responsibly managing public funds. We propose that the government adopt as one of the criteria for judging the merits of a particular reform that it reduces inequality or, at least, that it does not further increase it. A more egalitarian society: a benefit to everyone.

Quebec is the most egalitarian society in North America. This enviable situation is a result of our collective choices and is a significant economic and social asset. Inequality harms the economy, society and democracy, as experts from around the world have proven, and as we have seen through our day-to-day grassroots work throughout Quebec.

When inequality increases, there is a growing divide between citizens. Like the links in a chain that stretch and break, the links between members of a society also break, and the entire community suffers. Social issues worsen and pressure on public and community services increases, causing costs to rise. Everyone loses.

In the most inegalitarian countries, crime is higher and life expectancy is lower than elsewhere. Conversely, the most egalitarian countries are among the most economically prosperous and powerful countries in the world.

Over the years, Quebec has developed the means to reduce inequality through taxation, education, health care and adequate social services. Investing in everyone's potential allows everyone to contribute to the best of their abilities. When each individual can put their shoulder to the wheel, the economy and society are better for it.

Remaining vigilant

Today it is no doubt time to see if the means we have chosen are still the most effective. But one thing that Quebecers will not call into question is the goal of being a society that gives everyone a chance. We believe that it is worth remembering this strong Quebec consensus illustrated by, among other things, the unanimous adoption by the National Assembly, in 2002, of the *Act to Combat Poverty and Social Exclusion*.

> Despite such efforts, the level of inequality is greater in Quebec today than it was 30 years ago. We must therefore remain vigilant. The reforms will be more effective if they contribute to reducing inequality. This, we believe, is a winning proposition for all.
>
> Joint statement
> The signatories are directors of private foundations[5, 6]

Following the letter's publication, the group of foundations, encouraged by the chord that its public position-taking had struck, decided to organize a half-day of reflection on April 22, 2015. Entitled "Les inégalités au Québec: restons vigilants" (Inequalities in Quebec: we must remain vigilant), this event gathered several experts to address the thorny issue of measuring social inequalities as a result of government reforms. In addition to the open letter's signatory foundations, approximately 120 people from different backgrounds (unionists, public health administrators, international development representatives, academics and other philanthropic representatives) attended the event, after which several new foundations expressed their interest in joining the signatory foundations in pursuing their common reflection.

Spurred on by this enthusiasm, the Collectif continued its concerted work and submitted, in January 2016, a brief to a "Public consultation. Solidarity and social inclusion. Towards a third plan for government action". At this stage, the brief was signed by 20 public and private foundations. Explicitly referring to the first open letter dating back to March 2015, the foundations reiterated their call for vigilance:

Excerpt from "Reducing poverty and social inequalities, an issue that concerns us"

> Our brief is a follow-up to the letter that a number of the signatory foundations of this brief addressed to the Government of Quebec in March 2015. [...]
>
> The core of our message is the need to focus on improving living conditions and the prevention of poverty by drawing on methods with a proven track record as well as by properly assessing the impact of administrative choices and public policies on social inequalities and ensuring consistency across governmental actions.

One year later, on January 26, 2017, the Collectif joined forces with the *Centre de recherche Léa-Roback sur les inégalités sociales de santé de Montréal* to organize a second public event entitled

---

5   See Appendix to this chapter (pp. 213–14) for a complete list of the signatory foundations involved in the Collectif's mobilization.

6   Originally published in *Le Devoir* on March 11, 2015 as "Les risques de la rigueur budgétaire." https://www.ledevoir.com/opinion/idees/434025/de-grandes-fondations-privees-inquietes-les-risques-de-la-rigueur-budgetaire

"Un ensemble de politiques visant à réduire les inégalités" (A set of policies aimed at reducing inequality). This one-day event attracted roughly the same number of participants as the first. An even greater focus was put on the need to adopt concrete tools to measure and reduce social inequalities in Quebec, including presentations on the key indicators for comparing inequalities between OECD countries and proposals for more progressive education and fiscal policies.

After almost two years, the members of the Collectif also decided to formalize their organization to secure the continuation of their initiative where previous initiatives had faltered. The Collectif members pooled financial resources, set up a website and hired a part-time liaison officer to coordinate the network and alleviate the burden of the two initiating foundations, which had invested considerable resources and internal expertise to handle coordination and media relations. Moreover, in 2017, the Collectif decided to solicit the services of two coaches in impact and strategic clarity to develop an action plan – their theory of change.

It was during the fall of 2017, with this theory of change in hand, that the liaison officer took over coordination and supported the Collectif in releasing a second public letter. The letter (see below) was published in the newspaper *Le Devoir*[7] on November 15, 2017 – Philanthropy Day – prior to the release of the action plan and the provincial government's economic update. It was also sent to the Premier, the Minister of Labour and Social Solidarity, and the province's Official Opposition team. This time, the list of Collectif signatories grew with the addition of two more foundations. The letter, slightly milder in tone than the first, urged the government and opposition parties to adopt a broader vision for combating poverty, one that involved mobilizing and supporting a vast array of stakeholders for this cause. The letter also reiterated the importance of the *Act to Combat Poverty and Social Exclusion* adopted in December 2002 in preparation for the release of the third government action plan to combat poverty and social exclusion.

"Engaging a community of stakeholders in the fight against poverty"

As philanthropic foundations that support hundreds of organizations working to assist families, youths, the elderly and communities, every day we see first hand the impact of concerted action by a multitude of stakeholders committed to diminishing social inequalities. When an entire community comes together to take charge of the situation in its own environment, when a host of small and large actions are combined – that is when we see the best results.

---

7 Collectif des fondations (2017, November 15) 'Engager une communauté d'acteurs dans la lutte contre la pauvreté', *Le Devoir*. Retrieved from: https://www.ledevoir.com/opinion/idees/512968/journee-nationale-de-la-philanthropie-engager-une-communaute-d-acteurs-dans-la-lutte-contre-la-pauvrete

Our position also leaves us well placed to appreciate the vital role of the government in creating the conditions for this generalized commitment to solidarity and inclusion. Unlike each of the organizations we represent, the government has levers at its disposal to act on a myriad of economic and social factors that contribute to diminishing or increasing social inequalities, and which cascade through its decisions and public policies.

On this subject, the government adopted governmental action plans to combat poverty and exclusion in 2004 and then 2010 with ambitious orientations and involving an array of societal actors with the ability to act on several determinants of poverty.

Unfortunately, in spite of the adoption of the *Act to Combat Poverty* and two subsequent action plans, Quebec has not achieved its goal of joining the ranks of the nations with the lowest numbers of poor, as evidenced by the report of the Ministère du Travail, de l'Emploi et de la Solidarité sociale entitled "Résultats des actions menées dans le cadre de la stratégie nationale de lutte contre la pauvreté et l'exclusion sociale, 2002–13" (Results of the actions carried out within the framework of the national strategy to combat poverty and social exclusion, 2002–13).

Going further

In this context, the third governmental action plan anticipated for this fall should go further. As the Minister of Employment, François Blais, recommended this past March, the plan should set clear targets for poverty reduction and establish the means to achieve them, along with the investments required. It should also provide for additional assistance to the organizations that help people facing poverty and exclusion, who lack social networks.

Moreover, this new plan arrives in a very different context. The economy is on the upswing, public finances are in balance, and unemployment is at a record low. However, despite its tremendous importance, employment is not the only criterion for progress.

The favorable economic context lends itself to the government's establishment of even more ambitious targets to combat poverty, and a continued focus on a range of diversified actions beyond supporting employment. As the strategy to combat poverty and social exclusion points out, it would be important for the action plan to include measures to combat prejudices against people living in poverty, and measures to improve access to public services.

Finally, we urge the government to stay true to this third action plan and adopt mechanisms to ensure consistency across its actions and to measure the impacts of its policies on inequalities.

This third governmental action plan to combat poverty and social exclusion is an opportunity for the government to embark anew on efforts to mobilize all ministries, governmental agencies, socio-economic stakeholders and citizens around this shared goal.

We hope the government will send a powerful message that it intends to use all the levers at its disposal. One of the most powerful is taxation, which remains one of the most effective tools for diminishing inequality. It would be interesting to seize this opportunity to advance reflection and social dialogue on the best options available in this respect.

We, the directors of nine foundations, commit to collaborating on this strategy by contributing our expertise, our passion and our ability to mobilize stakeholders from a diversity of backgrounds.

Starting from the first public statement, the Collectif's actions can be understood in two contexts. First, the foundations clearly wished to have a space where they could come together to pave the way for a collaborative partnership. Member foundations' desire for a coalition that could take collective action on social inequality was supported by their pooling of resources, hiring of a liaison officer and creation of a website. But this consolidation was not intended solely to support their ability to take public positions and to enter into dialogue with government; the Collectif also wanted to stimulate broader public reflection on social inequality by initiating public events and, most importantly, internal debates on the topic.

In the two-and-a-half years following the first open letter, the Collectif did attempt to engage with government officials with a view to establishing an ongoing dialogue about what the government could be doing to combat poverty and reduce social inequalities, and to offer to collaborate towards these ends. They did this from their position as philanthropic foundations, presenting themselves as having a privileged vantage point and a neutral capacity to represent civil society perspectives. While a couple of meetings with representatives of the Ministry of Labour, Employment and Social Solidarity did take place, Collectif members quickly came to understand that their government interlocutors suffered from some misconceptions about the foundation sector, and that the basis for greater mutual understanding would first need to be established before engaging in further dialogue about potential collaborations.

Finally, since 2018, the Collectif's foundations have been in a dialogue with one another on the issue of tax privileges (related to Canada Revenue Agency's regulatory framework for charities) and their own "inequality footprint" as foundations. To this end, they reflected on how the the tax privileges they benefit from may reinforce certain socio-economic inequalities. As an increasing number of calls are made to review and modernize federal charity regulation[8], the Collectif's own reflections are timely, as some of these tax privileges may well come under renewed scrutiny. Yet this reflection is designed first and foremost to feed their own internal practices. As part of this process, several member foundations engaged their boards and management teams in a dialogue on this subject. This ability to engage in a collective discussion around tax issues, a sensitive subject within the philanthropic sector, is a measure of the progress made in building trust between members of the Collectif.

Evaluating the results

Given the absence of a positive government response to the Collectif's appeal to adopt a tool to measure the impacts of its policies on social inequalities, one might at first glance judge the Collectif project a failure. During our first interviews in the summer of 2015, the government issued no response to the Collectif, aside from acknowledging receipt of their statements. For some stakeholders, the absence of a swift response on the part of the provincial government constituted the project's main failure.

Nevertheless, it is worth noting that most member foundations never expected at the outset that they would encounter much success in getting the government to change its practices in matters of social inequalities. Based on the interview statements of the project's initiators, the main goal was simply to "introduce doubt". Moreover, over time the range of potential government interlocutors expanded to include people at the federal as well as the provincial level.

The evaluation of the mobilization thus becomes more nuanced when considering the impact of its favorable coverage in the media and its reception by not only community organizations but also players who are generally critical of foundations. The Collectif's arguments in some ways run counter to the usual criticism of foundations as agents of social policy privatization. Above all, the Collectif's greatest effect has been to spark a new dialogue among the foundations of Quebec. Since its creation, other foundations have shown an interest in the Collectif's reflections on the role of foundations in public debate, their relationship with the state and taxation, and on social inequalities.

In the end, Quebec's Ministère du Travail, de l'Emploi et de la Solidarité sociale agreed to meet the Collectif's representatives, but it seems (at the time of going to press) that discussions are still in their infancy and the ministry continues to show little understanding of the Collectif's atypical

---

8   See, for instance, the report issued in 2019 by the Special Senate Committee on the Charitable Sector.

mobilization. In the face of this problem, the Collectif's representatives should clarify their public stance, since they refuse to be recognized as either a lobby, advocacy group or mere funder. If anything, they wish to be recognized as a unique entity, and they propose that government explore possibilities to further collaborate for social equality by leveraging both parties' resources.

Despite the fact that the government calls upon foundations to financially support the community sector and to give its support to government policies, the government does not seem to acknowledge foundations as a legitimate policy actor. The government's lack of openness to cooperate in this manner remains a significant disappointment to the members of the Collectif. In 2019, however, the Collectif was one of the rare actors of the philanthropic sector invited by the Government of Quebec to submit a new joint brief in the framework of the consultation leading up to the new government action plan for supporting community action.

Media coverage of the first letter still represents a success for members of the Collectif. The reaction gave it credibility and confirmed the importance of having taken a public stance. Community groups, in particular, expressed to the foundations how warmly they welcomed this action. Several foundations stated that they had received words of thanks and encouragement, thus marking a break from the sometimes much tenser relationships between foundations and community organizations: "It was very spontaneous and came from groups, group networks or closely involved individuals the very morning after the letter went out. I remember that feedback started coming in as early as a quarter to seven in the morning. Brief messages like, 'Hey thank you!' 'Wow, that's fantastic!'" The public letter contributed to a sense of relief among the funded organizations, given that they are in a position where taking a stance might jeopardize their financial capacity.

Accordingly, foundations reported that the community organizations felt encouraged and endorsed: "They find that the letter added another voice. It's one more voice speaking up for greater social justice"; "Our organizations were telling us that it's supportive of, and substantiates, what we're saying." In turn, these thanks fueled a sense of pride among the Collectif's members and work teams: "We're proud to have taken part in the Collectif"; "It's like, wow! We really supported them in their efforts."

Going forward

Several questions put to our interviewees dealt with the future of this Quebec coalition of foundations and the potential participation of the interviewed foundations. Their responses allowed us to identify three points of tension that shed light on potential issues going forward.

The issue of inequalities ... between foundations

Quebec's philanthropic sector struggles with its own disparities and tensions with regard to:

- affinities with different fields of endeavour (e.g. religion, politics, community action, sports, medicine)
- scale of intervention (e.g. local, provincial, federal, international)
- sub-categories with their own networks (e.g. the Centraide/United Way foundations, community foundations)
- size and scale of economic resources (e.g. size of endowment, amounts raised by fundraising or through partnerships)
- social capital (e.g. pool of contacts, ability to mobilize other stakeholders, quality of relationships with community, political and religious organizations)
- symbolic capital (e.g. age/maturity of the foundation, prestige associated with the founder's name, board members' reputation, recognition conferred by awards, testimonials from grantees)

Considering this heterogeneity, it is not surprising that the composition of the foundations comprising the Collectif are diverse, including significant differences in terms of financial resources, territory (local, provincial, Canadian) and relationships to the state (partnership/distance).

Predictably, the most striking disparity lies in the foundations' financial capacity. Since the Collectif includes two of Canada's ten largest foundations and other much smaller ones, it may face a challenge in terms of managing financial inequalities among its own members. This gap in size often goes hand in hand with different organizational cultures, ranging from a more entrepreneurial culture to what one interviewee described as "activist at heart". Some of the member foundations have few or no salaried permanent positions, which can represent a problem for follow-ups and participation in meetings. The Collectif was also challenged to do justice to the smaller foundations, proving unable to give their words greater weight or to allow for a less costly participation in meetings and events.

To take this disparity into account, the Collectif adopted a lenient and flexible approach to the contributions to expenses. The Collectif's members agreed that each member could contribute according to its own financial means and that no foundation would be excluded due to a lack of financial contribution. However, this threatened to become a source of tension in the longer term if the absence of a contribution by certain medium-sized or larger foundations was noticed or if the words of a given foundation weren't heard and acknowledged in quite the same way during discussions.

Along similar lines, the disparity of resources between the foundations risks significantly influencing their commitment to the coalition's continuation. Small and medium-sized foundations, for example, experience the "cost" of their participation more directly on the rest of their activities, and their members (employees or other) have less time to devote to the project. At a time when some foundations would like to fund a larger number of projects in order to foster more initiatives (or to keep others going), questions arise about the "profitability" of invested resources: Can these foundations afford to invest in the Collectif? What are the potential and measurable impacts of this commitment?

A final important difference between foundations around the table is the decision-making power of their management, which is itself dependent on the philanthropic capital structure of their foundation. Based on our observations, we posit the following hypotheses in this regard:

- First, foundations that rely on fundraising from large private donors or the general public are reluctant to politicize their image through overcommitment
- Second, among the capitalized foundations, differences between managements' power appear to be determined by the degree of presence of the donor

At one end of the spectrum there are foundations in which the donor and her or his family still have the "hands on the wheel". At the other end of the spectrum there are foundations in which managers with no ties to the history of philanthropic capital hold significant power, as is the case especially when a donor relinquishes any place in the foundation's governance. These differences in management power and capital structure can lead to complex exchange dynamics. Thus, discussions on the investment of capital and its sustainability or use have different implications in foundations, depending on whether the donor (or her or his heirs) is absent or present within the governance. These differences between foundations are sometimes revealed when it comes to "talking politics".

The fear of "talking politics"

The second point of tension revealed during our interviews is to do with the Collectif's future mode of operation. Despite a sense of being able to speak freely, some foundations worry about the repercussions of public position-taking and the legal framework governing their organizations. They fear that federal regulatory control will become more stringent, either spontaneously or in the definition of their activities (charity versus political).

In addition to the Collectif, the foundations also have various partners to whom they feel accountable or with whom they seek to secure a bond of trust. Their autonomy is dependent on their various connections within society. Among other things, some foundations, even in the absence of formal partnerships, seek to preserve their privileged ties with the state and therefore prefer to "refrain from criticizing". Others, conversely, are more demanding in voicing expectations of a strong welfare state. As one respondent summarized:

→ You know that foundations enjoy a good relationship with the government … Yet at the same time no one can deny the need to balance our budgets and better manage our collective assets. So … it's a dance [laughs], a sort of tango where you inevitably learn to dance, since the dance is something you make up as you go, as the measures are being implemented.

Finally, the foundations' fear of "talking politics" stems from the fear that public interventions would lose their "special" status if they were to become too frequent. They fear that, by expressing their views more frequently in the media, they might lose their credibility (accorded to them). Hence, they conclude that "strategy" and targeted intermittent interventions might be the wiser option. Already, more recent media releases attracted less attention than the first one.

This concern also ties in with the desire by some foundations to maintain a certain distance from public debates. Indeed, for public foundations that rely more heavily on donors (especially major and wealthy grantors), "talking politics" may well give them a more contentious public image, which then runs the risk of scaring away any donors who are more reluctant to associate with an advocacy movement. Roughly half of the foundations mentioned that they prefer not being associated with the "rhetoric" of an activist movement or lobby.

Observers from the field (Cave, 2016; Northcott, 2016) believe that the election of the Trudeau Liberals in 2015 has sent a positive signal to a considerable group of Canadian charities and nonprofits, following many years of tension with a federal government accused of putting a "chill" on activities (Floyd, 2015). In 2018, the Ontario Superior Court ruled in favor of an organization threatened with the loss of its charitable status, which was contesting the ten-percent limit for political activities. As a result of this ruling, the government established a new framework, abolishing the ten-percent limit for political activities but continuing to prohibit partisan activities (Grant-Poitras & Alalouf-Hall, 2019). Nevertheless, the challenge of the difficult relationship between politics and philanthropy, as highlighted in 2012 by Stephen Harper's Conservative government, is not just a thing of the past. Only recently, Alberta's premier, J Kenney, warned environmental foundations about being critical of the province's extractive activity (Lum, 2019).

The relationship between philanthropy and inequalities

The final point of tension about the Collectif's mobilization concerns the societal position of the foundations themselves. Even if they would like to formulate a solution to inequalities, structurally speaking, they are themselves a product of inequalities of capital. Indeed, the Collectif is not entirely in control over how it is perceived by grantee organizations or the general public. The organizations attached to the philanthropic foundation label or to a specific foundation can sometimes have more weight than the Collectif's voice. This context of heightening social inequalities brings back into the public debate the complex and delicate issue of wealth creation and redistribution and, more generally, the role of philanthropy in combating social inequalities.

Foundations appear to be the bearers of an inherent contradiction in their discourse, given that they are at once a result and a cause of wealth inequality. Capital has accumulated and become ever more concentrated since the 1980s. This capital accumulation has occurred in correlation with a decline in states' redistributive capacity, especially from a taxation standpoint (Piketty, 2014). Structurally, the central problem stems from the fact that foundations' revenues or endowments depend on the health of financial markets, known to be precarious and volatile – an economic health that is disconnected from the health and well-being of our societies.

It is not surprising, then, that several of the individuals we interviewed proved rather cautious about publicly voicing their views on this issue.[9] This even included those from foundations with less capital or those relying more heavily on fundraising, who might be expected to be more vocal about issuing warnings about rising inequalities. But, as our interviews uncovered, some of these representatives feel that their modest infrastructure gives them a limited role, or fear that run-ins with public opinion might cost them a large swath of their potential donor pool.

Despite repeated affirmations on the part of interviewees that their foundations did not wish to replace the state, vagueness continues to prevail around their legitimacy in publicly voicing their views on inequalities. Indeed, foundations spoke to us of the contradictions and questions with which the responsibility of speaking up in public is fraught: Should the role of foundations be, instead, to encourage or empower the groups they fund to voice their own views? Can they reconcile the role of mouthpiece to the government with continuing to act as supporters of the organizations that combat inequalities? And what can they do internally to diminish inequalities?

---

9 This is, in fact, a question that one radio show host put to the Collectif's spokesperson following the March 11, 2015 media release: "People question how foundations exist, why they exist, and how they manage money that should have been distributed to society, in the form of taxes, in the first place. [...] Surely, the best redistribution of wealth is to pay your taxes [...] Which foundations don't!" The host went on to explain how one foundation belonging to the Collectif had been created following the sale of the cable company Vidéotron, and how this was an example of tax avoidance. This criticism has continued to resurface since the beginning of the 20th century and the institutionalization of a tax privilege for foundations.

Clearly, speaking out in public also carries the risk of being answered publicly. Among other things, the matter of tax avoidance through the creation of foundations may well be brought up, which foundations would find it hard to answer. Further, any defined point of view on this issue is unlikely to be shared by all other members of the Collectif. For example, one respondent's view was that taxes were no longer enough to meet social needs anyhow, and that paying one's taxes therefore comes down to "paying off deficits ... But you don't get any leverage." Keeping one's money within a foundation allows for "stretching your dollar further than if it went to the government".

Foundations thus appear to be split into two camps: one that follows a more "offence-focused" discourse of demanding public policies geared toward diminishing inequalities, and the other adopting a less conflictual posture and one that praises existing accomplishments and achievements. This issue is all the more delicate for the foundations that rely on fundraising, especially from major donors, who are not particularly open to the idea of being more heavily taxed. For this reason, it is critical that the Collectif provides a meaningful and safe space for foundations to reflect on their public engagement of social inequalities.

Conclusion: "A good conversation"

At first glance, the Collectif's actions seem to be directed outwards, given that it addresses the provincial government and more broadly the stakeholders involved in combating poverty. However, a number of elements indicate that these actions have been primarily directed inward, with Quebec foundations participating to build a new philanthropic field. Indeed, the Collectif's greatest success lies in the ties forged between foundations, as this strengthened their capacity to influence the agenda of the foundations themselves and to tackle the question of social inequalities.

Moreover, the project created an uncommon opportunity to open the way for internal discussion between colleagues within foundations. The Collectif made it possible to discuss and to reflect on social inequality issues, a topic not often addressed in the everyday work of many foundations' teams. Even in cases where internal conversations became relatively tense, the interview respondents evaluated them positively, underlining the value of this unifying experience for the team.

Another aspect appreciated by the interviewees was the opportunity for foundations to come together, develop a new form of collaboration, and position themselves with respect to other foundations. In the context of our interviews, nearly all the foundations emphasized the quality of the discussions that took place. The recognition of the Collectif as a forum for exchange has been the central element of its sustainability over the past four years – and, even though it has not made many public pronouncements in recent months, the exchanges and internal reflection sessions have continued. Reflecting this organizational transition, the Collectif now presents itself on its website as: "A place to network, learn and share ideas about social inequalities and the role of foundations in the current social context" (Collectif des fondations, 2019).

Nevertheless, it is difficult to predict whether and how the Collectif will be able to maintain this resolve throughout variegated political contexts once the initial enthusiasm has waned. At the very least, there can be no doubt that creating a network of foundations in Quebec has spurred many stakeholders to reflect on their role and their positioning with respect to the state. Such reflection will have, at least in part, been a response to the "identity crisis" that had preoccupied the foundations that were the first to join the Collectif, as well as those who joined later on. Indeed, over and beyond its immediate public message, the founding hallmark of the Collectif lies in the will to deepen the dialogue between foundations, and to voice a common position.

Foundation representatives' satisfaction with the internal cohesion created during the preparation of the first media release and the ensuing events cannot be understood without taking into account the earlier approval and significant positive feedback received from community milieus. The initiative enabled the foundations closest to these milieus to maintain their close ties and allowed others to warm up relations or ameliorate a climate of mistrust, if only temporarily. Over and beyond the power relations inherent in the grantor–grantee relationship, the foundations' public statements brought to light overlapping interests, whether in terms of the need to maintain public funding for social services or the issue of social inequalities. Representatives of community organizations have given foundations the legitimacy to intervene on the issue of social inequalities, an issue on which they have historically claimed their own legitimacy vis-à-vis the Quebec government. And in this sense, it would have been difficult to envisage that the Collectif publicly release a political discourse contradictory to the one of community organizations.

One of the keys to the success of the Collectif initiative is ultimately that it enabled foundation representatives to come to know one another and community organizations to feel listened to. Beyond its unifying dimension, the discussion around social inequalities continues to provide an arena for debating and defining a broad and diverse philanthropic field. Moreover, in the wake of the initiative, the foundations came to realize that they too – and not only the organizations they fund – are vulnerable and prone to work in silos and be consumed in inter-organizational competition. Viewed from this perspective, this collective action served to bring more consistency and coherence to foundations' discourse and ways of doing things.

Three key takeaways

1 Social inequalities concern all foundations, even if this is not their direct field of intervention. This is because assets are core to both their creation and subsequent disbursements across all fields of expertise, such as health, education, culture or environment.

2 The work of the *Collectif des fondations* is an example of a collective interlocutor with influence among participating foundations as well as public authorities and foundations in other provinces.

3 While the initial context that led to the creation of the *Collectif des fondations* has evolved, other issues such as the frontier between politics and philanthropy, and charity modernization and tax reform, still fuel the need for collective discussions.

Appendix A: Stakeholders involved

The following table outlines the stakeholders involved in the Collectif's actions.

Open letter #1 (March 11, 2015)	Béati Foundation Berthiaume-Du-Tremblay Foundation Dufresne and Gauthier Foundation Léa-Roback Foundation Lucie and André Chagnon Foundation McConnell Family Foundation Montreal Women's Y Foundation Solstice Foundation YMCAs of Quebec Foundation
Brief (January 26, 2016)	Béati Foundation Berthiaume-Du-Tremblay Foundation Centraide du Grand Montréal Centraide Duplessis Centraide Estrie Centraide Gatineau-Labelle-Hautes-Laurentides Centraide KRTB-Côte-du-Sud Centraide Lanaudière Centraide Mauricie Centraide Outaouais Centraide Québec Chaudière-Appalaches Centraide Sud-Ouest du Québec Dufresne and Gauthier Foundation Léa-Roback Foundation Léger Foundation Lucie and André Chagnon Foundation McConnell Family Foundation Montreal Women's Y Foundation Solstice Foundation YMCAs of Quebec Foundation
Open Letter #2 (November 15, 2017)	Béati Foundation Berthiaume-Du-Tremblay Foundation Dufresne and Gauthier Foundation Léo-Cormier Foundation Léa-Roback Foundation Léger Foundation Lucie and André Chagnon Foundation McConnell Family Foundation Solstice Foundation

Current members (as they appear on the Collectif's website in November 2019)	*Active members:* Béati Foundation Berthiaume-Du-Tremblay Foundation Centraide du Grand Montréal Centraide Québec Chaudière-Appalaches Dufresne and Gauthier Foundation Léa-Roback Foundation Léo-Cormier Foundation Lucie and André Chagnon Foundation McConnell Foundation Mission Inclusion Mirella & Lino Saputo Foundation Montreal Women's Y Foundation Solstice Foundation Trottier Foundation *Peripheral members:* Centraide des régions du Centre Ouest du Québec YMCAs of Quebec Foundation

References

Cave, J (2016, January 4) 'A shifting sector: Emerging trends for Canada's nonprofits in 2016.' Retrieved from: https://thephilanthropist.ca/2016/01/a-shifting-sector-emerging-trends-for-canadas-nonprofits-in-2016/

Coffman, J (2008) *Foundations and Public Policy Grantmaking* (p. 21). California: James Irvine Foundation

Collectif des fondations (2019) 'À propos du Collectif des fondations québécoises.' Retrieved from: https://www.collectifdesfondations.org/about

Elson, PR & S Hall (2017) 'System change agents: A profile of policy-focused grant-making foundation engagement in public policy', *Canadian Journal of Nonprofit and Social Economy Research*, 7(2).pp. 57–78

Floyd, G (2015, July 20) 'A chilly time for charities: Audits, politics and preventing poverty'. Retrieved from: https://thephilanthropist.ca/2015/07/a-chilly-time-for-charities-audits-politics-and-preventing-poverty/

Grant-Poitras, D & D Alalouf-Hall (2019, October 28) 'Les organismes de bienfaisance sont désormais les bienvenues sur la scène politique: Qu'est-ce que cela signifie véritablement et à quoi s'attendre pour l'avenir?' Retrieved from: https://thephilanthropist.ca/2019/10/les-organismes-de-bienfaisance-sont-desormais-les-bienvenues-sur-la-scene-politique-quest-ce-que-cela-signifie-veritablement-et-a-quoi-sattendre-pour-lavenir/

Lefèvre, S & A Berthiaume (2017) 'Les partenariats entre secteur public et fondations philanthropiques au Québec: Genèse, contestation et épilogue d'une réforme de l'action publique,' *Revue française d'administration publique*, 163(3), 491–506.

Lum, Z-A (2019, April 17) 'Environmental Charities Not Fazed By Kenney Vow To Probe Foreign Funding.' Retrieved from: HuffPost Canada website: https://www.huffingtonpost.ca/2019/04/17/jason-kenney-foreign-funding-charities_a_23713600/

Neveu, É (1999) 'Médias, mouvements sociaux, espaces publics', *Réseaux. Communication – Technologie – Société*, 17

Northcott, A (2016, February 1) 'Charities Have a Moral Obligation to Help Develop Public Policy'. Retrieved from: https://thephilanthropist.ca/2016/02/charities-have-a-moral-obligation-to-help-develop-public-policy/

OECD (2014) *Focus on Top Incomes and Taxation in OECD Countries: Was the crisis a game changer?* Retrieved from: http://www.oecd.org/els/soc/OECD2014-FocusOnTopIncomes.pdf

Piketty, T (2014) *Capital in the Twenty-First Century* (A Goldhammer, trans.). Cambridge Massachusetts: Harvard University Press

Stiglitz, JE (2013) *The Price of Inequality: How Today's Divided Society Endangers Our Future* (1st edn.). New York: WW Norton & Company

Part three
Chapter ten

Community foundations at work: Mobilizing and connecting place-based philanthropy

Laurel Carlton and Sara Lyons

Philanthropic organizations are called to the table around a range of complex issues, such as reconciliation and restoration, the future of community journalism, and the Sustainable Development Goals (SDGs), which require action on root causes including poverty, racism and inequality. In recent years, philanthropy has stepped far outside its traditional grantmaking role into new areas like social innovation, social finance, collective impact, public policy work and systems change. Across many sectors, interorganizational collaboration, partnerships, and network-building have been recognized as fundamental to innovation and achieving impact when working in complex areas (e.g. Wei-Skillern & Marciano, 2008; Pearson, 2010; Pole, 2016; Glass and Pole, 2017).

With an eye to deepening the impact of its work, Community Foundations of Canada (CFC) has expanded its partnership practice over the past decade, working with Canada's 191 community foundations and a mix of federal and provincial governments, private sector organizations, and philanthropic partners. These partnerships have spanned a range of areas, including impact investing, community knowledge, food security, and the development of community philanthropy in Canada. As CFC has worked across sectors, two specific initiatives from the last four years stand out for their unique design, scale, and volume of learning and insight about the potential for mobilizing community philanthropy towards a common vision and in partnership with others: the Welcome Fund for Syrian Refugees and the Community Fund for Canada's 150th.

Both of these initiatives have offered important insights about the unique ways that place-based philanthropic organizations can mobilize towards outcomes that extend beyond their immediate geographies, with national or even global impact. In the context of a global movement of community philanthropy that continues to grow rapidly – 68% of the world's 1866 community foundations were created in the past 25 years (Community Foundation Atlas, n.d.) – the lessons learned by CFC point towards future opportunities for community foundations to align their efforts towards impact. Indeed, with increasing attention being paid to the SDGs as well as specific areas including gender (in)equality, demographic shifts, and the opportunities for alternative approaches to capital and finance, there is potential for a rapid scaling-up of partnerships and initiatives towards these shared agendas and global goals.

Following a brief overview of the existing literature that covers collaborations between philanthropic organizations, this chapter will examine the Welcome Fund for Syrian Refugees and the Community Fund for Canada's 150th, as two case studies that demonstrate the potential of mobilizing place-based philanthropy towards national or global impact. We will briefly explore these initiatives as they relate to the conventional understandings of philanthropic collaborations, and will then explore core themes that emerged through the experience with the Welcome Fund for Syrian Refugees and the Community Fund for Canada's 150th related to navigating partnerships, accountability, and power dynamics.

Interorganizational collaboration: The literature

Collaboration between organizations and across sectors has been recognized as a key component of effective efforts towards tackling complex challenges (Lawrence *et al.*, 2002; Woodland & Hutton, 2012; Marek *et al.*, 2014; Fine *et al.*, 2018). In her extensive literature review of funder collaboratives, Pole (2016, p. 2) identifies that "collaboration is often seen as the only way to achieve ambitious change goals, based on the recognition that multiple actors need to work together to solve complex problems". Indeed, "collaboration" between funders has also become a long-discussed topic, with books, conferences, articles, journals and panel discussions dedicated to exploring the opportunities, drivers, wise practices and pitfalls that they present. Some (Pearson, 2010, Pole, 2016, p. 2) note that the proliferation of thinking and support for collaboration has become somewhat of a "buzzword" in sector literature.

A number of authors have focused on collaboration between philanthropic organizations, seeking to identify the drivers and benefits. Primary motivators of funder collaborations include economic necessity, generational shifts among donors as well as their changing expectations, and growing diversity in the sector identifying collaboration as a key to impact (Gibson, 2009, Pearson, 2010). Others have identified the ability for parties to increase their impact, influence, efficiency and organizational learning as driving forces behind collaborative efforts (Prager, 2011, Glass & Pole, 2017). Greater innovation and impact can also be unlocked through interorganizational collaboration and shared learning (Huang & Seldon, 2015).

Others have noted the challenges that face organizations that wish to collaborate, which include an inability to relinquish control, a desire for credit, institutional shifts like staff turnover, and interpersonal tensions (Gibson, 2009). Collaborative efforts can also be more costly than "going it alone", in terms of time, staff effort and organizational resources (Gibson, 2009; Prager, 2011). When organizations enter into deep forms of collaboration, they are required to adapt their own systems, operational procedures, cultures, institutional norms, and even accountability structures – all of which can be significant impediments to successful interorganizational working relationships (Gibson, 2009; Kabel, 2016; Pfitzer & Stamp, 2010).

A number of authors have divided collaborative efforts into various taxonomies (e.g. Glass & Pole, 2017; Huang & Seldon, 2015; Prager, 2011). In their literature review on funder collaboratives, Glass and Pole note that they fall into two major groupings: "'light-touch' collaboration types where participants generally retain their full autonomy over strategies and granting procedures [and] deeper, more integrated forms of collaboration requiring partners to establish joint objectives and ways of working" (2017, pp. 66–7).

Less attention has been paid to either the potential for collaboration between place-based philanthropic organizations like community foundations, or their mobilization towards shared goals – largely on the assumption that their place-based focus meant that these organizations work with others within their own geographies, but not beyond them. Within the literature on place-based foundations and collaboration, attention tends to focus on these foundations' relationships with businesses or organizations located in one place, or with other funders that are interested in specific, local goals, including United Ways and Tides Canada (Glass & Pole, 2018). In her review of the literature, Pole (2016) suggests that "impediments to collaboration can be amplified" for place-based funders because of a sense of local competition for donors and for a perceived sense of local leadership (Paarlberg & Meinhold, 2012; Graddy & Morgan, 2006; Bernholz, *et al.*, 2005). Ostrower (2007, p. 524) also notes that in their commitment to serving a wide range of interests and needs in a specific geographic area, community foundations' abilities to partner meaningfully is undermined by their "definition of effectiveness that leads them to try to be all things to all people".

Those who have considered working relationships between community foundations have focused on efforts to strengthen organizational capacity or the business model itself, whether through alliances, affiliations, or mergers (Elliott, 2009; Graves & Marston, 2011) as well as knowledge-exchange and learning opportunities between community foundations. There are a few examples where community foundations have mobilized their assets by building direct relationships with other community foundations in order to pool funds in response to a common goal, as in the case of Canadian community foundations around the 2013 flooding in Southern Alberta and the 2016 fires in Wood Buffalo (CFC, 2017).

The case studies that follow build on these examples by exploring much larger-scale mobilizations of a network of community foundations around two specific national efforts: the settlement of refugees, in the case of the Welcome Fund for Syrian Refugees, and support given to community-led initiatives connected to inclusion, belonging, and reconciliation in the case of the Community Fund for Canada's 150th. With the rapid growth in community philanthropy and the wide range of complex issues that philanthropic organizations are asked to tackle, these two case studies offer insights into different ways that place-based philanthropic organizations and cross-sector partners can be rallied around a shared vision or outcome for future national or global efforts for impact.

It is important to acknowledge from the outset that the Canadian community foundation network stands out on the global stage for its cohesion as a "movement" and for the fact that CFC is a network organization that is uniquely dedicated to community foundations, rather than being an "omnibus association" that serves all philanthropy (Phillips et al., 2016, p. 70). In both case studies described here, CFC played a central role by promoting a shared vision, managing relationships with partners, designing the initiatives, and coordinating implementation at the national level, while the community foundations themselves led and coordinated these efforts at the community level. Most jurisdictions do not currently have a coordinating body that is positioned to lead in this way, nor such strong partnership-based relationships between individual community foundations and a network organization. CFC is grateful for the opportunity to lead in this way, and recognizes the vital leadership role that community foundations and partners played in each of these efforts, all of which made these initiatives and this subsequent analysis possible.

Case study I: The Welcome Fund for Syrian Refugees

Philanthropy has received ample attention for its slow and intentional pace (e.g. Zinmeister, 2016). That said, philanthropic organizations can also respond rapidly to emergent and developing situations, such as a humanitarian crisis and natural disasters. Such a moment arrived for Canada's community foundation movement at the end of 2015. Following the November 2015 federal election, Canadians broadly united around a campaign promise by the newly elected Liberal government to welcome 25,000 refugees from Syria to Canada. The newly appointed Minister of Immigration, Refugees and Citizenship, John McCallum, issued a call to corporate Canada to contribute to the effort, alongside government and individual Canadians. Shortly thereafter, seed funding from first-mover Manulife was augmented by an historic $5 million donation from CN, as well as generous support from GM,[1] and a number of anonymous contributors – bringing the full pooled fund to $6 million.

CFC took up the role as focal point for these donations at the invitation of government and in response to engagement from corporate sector partners. As a result, CFC created the Welcome

---

[1] Manulife (Manufacturers Life Insurance Company); CN (Canadian National); and GM (General Motors).

Fund for Syrian Refugees to deliver these resources to local organizations that were working directly with arriving families. By working in regular dialogue with the corporate partners and the federal government, CFC used its capacities and networks to scope and understand the challenge, to identify the most urgent and impactful funding opportunities, and to direct appropriate proportions of the pooled fund to the identified organizations and programs. In delivering the Welcome Fund for Syrian Refugees, CFC entered into relationships with large corporate donors, with the government of Canada, community foundations and local agencies.

The Welcome Fund for Syrian Refugees worked in partnership with community foundations in a number of ways. First, many community foundations added to the momentum by raising and/or contributing additional dollars beyond the initial corporate donations, roughly $2 million in total. This money flowed directly from community foundations to local agencies rather than through the pooled Welcome Fund for Syrian Refugees that was held at CFC. Second, local community foundations played a key role in helping CFC disperse the funds in a way that complemented the central settlement effort driven by the federal government. By contributing local knowledge and contextual perspectives on real actors, needs and developments in communities that were receiving significant numbers of refugees, the community foundations were able to identify meaningful opportunities for impact in a very compressed timeline (CFC, 2016).

By engaging community foundations as partners, CFC tapped into existing relationships with settlement agencies, local leaders and emerging coalitions to support new arrivals. At the national level, decisions about which cities and communities would receive funding were driven primarily by the number of refugees arriving in a community and, in a more minor way, by the ease with which settlement processes were unfolding locally. Local decisions about the destination of funds and their use was determined by a series of "coalitions" comprised of local agencies, community foundations (with a few exceptions) and CFC, each operating from a different set of insights, parameters and desires.

In this work, CFC drew on a long history of movement-building. While CFC held the ultimate responsibility and accountability for decisions and outcomes, it was the significant level of trust between community foundations and CFC that made the pan-Canadian/local dialectic work. CFC emphasized and respected the relationships and leadership roles that community foundations had locally. Further, CFC counted on community foundations to define for themselves the role they wanted and could play, roles that ranged from making an introduction to leading local consultation and fundraising tables. Most importantly, CFC and community foundations relied on each other to do the work of understanding local needs and funding opportunities with skill, integrity, urgency and care. The dynamic of trust that characterized these partnerships was not formally documented but was perhaps the most important element of delivering impact and honouring the purpose and reputation of the community foundation movement.

Ultimately, $6 million was given to organizations working in 27 communities in proportion to the number of government-sponsored refugees arriving from Syria. Contributions were made in every province and were used for rent subsidies for families, emergency loan funds, urgent mental health care, start-up kits of household goods, language and employment training, and much more. For example, in Calgary, AB, more than 100 families (600 individuals) in financial distress were screened, and a rent subsidy was provided directly to them based on the gap between their monthly budget and their housing costs. In St John's, NL, an Emergency Housing Fund was established to provide refugees with an interest-free short-term loan (or non-repayable grant in certain circumstances) to assist those who were experiencing difficulties in meeting essential living expenses. In Abbotsford, BC, funds were used to cover moving and start-up living costs (moving trucks, damage deposits, key household and gardening supplies) for 22 families, ultimately reducing stress and improving their quality-of-life.

As the flow of refugees ramped up in early 2016, bottlenecks were caused by a lack of affordable rental housing options, particularly in large cities like Toronto, ON, and Vancouver, BC. The federal government brought forward the idea to use the Welcome Fund for Syrian Refugees to top-up the monthly income of families. With more income, families were able to afford the rental units available in their local market and were able to focus on next steps in their settlement journey, including language training, education, employment, attending to medical needs, etc. Ultimately, about 70% of the Welcome Fund for Syrian Refugees resources were used in this way.

As a case study, one of the most interesting elements of the Welcome Fund for Syrian Refugees is that it was created and entirely operationalized in a very short timeframe: five months. Doing so involved a variety of relationships and multiple sectors, all reacting in real time to real-world developments. These ingredients pushed everyone involved into nimble and iterative frameworks and relationships.

Case study 2: The Community Fund for Canada's 150th

While the Welcome Fund for Syrian Refugees demonstrated responsive action to a rapidly developing and unforeseen need, the Community Fund for Canada's 150th emerged following years of intentional engagement with Canadians from coast to coast to coast, as well as relationship-building with civil society organizations and government developments.

In 2013, CFC partnered with CBC/Radio-Canada and Via Rail on CANADA 150/2017 STARTS NOW, a series of local, regional and national conversations intended to "start a conversation with Canadians in all corners of the country, and to use these conversations as a catalyst for action to connect and engage Canadians in 2017 and the 150th anniversary of Confederation" (CBC *et al.*, n.d.). In 2015, these conversations were extended by the creation of the Alliance 150, a network of individuals and organizations from all sectors that shared a desire to mobilize around Canada 150 (CFC, 2015). Through these dialogues, Canadians expressed a desire for 2017 to be a moment that was more than a celebration. Participants recognized that the sesquicentennial could offer a focusing moment to engage Canadians in dialogue about the past and future of Canada, and to inspire action on pressing issues and community priorities (CFC, 2015; CBC *et al.*, n.d.).

Based on these dialogues, CFC issued an invitation to the government of Canada in early 2015, inviting the federal government's collaboration with community foundations in all parts of Canada to create a locally driven fund that would support issues that mattered most to Canadians. Over the months that followed, CFC worked with the Department of Canadian Heritage to identify the following shared values: an openness to collaboration, a commitment to the inclusion of many voices, and a desire to empower Canadians to shape the local narratives and impact of Canada's 150th.

Ultimately, the government of Canada seeded the Community Fund for Canada's 150th, which was matched by community foundations and made available to Canadians in all parts of Canada. Community foundations issued grants of up to $15,000 to a wide range of local projects that fitted within three pillars: encouraging participation in community activities and events to mark the anniversary, inspiring a deeper understanding about the people and places that shape communities and Canada, and building community with the broadest possible engagement of citizens. The Fund had a specific focus on supporting projects led by youth, Indigenous peoples, groups that reflect Canada's cultural diversity, and official language minorities (francophones outside Quebec and anglophones in Quebec). Its intended outcomes were around inclusion, belonging and reconciliation (CFC, n.d.).

In order to participate, community foundations were required to match the contributions from the government of Canada. As a result, the Fund was a collaborative investment: every grant comprised both federal dollars and funds from the local community. CFC invited the participation of municipal governments in areas without an active community foundation.

As with the Welcome Fund for Syrian Refugees, CFC held ultimate accountability for the funds from the federal government. The Fund was held centrally at CFC, and, to the extent possible, it was designed around a core principle of upholding the priorities and leadership of Canadians at community level. Funding decisions on the contribution from the federal government were made by the boards of directors of individual community foundations, and the staff team at CFC were actively engaged to ensure that funding decisions were in line with the terms of the partnership with the federal government.

Under the principle of local leadership, each foundation had the freedom to set priorities for the fund in their own community. As a result, the Fund took on a unique local flavour across the country. In some communities – particularly in rural areas – the Fund focused on local celebratory events for the 150th, while in many others the community foundation identified priority areas and invited community members to use the occasion of the 150th as a call to action in regard to those priorities. For example, in St John, NB, the community foundation focused the Fund on youth-led initiatives; in Montreal, QC, the Fund prioritized initiatives that addressed education, domestic violence and food security; and in Clayoquot Sound, BC, and Peterborough, ON, an emphasis was put on initiatives that built relationships between Canadians of diverse cultural backgrounds, including Indigenous and non-Indigenous peoples.

Notably, because the Community Fund for Canada's 150th was seeded by public dollars, a high level of operational rigidity was required to create national coherence, reporting and accountability. For example, each community foundation was required to use the same core messaging associated with the Fund, and to follow the timelines set by CFC to operationalize the grantmaking process. Further, each one of the 176 participating community foundations was required to conduct the call for grant applications through one shared application portal, which it had access to for the purpose of reviewing applications, and which was ultimately administered centrally by CFC. As described in the literature, this meant that participating community foundations had to give up some autonomy and control over operations in order to access the opportunity to leverage matched funding and amplify their work through the national Community Fund for Canada's 150th.

In total, the Fund supported 2,124 projects in over 630 communities in every province and territory. A total of $16 million was granted, of which half came from the government of Canada, and the other half came from community foundations, municipalities, and other local partners. As eligible projects were also required to demonstrate that they had other contributions in cash or in kind, these funds were further leveraged – $20 million in cash from municipal and provincial governments, private contributions, businesses and individuals, and $24.4 million worth of in-kind contributions of volunteer hours and other donations.

Projects reported that they engaged more than 20 million Canadians, including over 110,000 volunteers, and that they had left a lasting legacy in many Canadian communities. Many of the supported projects created new relationships between Canadians – for example, the gathering of Atlantic francophone families held in Cap-Egmont, PEI, and the summer camp that used sport to build bridges between Indigenous youth and police in Corner Brook, NL. Other initiatives increased connections between Canadians of different cultural backgrounds, as in the case of a series of multicultural dinners hosted in Montreal, QC, and a two-week hide-tanning camp in Yellowknife, NT. Some projects, such as one that connected isolated seniors in rural Nova Scotia, continued to grow resilience in their communities, while others left physical legacies, such as a playground made more accessible in Nanaimo, BC; outdoor learning spaces in Warman, SK, and Shoal Lake, MB; community gardens in Calgary, AB; and a coastal clean-up near Fredericton, NB.

Uptake of the Community Fund for Canada's 150th was not always smooth. In many communities, Canadians were hesitant to engage in a national conversation at all, and expressed a sense of disconnect or isolation from Canada as a country. In these cases, there was more enthusiasm for

Canada 150 and its goals once CFC was clear that interested applicants could interpret the 150th as a moment for community-level impact, one that was reflective of local leadership, decision-making and priorities. This seemingly reflected that Canadians identified more closely with their local communities than with Canada overall.

Beyond the funded individual projects and the thematic challenges, the Community Fund for Canada's 150th demonstrated the potential for mobilizing community-based leadership around a national narrative or goal. In delivering the Fund, community foundations, municipalities, and other local leaders worked towards a shared vision in an unprecedented way, and this experience has left civil society with new capacity for grappling with complex issues in a manner that is both nationally connected and uniquely local.

Scaling place-based connections

Through both the Welcome Fund for Syrian Refugees and the Community Fund for Canada's 150th, CFC explored new ground in terms of unique ways that community foundations can be mobilized to combine and scale local leadership with a national vision, while working alongside other partners, including government. The two initiatives shared some key common elements: national-level coordination by CFC, local input from the individual community foundations, and the involvement of a range of other partners, including the private sector and the federal government. These case studies also feature some significant differences, most notably that, in the case of the Community Fund for Canada's 150th, the Fund was seeded by the government of Canada and then matched by community foundations, whereas it was the private sector that seeded the Welcome Fund for Syrian Refugees. While the federal government was a major stakeholder in the rollout of the Welcome Fund for Syrian Refugees, no public dollars \were involved.

In terms of other similarities, the two initiatives involved shared motivations and benefits, ones that align with the existing literature on collaboration, including a growth in impact, influence, and learning opportunities (Prager, 2011; Glass & Pole, 2017). Each organization involved in these collaborations had their impact extended in terms of dollars available, geographic areas served and number of Canadians engaged. CFC and participating community foundations also extended their influence as a result of these collaborations, reaching new audiences, new media, and new partnerships. There were extensive learning opportunities from both of these initiatives for CFC and the individual community foundations, which may open the door for mobilization of more place-based foundations in the future.

While these two case studies reflect some of the motivators and benefits behind funder collaboration, they challenge the assumption in the literature that community foundations only engage in collaborations that are place-based. Indeed, the Welcome Fund for Syrian Refugees and the Community Fund for Canada's 150th demonstrate that community foundations can develop powerful mobilizations towards shared inter-regional or national outcomes that go beyond capacity-building, mergers, alliances, and knowledge exchanges. In both cases, community foundations led through their deep roots in their local community and, when aggregated, collectively created a groundswell of local efforts that worked towards national objectives.

As previously mentioned, Glass and Pole group the taxonomies of collaboration into two broad categories: "'light-touch' collaboration [where] participants generally retain their full autonomy over strategies and granting procedures [and] deeper, more integrated forms of collaboration requiring partners to establish joint objectives and ways of working" (2017, pp. 66–7). Both the Welcome Fund for Syrian Refugees and the Community Fund for Canada's 150th were hybrids of these two models. On the one hand, participating community foundations entered into the space of "deeper" collaboration, aligning strategic efforts, funds and operations towards the shared goals of rallying support for the settlement of refugees or the engagement of Canadians in community-building initiatives. This was particularly true in the case of the Community Fund for Canada's 150th, which involved deep operational collaboration that was necessitated by the funding relationship with the government of Canada.

On the other hand, through both the Welcome Fund for Syrian Refugees and the Community Fund for Canada's 150th, CFC was committed to keeping these collaborative efforts as "light touch" as possible by creating space for participating community foundations to maintain autonomy over the broader strategies of their foundation. This interplay between "deeper" and "lighter-touch" collaboration was a balance managed by CFC, one that was made more delicate when also accommodating the needs of partners including private contributors and the government of Canada.

This balance reflected two of the main challenges that the literature identifies with collaboration between funders: the loss of control and operational autonomy (Gibson, 2009; Morris, 2014; Kabel, 2016, Pfitzer & Stamp, 2010). CFC worked to accommodate and create operational flexibility for community foundations whenever possible, and in some cases was required to uphold core design elements that had been agreed upon with corporate or government partners. At times, this was a source of frustration for the individual community foundations that were not accustomed to working with CFC or another external partner in this way.

Beyond the challenges identified in the literature, CFC experienced a range of other dynamics when leading on the Welcome Fund for Syrian Refugees and the Community Fund for Canada's 150th that expand the understanding of the challenges raised by interorganizational collaboration. A few key areas were particularly salient: navigating multi-layer partnerships, broader power dynamics, and questions about accountability. The pages that follow will highlight those dynamics, as well as the core questions and lessons learned by CFC.

Navigating partnerships in rapidly changing contexts

As described in the overview of the two funds, neither the Welcome Fund for Syrian Refugees nor the Community Fund for Canada's 150th were strictly collaborations involving community foundations – both involved the active participation and financial contributions from other partners, including private-sector organizations and the government of Canada. Navigating the many layers of these relationships while also delivering robust initiatives required nuanced and principled decision-making.

In the case of the Welcome Fund for Syrian Refugees, the government of Canada was a main stakeholder and partner in the design of the program, despite the fact that the funds themselves came from the corporate sector. It was CFC's perception that the government hoped that the Welcome Fund for Syrian Refugees would align with their own process and, in particular, would assist with the pressures to move refugee families through shelter/hotel housing and into permanent housing (local rental). CFC and corporate donors shared this vision and generally focused on different priorities only when local community foundations and service organizations reported that other local priorities had been identified that needed resources.

In the case of the Community Fund for Canada's 150th, the moment of Canada 150 arrived in the midst of a political transition. Early conversations about a potential Fund and Canada 150 had begun under the Conservative government led by Stephen Harper, with an initial focus on "encourag[ing] Canadians to learn more about their history, commemorate events, celebrate accomplishments and honour people that helped shape what Canada is today" (Levitz, 2015). The election of Justin Trudeau's Liberal government in October 2015 saw a pivot in the narrative around Canada 150, with a new emphasis on "diversity and inclusion, reconciliation from nation to nation with Indigenous people, the environment and youth" (Wherry, 2016). CFC adapted to this pivot while continuing to uphold the primacy of local leadership and community priorities, which required careful relationship management. Despite these changes, however, both the Conservative and Liberal governments shared an expressed desire to work with community foundations to complement their own larger, concurrent grantmaking efforts, and to ensure that Canadians were directly engaged in Canada 150 at the community level.

As far as both the Welcome Fund for Syrian Refugees and the Community Fund for Canada's 150th are concerned, CFC and community foundations grappled substantially and continuously with the challenge of balancing the needs of government stakeholders; the moral obligation to understanding community-level contexts, insights and priorities; and a commitment to upholding local decision-making. For example, CFC repeatedly wrestled with the ethical elements of collaborating with the federal government on a national narrative that was connected with a contested space – 150 years of confederation – while CFC was, at the same time, working to build authentic relationships with Indigenous peoples and increase its organizational capacity as an ally in reconciliation and restoration. While CFC generally wanted to act collaboratively with government, it was also clear that the local knowledge and leadership of community foundations was fundamental to the Fund's ability to achieve the most impact with limited resources.

Throughout both case studies, CFC grappled with the tension between a desire to be thoughtful and deliberate in design and implementation, and non-negotiable timelines: the Liberal government had publicly set an ambitious "deadline" for achieving the settlement of 25,000 refugees, and the "2017" timeline associated with Canada 150 was understandably immovable. Ultimately, CFC staff created a distinct set of principles for each initiative that would act as a "playbook" in relationship management, decision-making and implementation.

In the case of the Welcome Fund for Syrian Refugees, the following principles guided decision-making when CFC was navigating relationships with community foundations, corporations and government:

- Prioritize the needs of refugees at all times, and align resources with and for refugees arriving in Canadian communities
- Use funding for the highest priorities, recognizing that there's not enough to fulfil all needs
- Stay true to the purpose of the Fund, but be nimble enough to respect and respond to local needs shared by communities
- Look for opportunities to build a legacy of lasting relationships and best practices
- Respond to the urgent nature of the situation, while keeping an eye on sustainability and a focus on the long-term

CFC used a similarly principled approach when navigating the needs of the 176 community foundations for the Community Fund for Canada's 150th:

- Create space and respect for local leadership
- Align the national narrative and vision with local priorities, and broaden that narrative as much as possible to be inclusive of new/alternative perspectives
- Prioritize the inclusion of many perspectives
- Make all operational and funding decisions in collaboration with local partner who can advise on what's best in a specific community

- Look for opportunities to build relationships in distinct geographies (e.g. Northern Canada) to ensure that funds reach the broadest number of Canadians possible

These sets of principles are not directly comparable to one another, as they were used to make different kinds of decisions. In the case of the Welcome Fund for Syrian Refugees, these principles helped guide the Fund's design and spending decisions. By contrast, the principles used to guide the Community Fund for Canada's 150th were specifically about the program design and the broad allocation of funding to various geographies – the funding decisions themselves were made by individual community foundations, and were based on criteria identified through their own local leadership.

These differences aside, this principle-oriented, decision-making approach proved fundamental to managing nuance and complexity in collaborative relationships – especially as both initiatives saw rapid change and emergent developments to which community foundations and CFC had to respond.

Accountability: To whom and for what?

A host of accountability-related dynamics emerged through the experiences of the Welcome Fund for Syrian Refugees and the Community Fund for Canada's 150th, raising questions about philanthropic–government partnerships as well as the nature of philanthropic accountability more generally.

In leading the Welcome Fund for Syrian Refugees, CFC navigated partnerships with government and the corporate sector alongside the goal of leading a philanthropic response to a real-time effort to help families fleeing Syria and arriving in Canada. These efforts played out in January 2016 – the same January that saw the ramp-up of Donald Trump's election campaign in the United States and the release of his first television advertisement that promised to "ban Muslims" and "build a wall" (Holpuch, 2016). By contrast, the government of Canada had recently declared a goal of granting asylum to 25,000 Syrian refugees (Zilio, 2016). CFC was aware of potentially divergent perspectives across the Canadian landscape on the arrival of the wave of refugees from Syria when it undertook the Welcome Fund for Syrian Refugees, and began conversations early with over 25 community foundations across the country as the project was seeded. Ultimately, one community foundation did decline to participate out of concerns about how their local community felt about the arrival of newcomers but, in general, both CFC and its members were excited to express shared values around belonging and diversity.

Issues of fairness and justice are always relevant to funders, and the large scale and public nature of these two funds put these questions in sharper focus. CFC was accountable to partners but also understood the work and the role in a broader context of the Canadian welfare state, the rights of residents and social cohesion. For example, throughout the Welcome Fund for Syrian Refugees, staff at CFC were repeatedly challenged by a core question: What did the need for the Welcome Fund for Syrian Refugees, and in particular its focus on (temporarily) supplementing the monthly budgets of refugee families above the level being provided by government, say about the adequacy of that core support to refugees in the first place? Further, given that the federal monthly Refugee Assistance Program cheques provided to refugee families are pegged to provincial monthly social assistance rates, was CFC now operating at the margins of the fairness and adequacy of Canada's social safety net? How could the CFC grapple with its role in specifically supporting Syrian Refugees, when so many others who also had acute housing needs – other refugees and Canadians alike – were not afforded similar support? What were the risks of providing one group of people with a benefit that others were not receiving? There are no sure answers to these questions, but CFC benefited from raising them continuously. Reflections of this nature are integral to strengthening collaboration.

The Community Fund for Canada's 150th posed very different questions about accountability. On the one hand, the government of Canada's contribution of $8 million in grantmaking dollars was granted to local projects on the basis of decisions made by the boards of directors at community foundations across Canada, ultimately involving over 800 Canadians in making decisions about the best use of federal funds in their own communities. This model presented a unique opportunity for Canadians to be responsible and accountable for decision-making on federal dollars, as the boards of directors of community foundations typically comprise local leaders with roots in the community and deep local knowledge. Their involvement in the decision-making process introduced an element of grassroots, "democratic" decision-making, rather than centralized, ministerial-directed grantmaking from Ottawa. Government officials and community members alike identified this as a unique and important offering, which raises the question: how can community foundations or other local leaders engage in decision-making about community-level funding priorities?

On the other hand, through the Community Fund for Canada's 150th, participating community foundations were required to provide matching dollars to the seed contribution from the federal government. The Fund's emphasis on reconciliation, inclusion and belonging – and the fact that it was seeded by the government of Canada – raised questions for some as they reflected on Canada's colonial history and the persisting inequalities that run along socio-economic, gender and ethnic lines. In response, community foundations and CFC sought to create space for critical dialogue, and to balance the projects that were celebratory in nature with those that involved difficult conversations and tackled deep community priorities. Nonetheless, this challenge does raise core questions: if community foundations serve, and are accountable to, their immediate local community, to what extent should they be involved in forwarding national objectives that originate outside the community? More broadly, as explored by others (Hall & Reed, 1998; Cohen,

2012; McPhee-Knowles & Bowland, 2016), to what extent should philanthropy be involved in advancing government priorities?

Power dynamics

A number of authors have noted that when funders work together to increase their own efficiency and effectiveness, they can amplify existing inequitable power dynamics between funder and grantee (Glass & Pole 2017). Through both the Community Fund for Canada's 150th and the Welcome Fund for Syrian Refugees, CFC reflected regularly on the ways that power dynamics emerged from a number of different angles.

Regarding both the Welcome Fund for Syrian Refugees and the Community Fund for Canada's 150th, government leaders and corporate partners expressed interest in working with community foundations with the intent to move decision-making power into the hands of community members. While this segmented some of the larger power dynamics at play, local leaders who sit on the boards of directors of community foundations tend to already have positions of power in the community. A regular point of discussion among community foundations is the ongoing need to increase the diversity of representation at the board table. With changing demographics in Canadian communities, to what extent do the boards of directors of community foundations reflect their community and truly understand their needs? A partial answer is that, in both case studies, gaps between the community foundations' power and local community members' experiences were narrowed through community/local organizational engagement and public dialogue about local priorities.

In both cases, there was also a question about the way power and available funding can influence local priorities. In what way does introducing new funds in a community alter or distract from ongoing and pressing local needs? In the case of the Community Fund for Canada's 150th, CFC received feedback from individual community foundations that, while the funds were appreciated and dedicated to meaningful local initiatives, the large-scale, national initiative diverted the community foundation from their own strategy and reduced their sense of autonomy. Further, the Community Fund for Canada's 150th stated in its eligibility criteria that projects were required to demonstrate an ability to match the value of the grant requested in cash or in kind. While this helped grow the overall impact and momentum around the Fund, it also privileged applications from groups that had access to other forms of support.

The very occasion of Canada 150 meant that the Community Fund for Canada's 150th was laden with complex power dynamics. The Fund's vision for the sesquicentennial was one of reconciliation, inclusion, and belonging – an outlook that raised questions for some as they reflected on Canada's colonial history and the persisting inequalities that run along socio-economic, gender and ethnic lines. To address this, CFC sought to listen and learn from these perspectives, and to be inclusive of alternative narratives that enriched the local and national conversations about Canadian communities and Canada as a country.

Looking ahead: Moving from responsive action to agenda setting

A final feature shared by both of these case studies is their responsive nature. While CFC and participating community foundations played key roles in shaping the initiatives, both the Welcome Fund for Syrian Refugees and the Community Fund for Canada's 150th arose in response to external forces including world events and public policy decisions – the decision to welcome 25,000 Syrian refugees to Canada, and the occasion of Canada's 150th anniversary of Confederation. As CFC closed these initiatives and looked to the future, a new set of questions emerged: What opportunity is there for place-based foundations to mobilize around persistent and systemic issues at scale? How can philanthropy work together to set the agenda for change through collaborative action?

At the time of writing, in November 2019, CFC is engaged in three pan-Canadian initiatives that developed from the partnerships and learnings that were first laid by the Welcome Fund for Syrian Refugees and the Community Fund for Canada's 150th:

- The RBC Future Launch Community Challenge, a partnership between CFC, the RBC Foundation, and 81 participating community foundations. The Challenge supports youth leadership in small and mid-sized communities – those with fewer than 150,000 inhabitants – through grants to youth-led projects as well as community convenings.
- The Investment Readiness Program, funded by the government of Canada. This initiative created opportunity for community foundations to work with local organizations focused on social enterprise to promote readiness for investment and social finance activities among social purpose organizations, at the local level.
- The Gender Equality Fund, a multi-year collaboration between CFC and the Equality Fund, with support from the government of Canada (Department for Women and Gender Equality). This initiative will work with community foundations in every province and territory to advance gender equality through a mix of grantmaking, gender-lens investing, and learning opportunities.

Each of these initiatives is still underway, and early observations identify core commonalities with the observations from the Welcome Fund for Syrian Refugees and the Community Fund for Canada's 150th. In addition, these newer initiatives have highlighted unique and distinct dynamics.

First, when inviting collaboration in systemic areas, the different collaborating foundations have come to the table with a range of familiarity and capacity. Whether related to the initiatives seeking impact related to youth employment, social finance, or gender equality, there are community foundations that have been long-time leaders and others that are entering these conversations for the first time. The community foundations' range of experience and capacity has provided CFC with an opportunity to invest in resources to ensure that all participating foundations have a shared understanding and set of tools to support their engagement. In many cases, this has presented opportunities for peer-learning between community foundations, and in others it has involved collaboration between community foundations and other local organizations with deep subject-matter expertise.

Growing on the groundwork laid by the initiatives discussed earlier in this chapter, these current opportunities for collaboration recognize that foundations need to shift power and involve different decision-making processes to seek deeper, systems-level change. Increasingly, CFC has required, or at least created opportunities for, collaborating community foundations to include other voices in their decision-making processes – voices that have a depth of lived experience and subject-matter expertise. For example, community foundations that participated in the RBC Future Launch Community Challenge were required to involve at least two community members between the ages of 14 and 29 in the decision-making process. The Investment Readiness Program invites participating community foundations to partner with a host of other local organizations with expertise in social finance. The emergent work around the Gender Equality Fund encourages community foundations to include gender specialists in the decision-making process. These commitments to engaging new voices in the decision-making processes has opened opportunities for greater impact, and has also added complexity to the initiatives and the collaborations involved.

A third and distinct development of these newer initiatives is the move beyond grantmaking and convening (which were the primary levers of the Welcome Fund for Syrian Refugees and the Community Fund for Canada's 150th) to efforts to set the local agenda and shape local dialogue in the areas related to youth employment, social finance and gender equality. Each of these three new initiatives has a focus on some combination of local dialogue, community events, monitoring, and developmental evaluation, which will gather important key learnings not only about the nature of the collaboration, but about the areas of impact themselves. They also involve public engagement and thought-leadership activities, like the creation of local and national Vital Signs reports that will highlight a range of indicators. In doing so, this collaboration between place-based foundations may offer important contributions in shaping public policy and advocating for "upstream" solutions at the local and national level.

Overall, the RBC Future Launch Community Challenge, the Investment Readiness Program, and the Gender Equality Fund each build from the earlier Welcome Fund for Syrian Refugees and Community Fund for Canada's 150th. Even at their early stages, these three current initiatives offer new learnings and highlight distinct opportunities and challenges as they engage action and dialogue around systems level changes. CFC will continue to monitor the further lessons they offer about the potential of collaboration between place-based foundations.

Conclusion

The limited attention that the literature gives to collaborative efforts between community foundations suggests that they rely on their immediate geographic areas as place-based funders. Community foundations have limited reasons to collaborate among themselves, such as the potential for capacity-building, learning and mergers. In recent years, however, CFC has led two distinct national, collaborative initiatives that demonstrate the potential for further collaboration between community foundations, and for the mobilization of a network of community foundations around a national-level vision. And at the time of writing there are three more collaborative initiatives underway!

The Welcome Fund for Syrian Refugees and the Community Fund for Canada's 150th demonstrate ways that place-based philanthropy can mobilize their individual local leadership towards a collective national outcome. These two initiatives were unique to the Canadian context, and yet they offer insights about the power of mobilizing place-based philanthropy that could be activated for future efforts in Canada or in other jurisdictions. These initiatives have demonstrated the potential for movement-wide collaboration, and have opened the door for further agenda-setting and leadership by the community foundation movement in areas including youth leadership, social finance and gender equality.

While these two initiatives achieved outcomes that far surpassed what would have been possible for any community foundation or national organization to achieve in isolation, they also raise a number of challenges. In both cases, community foundations had to grapple with core questions about their own organizational autonomy and decision-making. In addition, CFC gained an important understanding of how to manage political relationships, accountability and power dynamics – all of which offered important insights for future initiatives. They raised other important questions that merit consideration:

- How do partnerships between government and philanthropic organizations affect the accountabilities of each, and their interaction with democracy more broadly?
- How might initiatives like these increase our understanding of the leadership roles that community foundations can play locally?
- What similarities, differences and themes would emerge if these case studies were compared with

collaborations that involve a broader set of funders rather than exclusively community foundations?
- How does collaboration between foundations and other sectors accentuate or diminish issues of power and privilege that are often part of funding programs?
- With respect to collaboration with government, what is the relevance of core beliefs around the role of government and/or the appropriateness or adequacy of government programs and services?
- What other complex issues may benefit from these kinds of national/local mobilizations through community philanthropy?

As we look to the future, these methods of mobilizing community philanthropy around larger visions offer an important opportunity for other national and global visions. What might be possible when local leaders and place-based foundations are invited to identify the challenges in their own communities, and then to look beyond their geographic bounds at ways in which they can increase their impact by connecting with others? The SDGs, for example, take aim at enormous global outcomes like "no poverty", "zero hunger" and "ending poverty," calling for action at both the local, national and global scales. How might community foundations, each working in their own communities, be rallied around the SDGs to ultimately do their part to address these significant and complex challenges?

CFC appreciates that the Canadian network of community philanthropy is more connected and mobilized than in many other philanthropic contexts, and that these kinds of network-wide mobilizations might not be replicable in other countries. Nonetheless, community philanthropy is an area in the philanthropic landscape that continues to grow. When considering the potential for philanthropic organizations to collaborate in the service of the complex national and global issues, and the potential for philanthropic organizations to work together to address these issues as they manifest themselves at a local level, community philanthropy is an important, thoughtful and engaged component of the philanthropic ecosystem.

Three key takeaways

1 Place-based foundations are capable of simultaneously collaborating on national issues and local goals, as long as specific supports are in place.

2 When navigating cross-sectoral collaboration with the private sector and/or governments, a lead organization can play an important role in assuming accountability and responsibility for this partnership while upholding the primacy of local leadership.

3 Deep collaboration calls for the need for explicit principles to navigate multi-layer partnerships, broader power dynamics and accountability.

References

Bernholz, L, Fulton, K & G Kasper (2005) 'On the brink of new promise: The future of US community foundations'. San Francisco: Blueprint Research & Design and The Monitor Group. Retrieved from: http://australiancommunityphilanthropy.org.au/wp-content/uploads/2014/05/On-the-brink-of-new-promise-the-future-of-US-CFs.pdf

CBC/Radio-Canada, Community Foundations of Canada & VIA-Rail (n.d.) 'Conference Summary: 2017 Starts Now / A Canada 150 Conversation Series'. Retrieved from: http://museumsassn.bc.ca/wp-content/uploads/2016/04/CBC-Canada-150-conference-summary.pdf

CFC (Community Foundations of Canada) (n.d.) 'About the Fund: Community Fund for Canada's 150th'. Community Foundations of Canada. Retrieved from: https://www.communityfoundations.ca/initiatives/community-fund-for-canadas-150th/

CFC (2015) 'Alliance 150'. Community Foundations of Canada. January. https://www.communityfoundations.ca/wp-content/uploads/2019/05/CFC042_ConferenceSummaryReport_EN_Dec20.pdf

CFC (2016) 'Rolling out the Welcome Fund for Syrian Refugees', Community Foundations of Canada. June. Retrieved from: http://communityfoundations.ca/rolling-out-the-welcome-fund-for-syrian-refugees-in-canadian-communities/

CFC (2017) 'When disaster strikes: A guide for community foundations'. Community Foundations of Canada. November. Retrieved from: https://www.communityfoundations.ca/wp-content/uploads/2019/04/When-Disaster-Strikes-Guide-for-Community-Foundations.pdf

Cohen, R (2012) 'Philanthropy funding government work? There's a foundation for that – several, actually', *Nonprofit Quarterly*. Retrieved from: https://nonprofitquarterly.org/2012/04/13/philanthropy-funding-government-work-theres-a-foundation-for-thatseveral-actually/

Community Foundation Atlas (n.d.) 'Snapshot of the movement'. Retrieved from: http://communityfoundationatlas.org/facts/

Elliott, C (2009) 'Being alive to the potential benefits of collaborations and mergers: Can UK community foundations and other community foundations globally achieve greater social benefit for their communities and facilitate community philanthropy more effectively via collaborations and mergers?' Centre on Philanthropy and Civil Society

Fine, M, Lawrence, S & M Schultz Hafid (2018) '(Re)thinking funder networks and collaboratives'. *Stanford Social Innovation Review*, April. Retrieved from: https://ssir.org/articles/entry/rethinking_funder_networks_and_collaboratives

Gibson, C (2009) 'Funder collaboratives: Why and how funders work together'. Grantcraft. Retrieved from: http://www.grantcraft.org/assets/content/resources/funder_collaboratives_secure.pdf

Glass, J & N Pole (2017) 'Collaboration between Canadian grantmaking foundations: The expression of an increasingly ambitious and strategic philanthropic sector?' *Canadian Journal of Nonprofit and Social Economy Research* 8(2). Retrieved from: http://doi.org/10.22230/cjnser.2017v8n2a254

Graddy, EA & DL Morgan (2006) 'Community foundations, organizational strategy, and public policy', *Nonprofit and Voluntary Sector Quarterly*, 35(4): 605–30. Retrieved from: https://doi.org/10.1177/0899764006289769

Graves, R & H Marston (2011) 'Seeking shared success: Business model innovation through mergers, affiliations, and alliances'. *CF Insights*, Council on Foundations. Retrieved from:https://www.cof.org/sites/default/files/documents/files/Seeking_Shared_Success.pdf

Hall, MH & PB Reed (1998) 'Shifting the burden: How much can government download to the non–profit sector?' *Canadian Public Administration* 41.1: 1–20. Retrieved from: https://onlinelibrary.wiley.com/doi/abs/10.1111/j.1754-7121.1998.tb01525.x

Holpuch, A (2016) 'Trump re-ups controversial Muslim ban and Mexico wall in first campaign ad', *Guardian*, January 4. Retrieved from: https://www.theguardian.com/us-news/2016/jan/04/donald-trump-great-again-first-campaign-ad-isis-mexico-wall-muslim-ban

Huang, J & W Seldon (2015) *Lessons in Funder Collaboration: What the Packard Foundation has learned about working with other funders.* Boston: Bridgespan Group. Retrieved from: https://www.packard.org/wp-content/uploads/2014/07/Lessons-in-Funder-Collaboration.pdf

Kabel, CM (2016) 'Five lessons on successful philanthropic collaborations', The Centre for Effective Philanthropy. Retrieved from: http://effectivephilanthropy.org/five-lessons-on-successful-philanthropic-collaborations/

Lawrence, TB, Hardy, C & N Phillips (2002) 'Institutional effects of interorganizational collaboration: The emergence of proto-institutions,' *The Academy of Management Journal* 45(1): 281–90

Levitz, S (2015) 'Canada 150 ad costs rising but no plan in sight', *Canadian Broadcasting Corporation*, January 4. Retrieved from: https://www.cbc.ca/news/politics/canada-150-ad-costs-rising-but-no-plans-in-sight-1.2889551

Marek, L, Brock, D-JP & J Savla (2014) 'Evaluating collaboration for effectiveness: Conceptualization and measurement', *American Journal of Evaluation*, 36(1): 67–85. Retrieved from: https://doi.org/10.1177/1098214014531068

McPhee-Knowles, S & W Boland (2016) 'The policy shop: Innovation, partnerships and capacity-building', *Social Change* 46.1: 124–34. Retrieved from: https://doi.org/10.1177/0049085715619496

Morris, T (2014) *The Future of Freshwater Funding in Canada: Mobilizing collective resources for healthy watersheds.* Toronto: Canadian Environmental Grantmakers Network. Retrieved from: http://www.cegn.org/wp-content/uploads/2014/05/waterfunders-low.pdf

Ostrower, F (2007) 'The relativity of foundation effectiveness: The case of community foundations,' *Nonprofit and Voluntary Sector Quarterly*, 36(3): 3: 521–7. Retrieved from: https://doi.org/10.1177/0899764007303532

Paarlberg, LE & SS Meinhold (2012) 'Using institutional theory to explore local variations in United Way's Community Impact model', *Nonprofit and Voluntary Sector Quarterly*, 41(5): 826–49. Retrieved from: https://doi.org/10.1177/0899764011418123

Pearson, H (2010) 'Funder collaboratives: Trend or tool', *The Philanthropist*, 120–5. Retrieved from: https://thephilanthropist.ca/original-pdfs/Philanthropist-23-2-407.pdf

Pfitzer, M & M Stamp (2010) *Multiplying Impact through Philanthropic Collaboration. A Report for the European Foundation Centre.* Brussels: European Foundation Centre and FSG

Phillips, S, Bird, I, Carlton, L & L Rose (2016) 'Knowledge as leadership, belonging as community: How Canadian community foundations are using vital signs for social change', *The Foundation Review* 8(3). Retrieved from: https://doi.org/10.9707/1944-5660.1314

Pole, N (2016) 'Collaboration among grantmaking foundations: A review of the literature'. Montreal Research Laboratory on Canadian Philanthropy, Working Paper #14. Retrieved from: https://philab.uqam.ca/wp-content/uploads/2018/01/Synthèse-cahier-14-eng.pdf

Prager, J (2011) *Promise or Pitfall? How foundations collaborate and develop partnerships.* York, UK: Joseph Rowntree Charitable Trust. Retrieved from: https://www.issuelab.org/resource/promise-or-pitfall-how-foundations-collaborate-and-develop-partnerships.html

Wei-Skillern, J & S Marciano (2008) 'The Networked Nonprofit', *Stanford Social Innovation Review*, Spring. Retrieved from: https://ssir.org/articles/entry/the_networked_nonprofit#

Wherry, A (2016) 'Justin Trudeau's Canada Day debut and the patriotic debate', *Canadian Broadcasting Corporation*, July 1. Retrieved from: https://www.cbc.ca/news/politics/wherry-trudeau-canada-day-1.3660354

Woodland, RH & MS Hutton (2012) 'Evaluating organizational collaborations: Suggested entry points and strategies', *American Journal of Evaluation* 33(3): 366–83. Retrieved from: http://doi.org/10.1177/1098214012440028

Zilio, M (2016) 'Liberals' revised goal met as 25,000th Syrian refugee arrives in Canada', *The Globe and Mail*, February 26. Retrieved from: https://www.theglobeandmail.com/news/national/liberals-revised-goal-met-as-25000th-syrian-refugee-arrives-in-canada/article28944527/

Zinmeister, K (2016) '12 Common criticisms of philanthropy – And some answers', *Stanford Social Innovation Review*, May 17. Retrieved from: https://ssir.org/articles/entry/12_common_criticisms_of_philanthropyand_some_answers

Part three
Chapter eleven

Vancouver Foundation: Fostering meaningful engagement with youth

Natalie Ord

As a community foundation[1] with a provincial mandate, Vancouver Foundation's purpose is to bring together community assets to address current and emerging community needs across British Columbia. To do this, the Foundation takes a broad view of philanthropy: in recognition that raising funds to tackle an issue is only part of any solution, citizens, organizations and governments are engaged and invited to work together and contribute their time, ideas, expertise and energy to an issue. One of the current priorities of the Foundation is systems change, that is, to support projects, processes and programs that improve a social system and go beyond treating symptoms to address the root causes beneath an issue.

Vancouver Foundation was previously known as a broad-based, responsive funder. Indeed, most of its funding is distributed through donor-advised and designated funds, with the balance going towards the activities of the Grants and Community Initiatives department: responsive grantmaking, grassroots grantmaking, capacity-building for other BC-based community foundations, learning and evaluation, and youth engagement. As a Foundation executive described, "We were granting in eight different fields of interest, province-wide. Grants were having a broad but maybe not a deep effect on any issue. We decided we wanted to have more of an impact on root causes" (Glass, 2018, p. 8). One example of focusing on upstream solutions to create systemic change is the Fostering Change initiative, in which the Foundation was able to build on existing relationships, skills and knowledge both internally and in the community to make an impact on the lives of young people leaving care at nineteen. The rest of this chapter will focus on the evolution of the Fostering Change initiative and the lessons learned through taking on a more vocal, engaged role in policy advocacy.

---

1 Community foundations are described in detail in the previous chapter (Chapter 10).

Youth Homelessness Initiative

Vancouver Foundation's Fostering Change initiative developed out of a previous program, the Youth Homelessness Initiative (YHI). Understanding that "the greatest asset of a community foundation is not the size of its endowment, but its knowledge of community and its ability to use this knowledge for community benefit and positive change", the Foundation used information collected from the 2006 Vital Signs report as the basis for its 2007 strategic planning process (Phillips *et al.*, 2016, p. 67), which identified poverty and homelessness as priority areas. Starting in 2008, the Foundation took a lead role or partnered in three key strategies to address homelessness, each representing human resources and/or financial investment from the organization.

First, the Foundation incubated the Streetohome Foundation, which is focused on leveraging and brokering a comprehensive systems response to homelessness in Vancouver (http://www.streetohome.org). Seed funding was provided by way of a $500,000 grant in 2008, and subsequent grants of decreasing amounts were provided until 2016. Second, a partnership initiative was developed with the Mental Health Commission of Canada for the national, 5-year At Home/Chez Soi study, focusing on a Housing First approach to ending homelessness. The Vancouver Foundation Board approved a grant of $275,000 towards the study and Catharine Hume, a program director who oversaw the organization's own homelessness initiative, was seconded to lead the project in Vancouver for 3.5 days a week (C Hume presentation, 2009). In 2011, Catharine left the Foundation to work on the project full-time. Finally, in December 2007, Vancouver Foundation made the decision to develop the Youth Homelessness Initiative, with an initial focus on the city of Vancouver. In 2009, the focus was expanded to encompass the Metro Vancouver region.

Through a series of internal and external conversations, including with over 100 young people who all were or had been homeless, youth homelessness in Vancouver was identified as an area that needed particular attention. Young people experiencing homelessness are less visible than their adult counterparts and had been traditionally under-served, with limited access to social housing. At the same time, many people who experience chronic homelessness often first experience homelessness as a child or youth. Youth homelessness was thus seen as an area where Vancouver Foundation could have a real and measurable impact over time – both in terms of preventing homelessness and in terms of preventing longer-term or more chronic homelessness among youth (Legare & Rootman, 2011).

The goals of the initiative were: to make a significant contribution to addressing youth homelessness through granting, convening and partnership activities in Metro Vancouver; to support approaches that increased access to housing for young people aged between 16 and 24 experiencing homelessness in Metro Vancouver and to help young people maintain their housing; to support initiatives that involve young people in developing, implementing and evaluating the projects; to encourage projects that build on strategies that are proven to be effective, as well as innovative approaches with a strong change of success that could serve as a model to others; and to foster projects that strengthen the community's capacity to respond to youth homelessness and which emphasize collaboration and formal partnerships with other agencies in the field. A 2011 evaluation of the initiative noted that the Foundation was well on the road to the successful accomplishment of all its goals (*ibid.*).

The Youth Homelessness Initiative may have been the first Foundation-wide priority area to be established at Vancouver Foundation, but it did build upon existing work and on the organization's strengths. Before entering into this work, strong partnerships already existed with youth-serving organizations in BC through the work of the Children, Youth and Families granting program. A significant number of grants had already been given to areas related to poverty and homelessness over the years, and continued to be given through other granting programs such as Health and Social Development. YHI's granting process built upon existing grantmaking practices such as having a volunteer advisory committee, made up of local experts, that made grant recommendations. The Foundation already had experience of directly engaging young people in grantmaking through its Youth Philanthropy Council and so YHI's advisory committee also included two young people with experience of homelessness.

Where YHI's grantmaking differed from other granting programs was in providing additional funds above and beyond the grant request to be used towards program evaluation, a practice which was seen as having potential to strengthen the sector (*ibid.*, p. 15). The initiative also gave development staff a new way to attract and engage donors through a Homelessness Fund, which was established in 2009. Finally, YHI provided Vancouver Foundation with an opportunity to strengthen its community leadership profile and build on its unique strengths in convening a diverse set of stakeholders around an issue. Interviewees in the 2011 YHI evaluation strongly encouraged the Foundation to take a stronger and more proactive role in influencing public policy, noting its strengths in "giving a voice to youth and bringing their stories forward for governments, funders, policy makers and the public to understand the issues and the solutions" (*ibid.*, p. 23).

Despite the Foundation's "exceptional ability to convene, communicate and to lead, which can be used for influence, public education, advocacy", the 2011 evaluation also noted the awareness that this "represented a steep learning curve for the volunteer board" as well as some "uncertainty whether taking on the role of policy advocate would weaken the Foundation's overall credibility with donors and strategic partners" (*ibid.*, p. 19). These concerns aren't restricted to Vancouver Foundation; many community foundations resist participating directly in advocacy, preferring instead to play an indirect role through funding, knowledge creation and convening (Phillips *et al.*, 2016, p. 76). And, until recently, limitations on non-partisan public policy activity imposed by the *Income Tax Act* created an overall chill on charitable advocacy. That said, based on the recommendations of the evaluation and despite those concerns, in October 2011 Vancouver

Foundation's board renewed their commitment to youth homelessness and prioritized the development and implementation of a three-year strategy (2012–15) to reduce youth homelessness in Metro Vancouver.

The second phase of the initiative began in a similar way to the first: through a series of conversations. Within a context of rising numbers of homeless youth, Vancouver Foundation posed a number of key questions aimed at increasing impact over the three years: What are the key paths to homelessness for youth, and can we prevent them? How do we share knowledge among young people, service providers, funders and researchers and act on what we've learned? How do we communicate to citizens and decision-makers in a way that builds a sense of common cause and responsibility? Along with the Youth Homelessness Advisory Committee, nearly 40 stakeholders were engaged through group discussions and individual interviews, including a range of service providers, funders, researchers and youth (Vancouver Foundation, 2012b).

As a result of those conversations, the Foundation chose to commit to a prevention-based initiative with a focus on one of the populations most vulnerable to homelessness: young people who have experienced government care. Involvement in the child welfare system is a pathway into youth homelessness, particularly as young people hit the age of majority (which in BC is 19 years of age); indeed a 2003 survey by the Public Health Agency of Canada (2006), found that over 40% of street-involved youth across Canada had been in foster care. In British Columbia, approximately 700 young people age out of care each year out of a total of approximately 8,200 young people in care at any given point. As noted in Chapter 8, the majority of young people in care are Indigenous, part of a history of assimilationist child welfare programs that resulted in what the final report of the Truth and Reconciliation Commission of Canada called "cultural genocide" (Blackstock, 2019, p. 5). Older youth in care in particular are disproportionately Indigenous, LGBTQ and/or young mothers (M Gifford presentation, 2012). The conversations with stakeholders established that youth involved in the foster care system are under-served, over-represented among the homeless population, and in definite need of focused support.

It was also suspected that the connection between child welfare system involvement and homelessness was not well understood, which meant that, unless there was a concerted effort to address youth homelessness, it was unlikely that any systemic change on the issue would be made. Based on a belief that "strengthening systems and services that ensure youth are connected, valued and safely housed before and after they transition out of care will reduce youth homelessness in metro Vancouver", the decision was made to focus the second phase of YHI on young people aged between 14 and 24 in the Lower Mainland who are or were in government care and at risk of homelessness (Vancouver Foundation, 2012a, p. 4). In order to achieve the goal of preventing homelessness by strengthening policies and practices that enable young people to successfully transition out of care and into adulthood, a four-pronged approach was developed as outlined in Figure 1: youth engagement; community grants; shared learning, evaluation and research; and public engagement (*ibid.*, pp. 3–4). The program was initially intended to run until 2015, but a few years into the initiative the board took the decision to extend the timeline to 2018. And thus, Fostering Change, our Youth Homelessness Initiative, was born.

Vision: Every young person leaving foster care will have the opportunities and support needed to thrive as adults

Mission: To improve policy, practice and community connections for young people transitioning from foster care to adulthood

Outcome	A growing public constituency is aware and engaged in issues facing young people in transition from care to adulthood.	Young people have increased voice and influence in planning and decision-making.	Community organizations have increased resources, knowledge and connections to better support young people.	Research, evaluation and learning expand knowledge and effectiveness.
Community grants	• Arts and media projects highlight the issues for public understanding • Public participation projects directly engage people in the issues	• Projects led by young people highlight issues of importance to young people and provide an opportunity for the practice of meaningful youth engagement	• Projects increase inter- and intra-organization capacity, as well as community capacity • Multi-year support for program services provides direct support to young people making the transition from foster care to adulthood	• Real-time, supported, collaborative learning contributes to improvements in practice and highlights gaps – "what we don't know"
Youth engagement	• Young people advise and participate in public engagement and communications work and act as co-hosts for events	• Young people are involved in the development, implementation and evaluation of everything that we do	• Expanded number and improved quality of tools and supports for young people and adult allies collaborating in community • Community organizations and communities are better able to engage in meaningful youth engagement	• Train and support young people to advise on research • Train and support young people to participate as active researchers and respondents
Shared learning, evaluation and research	• Public release of findings from shared learning, evaluation and research help public understand issues facing young people in transition	• YAC captures and shares learning about meaningful youth engagement • Youth-led and youth-directed research and learning highlight issues of importance to young people and expand evidence base of what we know	• Shared Learning and Evaluation (SLE) workgroup learning products support better practice in work with young people and inform possible system and policy changes • A community of providers is built, providing a foundation for greater sharing of knowledge, resources and opportunities	• SLE workgroup collectively identifies issues and learns together (practice-learning feedback loop) • Contracted research contributes to evidence base of what we know • Ongoing measurement of experience of young people contributes to evidence base of what we know (measure key indicators: health, housing, employment, education, support networks, finance)
Public engagement	• Increase broad public awareness of key issues • Invite participation and grow constituency • Engage public in developing possible solutions and actions	• The voice of young people and the expertise of youth leaders are amplified • Provide a platform for young people to directly interact with and influence decision-makers	• Capacity of communities is developed to be able to confidently take public roles in promoting goals for youth in care • Build credibility of organizations • Showcase what is working and amplify success • Highlight gaps in the system	• Learning with communities about issues of importance to them and where they see strengths/gaps • Generate a set of community tested "asks" that are meaningful and can be taken forward by stakeholders and assessed for relevance with broader public audiences and potential allies
Why this matters	Research shows that systems change is enabled by public which requires increased visibility of and engagement with the issue.	All people have the right to be involved in decisions that affect them. Research shows that authentic youth engagement leads to better individual, programmatic and policy outcomes.	Research shows that fragmented services lead to poor outcomes, so communities need to be supported to collaboratively surface and demonstrate programs and practices that enable better outcomes for young people.	Developing a collective understanding of what works in a BC context and what we still need to learn supports effective practice and can inform policy and system change.

Youth engagement

Vancouver Foundation has a strong track record of prioritizing the involvement of youth in the development of programs, policies and infrastructure that affect their lives. Guided by the principle of "Nothing about us without us", Fostering Change built on this legacy by creating the Youth Advisory Circle (YAC), which was involved in all aspects of the Fostering Change initiative. Vancouver Foundation's *Youth Engagement Report: Learning from Fostering Change and Fresh Voices* (Glass, 2018) outlines nine key steps that were integral to the youth engagement work of Fostering Change.

1 Involve youth early in the process, and keep them in the centre throughout the initiative

One of the first actions in developing the Fostering Change initiative in 2012 was the formation of the YAC. As a Foundation executive noted, "The biggest advice I received came from a young person who said, so often organizations decide what they are going to do, and then they invite youth in. Young people want to be involved early, in the thinking, the planning, the decision-making" (*ibid.*, p. 10). Much of the first year was spent developing relationships, building trust, learning how to engage in group dialogue and exploring the relevant issues. This meant that when the time came to set goals and create strategy, young people were already full, informed partners. This also meant that the work of Fostering Change was more effective and reflective of the wisdom of those with lived expertise of the issue. As a staff member put it, "When we put young people in touch with the communications team and involved them in every stage, including the design, colour, content of the website, that shifted the ownership for the campaign. It became clear that we had to continue this practice of deep youth engagement" (*ibid.*, p. 19).

2 Be intentional about which youth are being engaged and why

The YAC was made up of six young people aged between 19 and 24, all of whom had lived expertise of foster care and homelessness. As a youth advisor pointed out, "The people who have the answers are the ones who are directly affected by the issue" (*ibid.*, p. 10). It was important to acknowledge that not all young people have the same access to power and to prioritize those with lived expertise on the issue.

3 Acknowledge power; don't ignore it

Taking the time to build trusting relationships between staff and young people, and between young people themselves, made it easier to have open conversations as well as reciprocity and respect, regardless of power imbalances. The Ladder of Young People's Participation (shown in Figure 2) was a useful tool to illustrate different levels of engagement. While there were times when decisions and activities were reflective of true adult–youth partnerships, sometimes these were being made or taking place on one of the lower rungs. Being transparent about the extent of youth decision-making power in different situations was an important part of navigating the power dynamics at play.

Figure 2 – Ladder of young people's participation

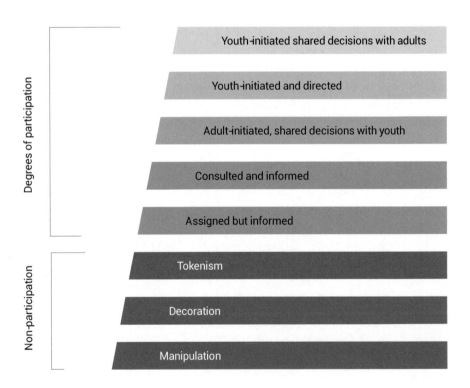

4 Sharing power means sharing information and responsibility

A key step in acknowledging power dynamics was for the Foundation to be comfortable with sharing power. As a staff member put it, it was important to "recognize that the whole organization needs to be on board. There's a lot of internal work that needs to happen before being ready to take on an inclusion program. If adults are not engaged in their own learning process to address fears about making mistakes and sharing power, it is hard to engage young people" (*ibid.*, p. 25). Being transparent about things like budgets, workloads, timelines and administrative requirements helped to keep young people in the loop and able to participate in an informed way. Terms of reference were also created to clarify the roles and responsibilities of the youth advisory, adult allies and foundation staff. As a YAC member described, "I am expected to come prepared because it is part of my commitment. Be clear on what's expected of the young people and what young people are expecting of the organization supporting them" (*ibid.*, p. 12).

5 Staff who build bridges between youth and the institution are the key to success

The program manager leading the youth engagement work had the professional skills to lead deep community engagement as well as personal experience of what it was like to be both a foster kid and a foster parent. This combination of professional and lived expertise was an integral component of the success of the youth engagement work of the Fostering Change initiative. However, lived expertise is not something that is typically valued through traditional recruitment processes. Bringing in youth engagement staff on a short-term contract was a way of demonstrating the importance of the role before the Foundation committed to a permanent position.

6 Youth engagement staff need to be well supported in order to support everyone else

Youth engagement staff work at the intersection between overall vision and daily practice, between adults learning to share power with youth and youth learning to work with an institution, and between the day-to-day realities of young people and systems that were not built for them. As a staff member commented, "It's hard work to hold. This is something for foundations to understand when bringing people on to do real community engagement. They are coming in deeply connected to these issues and communities. Foundations are trading on staff's credibility and relationships, whether they think about it or not. That is why it's essential to demonstrate that their work is respected throughout the organization, not pigeon-holed or minimized" (*ibid.*, p. 14). Supports needed to allow youth engagement staff to do their best work include: job security, decent pay, trust and openness with leadership, commitment to reducing barriers to youth within the organization, and efforts to ensure the youth program is understood and valued by all staff and board members.

7 Respect the knowledge youth bring with them while supporting them to increase their capacity to lead

The YAC had a dedicated training budget that youth could use for their learning priorities, such as group workshops in public policy or media training or facilitation skills. Staff and adult allies also provided ongoing informal coaching and ensured that young people were well prepared and supported before speaking at a conference or with elected officials, for example. As a community partner and grantee explained, "Fostering Change identified each young person's gifts and linked them up with mentorship that was meaningful and effective. That reflects an Indigenous concept because, in our traditional community, you were identified for your gifts at a young age and mentored. The act of honouring young people is so profound for their development, for their sense of belonging, especially when they don't have a family" (*ibid.*, p. 14).

8 In the Youth Advisory Circle, take time to get to know each other and to stay on track with the work

YAC members are most proud of two things: the relationships they built with each other and the achievements they accomplished together. Each YAC meeting started with a meal and a check-in question, both intended to contribute towards building relationships between members and with youth engagement staff. Sometimes the YAC would come together at someone's house to prepare the meal, taking time to be in each other's company outside official business. Having strong relationships between YAC members and with the youth engagement staff made it easier to stay on track and support each other through challenges and when the work invariably got messy.

9 Designated adult allies play a quiet but essential role in the Youth Advisory Circle, supporting young people to contribute to their fullest

The YAC was supported by three adult allies who were interviewed and chosen by YAC members themselves. Each of them had experience working with youth and were dedicated to the goals of the initiative. Their role was to attend meetings and build relationships with the young people to assist the group to learn, discuss and work together. As one of them noted, "My practice was to really engage youth members as knowledgeable people that deserve mentorship. They deserve to be treated as people who have capacity and ability and who are also there to learn. I asked a lot of questions and mediated what came up in the group as respectfully as I would with any other colleague" (*ibid.*, p. 15).

The Youth Engagement Report also highlights some key practices that ensured that young people were able to participate in the Fostering Change initiative:

- Food at meetings (healthy full meals, not just pizza!)
- Honoraria
- Transit tickets
- Meeting times that work for youth (it might be Friday evenings!)
- Variety of communication methods (graphic recording, silent reflection, sharing circles)
- Registration and travel to events and conferences
- Printed material for youth to review, rather than relying on electronic communications
- Individualized support (like assistance getting a passport to present at an out-of-country conference)

Being able to effectively support young people's participation in the work of Fostering Change required dedicated human and financial resources. It also required adjusting internal practices to support the work, which at times created challenges. Organizational choices such as whether or not to allow evening or weekend meetings in the office or how honoraria should be disbursed, along with questions around the frequency of meetings, amount of the food budget and how long processes took, had an effect on the overall climate of inclusion/exclusion.

Community grants

The approach to grantmaking evolved over the lifespan of Fostering Change. As with YHI, all grants were reviewed by a volunteer advisory committee made up of community members with expertise in the issue, ranging from young people with lived expertise (including a few members of the Youth Advisory Circle), researchers, direct service providers and foster parents. Together they made funding recommendations to Vancouver Foundation's board for final approval. Also similar to YHI, Fostering Change's grantmaking contained an evaluation component but, rather than funds being provided to organizations for them to conduct their own evaluations, funding was instead given to compensate for the time it took staff to participate in shared learning and evaluation activities led by the Foundation's in-house evaluation staff. The goal here was to ensure that learning was being shared between grantees and used to benefit the network, and initiative, as a whole. As one grantee explained, "Vancouver Foundation worked really hard to be a network medium, bringing grantees together to learn and share. We realized we have the same objectives and can collaborate instead of being siloed and competing for funding" (Glass, 2018, p. 20). Having a close relationship with grantees allowed Fostering Change to adapt its approach to grantmaking to better serve the overall goals of the initiative.

In the early years, larger multi-year grants were given for single-agency, direct service approaches to supporting young people aging out of foster care. This filled an important need in the community and allowed critical services to be delivered to young people, but it was not necessarily the most effective way to create change at a systemic level. There was a willingness from both the granting advisory committee and staff working on the initiative to fund prototypes and take risks to test out new ideas and ways of doing things as well as provide funding for activities that it is not always easy to get a grant for, such as engaging young people, bringing community together, creating and implementing advocacy campaigns, and working across agencies. The willingness to take risks and provide flexible funding supported grantees in delivering projects with greater impact. As one grantee put it, "We were listening to the interests and needs of the youth, and that would sometimes be different than what we had planned. The Foundation was flexible with us in terms of changing the project to meet the needs of the youth. That allowed us to do more meaningful work" (*ibid.*, p. 21). Over time, grants of varying sizes with different granting criteria were eventually developed, with the aim of supporting different aspects of the overall work of Fostering Change. In the five years between 2012 and 2017, $5 million in grants were given to community organizations through five different types of grant, as described below.

Youth Engagement/Youth Partnership Grants

Youth Engagement/Youth Partnership Grants were grants for up to one year for a maximum of $25,000. A condition of the grants was that young people had to be included in the design and delivery of the projects, which were intended to amplify the voices and engagement of young people. The purpose was to support creating knowledge, awareness and dialogue about experiences of youth transitioning from care to adulthood; connections between young people in, and from, care and their local community members; youth-led research and/or creative arts-based projects. These grants were reviewed first by the Youth Advisory Circle, who provided their recommendations and rationale for funding to the advisory committee.

Community planning and engagement grants

Community planning and engagement grants were grants for up to 18 months for a maximum of $50,000. Their purpose was to support strategies that built capacity and common ground for shared action and learning by community stakeholders. Grants could support work such as convening and scoping early-phase engagement of stakeholders in development of practice and/ or policy innovation, coordination of initial collective impact strategies, and local advocacy and awareness work connected to the goals of the Fostering Change initiative.

Multi-year strategies

Multi-year grants were for up to three years for a maximum of $150,000. The expectation of these grants was that they would generate evidence to improve practice, policy and levels of collaboration and community engagement. In later years, the focus was explicitly on applications that extended beyond direct service and case management approaches. The expectation of grantees was that they would participate in the Foundation-supported shared learning and evaluation agenda as well as communications, public engagement and youth engagement activities.

Small grants

Small grants for $10,000 were given for youth- and community-led initiatives focused on youth engagement, relationship building, community convening and public engagement. Given the small amount of funding, decisions on small grants were based upon the submission of the letter of intent alone and not a full application. To provide a quicker response, decisions on funding were made by staff in partnership with at least one volunteer advisory committee member.

Legacy grants

Legacy grants were provided in 2017, the final year that Vancouver Foundation housed the Fostering Change initiative, for a maximum of $150,000 over two years. These were grants to build upon and carry forward the work of Fostering Change, in the following categories: youth engagement, capacity development, shared learning and research.

Shared learning, evaluation and research

Fostering Change's approach to shared learning and evaluation also evolved over the lifespan of the initiative. As indicated above, shared learning and evaluation activities were led by a staff member on the Fostering Change team, which was the first time that the Foundation had a dedicated staff person for learning and evaluation. Understanding that "Foundations need to become good learners and to position learning itself as a core strategy" when working on complex systems change, Fostering Change wanted to have the capacity for learning and evaluation embedded within the team as a key resource for both the Foundation and grantees (Patrizi et al., 2013, p. 52). Just as with youth engagement staff, the position was initially a short-term contract, in order to demonstrate the importance to the organization of having a permanent staff member responsible for this work. In fact, this work proved to be so important that the Foundation currently has a Learning and Evaluation team within the Grants and Community Initiatives department, which is now staffed by three full time employees.

At the outset, only multi-year grantees were involved in the shared learning and evaluation (SLE) working group, but after almost a year the group was made accessible to all grantees (at their request), no matter what size or type of grant they received. Given the increased number of agencies involved, the SLE work evolved from one working group into multiple learning pods, each focusing on one theme related to the work, such as housing, education, culture, etc. Grantee staff self-selected into a pod based on its relevance to their work, and each worked through a prototyping cycle (planning, studying, prototyping, reflecting, and sharing) by selecting a practice that they were interested in trying. All grantees across the pods came together at least three times a year for Grantee Learning Days to share what they were doing and to learn from each other. Initially only grantees attended the Learning Days, but these evolved into an opportunity to bring together people across the community – with grantees being invited to extend the invitation to young people they worked with as well as other partner organizations, including the BC Ministry of Child and Family Development. These days were hosted by Vancouver Foundation in partnership with an external facilitator, and the process for each day was designed with interested participants, including young people.

The shared learning and evaluation work changed the Fostering Change team's relationship with grantees from one based on accountability to that of a learning partner. One grantee expressed it like this: "The Foundation worked closely with grantees. They got an intimate look at the barriers and opportunities so agencies were less afraid to give legitimate feedback. The Foundation didn't want the initiatives to fail. They encouraged us to look for what was working and expand it. Most funders think they can't take that risk and we have to pretend the proposal is perfect, that the organization always knows exactly what it's doing" (Glass, 2018, p. 21). Being a learning partner also meant approaching the work with a beginner's mindset and acknowledging that Vancouver Foundation is not the expert. Instead, the role of the Foundation was to honor the wisdom held by community groups by creating the space for grantees to reflect, share and build collective learning into their own work.

Beyond working with grantees and community partners, another way that the Foundation supported learning was through commissioning research. In 2013, Vancouver Foundation worked with Sentis Market Research to survey 1,820 adult British Columbians to "gain a better understanding of public attitudes, values and perceptions about youth transitioning to adulthood and, more specifically, for youth aging out of government care in the province" (Vancouver Foundation, 2013, p. 3). The results of the survey indicated that 80% of parents who have 19–28-year-olds living away from home provided their children with some form of emotional, social and financial support, and most British Columbians believed that 19-year-olds do not have the necessary skills and resources to live away from home and support themselves independently: 68% of British Columbians were thus in favor of increasing the age at which government support is cut off to at least 21 (*ibid.*, p. 4).

252   Vancouver Foundation: Fostering meaningful engagement with youth

The survey also, however, pointed to a lack of knowledge about young people in government care: only 28% of those surveyed were aware that government support ends when young people in care reach their 19th birthday and 71% underestimated the percentage of young people who are currently in foster care or in a group home (*ibid.*, p. 7). Given that systems change is enabled by public support, this information helped the Fostering Change team design their public engagement activities to increase visibility of and engagement with the issue, as will be described further in the next section. Indeed, a second public opinion survey, conducted three years later in 2016, indicated that public awareness and understanding of the scale and significance of issues facing young people in foster care had increased, with 38% of British Columbians aware that government support ended at 19 and less than half underestimating the number of young people living in care (Fostering Change, 2016, p. 4). The survey also found that an increased number of British Columbians (76%) were in favor of extending the cut-off for receiving assistance and support beyond the age of 19 (*ibid.*, p. 2). Knowing that there was broad public backing for better supporting young people aging out of foster care helped make the case for the Foundation to step into an advocacy role and dedicate human and financial resources to making policy change on the issue.

As well as conducting research to understand the public perceptions of and support towards the issue of young people transitioning from foster care, the Foundation also supported research to increase public and political will. The most high-profile piece of research to come out of Fostering Change was *Opportunities in Transition: An Economic Analysis of Investing in Youth Aging out of Foster Care*, (Shaffer *et al.*, 2016) The purpose of the study was threefold:

- to document what is known about the outcomes for youth aging out of care
- to estimate the costs of adverse outcomes
- to identify measures that could improve outcomes and assess their incremental costs in relation to the potential benefits they may generate

This was the first time that an economic analysis had been done with data specific to British Columbia. The research showed that educational, economic, social and wellness outcomes for many youth aging out of care were poor when compared with most young people, and the costs of those adverse outcomes were extremely high – up to $268 million per year (*ibid.*, p. 1). Conversely, a basic package of increased supports from age 19 through 24 for living costs, education, community connections and social supports that could build on existing services and programs was estimated at $57 million per year (*ibid.*, p. 2). This piece of research proved critical to building public will and advocacy efforts by proving that not only do youth aging out of foster care in BC deserve the same support and opportunities as all young people, but that it also makes economic sense to provide these.

Public engagement

A key component to the Fostering Change initiative was engaging the public to create the conditions for policy change. As a staff member put it, "Early on we realized we don't have an evidence problem; we have a policy problem. How do we influence public will to provide political licence for the policy shifts that need to happen?" (Glass, 2018, p. 18). Part of the approach was to work under the belief that government both wants to do the right thing and is more likely to work hard to change policy when it thinks the public is behind it. Another belief the team was driven by is that it is within the role of a community foundation to influence public policy and advocate for change. Indeed, as Gibbins (2016) argues, "Policy advocacy is an inherent part of the charitable mission" and charities, which include community foundations, have a "moral imperative to pursue the public good and to be engaged as policy advocates in political and ethical debates about policy and social change." In the case of Fostering Change, policy advocacy took place in a few different forms, including grassroots organizing, active campaigning, public awareness-raising, research, network-building, convening, and communicating with elected officials.

Building off the public opinion surveys This issue is, which indicated a willingness to get behind increased supports for youth aging out of care but a lack of awareness about the issue, one of the first projects Fostering Change took on was to change the narrative around youth in and from care. The team recognized that "sad images of marginalized youth might provoke a cheque-book response, but they won't provoke a policy response. And youth won't want to stick around, either. It's their stories. It's their lives" (Glass, 2018, p. 16).

Young people were trained and supported to talk about systemic issues, combining personal storytelling with a clear policy ask. As a YAC member pointed out, "This issue is about all of us, not one of us" (*ibid.*, p. 12). In 2015, the *Messaging & Communications Guide* was created based on input from youth, service providers, front-line workers, policy makers, funders, engaged parents, communications specialists and advocates. Its goal was to provide a resource for organizations, journalists and other people interested in the issue and to reframe it from one of stigma and hopelessness to one of hope and opportunity to make change. It also tried to get the public to think of youth in care as "our kids" instead of "those kids", redefining how we perceive our role and responsibility as individuals and as a society to help them reach their potential.

That same year, a series of five community conversations held alongside community partners convened more than 350 people across the Lower Mainland. The conversations were designed to get participants sharing knowledge and networks with each other, spark new thinking from local perspectives map local assets and capacities for supporting young people leading up to and following aging out of care, and identify trends that would help establish shared interests in new granting, public policy, and youth and community engagement priorities (Fostering Change, 2015, p. 3). This was a starting point for building on the knowledge that exists in communities, to better serve, support and enable healthy transitions to adulthood for young people in our care. The year 2015 culminated with the launch of a standalone Fostering Change website in order to share stories, resources and information – and to gather a network of supporters.

The next phase of the public engagement work was focused on active campaigning. Using a petition to build a list of supporters, a combination of online outreach and street teams were used to gather petition signatures as part of a campaign titled "Write the Future". In six weeks of active campaigning more than 15,000 signatures were gathered from members of the public who backed increased supports for young people aging out of foster care. The campaign was a mechanism to increase public awareness of the issue and further proved that there was broad public support for it – which was important leading into the 2017 provincial election in British Columbia.

The next phase of that campaign was #supportthe700, focused on the candidates for the election. A pledge was developed asking candidates to commit to up to four actions related to improving supports for young people aging out of foster care. Through mobilizing the 15,000 supporters and conducting direct outreach to candidates, 147 candidates (40% of the total candidature) signed the pledge, 41 of whom went on to be elected. Additionally, the platforms of all three primary parties mentioned young people aging out of care, and in one of the televised debates leading up to the election the leaders were asked what they would do to improve support for young people aging out of care.

Engaging in advocacy at this scale was a new activity for the Foundation, one that required different skills and expertise than existed on the Fostering Change team. With just 3.5 full-time employees covering all aspects of the Fostering Change initiative, additional human resources were also required to run effective campaigns while maintaining the grantmaking, youth engagement and shared learning, evaluation and research work. In order to both develop the capacity of the Foundation to engage in this work and also involve young people in as many aspects of the campaigns as possible, Fostering Change partnered with contractors who had the skills and capacity to teach and learn as they worked. External consultants provided expertise in campaign strategy, communications, facilitation, public engagement and Nationbuilder web platform training.

To engage in advocacy as a registered charity, Vancouver Foundation had to remain staunchly non-partisan throughout the campaign work. Staff, board and young people needed to be educated on the rules as they pertained to election campaigns in order to reduce the sense of risk and ensure that the Foundation's reputation would not be damaged. This work resulted in what one city councillor described "the best example I can point to of grassroots organizing and public policy campaigning in BC in the last five years" (Glass, 2018, p. 6). Recently, the BC government made significant policy improvements to the eligibility of former foster care youth to access financial support, the amount they can claim and the length of time they can continue to access it, by investing $30 million in the program over three years, starting in 2018–19.

Lessons

Over the past few years, Vancouver Foundation has been working to better understand its role in supporting change. To do so, it has developed a theory of philanthropy, intended to "articulate how and why [it] will use its resources to achieve its mission and vision" (Patton *et al.*, 2015, p. 7). What has emerged is that Vancouver Foundation's primary contribution to social change is influence, which is used to inspire community change through raising and granting money, convening formal and informal conversations, providing sectoral leadership and maintaining a solid professional reputation. This is evident in the work of the Fostering Change initiative.

As a community partner recounted, "Fostering Change was a real game changer and a landscape changer. It created culture shifts: in people's attitudes towards youth aging out of foster care, and in the relationships among funders and community groups" (Glass, 2018, p. 6). It also brought increased attention and profile to organizations and individuals that had been in this work long before Vancouver Foundation made it a priority: "Our organization has been working with foster children for 30 years. When an actor as big as Vancouver Foundation entered the policy arena, it gave new legitimacy and visibility to these issues. Now we are able to attract MPs and city councillors to our events. We are more important to decision-makers than before" (*ibid.*, p. 20).

Making young people central to the initiative and making youth engagement a criterion for organizations seeking grants encouraged community organizations to improve their practice and see young people as significant assets: "The youth facilitators became legitimate advisors in our field. The initiative gave our network of organizations, even City Hall, access to an untapped network of young people who had become experienced in effective community engagement" (*ibid.*, p. 21). Recognizing, and growing comfortable with, its influence allowed Vancouver Foundation to amplify the voices and experiences of young people with lived expertise of the child welfare system, to invest in research and grantmaking on a targeted issue and to take on a new role as an advocate.

In order to address the root causes of complex social issues, foundations are finding that an emergent approach that "allows evolution and adaptation to challenges that arise as the strategy unfolds" is required, and Vancouver Foundation is no exception (McCarthy *et al.*, 2017, p. 64). The guiding principles of emergent philanthropy include: strengthening relationships between systems-level actors and the Foundation; co-creating strategy through collaboration with grantees, partners and those most affected by the issue; thinking at a systems level; adaptability supported by learning, self-reflection, critical thinking and experimentation; prioritizing equitable grant processes in which those most affected can both inform the process and successfully apply for grants; and committing to processes proven to lead to improved community outcomes such as through treating stakeholders as equals, focusing on the root problem and being authentic (*ibid.*, p. 66). Each of the four parts of the strategy described above required the Fostering Change team to work differently, which was only possible through strengthened relationships and adaptive processes.

Working in this way also required a significant commitment of both human and financial resources. In 2016, for example, the initiative's program budget was $468,500 excluding grants and staff. Along with the 3.5 full-time employees (director, program manager, evaluation manager and grant administrator) who made up the Fostering Change initiative, additional support was also provided by communications, finance, donor services and executive staff, in addition to the external consultants previously indicated. Working across the Foundation meant that internal practices in other departments also needed to adapt and change in order to support the work.

In the words of one Foundation executive, "We had an obligation to protect the organization. At the same time we had to acknowledge that we were asking youth to step into our box, not the other way around. So we had to face that there would be some things we needed to adjust internally" (*ibid.*, p. 25). That said, program staff reflected that the responsiveness of the organization to adjusting internal practices to support meaningful youth engagement was uneven. For example, Foundation administration twice changed the way YAC members received compensation out of concerns about accountability – from cash at each meeting to a cheque at each meeting to a lump sum termed a bursary. In one case, a YAC member living in social housing became ineligible for his apartment because he had to declare the bursary as income. Practices and changes such as this may have seemed small and more efficient for the Foundation, but they could have (and did have) huge consequences on the lives of young people. Balancing the Foundation's need for risk management with the creation of conditions for new ways of working needs to be spread across the organization; the commitment towards youth engagement and advocacy can't be confined to one department or initiative.

Working closely with young people and in community meant that Fostering Change evolved in a fluid way, with staff constantly learning as they went and adapting activities and strategies accordingly. This meant that sometimes the work moved very slowly, while at other times it had to move quickly. Keeping both internal and external stakeholders in the loop occasionally proved challenging. As a donor services staff member pointed out, "It was important for our team to understand why the Foundation is running a program instead of just making grants. What makes the program unique? How does it relate to the organizational objectives? It was not always easy for us to explain to donors" (*ibid.*, p. 23). Program staff often struggled when asked to report back to donors about the impact of their donation, because the initiative was not about service delivery. And challenges also arose when staff in other parts of the organization used language to describe the initiative that diverged from the narratives developed by youth and program staff.

These issues highlighted the need for better communication and understanding within the Foundation as well as, again, the need to have the entire Foundation on board with new ways of working. Likewise, sometimes external partners felt out of the loop as the initiative grew and changed. As a community partner described it, "You create a network, and the community supports the public policy campaign. People put a lot of effort and time into it. When it all gets going, you need a feedback mechanism that shows the progress being made towards the stated goals" (*ibid.*, p. 21). While Fostering Change made sure to get buy-in from community partners at the start of the campaigns, more communication and transparency was needed throughout the initiative to keep everyone engaged.

Throughout the initiative, Vancouver Foundation acknowledged that the wisdom and commitment to this work resided in community, and in 2018 the Foundation returned Fostering Change to the community that had inspired it. The 2017 legacy grants provided funding for organizations to continue aspects of the initiative, with First Call: BC Child and Youth Advocacy Coalition taking on the continued advocacy work of the initiative. As a non-partisan coalition of 101 provincial and regional organizations, First Call is well positioned to expand the work of Fostering Change across the province and hold government accountable to better supporting youth aging out of care.

The sunsetting of the Fostering Change initiative at Vancouver Foundation was, however, not without challenges. While the board "saw the Foundation's role as an incubator" (*ibid.*, p. 22) this was not always clearly communicated. Given that the initiative had previously been renewed twice (from 2012 to 2015 and then again from 2015 to 2018), many people and organizations assumed that the initiative would continue to be renewed, despite being told that it would end in 2018. And even though people understood that no further grants would be made to support work related to Fostering Change, it was more challenging for them to recognize that there would no longer be dedicated resources, such as staff and a program budget, at Vancouver Foundation for the initiative.

In a recent study looking at funders who managed a "successful exit" of major, time-limited, place-based initiatives, the authors found that the following components were vital: "[an exit] guided by respect for the relationships the foundation has forged with grantee partners; a clear intention to sustain the change-making efforts at the core of the initiative; inclusive and evidence-based decision-making; thoughtful and advance consideration of what comes next; and proactive management of the internal changes likely to accompany the transition to new efforts and focuses" (Cau Yu *et al.*, 2017, p. 65–6). These are important considerations for the Foundation as it takes on further time-limited strategic priorities.

Conclusion

While Vancouver Foundation is no longer housing the Fostering Change initiative, youth engagement remains a permanent focus of the Foundation. The current youth engagement initiative, LEVEL, builds upon the relationships, lessons and capacities developed out of Fostering Change and includes a grantmaking, grassroots-organizing and a public policy program component to address racial equity within the nonprofit sector. LEVEL also continues the practice of having clear plans about which young people are to be engaged, with an explicit focus on Indigenous and racialized immigrant and refugee young people. Additionally, Vancouver Foundation continues to prioritize addressing the root causes of issues through its focus on funding systems-change work through its responsive grantmaking program. By continuing to work in this way, the Foundation is indicating its desire to embrace its role as a changemaker, advocate and active community participant.

Three key takeaways

1 It's all about relationships: making time and space to build upon and strengthen relationships with and between grantees, partners, staff and young people is crucial. Don't attempt to tackle an issue unless you have existing relationships and experience in that area.

2 "Nothing about us without us": place at the centre the voices and lived expertise of those most affected. Approach the work with a beginner's mindset and acknowledge that you are (probably) not the expert.

3 Understand and be willing to shift power dynamics: engaging in advocacy and changemaking requires flexibility and different ways of working (which will likely include changing or adapting internal policies and procedures) for the entirety of the organization. If it's a time-limited strategy, make sure to plan the end from the beginning and be clear and transparent about timelines and commitments.

References

Blackstock, C (2019) 'Indigenous child welfare legislation: A historical change or another paper tiger?', *First Peoples Child & Family Review, 14* (1), 5–8. Retrieved November 29, 2019 from: http://journals.sfu.ca/fpcfr/index.php/FPCFR/article/view/367

Cao Yu, H, Jhawar, MK & D Berman (2017) 'Exiting from large-scale initiatives: Lessons and insights from a national scan of philanthropy', *The Foundation Review, 9*(1). Retrieved on November 29, 2019 from: https://doi.org/10.9707/1944-5660.1351

Fostering Change (2015) *Community Conversations May–June 2015*. Vancouver, Canada: Vancouver Foundation

Fostering Change (2016) *2016 Youth Transitions Survey: Early Results*. Vancouver, Canada: Vancouver Foundation

Gibbins, R (2016) 'The moral imperative for policy advocacy', *The Philanthropist*. Retrieved on November 29, 2019 from: https://thephilanthropist.ca/2016/02/the-moral-imperative-for-policy-advocacy/

Glass, J (2018) *Vancouver Foundation's Youth Engagement Report: Learning from Fostering Change and Fresh Voices*. Vancouver, Canada: Vancouver Foundation

Hart, R (1992) *Children's Participation: Tokenism to Citizenship*. Florence, Italy: UNICEF International Child Development Centre, Spedale degli Innocenti

Legare, J & J Rootman (2011) *Evaluation of the Vancouver Foundation Youth Homelessness Initiative*. Vancouver, Canada: Legare Associates

McCarthy, A, Bornstein, J, Perrin, T, James, J & B Fulton (2017) 'Insights from deploying a collaborative process for funding systems change', *The Foundation Review, 9*(2). Retrieved on November 29, 2019 from: https://doi.org/10.9707/1944-5660.1366

Patrizi, P, Heid Thompson, E, Coffman, J & T Beer (2013) 'Eyes wide open: Learning as strategy under conditions of complexity and uncertainty', *The Foundation Review, 5*(3). Retrieved on November 29, 2019 from: https://doi.org/10.9707/1944-5660.1170

Patton, M, Foote, N & J Radner (2015) 'A foundation's theory of philanthropy: What it is, what it provides, how to do It', *The Foundation Review 7*(4). Retrieved on November 29, 2019 from: https://doi.org/10.9707/1944-5660.1263

Phillips, S, Bird, I, Carlton, L & L Rose (2016) 'Knowledge as leadership, belonging as community: How Canadian community foundations are using vital signs for social change', *The Foundation Review, 8*(3). Retrieved on November 29, 2019 from: https://doi.org/10.9707/1944-5660.1314

Public Health Agency of Canada (2006) *Street Youth in Canada: Findings from enhanced surveillance of Canadian street youth, 1999–2003*. Canada: Public Health Agency of Canada

Shaffer, M, Anderson, L & A Nelson (2016) *Opportunities in Transition: An economic analysis of investing in youth aging out of foster care*. Vancouver, Canada: Fostering Change

Streetohome (2018) 'About us'. Retrieved October 10, 2018, from: http://www.streetohome.org/about/

Vancouver Foundation (2012a) *Ending Youth Homelessness in Metro Vancouver: Vancouver Foundation's strategic plan 2012–15*. Vancouver, Canada: Vancouver Foundation

Vancouver Foundation (2012b) 'Vancouver Foundation YHI strategy 2012–14: Addressing the pathways to housing, capacity and community for youth in care.' Vancouver, Canada: Vancouver Foundation

Vancouver Foundation (2013) *Perceptions on the Challenges Facing British Columbia Youth Transitioning out of Government Care: Results of the Vancouver Foundation Transitions Survey*. Vancouver, Canada: Vancouver Foundation

Part three
Chapter twelve

Centraide's Collective Impact Project: Poverty reduction in Montréal

Nancy Pole and Myriam Bérubé

Launched in late 2015, Montreal's Collective Impact Project (CIP) is a five-year collaborative philanthropic initiative that describes itself as an accelerator of community change. As of June 2018, the CIP was composed of ten philanthropic partners, including Centraide of Greater Montreal (Centraide) as project manager and nine grantmaking foundations acting as financial partners. Three non-financial partners are also involved in the CIP's governance.

Through the pooling of financial and non-financial resources, the CIP aims to intensify and ensure greater coherence to supports given to comprehensive community change processes in Montreal. The project is based on the assumption that, if both funding support and funders' strategic actions are coordinated, local communities will be able to achieve more meaningful results with regard to poverty reduction.

This chapter discusses the CIP as a case study highlighting possibilities and challenges relating to funder collaboration as a means of shifting the dynamics associated with complex funding ecologies. This case study also shines a light on the evolving expression of community leadership by place-based foundations.

The CIP follows in the established tradition of place-based philanthropy, and wrestles with challenges related to the funder's role in collective impact. As an initiative, it represents continuity as well as a new development in Montreal's funding ecology. By introducing a new opportunity for funders, grantees and policymakers to come together and test out new ways of working, this initiative shines a light on existing relationships and system dynamics, while casting ripples that may (or may not) have a lasting effect elsewhere in the system. In addition, the CIP signals philanthropy's intention and capacity to occupy a more significant place within Montreal's funding ecology.

The partners of the Collective Impact Project as of June 2018

- Centraide of Greater Montreal (project manager)
- Lucie and André Chagnon Foundation
- Pathy Family Foundation
- McConnell Foundation
- Mirella and Lino Saputo Foundation
- Silver Dollar Foundation
- Foundation of Greater Montréal
- Molson Foundation
- Marcelle and Jean Coutu Foundation
- Trottier Family Foundation

This chapter draws upon the findings of a commissioned action research project that was carried out by Nancy Pole and Jean-Marc Fontan of PhiLab in 2016–17.[1] Its findings were drawn from 25 semi-directed interviews with partners, local representatives and other key informants, as well as a review of project documents and a literature review that provided a reading of relevant elements of the context.

The study described the vision of the CIP's original co-architects, Centraide and the Lucie and André Chagnon Foundation, and reviewed key moments of the design and early implementation phases. It focused in particular on how the partnership formed and how it changed over the first year of the initiative, on how the initiative was rolled out, and on the kind of reception it was given by grantees and other constituents. The original study produced findings and recommendations that were actionable in the short term, supporting greater awareness among partners and suggesting possible future adjustments. In the spring of 2018, an in-depth interview with the CIP's program director, Myriam Bérubé, provided a further update on evolving conditions and emerging challenges, as well as recent adaptations and adjustments to the project's management and governance.

Written at roughly the half-way point in the CIP's five-year trajectory, this chapter captures a point in time in a highly developmental initiative. Designed as an adaptive initiative, from one year to the next the CIP remains open to an ongoing and continuous process of discovery and adjustment. Thus, the chapter describes only the first half of the CIP's trajectory, not the outcomes or the final lessons. As a reflection on a still-unfolding initiative, its aim is to describe the project's specificities and engage with elements of the experience that may have some resonance for the broader field, including place-based foundations, private and public funders that are looking for ways to engage differently in complex funding ecologies, and practitioners and researchers involved with the still-unfolding field of collective impact.

---

1 The report, Montreal's Collective Impact Project (CIP) and the first stages of its partnership and operationalization, can be downloaded at: https://philab.uqam.ca/wp-content/uploads/2018/01/rapportPIC.pdf

Context

Reference points: comprehensive community change and collective impact

The CIP is inspired by the traditions of place-based philanthropy and of foundation support for comprehensive community initiatives (CCIs), also referred to as comprehensive community change efforts. In adopting a place-based approach, funders are often motivated by a recognition that their grantees do not operate in isolation but are part of an interdependent geographic "system" or "ecology", whose resilience and adaptability depend on collaboration rather than competition (Institute for Voluntary Action Research – IVAR, 2015, p. 1).

Foundation-supported comprehensive community change, for its part, rose to prominence in the United States in the 1990s and 2000s, while in Canada the flagship initiative in this area was Vibrant Communities, supported by the McConnell Foundation from 2002 through 2012 (Gamble, 2010; Cabaj, 2011). Defining characteristics are:

- a comprehensive and integrated orientation to community change involving work across multiple areas such as housing and the built environment, social services, and economic and social development
- a community-building orientation focusing variably on communities' participation or control over their own agenda for development
- an intention to catalyze some kind of systems change leading to more effective supports for devitalized communities (Aspen Institute, 2012)

Following its emergence in 2011, the collective impact framework has come to provide community change practitioners with a common language and frame of reference to succinctly describe the underlying principles of comprehensive community change and other collaborative initiatives (Weaver, 2014; Christens & Inzeo, 2015). The framework is built on the premise that solving complex problems requires the intensive engagement of influential partners across a variety of sectors, who then collaborate to leverage the resources at their disposal to drive toward outcomes in line with the desired changes (Weaver, 2016). More recent writings on collective impact have helped to bring the framework more in line with the principles and practices of community development, infusing it with the lessons learned from the older community-change tradition (Brady & Juster, 2016; Cabaj & Weaver, 2016; Kania & Kramer, 2016; Wolff, 2016).

The CIP's very name – Collective Impact Project – indicates that the project's designers and partners find this framework a useful reference point in their own thinking about how community change occurs. They are not alone; the collective impact concept has attracted particular attention from funders of collaborative initiatives, who appreciate the shift in emphasis away from the organizing *process* towards the *outcomes* to be achieved (Christens & Inzeo, 2015). Inspired by these and other trends, these funders have for some time been communicating expectations that collaborative initiatives be able to measure and demonstrate their own impact (Walzer *et al.*, 2016).

Regional context

The CIP was made possible by a particular context and set of enabling conditions in Montreal. Nonprofit and public sector organizations already had an established tradition of place-based collaboration, supported by various funders, public programs and structures in Montreal and elsewhere in Quebec (Klein & Champagne, 2011; Longtin & Rochman, 2015; Opération veille et soutien stratégique, 2017).

Of particular relevance to the CIP, between the late 1980s and the early 2000s, 30 local cross-sector and multi-stakeholder neighbourhood roundtables had emerged across the city of Montreal. Over the years a good number of these neighbourhood roundtables had come to occupy "backbone" roles, supporting the development of a shared vision of community change for their neighbourhoods, and then leading a joined-up action plan that served as a guidepost to help local organizations align their own actions with collectively determined priorities. Centraide already had well-established relationships with these roundtables, providing core and project funding for over a decade prior to the advent of the CIP. Alongside this, many roundtables also managed project funding from various other sources that was specifically earmarked for cross-sector, collaborative local initiatives focused on poverty reduction, neighbourhood revitalization, or the development of healthy environments for children, youth and families.

In the year leading up to the CIP's launch, a number of shifts began to be felt within the funding landscape for community change, including the end of a series of funding partnerships (described below) that had supported the funding and roll-out of hundreds of cross-sector community change initiatives across Quebec. On top of this, a series of austerity-motivated administrative reforms and government funding cuts had an immediate impact on the infrastructures that supported local and regional social development processes in Quebec (these are further discussed in Chapter 9 by Annabelle Berthiaume and Sylvain A. Lefèvre). This scale-back of institutional supports for community-change processes left many communities uncertain about how to hold on to the gains that they had worked so hard to achieve. In the context of such sector-wide upheaval, the scene was somewhat fortuitously set for a major new philanthropic funding initiative to emerge.

The idea for the CIP takes shape

The idea for the CIP emerged out of a dialogue between Centraide of Greater Montreal and the Lucie and André Chagnon Foundation. The two organizations had been in contact with each other for a number of years, as each had its own history of supporting broad-spectrum community development approaches.

From the late 1990s onwards, Centraide had progressively developed a comprehensive approach to supporting community development, providing funding and other supports to neighbourhood roundtables to help them develop their capacity to lead comprehensive community-change processes. Between 2007 and 2009, the Chagnon Foundation had set up three province-wide funds (Québec en Forme, Avenir d'enfants and Réunir Réussir) in partnership with the government of Quebec. The parameters of these funds had called for cross-sector organizing and collaborative engagement in local communities across the province (Brunet, 2014).

Starting in 2012, the two foundations together began to explore opportunities to develop a more purposeful strategic partnership focused around comprehensive community-change approaches in Greater Montreal. The context was conducive for each organization. As the sunset period approached for the three funds set up by the Chagnon Foundation, the foundation was engaging in a strategic reflection about the next direction for its community-change investment strategies. Centraide, for its part, was aware of the limits of its own capacity to scale up its support for comprehensive community-change work, whether this be on its own or as a partner within the *Initiative montréalaise (IM)*,[2] and was wanting to explore new ways to reach beyond these limits.

Centraide was also contending with major ongoing changes in the fundraising environment, as its federated model came to be challenged by the proliferation of new fundraising channels and platforms (Pereša & Viens, 2015; Centraide, 2016a). To help counter the impact these trends were having on its campaign, Centraide undertook two strategic shifts:

- It publicly repositioned itself as a value-added philanthropic actor, acting to raise its own profile as an expert, convener and leader in regional social development. In making this move, Centraide followed in the footsteps of other North American community philanthropy organizations that have sought to position or brand themselves in ways that give them a comparative advantage with donors, in particular by taking up a "community leadership" role in the social development of their city or region (Graddy & Morgan, 2006; Paarlberg & Meinhold, 2012).

---

2   A funding and strategic partnership of Centraide of Greater Montreal, the Montreal Regional Public Health Department (Direction régionale de la santé publique de Montréal – DRSPM), the City of Montréal and the Montréal Neighbourhood Round Tables Coalition (CMTQ).

- It devised a new campaign strategy that involved soliciting "transformational gifts" from major donors – large donations spread out over several years – and engaging these donors in establishing and rolling out specific granting initiatives (Centraide, 2015). The CIP offered itself up as a first opportunity to test out this new transformational gift strategy.

As the CIP began to take shape, a first key decision was that Centraide would act as the project's lead and manager. In setting itself up to play this role, Centraide put forward a value proposition that hinged on its deep knowledge of the CIP's content area, its existing relationships with community and institutional stakeholders, and its established capacity to manage the project. With respect to this last element, since 2010 the role of Centraide's program officers has shifted towards a more proactive one based on close, embedded relationships with neighbourhood stakeholders across Montreal (Centraide, 2016b).

The CIP's specificities

A shift towards trust-based funding mechanisms

The CIP was designed to address a specific issue: available funding for neighbourhood revitalization processes was limited in scope, standardized in nature and highly fragmented, as each funding source had its own set of guidelines and parameters. Neighbourhoods relying on these existing funding sources were challenged to coordinate and fit the different pieces of funding together in ways that would support the integrity of their neighbourhood's development plan. In the two years leading up to the CIP, some representatives of local roundtables had challenged Centraide to use its influence to find a solution to this problem.

As a direct response to this issue, the CIP set out to make more substantial amounts of funding available to neighbourhoods to support them in implementing their comprehensive action plans. In contrast to most funding programs' normative constraints, CIP funding would be flexible and adaptable to the different needs expressed by stakeholders on the ground.

The thinking that informed the CIP's design was aligned with research findings about the conditions and requirements for successful design, coordination and support of comprehensive community-change efforts (Karlström *et al.*, 2007; Kubisch *et al.*, 2010; Burns & Brown, 2012; Auspos & Cabaj, 2014; Hopkins, 2015). A core principle of the CIP's design was that communities should be able to articulate what kinds of outside supports they need, based on the priorities for change that local stakeholders and residents have established together. Communities receiving CIP funding could set their own goals and targets for change, including improvements to community engagement processes and dynamics, improvements to living conditions and quality of life in the neighbourhood, or systemic issues that affect the welfare of local populations.[3]

In taking this route, the CIP's originators chose a complexity-friendly funding model built on devolution of decision-making and trust in local communities' intrinsic motivation to determine and drive the changes that will most benefit them. This stands in marked contrast to other strong trends in the funding landscape (inspired by the New Public Management paradigm) that incur transaction costs for applicants and funders alike, such as competitive grant-awarding processes, payment-for-results schemes, and public–nonprofit sector contracting and procurement (Knight et al., 2017).

Based on their previous experience with funding community change efforts in Montreal, the CIP's co-architects believed that some neighbourhoods had reached a certain level of maturity in their stakeholders' ability to work together and achieve results. They considered that the conditions were there for these neighbourhoods to achieve appreciable progress in poverty reduction and in improving their residents' living conditions and quality of life.

Following up on this, five neighbourhoods were selected to receive substantial resources for implementation of their entire neighbourhood plan; these five neighbourhoods were intended to be the primary testing ground of the CIP's central intention. Twelve other neighbourhoods received more moderate amounts of funding for specific pieces of their neighbourhood development plan.

The CIP's design also featured a range of customized capacity-building supports for funded communities. This is in keeping with research findings that note that communities need to have strong and well-established collective capacity in order to be able to generate significant impacts (Gamble, 2010).

Lastly, the CIP was designated as a learning project. Because of the inherent complexity of comprehensive community-change processes, observers of the field call for a continuous learning approach that can support flexible and adaptive management strategies (Kubisch et al., 2010; Auspos & Cabaj, 2014). The CIP's evaluation, knowledge mobilization and knowledge transfer activities were designed to occur within and across funded neighbourhoods, as well as between neighbourhoods and funding partners. Lessons would be shared with other communities engaged in comparable initiatives elsewhere in Quebec, Canada and the United States.

---

[3] The CIP's website (http://pic.centraide.org/en/#) provides a brief description of community change initiatives in all 17 neighbourhoods.

Expansion of the partnership to form a funder collaborative

The comprehensive community-change research literature also points to the need for foundations to recognize the broader funding ecosystem in which they are operating. Rather than go it alone, they should reach out to prospective partners from the start and build in opportunities for still more partners to align with the initiative over time, sometimes in ways that require some adaptation of the overall scope and direction of the place-based effort (Burns & Brown, 2012).

As Centraide and the Chagnon Foundation worked to develop the project, a second key decision made was to expand the partnership beyond the two originators. The CIP's co-architects believed that a broader funder collaborative could better impact systems-level outcomes by modelling new types of funding practices, and by influencing regional policy alignment in support of poverty reduction and community change.

During the ten months leading up to and immediately following the CIP's launch, the senior leadership of both Centraide and the Chagnon Foundation leveraged their existing relationships to bring in five other philanthropic foundations with roots in Montreal.[4] After the CIP's launch, three more foundations[5] joined the CIP during the first years of its rollout, bringing the total number of foundations involved in the partnership to ten, Centraide included.

Two reasons guided the choice to look to philanthropic foundations to form a funder collaborative rather than to public sector funders, even though many of those engaged had little background with funding comprehensive community change. First, rather than attempt to create cross-sector alignment right from the start, the idea was to engage a group of more agile, independently resourced funders to build the template for funder alignment from the ground up. Second, as eligible major donors to Centraide, philanthropic foundations could be engaged in the CIP as the test case for the organization's new transformational gift strategy.

Two major public sector institutions – the City of Montreal and the Montreal Public Health Department *(Direction régionale de la santé publique de Montréal – DRSPM)* – were also approached to join the project as non-funding partners.[6] Their association was strategic, as they provide core funding (with Centraide) to the neighbourhood tables through the *Initiative montréalaise* and manage a number of other funds that support local collaborative initiatives. It was hoped that their participation in the CIP steering committee would lead them to use their leverage within their own institutions in order to foster greater alignment between CIP-funded programming and these other funding programs, as well as other policy leverage points. If these players could help to

---

4 The Pathy Family Foundation, the McConnell Foundation, the Mirella and Lino Saputo Foundation, the Silver Dollar Foundation and the Foundation of Greater Montréal.

5 The Molson Foundation, the Marcelle and Jean Coutu Foundation and the Trottier Family Foundation.

6 A third non-funding partner, the Coalition of Montreal Neighbourhood Roundtables, is discussed later in this chapter.

shift the dynamic of collaboration and alignment at the regional level, this would positively affect local communities' capacity for action.

In joining the CIP partnership, each partner foundation agreed to make a five-year financial commitment; beyond the entry-level contribution that was established, these ranged in size according to each partner's capacity. The end result: a total pooled amount of $23 million was made available over five years for communities selected for CIP support.[7] Funds would be disbursed annually according to individual partner agreements, and a steering committee was formed bringing all partners together. Centraide would act both as project manager and as funder intermediary, receiving partners' contributions and allocating funds to communities.

Negotiating funder collaboration: adapting the model to support engagement and buy-in

The CIP's original operating model represented a form of funder collaboration that placed relatively few demands on the organizations involved. Especially in the first year, the partners' role in decision-making was limited. Rather, they signed on to a project in which they would be "learners" and in which Centraide would take on both risk and responsibility as project manager, fulfilling coordination and community relations roles, providing analysis and expertise, and mediating between partners and neighbourhood roundtables.

Various aspects of the project originators' proposal appealed to the funding and institutional partners who signed on to the CIP, including the opportunity for grantmaking foundations to work together, to be better able to measure the impact of their grants, to learn about ways to support comprehensive community change efforts that were most likely to produce lasting results, and to have an effect on the broader ecosystem.

However, as most of the funding partners did not participate in the project's design, it turned out that their buy-in and engagement were somewhat transactional. Beyond the intentions laid out in the co-architects' proposal, most of the funding partners had their own interests and intentions. Each was coming at the CIP from their own particular frame of reference, whether that be social innovation, social entrepreneurship, or philanthropy's role in shaping placemaking practices and new urban development. Some funding partners were less interested than Centraide and the

---

7   These are confirmed financial commitments at the time of writing.

Chagnon Foundation in building upon existing features of an established community change ecosystem, seeking rather to open it up to new influences and different ways of thinking about and embracing change, or looking to disrupt established ways of operating and providing funding.

Before the end of the CIP's second year, it became clear that the project would need to find ways to reconcile and respond to partners' different expectations. The initial operating model was well suited to certain purposes (granting efficiency and funder learning) but, as time went on, partners had begun to express intentions and expectations that fitted better with a more integrated and high-engagement operating model in which partners would need to collaborate to establish common objectives, coordinate strategies and leveraging capacities, and work together to exercise joint influence. At the same time, if the CIP were to evolve in this direction, it might cease to be "Centraide's project", as most saw it, and become a project where risk, responsibility and authority for decision-making would be more distributed.

At the project's half-way point, shifts were made to the project's governance and operations models to try to accommodate these different intentions and ambitions.

Decentralized governance

First among these, a new governance model was proposed that allowed for differential levels of engagement among partners. Beyond statutory steering committee meetings, partners could get involved in working groups, conference calls focused on funding decisions and opportunities, and in roll-up-the-sleeves, unstaged, deep-dive working sessions with funded neighbourhoods. Those partners with less capacity or interest could simply be kept in the loop.

While these adjustments were made to respond to partners' expressed needs and expectations to step into a more active role, further adjustments may be necessary as the project continues to evolve. An emerging concern is that the pendulum may have swung too far in the direction of decentralization, without leaving enough oversight mechanisms in place to allow everyone on the steering committee to keep the overall strategic vision for the project firmly in view.

Brokering partner–community relationships and contributions

Second, Centraide shifted away from its position of sole community interface, to allow funding partners to enter into more direct relationships with funded communities. The potential advantages were clear: a more direct relationship with neighbourhoods could increase partners' sense of buy-in and commitment and allow them to identify new opportunities for funding or other supports that are connected to actual needs on the ground.

On the other hand, these new direct relationships between partners and neighbourhoods would need to be forged in a way that respects communities and helps to preserve their trust and buy-in to the CIP. Poorly brokered connections could risk disrupting local relationships that are both the bedrock of community collaborations and also the basis for trust and good communication between funders and communities.

In this context, the relational capital that Centraide had built up over the years with neighbourhood tables and other community stakeholders represented an undeniable asset, and it made sense for Centraide to help broker and mediate this linking-up process, setting the stage for direct conversations to take place between funding partners and community representatives while preventing miscues and misunderstandings.

Emergent opportunities for new partner contributions

In parallel to the core CIP-pooled funding envelope, funding partners can also channel complementary contributions to CIP neighbourhoods. This opens up the possibility for partners to grant or to leverage resources towards communities both as needs and opportunities arise, and in ways that align with their own strategic orientations beyond the CIP.

As this has happened, the CIP has also become a point of encounter between stakeholders associated with different generations of urban collective action, each responding in their own way to the complex dynamics of metropolitan development and renewal in the early 21st century: on the one hand, pragmatic comprehensive community-change traditions rooted in specific neighbourhoods, and on the other, newer movements focused on reclaiming and redesigning public spaces, led by emerging social entrepreneurs that are not tied to place or neighbourhood in the same way as older nonprofits (Hamel, 2016).

The points of encounter between the CIP originators' intentions and foundation partners' other involvements can be both generative and disruptive as they play out on the ground. In attempting to broker some of these meeting points and offer a more curated experience of joining up the established and the new in some CIP-funded neighbourhoods, the challenge for Centraide has been to strike a balance, "adding new ingredients to the recipe without completely changing the dish that we are cooking".[8]

In the best case scenario, the CIP's focus on place – and the granular, real-world challenges that it presents – offers an opportunity for funding partners to reach a negotiated understanding of the most valuable contribution that each one can make, based on their respective specializations as funders (Kippin & Reid, 2015). However, this challenges the partners to arrive at a common reading of the environment in which they are operating, one that they did not share at the project's outset. In this context, the curated, on-the-ground experiences become sites of *bricolage*[9] that in themselves are likely to yield insights, whether they succeed or fail.

---

8   Interview with CIP program director, May 29, 2018.

9   In social innovation scholarship and practice, the term *bricolage* refers to the recombining of existing and new ideas and elements to form something novel.

The CIP, collective impact and funder-grantee relations

Across much of the landscape of North American collective impact practice, funders play a lead role in convening multi-stakeholder initiatives that include their own grantees, staying on as active participants in the governance bodies and working groups of the initiative, and sometimes even positioning themselves to play a backbone role. This is consistent with the "grasstops" orientation of many of the earlier writings on collective impact, which place an emphasis on bringing together decision-makers and influential people to channel change. Numerous place-based funders, including the United Ways in the United States[10] (United Way Worldwide, 2013), have embraced this understanding of their role in collective impact.

More recent reframings of collective impact criticize the grasstops orientation of these earlier writings, pointing to a need to pay more attention to power relations and equity issues within collective impact partnerships (Williams & Marxer, 2014; McAfee et al., 2015). Other voices echo these points, shining the light even more directly on the funder–fundee power dynamic and noting that its distortions become even more acute when foundations act as both funder and member of an implementing coalition (Kubisch et al., 2010; DP Evaluation, 2012). Collective impact funders themselves have begun to grapple with how to better bring an equity lens into their work (Collective Impact Forum and GEO, 2015).

Neither entirely funder-led (grasstops) nor entirely community-led, the CIP is at the confluence of these two dynamics. While its goals and supports are funder-defined, the CIP has, from the start, respected and deferred to local processes for priority-setting and implementation; community stakeholders convene and facilitate their own collective impact initiatives at the neighbourhood level. Thus issues around equity, engagement, voice and representation take on a nested dimension, applying both within communities as well as to the relationship between CIP partners and grantee communities.

In this hybrid configuration, the CIP partnership has been grappling with its own set of challenges in relation to constituent engagement, equity and power-sharing. The CIP partners' main concern has been with ensuring that community stakeholders have a voice in the initiative's governance and operations.

There are two levels, or dimensions, to the process of opening up to grantee communities and bringing in their voice. The first dimension involves instilling greater openness in the relationship

---

10 United Ways in Canada have not embraced collective impact in quite the same explicit way, adopting instead a language of "community impact".

through transparency and feedback mechanisms. The second involves giving grantee communities a voice in decision-making about the project.

Trusting relationships are crucial to the success of both place-based philanthropy and complexity-friendly funding (Karlström et al., 2007; Knight et al., 2017). Observers have argued that the very legitimacy of place-based philanthropy's changemaking ambitions and capacity depends on its ability to be transparent about goals, strategies, underlying assumptions and expectations, as well as on a willingness to engage in an ongoing dialogue with other important stakeholders (Brown, 2012; Fehler-Cabral et al., 2016). At the time of the CIP's inception, the project could draw upon an existing wellspring of trust and goodwill between Centraide and Montreal neighbourhoods. However, that trust should not be taken for granted and will need to be maintained throughout the entire project.

Like others in the field (Albright, 2016), CIP partners have come to understand that if they want to maintain the foundations of trust and buy-in from local communities, they need to consider setting up mechanisms for feedback and dialogue with local communities. Adopting and modelling openness practices takes on even more importance in a project, like the CIP, that is predicated on shared learning. In order for everyone to learn from failure as well as from success, "intel" from the ground needs to be shared freely. As risk in the project is unevenly distributed, the partners who are less exposed to risk have come to realize that it is up to them to demonstrate that they wish to create conditions where failure is not only allowed but also welcomed as an opportunity for learning.

The CIP partners are aware of the challenges here; because of the inherent power dynamic in the funding relationship, grantees will often self-censor in their communications with funders, holding back on useful feedback. In cases where it is not possible to create anonymous feedback mechanisms,[11] funders need to model transparency, for instance by publicly sharing the feedback that they receive, and they need to demonstrate that feedback will be used to make improvements (Ranghelli & Moore, 2015). As project lead, Centraide has already made observable efforts in this direction, making changes to the CIP's parameters and capacity-building supports in response to grantee feedback.

Beyond feedback: voice, representation and power-sharing

Issues of genuine constituent representation likewise pose challenges in collective impact initiatives in which funders play a dominant role. The voice of communities is nominally represented in the CIP's governance, as the coordinator of the CMTQ (Coalition of Montreal Neighbourhood Roundtables) sits on the steering committee as one of the project's strategic

---

11 For example, the grantee perception reports that the Center for Effective Philanthropy issues for the benefit of client foundations, or the platform created by the Philampify initiative of the National Committee for Responsive Philanthropy.

partners. Even if the CMTQ were to feel authorized and empowered by its own membership to represent community voice on the steering committee, the presence of one community voice alongside thirteen other partners, most of them funders, reproduces a significant imbalance in perspective between funders and communities.

As the partners search to ensure less tokenistic and more substantive engagement of community voices in the project, they may once again turn to lessons imparted by other funders, and consider different mechanisms for different purposes (Collective Impact Forum, 2018, p. 19).

One opportunity presents itself in connection with the CIP's systems-change ambitions, discussed in the next section. The CIP aims not only to help communities to make greater progress in their poverty reduction efforts, but also to tackle systemic barriers that can impede neighbourhoods' ability to move towards the change targets that they have established. Concretely, this would imply designing a strategy in consultation or in coordination with community stakeholders, based on the barriers and obstacles that they have identified. At the very least, these kinds of strategies would require setting up a dialogue mechanism allowing neighbourhood stakeholders to identify and share the systemic obstacles or barriers that they are encountering, and that might fall within the partners' sphere of influence. If this were to happen, the CMTQ could take on a more explicit role as an interface and spokesperson for the neighbourhood tables, helping to relay the issues that affect them locally but that are beyond their control to change. Here, to echo the recommendations of Dewar (2010) and Auspos and Cabaj (2014), it would be important to allow neighbourhood actors to define the influence strategies in which they can take leadership, wherever possible and relevant.

Changing systems

The CIP's aims for systems change are in line with recent writings which argue that, in order to really tackle complex problems, collective impact initiatives need to expand their scope beyond programmatic outcomes, such as improving service coordination in a given area, to focus their efforts on policy and systems change.

Similarly, the current generation of place-based philanthropy in support of comprehensive community change recognizes that broader policies and market trends shape and constrain what local initiatives can undertake and hope to accomplish; these include public and philanthropic funding programs and investment policies, policies and regulations related to housing, urban planning and commercial development, and procurement and local hiring practices in the public and private sectors (Dewar, 2010; Hopkins, 2015). In seeking "systems change", current-generation initiatives aim to bring about sustainable changes to policies and practices within the broader ecosystem, in order to create an enabling environment for transformations to take place at the local level (Auspos & Cabaj, 2014; Mack *et al.*, 2014).

However, past experiences reveal that local communities tend to be unable to catalyze systems change on their own. Other actors with access to decision-making, including funders, are in a better position than local communities themselves to work to change practices and policies that hamper local revitalization efforts (Aspen Institute, 2012; Auspos & Cabaj, 2014). In recent years, this understanding has led foundations involved in supporting community change to carry out parallel strategies focusing on policy and systems change (Hopkins, 2015).

Systems change strategies may target practices in both the private and public sectors. Some comprehensive community-change initiatives have specifically sought to engage private-sector players to support local revitalization efforts in new ways, opening up new financing channels for impact investing or seeking to nudge urban development trajectories in a more inclusive and equitable direction (Mt. Auburn Associates, 2012; Ferris & Hopkins, 2015).

In keeping with these trends within the field, the CIP's funding and strategic partners have recognized that they have a role to play in leveraging opportunities and addressing systemic constraints that fall beyond local communities' range of influence. At the project's half-way point, opportunities have arisen to leverage new resources for broad strategies that span many neighbourhoods, and whose regional applications may extend beyond the CIP. These opportunities include:

- the alignment of funding strategies to fill gaps and better support the breadth and spectrum of local food-systems work taking place across almost half of CIP-funded neighbourhoods
- pulling in new resources and bringing new partners to the table to help CIP neighbourhood coalitions to become leaders in the redevelopment of abandoned industrial sites, quarries, even disused racetracks
- exploring opportunities to establish a public–private–philanthropic investment fund for building and renovating community infrastructure spaces, such as hubs for community agencies and social enterprises in the neighbourhoods they serve across the city – this last opportunity aligns with an emerging trend towards collaborative place-based impact investing (Ashley & Ovalle, 2018)

The CIP may also be able to act as a catalyst for alignment within and between public institutions. In Montreal's decentralized city government system, this is not a simple thing to achieve. As CIP neighbourhoods work to implement their locally prioritized development projects, many have run up against regulatory barriers at the municipal level. It was hoped that having the city's senior social development official on the CIP steering committee would make it easier to lift some of these barriers. The official in question has in fact taken a first step in this direction, calling a meeting of social development program directors across all the city's geographic jurisdictions in order to begin a discussion about better program alignment in CIP neighbourhoods.

In the future, actions to create an enabling environment for CIP neighbourhood development plans will likely call on other forms of cross-departmental alignment within the city administration that go well beyond the social development branch, including housing, economic development, urban planning and land use, and transportation and public works.

Beyond the CIP, other developments within the regional funding and policy ecosystem may also be working to nudge players towards greater alignment. As an example, the City of Montreal's Policy on Social Development, launched in 2017 as the result of a lengthy engagement process involving over a thousand stakeholders and citizens, targets alignment both among city departments and across institutional boundaries, recognizing foundations among its major social development partners (Ville de Montréal, 2017).

As this illustrates, CIP partners will not be alone in working towards these kinds of outcomes, and indeed, the boundaries between the CIP and other processes of influence are likely to blur. Many CIP partners are also participants in various other multi-stakeholder regional governance initiatives in areas such as housing and built infrastructure, homelessness, education and food systems, all of which may at various points have cause to advocate for better cross-sector institutional alignment. A dense webbing of networks overlays the boundaries between these different regional governance spaces, allowing intentions to form and opportunities to be identified in ways that loop back and forth between the CIP and these spaces. As governments have increasingly come to cultivate private and third-sector contributions towards developing innovative solutions to complex social problems, these configurations are typical of the new networked governance that has come to shape policy and programs within cities and regions (Tibbitt, 2011; Tomalty, 2013; Cattacin & Zimmer, 2016).

The CIP's significance to Montreal's funding ecology and beyond

The CIP's arrival in the Montreal landscape can be read in a number of ways. With the inauguration of a trust-based model that provides flexible support for community-set priorities, the CIP represents a significant innovation in the community change funding ecology. Recognizing this, many community stakeholders have heralded its arrival, stating that the CIP has helped to fill a very real funding gap.

The CIP has offered Centraide the means to act on ambitions that it had long nurtured for its work in place-based philanthropy. It has also signalled a significant "win" for Centraide as it has sought to position itself in a community leadership capacity, as an influential broker with the ability to set agendas. This accomplishment, for all its rootedness in a specific context and history, may point to a way forward for other United Ways that are looking to focus their identity and renew their campaign strategies. At the same time, in choosing the route of convening and facilitating a funder collaborative, there is a tension to navigate between upholding a community leadership positioning and engaging in the type of adaptive, humble systems leadership required to engage a group of foundations as peers in a collaborative venture.

The CIP also signals a shift in Montreal's funding landscape, in which philanthropy takes on an even greater role in setting the parameters and sculpting the contours of comprehensive community change work in Montreal. A shift of this nature has particular reverberations in Quebec where, in comparison with the rest of Canada, the state has continued to play a stronger role both in setting and delivering on social policy and in recognizing and supporting civil society and third-sector organizations (Hamel & Jouve, 2006; Laforest, 2011; Savard *et al.*, 2015; see also Chapter 1 in this volume by Sylvain A. Lefèvre and Peter Elson).

With its avowed intentions to engage with policy and to try to influence certain development trajectories within the region, the CIP partnership also signals philanthropy's concomitant rise to greater prominence within regional governance networks. In Montreal as elsewhere, philanthropic foundations are increasingly recognized and sought out for their role in these spaces of networked governance (Jung & Harrow, 2015; Funders' Forum on Sustainable Cities, 2016). As Jung and Harrow (2015) contend, foundations' resource independence allows them a high degree of self-organization, which in turn lends them a stronger influence, relative to their size and numbers, within complex governance processes. Observers of philanthropic foundations' increasing presence and power in these spaces have consistently raised issues of legitimacy, transparency and accountability (Jung & Harrow, 2015; Lefèvre & Berthiaume, 2017). CIP partners would do well to engage proactively with these issues, in dialogue with the CIP's proponents and detractors, and seek to articulate their understanding of their social licence to occupy these spaces and of their corresponding accountabilities.

Implications for philanthropy and philanthropic practice beyond the CIP

For most key informants consulted in the original study that helped to shape this chapter, beyond any results and learnings that the CIP engenders for its partners during its 5-year span, the initiative's real interest lies in the ripple effects that it has beyond itself.

1 For some, the CIP is first and foremost a philanthropic action model (co-investment with joint strategy) that should be scaled out to augment and sustain foundations' support for community change efforts. Alongside the benefits (greater coherence, increased impact) that CIP partners associate with funder collaboration, a few project stakeholders and external key informants noted that funders working together can also have perverse effects.

Indeed, issues about the boundaries of the CIP – where it starts and leaves off, what's in and what's out – are already being felt within communities. Organizations in some neighbourhoods already had an existing tradition of relationships with specific CIP foundations before the CIP began. Since the CIP's inception, ambiguity now surrounds these relationships: what is to remain independent, and what is to be integrated into the CIP? Interests may diverge here, but the question invites a reflection regarding anticipated and unanticipated consequences.

By creating a single gateway for federating community support from most of the major philanthropic foundations active in Montreal, the CIP or its successor could have the effect of reducing the diversity of funding options available to communities, and in particular to those that have been turned down for CIP support. One respondent illustrated this point by referring to a similar experience observed elsewhere, where the bargaining power of grantees was reduced when they faced a united front of funders.

2 In the second ripple-effect scenario, the CIP serves as a demonstration project with the purpose of influencing public policies and practices that have an impact on community-led change. Here the evidence suggests that the intended influence rarely happens as planned, particularly in an era of constrained public budgets and funding programs. For one, philanthropic and government funding tend to occupy distinct and complementary niches in the comprehensive community-change field (Aspen Institute, 2012). Secondly, where comprehensive community initiatives have succeeded in influencing public policy and practice, this has not been because of a demonstration effect, but rather the result of active and focused advocacy efforts (Hopkins, 2015).

280 Centraide's Collective Impact Project: Poverty reduction in Montréal

3

A more promising trend in the field of support for comprehensive community initiatives appears to be the emergence of structures that foster complementarity and linkage of philanthropic, public and private sector resources (Ferris & Hopkins, 2015). For now, these structures remain the exception rather than the rule, but their ability to leverage and aggregate more significant financial resources makes it possible to support more ambitious and longer-term initiatives.

Negotiating these kinds of hybrid structures requires philanthropic, private, social and state actors to have a shared understanding at the outset of their respective roles and competencies. However, it cannot be taken for granted that these different actors' understanding and assumptions about each other all line up (Healy & Donnelly-Cox, 2016). The Integration Initiative of Living Cities[12] illustrates the complexity inherent in this quest for a shared understanding. Launched by philanthropic foundations, the Integration Initiative sought to mobilize public sector partners to become co-sponsors of local community change initiatives. This met with less success than expected. Government stakeholders were inclined to see foundations as substitutes for state action rather than as collaborators, and less inclined as a result to define a distinct and complementary role that they themselves could play within the initiatives (Hecht, 2014).

Even when this shared understanding can be reached, stakeholders aiming to reach cross-sector alignment run up against challenges relating to the fundamental differences in each sector's operating environment. Different accountability pressures, different governance and regulatory environments establish limits as well as parameters of possibility to be explored (Knight *et al.*, 2017).

---

12 https://www.livingcities.org/work

Conclusion

The CIP's central hypothesis is that:

→ [...] the action of a certain number of funders, if it is well organized and coordinated among them, will allow for greater local and regional coherence and consistency and will have a more powerful collective impact than the isolated outcomes achieved so far.

Centraide, 2016a, p. 36 [our translation].

The implications of this hypothesis are different depending on where attention is focused. At one level, the CIP offers itself up as a means to influence how communities work together, nudging them to shift the emphasis of their collective action more towards outcomes, towards the changes to be accomplished.

At another level, for partners and observers of Montreal's CIP, the CIP has established itself as a test case for a number of other things beyond this – in particular the effects of new philanthropic strategies upon Montreal's place-based funding ecosystem and upon regional governance networks.

The lessons that the CIP offers up at the end of the project will be of interest to practitioners and scholars engaged with any of the above subjects. In addition, the CIP's ongoing development will be of interest to collective impact practitioners who are grappling with the challenges of openness and authentic engagement between funders and grantees.

Comprehensive community-change initiatives operate in complex environments: the issues that concern them are deeply interconnected, and they seek to engage a broad and diverse range of people, organizations and structures. Rather than measure these initiatives' success by their ability to achieve predetermined objectives, funders in these environments instead need to embrace learning itself as the return on their investment (Auspos & Cabaj, 2014). This is a difficult commitment to make and follow through on, as it challenges current notions of accountability and requires that funders accept new risks (Knight *et al.*, 2017). If the CIP is able to deliver on this intention for its own stakeholders, it should be able to generate lessons and insights that are nuanced and complex enough to allow the rest of the field to advance its own understanding.

Three key takeaways

1 A shift towards trust-based funding mechanisms is disruptive both for funders and grantees. Even when this shift comes as a response to grantee communities' wishes and desires, one shouldn't underestimate the adjustments required on all sides.

2 There are no pathways to sure outcomes. Instead of defining success by the reaching of specific change targets, leadership and partners should map out the shared learning intentions that all key stakeholders can get behind.

3 Clarity and alignment need to be sought early on around purpose, leadership and governance mechanisms; these points of shared understanding should be reviewed and revisited at regular intervals, and the funder circle expanded beyond foundations to include public-sector partners.

References

Albright, R (2016, August 9) 'Four ways to bridge the grantee–grantmaker power gap in collective impact', *Stanford Social Innovation Review. Retrieved from:* https://ssir.org/articles/entry/grantee_grantmaker_gap_in_collective_impact

Ashley, SR & J Ovalle (2018) *Investing Together: Emerging approaches in collaborative place-based impact investing.* Washington, DC: Urban Institute

Aspen Institute (2012) *Listening to Voices from the Field III: Implications for place-based giving.* Transcript from Council on Foundations Annual Conference 2011. Washington, DC: Aspen Institute

Auspos, P & M Cabaj (2014). *Complexity and Community Change: Managing adaptively to improve effectiveness.* Washington, DC: Aspen Institute

Brady, S & JS Juster (2016, April 17) 'Collective impact principles of practice: Putting collective impact into action' Retrieved from: https://collectiveimpactforum.org/resources/collective-impact-principles-practice

Brown, P (2012) 'Changemaking: Building strategic competence', *The Foundation Review, 4(1)*, 81–93

Brunet, L (2014) 'Learning to tango on a tightrope: Implementing a collective impact approach', *The Philanthropist*, 26(1), 21–34

Burns, T & P Brown (2012) *Lessons from a National Scan of Comprehensive Place-based Philanthropic Initiatives.* Final report prepared for the Heinz Endowments. Philadelphia, PA: Urban Ventures Group

Cabaj, M (2011) *Cities Reducing Poverty: How vibrant communities are creating comprehensive solutions to the most complex problems of our time.* Waterloo, ON: Tamarack Institute for Community Engagement

Cabaj, M & L Weaver (2016) *Collective Impact 3.0: An evolving framework for community change.* Waterloo, ON: Tamarack Institute

Cattacin, S & A Zimmer (2016) 'Urban Governance and Social Innovations' in Brandsen, T, Cattacin, S, Evers, A & A Zimmer (eds.) *Social Innovations in the Urban Context* (pp. 21–44). Cham, Switzerland : Springer International

Centraide of Greater Montreal (2015) *Centraide, plus pertinent que jamais. Plan d'évolution philanthropique 2015–20.* Montreal: Centraide of Greater Montreal

Centraide of Greater Montreal (2016a) *Mémoire déposé par Centraide du Grand Montréal à la consultation publique sur le 3e plan d'action gouvernemental en matière de lutte contre la pauvreté et l'exclusion sociale au Québec.* Retrieved from Centraide of Greater Montreal website: https://medias.centraide.org/Docs/Memoire_Centraide_du_Grand Montreal_2016.pdf

Centraide of Greater Montreal (2016b) *Evaluation Report: 2010–15 social development strategy.* Retrieved from Centraide of Greater Montreal website: https://www.issuelab.org/resources/27004/27004.pdf?download=true

Christens, BD & PT Inzeo (2015) 'Widening the view: Situating collective impact among frameworks for community-led change', *Community Development, 46:4, pp. 420–35*

Collective Impact Forum and Grantmakers for Effective Organizations (2015) 'Collaborating to see all constituents reach their full potential: memorandum on research and resources on equity and collective impact.' Retrieved from: http://collectiveimpactforum.org/resources/collaborating-see-all-constituents-reach-their-full-potential-memorandum-research-and?utm_source=newsletter&utm_medium=email&utm_content=Read%20Now%20%3E&utm_campaign=20151026EquityGeoResearchScan

Collective Impact Forum (2018) 'Advancing funders' openness practices: Lessons for the field from the Collective Impact Funder Action Learning Lab.' Retrieved from: http://collectiveimpactforum.org/resources/advancing-funders%E2%80%99-openness-practices-lessons-field-collective-impact-funder-action

Dewar, T (2010) 'Aligning with Outside Resources and Power', Chapter 4 in Kubisch, AC, Auspos, P, Brown, P, & T Dewar (eds.), *Voices from the Field III: Lessons and Challenges from Two Decades of Community Change Efforts* (pp 77–88). Washington. DC: Aspen Institute

DP Evaluation (2012) *A Funder Conundrum: Choices that funders face in bringing about positive social change*. London: Association of Charitable Foundations

Fehler-Cabral, G, James, J, Preskill, H & M Long (2016) 'The art and science of place-based philanthropy: Themes from a national convening', *The Foundation Review*, 8(2), 84–96

Ferris, JM & E Hopkins (2015) 'Moving Forward: Addressing spatially concentrated poverty in the 21st century' in Hopkins, EM & JM Ferris (eds.) *Place-Based Initiatives in the Context of Public Policy and Markets: Moving to higher ground* (pp. 83–6). Los Angeles: Sol Price School of Public Policy, University of Southern California

Funders' Forum on Sustainable Cities (2016) *Philanthropy Input Paper to the New Urban Agenda*. Brussels: European Foundation Centre

Gamble, J (2010) *Evaluating Vibrant Communities 2002–10*. Waterloo (ON): Tamarack Institute for Community Engagement

Graddy, EA & DL Morgan (2006) 'Community foundations, organizational strategy, and public policy', *Nonprofit and Voluntary Sector Quarterly*, 35(4), 605–30

Hamel, P (2016) 'Mouvement social, une notion désuète? Les nouvelles formes de l'action collective et le renouvellement des perspectives théoriques' in Petropoulou, C, Vitopoulo, A & C Tsavadaroglou (eds.). **Κοινωνικά κινήματα πόλης και περιφέρειας** / Urban and Regional Social Movements. Thessaloniki, Research Group Invisible Cities: 381–407

Hamel, P & B Jouve (2006) *Un modèle québécois ? Gouvernance et participation dans la gestion publique*. Montréal: Les Presses de l'Université de Montréal

Healy, J and G Donnelly-Cox (2016) 'The Evolving State Relationship: Implications of "Big Societies" and shrinking states' in Jung, T, Phillips, SD & J Harrow (eds.) *The Routledge Companion to Philanthropy* (pp. 200–12). Oxford, UK: Routledge

Hecht, B (2014) 'Reflections on Living Cities' Integration Initiative'. Retrieved from Living Cities website: https://www.livingcities.org/resources/267-reflections-on-living-cities-integration-initiative

Hopkins, EM (2015) 'The State of Place-based Initiatives' in Hopkins, EM & JM Ferris (eds.) *Place-based Initiatives in the Context of Public Policy and Markets: Moving to Higher Ground* (pp. 9–30). Los Angeles: Sol Price School of Public Policy, University of Southern California

Institute for Voluntary Action Research (2015) *Place-based Funding: A briefing paper*. London, UK: Institute for Voluntary Action Research

Jung, T & J Harrow (2015) 'New development: Philanthropy in networked governance – treading with care', *Public Money and Management*, 35(1), 47–52

Kania, J & M Kramer (2016, May 16) 'Advancing the practice of collective impact' [Blog post]. Retrieved from: https://www.fsg.org/blog/advancing-practice-collective-impact

Karlström, M, Brown, P, Chaskin, R & H Richman (2007) 'Embedded philanthropy and community change'. Chicago: Chapin Hall Center for Children at the University of Chicago

Kippin, H & RS Reid (2015) 'A new funding ecology: a blueprint for action'. Retrieved from the Collaborate CIC website: https://collaboratecic.com/a-new-funding-ecology-a-blueprint-for-action-6065d12b3ce4

Klein, J.-L & C Champagne (2011) 'La lutte contre la pauvreté et l'exclusion sociale: approches et stratégies institutionnelles' in Klein, J.-L et C Champagne (eds.) *Initiatives locales et lutte contre la pauvreté et l'exclusion* (pp. 31–44). Québec: Presses de l'Université du Québec

Knight, AD, Lowe, T, Brossard, M & J Wilson (2017) 'A whole new world: Funding and commissioning in complexity'. Collaborate and Newcastle University. Retrieved from the Collaborate CIC website: https://collaboratecic.com/a-whole-new-world-funding-and-commissioning-in-complexity-12b6bdc2abd8

Kubisch, AC, Auspos, P, Brown, P & T Dewar (2010) *Voices from the Field III: Lessons and Challenges from Two Decades of Community Change Efforts*. Washington. DC: Aspen Institute.

Laforest, R (2011) 'L'étude du tiers secteur au Québec: comment saisir la spécificité québécoise?' *Politiques et Sociétés, 30(1)*, 43–55. DOI 10.7202/1006058ar

Lefèvre, S & A Berthiaume (2017) 'Les partenariats entre secteur public et fondations philanthropiques au Québec: genèse, contestation et épilogue d'une réforme de l'action publique', *Revue française d'administration publique 2017/3* (N° 163), 491–506

Longtin, D & J Rochman (2015) *Les enjeux du développement social à Montréal: évolution entre 1998 et 2014.* Cahier ET1503. Montréal : Centre de recherche sur les innovations sociales et l'économie sociale (CRISES).

Mack, KP, Preskill, H, Keddy, J & MK Jhawar (2014) 'Redefining expectations for place-based philanthropy', *The Foundation Review*, 6(4), 30–43

McAfee, M, Blackwell, AG & J Bell (2015) *Equity: The soul of collective impact.* Oakland, CA: PolicyLink

Mount Auburn Associates (2012) *The Integration Initiative Midterm Outcome Report.* Somerville, MA: Mt. Auburn Associates

Opération veille et soutien stratégiques (2017) *Riches de notre histoire: regard rétrospectif sur l'histoire récente du développement collectif au Québec.* Retrieved from Opération veille et soutien stratégiques website: http://www.operationvss.ca/

Paarlberg, LE & SS Meinhold (2012) 'Using institutional theory to explore local variations in United Way's community impact model', *Nonprofit and Voluntary Sector Quarterly*, 41(5), 826–49

Pereša, L & O Viens (2015) 'Rencontre avec Lili-Anna Pereša' in Institut Mallet (ed.) *Écosystème philanthropique: perspectives, perceptions et échanges.* Proceedings of the 2015 Sommet sur la culture philanthropique, Montreal (pp. 137–57). Quebec: Institut Mallet

Ranghelli, L & Y Moore (2015, June 8) 'Are nonprofits ready to give foundations direct feedback?' *Nonprofit Quarterly.* Retrieved from: https://nonprofitquarterly.org/2015/06/08/are-nonprofits-ready-to-give-foundations-direct-feedback/.

Savard, S, Bourque, D & R Lachapelle, R (2015) 'Third sector organizations in Québec and the new public action in community development', *Canadian Journal of Nonprofit and Social Economy Research*, 6(2), 28–41

Tibbitt, J (2011) *Localism, Place-making and Social Innovation.* PASCAL International Observatory, Policy Challenge Paper 2

Tomalty, R (2013) *Sustainable Cities: The role for philanthropy in promoting urban sustainability.* Toronto: Canadian Environmental Grantmakers' Network

United Way Worldwide (2013) *Charting a Course for Change: Advancing education, income and health through collective impact.* Retrieved from the United Way website: https://www.unitedway.org/blog/charting-a-course-for-change#

Ville de Montréal (2017) *Politique de développement social.* Retrieved from: http://ville.montreal.qc.ca/portal/page?_pageid=8258,142580108&_dad=portal&_schema=PORTAL

Walzer, N, Weaver, L & C McGuire (2016) 'Collective impact approaches and community development issues', *Community Development*, 47(2), 156–66

Weaver, L (2014) 'Q & A with John Kania and Fay Hanleybrown', *The Philanthropist*, 26(1), 125–32

Weaver, L (2016) 'Possible: Transformational change in collective impact', *Community Development*, 47(2), 274–83

Williams, J & S Marxer (2014, September 4) 'Bringing an equity lens to collective impact'. Retrieved from: https://collectiveimpactforum.org/sites/default/files/EquityandCollectiveImpact_UrbanStrategiesCouncil.pdf

Wolff, T (2016) 'Ten places where collective impact gets it wrong', *Global Journal of Community Psychology Practice*, 21. Retrieved from: http://www.gjcpp.org/en/resource.php?issue=21&resource=200.

Part three
Chapter thirteen

Foundation House: More than just sharing space

Jehad Aliweiwi, Marcel Lauzière and Bruce Lawson

→ "It has been said that foundations are the first to demand collaboration amongst grant recipients and the last to collaborate amongst themselves; we wanted to provide a visible and tangible demonstration that this was not the case here."

Bruce Lawson

In May 2014, following a conference of philanthropic organizations held in Banff, Alberta, the three authors of this chapter[1] found ourselves discussing the mundane but always important topic of office space on the journey back to Toronto. We knew one another by professional reputation, but not personally. Yet we were peers in the rarified world of foundation management. As such, we had all found ourselves, coincidentally, contending with a familiar dilemma: the need for new digs.

In the case of the Counselling Foundation of Canada, Bruce felt the organization required a new space. His office at the time was located in downtown Toronto in a cramped space which needed renovation to accommodate a growing staff team, and where the boardroom was both a substantial part of the total square footage and highly underused. For Marcel, the Lawson Foundation had recently made a decision to relocate from London, Ont., to Toronto, and they were looking for the right workspace. Jehad, who runs the Laidlaw Foundation, realized its offices were underused and impractical. In addition, their landlord was busy making several upgrades throughout the building, which meant Laidlaw might have been faced with a decision to relocate sooner or later.

As we were commiserating about our respective real estate headaches, a few other executives from other foundations chimed in with their own stories. A pattern was emerging, and a practical idea soon followed: what about sharing space?

The mere notion of combining resources seemed out of character. Foundations, as we all knew, tended to be the lone wolves of the philanthropic world. We expect the organizations that accept our grants to collaborate and carry out the work we support cooperatively and inclusively. Yet, from many years of experience, we

---

[1] Bruce Lawson is president of the Counselling Foundation of Canada. Marcel Lauzière is president and CEO of the Lawson Foundation. Jehad Aliweiwi is the executive director of the Laidlaw Foundation. The three founding organizations have collective philanthropic assets worth approximately $250 million. For clarity, this chapter occasionally uses the first-person plural to represent the voice of the three founders.

understood that foundations aren't inclined to work that way themselves. Those of us fortunate enough to manage these endowments are keenly aware of the fact that most foundations and their boards prefer to operate independently. It's true that as a sub-sector of the philanthropic world, we belong to various umbrella organizations and convene regularly for conferences or other industry events. But we don't, by definition, need to go out into the world to secure resources; we provide resources to others. And so when it comes to the day-to-day business of managing our investment portfolio, vetting applications and directing funds, we do our own thing as foundations.

In other words, while "shacking up", as Bruce likes to put it, seemed like a straightforward solution to an ordinary problem, the prospect clearly demanded more than just a mechanical approach. It would entail a shift in thinking, a change in outlook about our place in the philanthropic world, vis-à-vis one another and outside organizations generally. Sharing meant becoming more public and less private.

The potential benefit, we should stress, was not at all theoretical. As will be explained later in this chapter, there's a fast-growing movement – among small businesses, real estate investors, social enterprises, nonprofits and even a few foundations – towards co-location or shared workspaces. Bruce had visited the Centre for Social Innovation (CSI) (McConnell Foundation, n.d), a shared space for social entrepreneurs located in two converted industrial buildings in downtown Toronto on several occasions. He was taken with the way that the building, with its many common-area spaces, served as a kind of civic stage where people from different organizations would run into one another and share ideas.

What was evident, in fact, is that the narrow economic and logistical benefits associated with sharing offices were merely part of a much larger package. The surging demand for shared space flows from the recognition that many creative and socially minded organizations depend heavily on access to ideas and fresh ways of tackling problems. Innovation, increasingly, is not a solitary task, to be conducted within well-fortified corporate walls.

Of course, we live in a technology-driven age when knowledge and data circulate freely, and at unprecedented speed. But, perhaps paradoxically, the human element remains equally important. As any scientist will attest, the conversations with colleagues in the pub or the random encounters on the way to the coffee machine are indispensable elements within any discovery ecosystem.

In sum, we saw the possibility of sharing space as an opportunity to not merely solve our real estate headaches but to try something different, and perhaps create an opportunity to push the world of foundation management outside its comfort zone. We understood that, in taking this step, we were attempting something very new, with very few operating models that could provide us with guidance when we encountered the inevitable potholes. But knowing something about how the world of collaborative work was changing in so many positive and constructive ways, we felt this step was a risk well worth taking.

Foundation House, which opened its doors in December 2015 on an 11,000 sq.-ft. floor in an office building in mid-town Toronto, is the result of that casual conversation that began on the way home from Banff in 2014. Besides our three founding foundations, it has seven "roomies", as we affectionately refer to our "tenant partners".[2] There is also a busy shared kitchen and a boardroom/convening space that is constantly filled with people who have come to Foundation House for various events, workshops, seminars, convening activities and other social activities relating to philanthropic work.

On the wall next to the main entrance is a framed copy of the Philanthropic Community's Declaration of Action (in English and French), a June 2015 commitment to respond to the Truth and Reconciliation Commission's recommendations to the charitable sector (Pearson *et al.*, 2015). This document, which includes the signatures of our three foundations as well as some of our "roomies", not only offers principles for the charitable sector at large; it is fundamental to the way we've conceived of this project.

The journey that led to the establishment of Foundation House required not just good will and collaboration, but also plenty of trial and error. We broke new ground. We have made some mistakes, and we hope we learned from them. In truth, the learning is non-stop. This chapter builds on the Foundation House Case Study, which was published about six months after the doors opened, and seeks to provide a roadmap of how and why we got here, as well as a provocation for other members of Canada's philanthropic world to consider our experiences in terms of their own operations and relationships with the charitable sector.

---

2 Canadian Environmental Grantmakers Network, CERIC, Community Foundations of Canada, Grantbook, Ontario Non-profit Network, Philanthropic Foundations of Canada and the Circle on Philanthropy and Aboriginal People in Canada.

Clusters, creativity and shared spaces

→ "By sitting together, we can think up new ideas and schemes and create more synergies."

Marcel Lauzière

Creative individuals tend to cluster, in both time and space. This abundantly well-documented phenomenon includes examples as diverse as the writers and artists who converged on the Left Bank in Paris in the 1920s, the skilled glass artisans who gravitated to Venice from the 13th century onwards (History of Murano Glass, n.d.) and the computer pioneers drawn to Stanford University and Palo Alto in the 1960s. Much more recently, the University of Toronto geographer and author Richard Florida has described both the economic and social gains made by cities that understand how to attract and retain creative people.

Likewise, clustering is a well-understood form of economic behaviour, with commercial entities (from retailers to manufacturers, high-tech firms and other types of businesses) establishing themselves in particular neighbourhoods or regions that are home to many competing firms. Previous and current examples would include everything from Manhattan's Diamond district to the insurers that have historically clustered in the City of London, Toronto's mining finance firms and garment district, and the film industry in Los Angeles. While the individual entities may compete with one another for customers, these regions attract talent, capital and new ideas.

Since about the early 2000s, yet another form of clustering has appeared on the innovation landscape. Regions like San Francisco/San Jose, Toronto/Waterloo and Boston/Cambridge have seen the emergence of incubators and accelerators, which are purpose-built spaces that bring start-ups, entrepreneurs, venture capital firms, researchers and others under one roof. These places are designed to foster interaction and are guided by the assumption that there are broad-based benefits associated with creating spaces meant to encourage random encounters. In cases like MaRS, a Toronto incubator/accelerator geared at domains like green energy and biomedical research, the building – a renovated early-20th-century hospital with two modern office towers built at either end – is embedded in and connected to a cluster of downtown research hospitals as well as the University of Toronto.

It is perhaps not a coincidence that Ontario entities like CSI, Innovation Works in London or the Ottawa Impact Hub have emerged at roughly the same time as the incubator/accelerator sector, and are guided by similar assumptions about the social nature of work, creativity and innovation. The popularity of commercial shared workspaces has broken out of the worlds of technology and social enterprise. We Work, a leading co-workspace company, has emerged to become a global enterprise, with more than 200 buildings located in 70 cities worldwide and annual revenues (2017) of US$900 million (Huet, 2018). As the company describes its mission: "We transform buildings into dynamic environments for creativity, focus, and connection ... [T]his is a movement toward humanizing work."[3] Regardless of the challenges that We Work is currently facing, to their credit they recognized a new and real workplace need. Many other real-estate firms, in fact, are moving into this field, offering tenants a completely different spatial and social experience that is based on breaking down the traditional barriers between organizations that share an address.[4]

This movement has also firmly taken root in the charitable/non-profit sector. While the earliest non-profit centres have been in operation for two or more decades, a report in October 2015 on shared spaces, conducted by the Non-Profit Centres Network (Jakubowski, 2015), found that the number of such facilities across North America grew from 212 in 2011 to almost 400 by 2015 (the survey included several Canadian examples). About four in ten had tenants from multiple sectors within the non-profit world, while 28% were "themed". According to the study, the typical facility had about 35,000 sq.ft, a dozen tenants, about 70 employees on site and gross revenues in the $500,000 range. (The figures for the Canadian centres surveyed were similar.)

A survey accompanying the report, asking respondents to enumerate the benefits of shared spaces, included the following results:

- 82% said shared spaces allow them to meet organizational goals better by allowing them to spend their revenues on programs instead of rent
- 77% generated revenue that meets or exceeds costs
- average annual savings reported by tenants was about US$25,000

While the financial and operational savings are clear, an earlier evaluation commissioned by Tides (US) revealed some of the more intangible benefits: additional traffic due to greater access, better outcomes for clients due to use of co-located services, revitalization of surrounding neighbourhoods, and environment improvements. The report further pointed out that in many communities, the shared centres fostered arts and other cultural activities and played a role in "field building" within the non-profit sector, allowing individual organizations to improve their service delivery and increase their organizational capacity:

---

3 We Work. Retrieved from https://www.wework.com/

4 The shared office market is closely linked to another workplace trend, which is the move towards flexible spaces. Pioneered by technology giants like Google, which encouraged creativity among its employees, these workspaces are conspicuously lacking in not just walls, but even individual desks or work stations. The ubiquity of laptops and Wi-Fi allows employees to work at shared tables, in lounge areas or other non-traditional and notably fluid settings within the company's offices.

→ A number of centre managers reported either consulting to centres in other communities during their planning process or being approached for advice by planned and developing centres. Some foundations that have developed non-profit centres have gone on to build non-profit centres in other communities. Many centres in the study actively participate in the training and peer-learning forums of the Nonprofit Centres Network. These types of activities not only stimulate the development of new centres in new places, but also help to ensure that learning within the field translates into better centre development and management practices.

The Nonprofit Centers Network/Tides, 2011

Foundations, funders and others sharing facilities

By contrast to the proliferation of non-profit centres, there are very few examples of facilities shared mainly by foundations, funders or other similar groups besides Foundation House. "An early attempt by the Kahanoff Foundation in Calgary to engage philanthropic foundations and not-for-profits showed promise when it was launched in 1992," according to a 2016 case study on Foundation House. "The space is now under the leadership of the Calgary Foundation as a convention and meeting space, generating income that supports community programs and activities while offering reasonably priced office space to charities and not-for-profits."[5] As of this writing, the Max Bell Foundation is about to relocate to the Calgary centre, and another one is being planned in Montreal.

---

5 http://www.foundation.house/. See Case Study.

293   Foundation House: More than just sharing space

The Philanthropy Hub

The Philanthropy Hub (Alaska Community Foundation), Anchorage[6]

Developed in 2013, the Hub "allows philanthropic-minded organizations to co-locate and share services. The facility features state-of-the-art conference rooms, co-office management, a shared receptionist, accessible and open common areas, and other amenities. The Philanthropy Hub also provides for daily cross-organization collaboration and philanthropic synergy."

Its tenants include four foundations, an organization that allows Alaskans to earmark the annual dividends of a state-owned asset manager to the charity of their choice, an addiction treatment service, and an affordable housing service.

Philanthropy House

Philanthropy House (European Foundation Centre), Brussels, Belgium[7]

Opened in 2009, Philanthropy House was the outcome of an effort by several large pan-European foundations to establish a stronger presence for the philanthropic sector in Brussels, which is home to the European Commission (EC). The members include public and private foundations. The facility, located in a restored mid-rise building, has office space for tenants working in or with the sector, as well as exhibition halls, conference rooms and theatres for screenings or panel discussions that draw in both members and those they hope to educate about the value of organized philanthropy.

The mission of Philanthropy House reflects its location: establish a stronger presence for the philanthropic sector with the EC, convey a message about the importance of collaboration among funding organizations, and provide EC decision-makers with a venue for understanding the work of European foundations.

---

6   https://alaskacf.org
7   https://www.efc.be

Location, location and location

In a project like this one, the choice of stage wasn't just important; it was foundational. Once we had determined the core group of participants, we embarked on a process for making the most practical decisions in this entire journey.

The first of these involved the question of whether to buy or rent. The overheated state of the Toronto real estate market – coupled with our collective desire to situate this new space within the city's core – meant ruling out the purchase and renovation of a building.

We retained the Not-for-Profit Advisory Group at Colliers Canada to identify potential rental spaces that were accessible by public transit and had plenty of light. Marcel had worked with the group during his time with Imagine Canada and had witnessed their genuine interest in working with the non-profit sector. This assignment would be a great challenge for them, given our expectations and the market conditions. We also hired a project manager to handle the day-to-day aspects of the search and oversee our projected $650,000 renovation budget.

All the obvious but important mechanical elements arose immediately: we needed to determine how much space we needed in order to accommodate the three organizations and our tenants – a process that required considerable discussion about current and future requirements. We had about 25 staff between us (as of 2015) and wanted to ensure space for approximately 15–20 other people (six or seven organizations). The three of us also had to make choices about the lease. And we required a vision for the design and configuration of the space.

Initially, we contemplated leasing space in one of the CSI buildings, which have served for several years as a viable and lively model for how shared space in the non-profit world can function. But we soon decided that, for our specific needs as a group of funders, we wanted space that would be both more formal and more curated, in the sense that we could seek our own tenant partners based on synergies and common objectives (see Pegi Dover's "A 'roomie's' perspective 2", pp. 310–11').

Through our networks, we became aware of a suite of offices in an office building at Yonge and St Clair, in mid-town Toronto. This venue seemed to tick several boxes. It had previously been leased by the Mastercard Canada Foundation, and we were able to assume the lease at below-market rates, with the promise of substantial long-term savings. The location itself – very central and on transit – was attractive because we had conceptualized Foundation House as a hub that would attract visitors.

After identifying the Mastercard space, we worked with Susan Manwaring, lawyer and leader of the Miller Thompson Social Impact Group. The lease proved to be the most straightforward secondary decision: we briefly considered incorporating and assigning the lease to this new entity but opted (for simplicity's sake) to have the Counselling Foundation (Bruce) serve as head lessee, with the two others – Laidlaw (Jehad) and Lawson (Marcel) – as sub-lessees.

The lease arrangements are laid out in a memorandum of understanding (MOU) between the three founding groups. Like all sound partnership agreements, it contains language about breaking up. The key element of the MOU is that if one of the founding members decides to exit, that foundation must first identify a replacement that is acceptable to the two remaining partners. The MOU also contains a provision allowing for the re-apportioning of the Foundation House space on the basis of the evolving needs of the member organizations. To keep well ahead of those sorts of changes, we have adopted a practice of checking in with one another from time to time to assess changing space needs.

Early on, we further developed a consensus formula about dividing up the costs of creating and operating Foundation House. It became apparent, as we proceeded through this process, that there were two sorts of expenses: space-based and time-based. The former involved anything to do with the physical lay-out, while the latter referred to the retention of advisors or consultants who provided services to the entire operation. We have allocated space-related expenses (rent, furniture, etc.) on a pro-rata basis; with time-based expenses, we divide the bills equally among the three founders.

While Bruce [Counselling Foundation] oversaw the day-to-day aspects of the renovation project (the interior design was spearheaded by Taylor Smyth Architects), we first agreed on several high-level principles and developed these over the course of the weekly meetings that took place in the months leading up to occupancy. In terms of its overall appearance and "feel", Foundation House, we thought, should express a sense of openness but also conformity in design, furnishings and other décor elements. But it would also have to be sufficiently professional in ambience to give us the confidence to invite a wide range of individuals and organizations for visits, seminars, etc.

To accomplish the latter goal, but also to ensure consistency across the space, the three of us left our own respective organizations' furnishings behind and asked that the tenants not bring their old office furniture when they moved into Foundation House. The visual conformity, as Bruce points out, created a sense that all the Foundation House members, both tenant partners and founders, are on an equal plane, which is one of the objectives of the project. We wanted to break down barriers and build community – and that began with the layout and furnishings.

The common areas demanded special consideration, as these are the places in Foundation House where the anticipated social interaction would occur. In our office, these include the reception area, a flexible very large boardroom/convening space near the main entrance and the kitchen.

The design and configuration of the general area around the reception desk and a few adjacent small meeting rooms nearby is very much what one would expect in most well-built office suites today – seating, places for quiet conversation and so on.

The boardroom configuration begins to reveal some differentiation for Foundation House. The boardroom resembles many of the larger meeting spaces one finds in most offices, but it is fitted out with partitions that allow users to increase or decrease the scale depending on the nature of the event or the use. Given that everyone at Foundation House has a diverse range of programming needs, the adaptability of that room is very useful.

Finally, the kitchen. The lunchroom is fitted out with counter space, coffee machines, fridges, plenty of cupboards, and a set of comfortable longer tables that are in use throughout the day. The lunchroom, as we hoped, has evolved into the central meeting place of Foundation House, both for all the obvious reasons, but also because of a quirk of the building's design.

Unlike many office towers, our building has the elevator column located not through the centre of the structure but off to one side. Consequently, Foundation House's space is not broken up by the typical elevator shaft, as happens in many offices that occupy all or most of a floor in a high rise. Instead, the lunchroom is situated in a highly trafficked central location, with two sets of doors opening to different parts of our space. For this reason, it functions not only as a destination for people seeking coffee or lunch, but also as a physical connection across and through Foundation House. While the circuit of ordinary corridors among the offices and cubicles provides access to all of Foundation House's constituent organizations, it is nevertheless interesting to ponder how the kitchen's other role – as a kind of crossroads – has affected the way the people who work here interact and engage with one another.

The layout of the space, in our experience to date, has facilitated what Marcel [Lawson Foundation] describes as "the impromptu bumping into people". "I'm seeing people I would never see unless I made an appointment" is a sentiment that can often be heard from people who visit or work at Foundation House.

The tenant mix

Initially, five foundations were actively engaged in the discussion about entering into a shared space arrangement, but two opted for their own reasons not to pursue the idea.

We knew we wanted tenants, but we also sought tenants that would fit well with Foundation House's orientation and operating philosophy. A key consideration involved whether or not to include organizations that fundraise or might receive grants from any of the partners or tenants. Unlike the shared non-profit centres described earlier, Foundation House's mission was to foster better collaboration among funders. But determining the tenant mix created interesting conversations. In some cases, there were obvious synergies – for example, with umbrella organizations representing Canada's private foundations or the one representing the country's community foundations. We were also eager to involve Indigenous organizations that have been working with the philanthropic sector on implementing the Truth and Reconciliation Commission's (TRC) recommendations.

But when it came to other non-profits, the decision was more difficult. As a general principle, we felt it could be problematic to share space with organizations whose leaders or employees might take advantage of their proximity to three funding bodies. At the same time, we were seeking more and better exposure to the non-profit world as a means of keeping our respective foundations grounded and informed about what was happening at the grassroots level of the sector.

As a way of balancing those two aspects, we approached the Ontario Nonprofit Network (ONN), whose members belong to a sector that includes 55,000 non-profits and charities, employs about a million people and accounts for 2.6% of the province's GDP (Ontario Non-Profit Network, n.d.). Before ONN took occupancy at Foundation House, we met to discuss the relationship and how we would approach collaboration within the organization. The consensus came down to a pragmatic view, as Marcel recounts it: "If it works, fine. But if it doesn't work, we'll commit to finding a solution."

Governance and operations

→ "If there were egos at play, this would not have worked. People have to surrender some of their autonomy, but they didn't have to compromise the integrity of the organization."

Jehad Aliweiwi, Laidlaw Foundation

In order to manage this new facility, we set up some basic governance and management structures. There are a handful of committees – an executive committee, consisting of the three of us; a management committee, which includes representatives of all the member organizations; a communications committee, which emerged organically as communications staff from various organizations saw the opportunity to share ideas with new Foundation House colleagues. In terms of day-to-day operations, our respective executive assistants or office coordinators and the Foundation House receptionist, who works for the entire organization, oversee the management of the space.

The operational tasks are, in many ways, absolutely routine. But the smooth functioning of the facility serves as the foundation upon which the more creative and interactive aspects play out. We learned several valuable lessons about co-management during the first two years.

The basic operational tasks include tech support, maintenance, scheduling the use of various Foundation House meeting spaces, and the stewardship of the kitchen. In the case of the latter, we realized early that the use and upkeep of the kitchen, a communal space, represented an especially important mandate, as skirmishes over kitchen duty in other office settings can create bitterness and resentment.

Kinamark, a leadership consultant hired in the late spring of 2016 to assist us in developing norms and principles for Foundation House, outlined both the objectives and the decisions required to attain them. The kitchen, the consultant advised, should be treated as our personal kitchens, with users taking responsibility for cleaning up after themselves, loading or emptying the dishwasher, replacing supplies and so on.

We had to choose between a voluntary self-clean or rotation system, or hiring a service to look after the space. Focus group sessions conducted by the consultant elicited a range of responses and views:

- Make expectations clear, e.g. about assigning weeks to particular organizations in a rotation-based system
- Zero tolerance for mess: users must clean up after themselves
- Hire a cleaning service, because even well-intentioned rotation/voluntary systems break down
- Pay attention to the fact that some people will clean up after others but end up feeling resentful

After reflecting on this feedback, we decided to include basic kitchen management responsibilities in the role designed for the receptionist.

The evolution of the Foundation House approach to tech support provided another important lesson. Early on, one of us hired a technician to work on-site, but the decision, which was made unilaterally, seemed to focus more on the tech needs of one of the founding partners than the entire organization. The other two partners declined to cost-share in that case. But we did agree that this short episode offered a useful learning about hiring support staff, which is that advance planning and consultation within the executive committee was crucial if we were to achieve our aspirational goal of consensus-based decision-making.

A third example involved concerns about distraction expressed by one of our largest tenant members, the Ontario Nonprofit Network. As it happened, their zone within the Foundation House space was situated near the reception area. In any shared and open-concept office setting, issues of noise will inevitably arise, and many workplaces now provide small rooms or quiet spaces where employees can have private meetings, conduct phone calls and so on.

After two years of working in the space, ONN employees were struggling with the visual and noise distractions of facing the high traffic hallway between the kitchen and boardroom, and asked that the walls of their office partitions be raised by one level. The request, Jehad points out, "would change the look of the space". We had invested resources and intellectual effort in creating an open-concept design that was intended to enable the interaction we envisioned, but we also realized that Foundation House needed to be able to respond positively to these concerns. In the end, the decision was made to increase the height of the partition walls on one side in the ONN area, as this was a unique situation based on the placement of the reception area and the orientation of the desks towards a busy hallway.

In these and other examples of how we manage this space, we've proceeded according to a handful of core principles:

- decisions are to be made by consensus wherever possible
- consultation with member groups, forward-planning and clear communications represent the best ways of heading off conflicts or misunderstandings
- in any undertaking that is breaking new ground, course corrections are to be expected and indeed welcomed

Creating an "ideas marketplace" culture

Personally, from the very beginning of this process, we, as the three founders, discovered that we enjoyed a great deal of positive chemistry. We all brought personal professional experience of working within ecosystems. We were interested in learning from one another, and others in the charitable sector, about how to make such an experiment succeed. And, we recognized that the ultimate pay-off went far beyond logistics and cost. The vision was to create a new and more collaborative mode for funder organizations – an "ideas marketplace".

At the same time, we recognized that none of these gains would happen on their own. And we sensed that much depended on the culture we fostered within Foundation House. As Jehad points out, "This was not without risk. We went into Foundation House fully aware of this reality. At the end of the day, we're employers."

The challenge was two-fold: one involved establishing basic human resource policies that would be adopted and respected by several independent organizations; the other focused on moving beyond ground rules to foster a cohesive and integrated social environment that encouraged creative thinking and new forms of collaboration within the funder space.

It's worth enumerating some of the potential pitfalls and questions that could arise in this kind of setting:

- How would we address instances of real or alleged harassment between employees of different Foundation House member organizations?
- Were there guidelines for employee recruitment between Foundation House members?
- Where was the line between social interaction and distracting behaviour?

In order to begin building a shared culture with common norms and core principles, we asked our consultant, Kinamark, in the spring of 2016 to guide us through a process meant to elucidate answers to these questions. "We were sending a very strong message to everyone who worked at Foundation House by doing this," Marcel [Lawson Foundation] observed.

The process involved interviews with the executives of the ten Foundation House member organizations as well as discussions with individual staff and leadership groups. Kinamark also conducted a staff survey, drawing on answers provided by 31 respondents.

Some of the key findings of the survey:

- Respondents showed that most people had "great enthusiasm about cohabitation and about the collective," with many mentioning the promise of sharing ideas, knowledge, best practices and so on. Yet at the staff level within individual member organizations, many "did not understand how the vision is expected to play out at the tactical or operational level".
- While the respondents overwhelmingly grasped the notion that Foundation House, as an ideas marketplace, could encourage new approaches, some felt this collective goal didn't have relevance for the work they did.
- The prospect of inter-organization collaboration represents an exciting opportunity, but it also raises challenging questions, because it wasn't clear to member organizations how or when to initiate such work, and what to do about the problem of a lack of time or resources to pursue joint projects. (A quarter of all respondents felt their existing workloads precluded them from pursuing collaborative undertakings.)
- The other obstacles to collaboration had to do with the familiar human factors that almost all organizations experience: leadership signals from member organizations; interpersonal or personality issues among staff who may not know, like or respect one another, or feel pressured into doing what their peers want to do (or not do). The member organizations, moreover, could turn into silos that tacitly discourage inter-organizational communication and collaboration.

Based on the findings of the survey and the interviews, Kinamark drafted two documents – "Norms at Foundation House" and "Principles by Which We Live". In each case, the consultant then convened focus groups to elicit further feedback, which was then incorporated into the final versions (see next page). "The principles and norms are meant to convey the ethos of Foundation

House," the consultant noted in its report to the executive. "Neither one is intended to be prescriptive. Ultimately, the principles and norms should help to sustain the vibrant and cohesive culture that exists at Foundation House. For these guidelines to become a conscious way of living at Foundation House, intentional effort will be needed on the part of the leadership, including strategic communication. The guidelines will evolve as the collective does."

Norms at Foundation House

We're mindful of noise levels.

We are aware of how background noise affects colleagues in the open work areas. So we are attentive to volume – of our conversations and of our gadgets.

Examples of how we live this norm:

- The pods are either for quiet time or webinars/small meetings
- Be mindful of people trying to have phone conversations
- Socializing: go to the kitchen
- Keep side doors to the boardroom closed. At the same time, each organization needs to be mindful of, and informed about, the need for specific workplace accommodations, e.g. accommodation for claustrophobia
- Walk through interior hallways, not the middle of workspaces
- Group parties – use the kitchen (close the kitchen doors)
- Let visitors know people are working in the open space
- We encourage the use of the collaboration tables (as opposed to convening at desks)

We balance connecting and concentrating.

We sustain our productivity yet also nurture our connections and good ideas as they arise. We pay special attention to when we interrupt each other.

Examples of how we live this norm:

- Understand and respect each organization's work cycles and when people need to concentrate
- Small group conversations – if these last more than five minutes, move elsewhere
- Use Slack to inform others when you're busy
- Ask "Is this a good time?"

- To keep with the spirit of Foundation House, we do need to introduce outside visitors, particularly when we feel there are viable connections
- We encourage the use of the collaboration tables (as opposed to convening at desks)

We share our meeting spaces.

We use meeting rooms/pods for as long as we need, and we book them.

Examples of how we live this norm:

- If you have booked the pod, you get priority
- Always leave the room tidy
- Use Meekan to book meeting rooms and pods

It's a scent-free workplace (particularly, synthetic scents).

Examples of how we live this norm:

- Remove air freshener from the women's bathroom
- Purchase scent-free supplies whenever possible
- Affix a sign on the front door that says "We aim to be a scent-free environment"
- Ascertain the different between allergy and dislike. Nine survey respondents identified allergens, including animal fur, dust, mold, strong perfumes, air fresheners, sprays and synthetic scents

Principles by which we live

- We foster a fun, friendly, and welcoming workspace
- We work with an eye to inviting and igniting trust and relationship
- We create and nurture an environment of learning and collaboration
- We have respect for each other
- We are committed to resolving conflicts with respect and openness

How do we live the principles?

These principles all contribute to one another:

- We are intentional in applying them to daily life
- We commit to more face-to-face interactions
- We serve as connectors for each other

1. We foster a fun, friendly, and welcoming workspace

Examples of how to live this:

- A sense of curiosity can lead to unexpected encounters
- Be intentional, to carve out time
- How can we extend our organizational "fun events" to Foundation House
- Potlucks, special event days

2. We work with an eye to inviting and igniting trust and relationship

Examples of how to live this:

- Be intentional
- How do we tell our stories?
- Who to approach for a sounding board – as group or one on one
- Everyone has come to it with an open spirit
- Communications Crew
- Lunch and Learns (e.g. present individual projects; demo Fridays)
- Weekly: come sit with me, we can share about our projects
- Socially, informally, around festivals
- Kitchen is a gathering place: we sit together so we get to know each other

3. We create and nurture an environment of learning and collaboration

Examples of how to live this:

- Some can do orientation (see Norms)
- Formal opportunities through Lunch and Learns
- Informal opportunities – if we see ourselves as connectors/networkers
- Freedom to engage

4. We have respect for each other

Examples of how to live this:

- Respect is linked to principle on trust
- Respect regardless of roles
- Respect for privacy
- Boundaries are important, e.g. personal does not carry over into workplace
- How to respect introvert/extrovert styles?
- Orientation/website

5. We are committed to resolving conflicts with respect and openness

Examples of how to live this:

The approach to conflict resolution will differ, depending on whether it is internal conflict or intra-organizational, personal or work-related. Here is one possible process:

- Because of mutual respect – we first address conflict directly, between the two people involved
- Take it to the manager
  We could adopt a method, such as one used by Grantbook called **WRAP:**
    - **W**iden your options
    - **R**eality check
    - **A**scertain distances
    - **P**repare to be wrong
- CEO would figure it out with other leaders
- Mediator

How it's all working

One of the most direct by-products of the process of developing norms and principles was a concerted effort to create a sense of community among the people who work at Foundation House. Over the first two years, the steering committee organized numerous events meant to build and then nurture those social connections – family day events, potlucks, movie nights and other such activities. We held animation sessions that allowed the various member organizations to explain to other Foundation House employees who they are and what they do.

Having laid the foundation, both physically and culturally, we have also been able to observe how our collaborative "ideas marketplace" is functioning.

The most readily observed examples that validate the premise involve traffic. Because Foundation House sits at the intersection of many organizations with their own respective professional and social networks, we are able to say that this facility has become a destination for many people and organizations participating in the various events held in the boardroom, which has been booked for use about 78% of the available times, depending upon the time of year. As Marcel [Lawson Foundation] says: "We're all organizations that bring a lot of people into the office."

For example, early in 2017, 23 foundations participated in a session at Foundation House with the leadership of the Public Policy Forum, where Marcel Lauzière is a board member. The event not only situated Foundation House as an important convening space; it also provided a forum for a discussion about strengthening the funding sector's engagement with public policy development.

The social and professional connections made at such events, and among Foundation House member groups, have produced other gains. For example, one important but challenging issue facing the charitable sector in recent years has been the twinned question of how to assess grant applications and measure impact.

The evaluation process, in particular, has come in for criticism, and some non-profits have urged funders to move beyond "box-ticking" to a more holistic approach to vetting applications. Because the ONN is a Foundation House member and also has strong views on improving evaluations, our foundation members and related umbrella organizations have had the opportunity to engage in a timely discussion about how to shift the dynamics and develop more effective assessment tools. ONN was able to press ahead with this discussion, as Marcel points out, "because at Foundation House, we're right under their nose". The results will be amplified across the entire sector.

Building on the conversation about evaluations, the three foundations in mid-2018 sent out a joint survey to recipients of grants from our organizations, canvassing them (anonymously) on their views about topics such as flexibility, communications, reporting, non-financial assistance, and their comfort levels in raising concerns about the granting experience with our granting officers. Each foundation also had a small number of unique questions. The survey, administered independently by GrantBook, produced an encouraging average 60% response rate and fed into our collective efforts to become more responsive funders. The fact that the survey was conducted jointly, with results shared among the three foundations, also speaks to the links between Foundation House-enabled collaboration and our desire to improve the way we go about our work.

A fourth instance of the cross-pollination enabled by Foundation House is instructive. CERIC,[8] a charity that functions under the auspices of the Counselling Foundation and sponsors education and research into career counselling, was working on a handbook on career development aimed at small and medium enterprises (SMEs). When Marcel found out about this project, he suggested that CERIC could adapt this publication so it would be useful for an audience of senior managers of non-profits. Now, CERIC is collaborating with ONN and Imagine Canada to produce just such a handbook. The fourth participant is another Foundation House member, the Circle on Philanthropy and Aboriginal People in Canada, which is contributing a section on recruiting and advancing Indigenous employees within charitable organizations. "If Marcel hadn't been in the office," Bruce observes, "he wouldn't have known we had done [that handbook] for SMEs."

Such "casual collisions", as Jehad [Laidlaw Foundation] describes these and other encounters that have occurred in the space since it opened in late 2015, serve to affirm the premise that Foundation House is evolving into a collaboration-driven "ideas marketplace" that generates forward-thinking ideas about philanthropy.

---

8 https://ceric.ca

A "roomie's" perspective 1: Philanthropic Foundations of Canada (CEO and president Hilary Pearson)

→ "We've been part of conversations about co-programming and values and how we live in the space together. We were part of that and felt consulted."

Hilary Pearson

For many years, the small Montreal-based umbrella organization had been borrowing space or renting hotel rooms when it had to conduct business in Toronto. When the prospect of lease space within Foundation House arose, Philanthropic Foundations of Canada (PFC) leapt at the opportunity. "We knew we were going to be using the boardroom," says Pearson. "For me, it was a no-brainer."

By virtue of what it does, PFC has plenty of visibility about what goes on within Canada's foundation sector. Many PFC members, especially the smaller family-based foundations, traditionally work in isolation from one another, explains Pearson. In recent years, however, a growing number have sought out a more collaborative approach – a shift Pearson attributes, in part, to the shifting demographics among foundation leaders and staff.

Millennials, she says, are a product of their social networks and seek these networks out in their professional lives – a dynamic that is clearly accelerated by digital networks and platforms. The existence of those virtual communities has fostered greater interest in direct social encounters and shared spaces. Consequently, when PFC hosts events or meetings at Foundation House in Toronto (once or twice a month), the attendance has been robust. "People are curious about Foundation House," Pearson says. "Have we gained benefits from being able to ask members to attend meetings there? Yes."

A "roomie's" perspective 2: Canadian Environmental Grantmakers Network (executive director Pegi Dover)

→ "I really love that environment. It's diverse. I feel like I'm in a workplace where good and interesting things are happening."

Pegi Dover

Like PFC, Canadian Environmental Grantmakers Network (CEGN)[9] is a small umbrella organization representing 65 entities – private and public foundations, funds and one co-op retailer – that want to promote sustainability projects and responsible investing. Before moving to Foundation House, CEGN rented space in CSI's Environment for Profit hub.

Dover made the move in part to "get environment out of its silo [...] With the three [founding] foundations and members like ONN, there's an opportunity for us to get invited to gatherings where [in the past] we wouldn't have been on the radar."

The networking and collaboration opportunities provided through Foundation House have translated into specific initiatives, several of which involve forging stronger and more respectful relationship with Indigenous organizations.

Because of Bruce's [Counselling Foundation] particular interest in fostering more constructive relationships between the philanthropic sector and Indigenous Peoples in Canada, Dover says CEGN's presence at Foundation House has created many more opportunities for relationship-building with Indigenous organizations, especially smaller ones. The connections have allowed CEGN members to provide grant-writing support for smaller First Nations that may lack the experience or administrative capacity to pursue a range of funding opportunities.

CEGN has also forged connections with another Foundation House member, Community Foundations of Canada (CFC). The organization has been looking to expand its environmental philanthropy, and many community foundations are well positioned to fund such work. Dover has worked with CFC on the latter's sustainable cities working group, especially the small community foundations. She's also promoted the use of the United Nations 17 sustainable development goals (developed in 2015) as the framework for measuring the progress of such local initiatives (United Nations Foundation, 2015). "The connection to reconciliation and the community foundations are the big benefits to working here," says Dover.

---

[9] http:www.cegn.org

Learnings and conclusion

At the time of this book going to press, we have watched Foundation House grow and evolve for about three years. In some very important ways, we feel that the process for achieving two of the primary objectives of Foundation House – encouraging better collaboration between foundations and creating new avenues for post-TRC engagement between funders and Indigenous organizations – is well underway. Indeed, consistent with the goal that a shared space can function as both an "ideas marketplace" and a kind of commons for the overlapping social/professional networks of the member organizations, Foundation House can be seen as a proof-of-concept model for other funders seeking to establish these kinds of arrangements.

But it would be misleading to suggest that all the bugs have been worked out, or that this approach will work in every case. Here are some key learnings based on these first few years.

Chemistry

We can say with confidence that the three founders – Bruce Lawson, Marcel Lauzière and Jehad Aliweiwi – enjoy a high degree of mutual trust and alignment in both our outlook and approach to our work. In the case of Foundation House, the planets seem to have aligned. That sense of mutual understanding at the leadership level provides both energy and glue. For others who are considering this model, the participants early on need to reflect closely about their ability to work together, because collective decision-making is vital for ongoing success. "This is not for everybody," Jehad says. "You have to be able to let go of your power and your authorities."

Culture

No organization can snap its fingers and establish a corporate culture, much less one that consists of many independent, albeit like-minded, entities. Every one of the organizations working at Foundation House has its own quirks and eccentricities – that's a given. Our advice to anyone considering this kind of shared space venture is that the time and resources spent on developing both collective norms and social cohesion is well worth the investment. An intentional, progressive and collaborative culture doesn't develop organically, but misunderstandings and resentments can easily take root in a shared work space that lacks traditional accountabilities.

Cruise control

As of our third year, we are aware that there's been some waning of joint activities and programming, most likely because the members have settled in, and their employees now know one another. This development is a natural evolution, but the importance of finding new ways of fostering collaboration cannot be overstated. What's more, as the workforces of the member organizations turn over, it will also be important to provide new Foundation House employees with a taste of the broader culture beyond that of their own organizations. The time that we invested in the beginning to build a Foundation House culture will be at risk if we don't continue to work at it and renew the way we do this if necessary.

In our experience, the rewards have exceeded the risks. Foundation House is evolving into a philanthropic commons and a hub for both random and carefully planned collaborations. It is about much more than just shared office space; it has truly become a place where ideas and people are constantly crossing paths.

Three key takeaways

1

Trust: Trust is key to the development of any partnership such as the one that led to Foundation House. Without trust, problems and challenges – inevitable in any large-scale multi-stakeholder initiative – can quickly degenerate into conflict and discord.

2

Relationships: The success of Foundation House is based on a multiplicity of factors but none as important as personal and professional relationships – across all organizations and at all levels. And these relationships must be continuously nourished and strengthened as time goes by.

3

Culture: An important success factor in the Foundation House project has been the time that has been invested in building a culture of respect, of sharing and of collaboration.

References

Florida, Richard L (2002) *The Rise of the Creative Class: And How it's transforming work, leisure, community and everyday life.* New York, NY: Basic Books, 2002

History of Murano Glass (n.d.) Retrieved from Glass of Venice website https://www.glassofvenice.com/murano_glass_history.php

Huet, E (2018) 'We Work, with $900 in sales, finds cheaper ways to expand', Bloomberg, February 26, 2018. Retrieved from https://www.bloomberg.com/news/articles/2018-02-26/wework-with-900-million-in-sales-finds-cheaper-ways-to-expand

Jakubowski, L (2015) *State of the Shared Space Sector Survey Released.* The Non-Profit Centers Network, October 19, 2015. Retrieved from: https://www.nonprofitcenters.org/state-of-the-shared-space-sector-survey-released/

McConnell Foundation (n.d.) *Centre for Social Innovation.* Retrieved from: https://socialinnovation.org/member_auto/mcconnell-foundation/

Ontario Non-Profit Network (n.d.) Retrieved from: http://theonn.ca/about-the-sector/

Nonprofit Centers Network/Tides (2011) *Measuring Collaboration: The Benefits and Impacts of Nonprofit Centres.* Prepared for: The Nonprofit Centers Network/Tides. Mt. Audburn Associates

Pearson, H, Lawson, B, Nemtin, A, Brascoupé Peters, W, Santoro, L & V Grant (2015) 'The Philanthropic Community's Declaration of Action', *The Philanthropist*, June 15, 2015

United Nations Foundation (2015) *Sustainable Development Goals.* Retrieved from: https://sustainabledevelopment.un.org/

Reflections
and conclusions

Tim Brodhead

This volume helpfully lays to rest three misconceptions about foundations in Canada: first, that foundations are just an expression of "charity"; second, that we can understand the role and practices of Canadian foundations by extrapolating from the more extensively studied world of American philanthropy; and third, that foundations – and the not-for-profit sector in general – are somehow in a "bubble", protected from larger societal forces and uniquely insulated from the changes buffeting society.

Let us look at each of these in turn. In Chapter One, Peter Elson and Sylvain A. Lefèvre provide a historical overview that positions foundations as part of the charity sector, especially in their origins, but they took on a distinct character in the early 20th century as "problem-solving machines" at the intersection of philanthropy, the corporation and the state. Organized philanthropy, in the form of foundations, became intentional, goal-oriented investors rather than simply "givers". The essential difference between charity and philanthropy can be neatly summed up in the German proverb, "Charity looks at the need and not at the cause"; by contrast, philanthropy – in principle, though not always in practice – aims not to alleviate but to cure. This distinction underlines the continuing need for both charity and philanthropy as well as their different functions. To ignore pressing needs while searching for solutions is immoral, but to overlook root causes leads to futility.

Nevertheless, charity's "virtuous halo" continues to shield foundations from much serious scrutiny (this is now changing in the US, as we shall note later). Who can disparage altruism – giving at a cost to oneself that benefits another, with no expectation of reward? The motivations behind philanthropy, however, are not always so righteous.

Throughout the examples of foundation work in this volume this distinction is clear, perhaps nowhere more so than in the chapter written by Nancy Pole and Myriam Bérubé. Centraide du Grand Montréal was created in the 1960s to encourage and facilitate giving by Montrealers to address poverty, homelessness and other urgent needs. Its purpose was to make charity more efficient and effective. Now, partly in response to changing donor expectations, it has pivoted to address causes and not just needs through initiatives such as the Collective Impact Program analyzed in Chapter 13.

The second misconception about Canadian foundations arises from the sheer scale of the US philanthropic complex and the outsize influence this confers. With typical American self-assurance, much of the literature generalizes US experience as characteristic of foundations everywhere – but in many ways it is quite distinct. Indeed, Canadian foundation representatives often find in international meetings that they have more in common with their European and other peers than with their fellow North Americans. Academic studies, publications like the *Chronicle of Philanthropy* or the *Stanford Social Innovation Review*, a cadre of confident and articulate "thought leaders", and the candid self-scrutiny of some of the largest foundations generate a constant flow of knowledge, ideas, emergent trends and fads that influence foundation practice around the world, and nowhere more so than in Canada.

Yet, the Canadian context is very different. The growth of foundations is more recent and, as the chapters exploring the role of network organizations like Philanthropic Foundations Canada (Chapter 3), Community Foundations Canada (Chapter 5), or the Circle on Philanthropy and Aboriginal Peoples (usually, just "the Circle") (Chapter 4) demonstrate, the infrastructure of organized philanthropy here is just being built. To give one example, until recently there were no university-accredited programs in not-for-profit and foundation management in Canada. Academic studies, such as this volume, remain rare.

More importantly, the socio-political context is different. Canadians are less inclined than Americans to dismiss government as "part of the problem", to use former President Reagan's famous phrase. This is particularly true in Quebec. Berthiaume and Lefèvre (Chapter 12) analyze the historical roots of Quebecers' faith in the state as an effective collective instrument and defender of their status as a minority community in North America.

Even while expounding the differences between US and Canadian foundations, we must acknowledge that – as in other areas of shared experience – the US often serves as a harbinger of emerging trends, opportunities and threats. Concepts which were coined in the US – including "strategic philanthropy", collective impact, impact investing, backbone organizations and so on – have entered both the lexicon and practice of Canadian funders.

Finally, there is the criticism that foundations and the voluntary sector more generally are somehow insulated from change, ostensibly because they are outside the inherently disruptive dynamic of the marketplace. This, as anyone who has worked at a not-for-profit, let alone a charity, knows, is nonsense. Technology has created new ways of giving and participating. People are seeking a more direct connection to the causes they support and evidence that their donations are producing results. Faith in good intentions is no longer enough. The 2018 Edelman Trust Barometer, which tracks level of trust in institutions across the globe, worryingly reported that, while 8% of Canadians say the community sector is "least broken" (46% consider government "broken"), trust in voluntary organizations has fallen 9% from 2017 to 2018 (among both the "informed public" and the "general population") (Edleman, 2018).

Clouds on the horizon?

The contributors to this volume tell a mostly upbeat story of "benevolence and good works": Canadian foundations are growing in scale, number and professionalism. In many cases they are tackling bigger challenges, pioneering new strategies, finding new forms of collaboration. Are there any clouds on the horizon?

Once again, we need to pay attention to what is happening in our southern neighbour. The paradox of foundations is that their greatest asset is also their greatest vulnerability: their autonomy, or what critics would call their lack of accountability. We see through examples in this book how their independence allows them to take risks, to adopt diverse perspectives, to champion unpopular or emergent causes. But that autonomy can also produce arrogance, abusive power relationships, and funding priorities skewed to elite interests.

Foundations are uniquely a product of liberal capitalism. Capitalism allows for the accumulation of vast fortunes, particularly when inequality is at the level experienced during the Gilded Age of the early 19th century or today. Liberalism protects individuals' right to determine how those fortunes should be purposed. It is no coincidence that for authoritarian regimes and "illiberal democracies" foundations, and philanthropy more generally, are an early target.

The legitimacy of foundations rests on their ability to balance the discretionary character of private wealth with their public responsibility to contribute to the common good. In times of growing economic inequality and political polarization, maintaining this balance – and the legitimacy it confers – is challenging. In the US, it is already a topic of lively debate (as seen in recent works such as the contrasting views of Joel Fleishman's *The Foundation: A Great American Secret* and Jean Mayer's *Dark Money*, to cite just two examples).

The "dirty secret" of the use of philanthropic vehicles in the US as a deliberate strategy to promote explicitly partisan political agendas has no parallel yet in Canada. Our politics are less polarized, and the regulations governing charities prohibit overtly partisan activities. Yet, even here, the former Conservative government did not hesitate to attack some foundations' granting to environmental causes as illegitimate political activity and to unleash auditors to scrutinize their books.

Some people confound their personal interests and the public good: using their wealth or power to promote an individual agenda to them is an exercise of freedom. In a society riven by deep differences over fundamental issues such as the threat posed by climate change, the role of government or the purpose of education, the use of private wealth to set public policy can be deeply problematic. More generally, we are living in a time when many citizens are losing faith in the institutions underpinning our liberal democracy. The sentiment that governing elites are out of touch with the needs of citizens grappling with economic dislocation, changing values and social insecurity is leading some countries to embrace authoritarianism and "illiberal democracy". (And let us not forget younger citizens who feel betrayed by inaction over climate change!)

Foundations are vulnerable to this loss of legitimacy. In 2017 Oxfam announced that just 42 individuals have as much wealth as the bottom half of the world's population (Oxfam, 2018). Warren Buffett's "billionaires pact", committing a handful of the ultra-wealthy to leaving 50% of their assets to charity does not, by pointing to the good works they sponsor, negate questions about how foundation resources are amassed. Calls for greater inclusivity, accountability and transparency are gaining strength. Claims by foundations that they promote systems change ring hollow when they are themselves seen as manifestations of the very inequality they seek to redress.

For twenty-five years critics of US foundations have pushed for greater inclusion of women, African-Americans and other groups in decision-making roles. In Canada, it is only recently (and under pressure from Indigenous leaders, a more visibly diverse society and, over a longer period, women) that philanthropy is being urged to adopt an "equity lens" in its funding practices and management structures. There is still an uphill path ahead.

All Our Relations

One of the strengths of this volume is the inclusion of powerful statements from respected Indigenous leaders like Roberta Jamieson, the Circle, Diane Roussim and Gladys Rowe. The Truth and Reconciliation Commission's Call to Action in 2014 was a wake-up call to Canadian foundations – not just to inform themselves about the urgency of the problems faced by many Indigenous people, but to undertake, in Jamieson's words, to "decolonize philanthropy". This is not just a matter of social justice, to rectify centuries of neglect and exploitation, but a demand for philanthropy to examine some of its most basic premises.

One of the tenets of social innovation is that new ideas most often come "from the margins", from society's interstices. The Indigenous view of the world could help to rectify some of philanthropy's blind spots. Reciprocity, relationship and wholeness are integral to the Indigenous understanding of life. Some foundations recognize that lasting solutions to large, complex problems require some form of *system change*, while they themselves continue to work in silos and in isolation from government and others.

A *decolonized* philanthropy would integrate from the Indigenous worldview the inherent connectedness of all things: humanity and nature, economy and environment, physical and spiritual – and funder and *recipient*. In Jamieson's words, "Reconciliation is not about making space for the 'other', it is creating a new space for both" (Chapter 2).

Despite efforts to redress the imbalance, relations between those who give and receive grants are anything but reciprocal. The logic of philanthropy is basically transactional: What result will we derive from this grant? Is it greater or less than some alternative investment? The "relational logic" of reciprocity might instead ask: Do I trust these people to know what they need? Can we work together to help fashion an effective solution?

Foundations working for social justice recognize that the power of money must be balanced by the power of relations. Asking whether the decisions they take are fair, transparent and open to challenge can only be answered by those most affected by those decisions.

This is not of course to argue against evidence, prudence and intelligent risk-taking. But the notion that these qualities are more present in homogeneous, largely male and well-off groups is well past its "best by" date. The evidence that more diversity produces better results is compelling, even if it flies in the face of donor autonomy. The "risk" funders assume is more like an opportunity cost (the grant might have had more impact elsewhere); the risk grant-users take is existential ("if we fail, we may never get funded again").

Trust in the future

Canadians have been uniquely blessed by nature and by history. But we now face a testing time: economic disruption from new technologies and business models, the existential threat of climate change, an aging society – and the fear that our political and educational institutions and social infrastructure are not equipped to respond effectively and in a timely fashion to growing threats to our future well-being. There is a gap between what science and knowledgeable "experts" tell us is needed, and what electorates are willing to accept. This is even leading some to argue that the fate of democracy in such situations is to trend inevitably toward autocracy.

The "three-legged stool" of a healthy liberal democracy is a market sector that generates wealth, government that makes and enforces rules and ensures some redistribution of that wealth in the interest of equity, and a not-for-profit or community-benefit sector that meets needs not addressed by government or the market. Foundations, specifically, have been called the research and development arm of the social sector.

Foundations must ensure that their legitimacy as social actors and agents of change is not eroded by a loss of trust. They can borrow some of the methods of business to improve their effectiveness (program- and mission-investing being an example), but they cannot be driven solely by efficiency and profit. They need to work with government or else they risk being niche players and sponsors of short-lived pilot projects; however, they must not aspire to replace government in service delivery or public policy-making.

This brings us to the question of advocacy, a topic raised by many of the contributors, most directly in Berthiaume and Lefèvre's rich and detailed analysis of the *Collectif* of foundations in Quebec in Chapter 12.

Successful systems change requires a profound shift in structures, resource flows, norms and patterns of authority, none of which is achievable without government. For this reason, many foundations, and charities in general, have pressed for advocacy on behalf of the causes and people they work for and with. For foundations, though, one must ask from where they derive legitimacy to advocate. Is it from their money, or their knowledge, or their independence and presumed disinterestedness? In a democracy it cannot be the first; and mere expertise is seldom sufficient (as the deafness to scientists on climate change attests).

The credibility foundations are given must be based on their transparency, lack of self-interest and willingness to share their power and collaborate. As foundations become more outspoken and visible, they will be forced to become more accountable. This is a good thing. The need for more transparency and accountability is a *leitmotif* through many of the chapters in this book; but how can the creative and generative impulses of private initiative be reconciled with community oversight or the stifling effect of public opinion? Can Jamieson's notion, in Chapter 2, that it is *reciprocity that creates equilibrium* help us find a balance between encouraging personal generosity and ensuring public accountability?

Reciprocity could suggest, for example, that the tax benefits to people creating a foundation be based on their degree of diversity and public accountability. Closely held private foundations would receive less favourable treatment than foundations with diverse boards and management, explicit goals and publicly available impact assessments, and representation of the communities they serve whenever feasible (like the best community foundations).

Foundations' autonomy allows for support for obscure, unpopular or emergent issues, which is essential. But foundations also must be concerned with the health of the broader charitable sector. Charities are facing their own struggles, which have been exacerbated by the withdrawal of government funding, especially for core operational costs. As many foundations have adopted a "strategic" approach based on their own priorities, they have stopped accepting unsolicited requests. The old formula of foundation grants being used for pilot projects that, once proven, could then be scaled up by government money, has not worked for years. It is well to bear in mind a remark by Darren Walker, president of the Ford Foundation: "We frequently assume that foundations are central protagonists in the story of social change, when, really, they are the supporting cast" (Walker, 2014, para 7). Foundations cannot work without strong community partners, and their granting should reflect this reality.

There are other measures that could help to enhance public trust in foundations. Granting above the mandated quota, or the use of endowment assets for impact investing, could be encouraged and rewarded. The "warehousing of charitable dollars" decried by Carla Funk (Chapter 8), could be countered by sun-setting endowments over a generation or two, so that assets are not accumulated long after respect for "founder intent" loses all meaning. For example, the disbursement quota could be adjusted upward by a few percent each decade, which might shift attention from capital growth to program *impact*.

Philanthropy embodies and promotes many of humanity's most desirable qualities. More than money, its currency is trust. Trust in today's world is not given; it is *earned*. The 2018 Edelman Trust Barometer (2018) echoes this when it concludes that "trust depends on clarity, balance and validation". The chapters in this book not only give examples of why that trust is deserved but also why it must not be taken for granted. We may hope that this book opens a wider discussion on how trust can be earned.

The opening chapter of this book questioned philanthropy's relationship to social inequality, to business and to the state. As far as social inequality is concerned, and the question of whether a larger and more visible foundation sector is cause or effect, Berthiaume and Lefèvre's conclusion in Chapter 12 is incontrovertible: "The context of heightening social inequalities brings back into the public debate the complex, delicate issue of wealth creation and redistribution and, more generally, the role of philanthropy in combating social inequalities". Early in the last century Justice of the US Supreme Court Louis Brandeis warned, "We may have democracy, or we may have wealth concentrated in the hands of the few, but we can't have both" (Louis D Brandeis Legacy Fund for Social Justice, n.d.).

In its relationship to business and the state, the challenge is to collaborate while maintaining foundations' distinctive value propositions: autonomy balanced by accountability, a capacity to connect and collaborate across silos and categories, and the power to share agency and voice with those who are marginalized and excluded in our imperfect society. There is more cross-fertilization now between business and philanthropy, with the growing acceptance of corporate social responsibility (see Cathy Glover's useful examples in Chapter 6) and the emergence of hybrid models of "social enterprise" that seek to both "do well and do good".

There has been less willingness by foundations to engage with governments (and where the effort has been made, as in Quebec, the experience was discouraging). But governments do more than make policy; they create the context and conditions for philanthropy. There is an urgency to improving the way governments function because, in dealing with the effects of massive economic and social dislocation, government is the only collective instrument we have. Collaborative processes like "solution labs" and new social finance instruments are welcome innovations but more attention is needed on how to make government more responsive, nimble and effective.

Philanthropy is most needed when the future is unpredictable, when pressures to address urgent problems absorb most of the available funding, when the insights of the "outliers", the contrarians, the risk-takers are essential. The mantra "let a thousand flowers bloom" may foster creativity and experimentation, but little social value is created if the flowers merely embellish private gardens and gated communities.

The reflex of business is to do *more* (scale, growth!); the reflex of government is to do the *same* (standardize, routinize!). Philanthropy's value must come from asking, "What must we do *differently*?" (question, challenge, innovate!) This book shows that the *how* is as important as the *what*: answers are most often to be found at the edges, where strangers meet, disciplines and ideas collide and creativity flourishes. We don't need philanthropy to do more of the same or to substitute for other sectors; we need philanthropy to ask harder questions and take bigger risks.

References

Edleman (2018) *2018 Edelman Trust Barometer: Global report.* Retrieved from: https://www.edelman.com/trust-barometer

Louis D Brandeis Legacy Fund for Social Justice (n.d.) 'Louis D Brandeis Quotes'. Retrieved December 10, 2018, from: https://www.brandeis.edu/legacy-fund/

Oxfam (2018) 'Richest 1 per cent bagged 82 per cent of wealth created last year – poorest half of humanity got nothing'. Retrieved December 10, 2018, from: https://www.oxfam.org/en/pressroom/pressreleases/2018-01-22/richest-1-percent-bagged-82-percent-wealth-created-last-year

Walker, D (2014) 'Philanthropy in a complex world'. Retrieved December 10, 2018, from: https://www.fordfoundation.org/ideas/equals-change-blog/posts/philanthropy-in-a-complex-world/

Contributors

Jehad Aliweiwi

Jehad Aliweiwi is a strategic thinker with more than 20 years of experience in senior leadership roles in social, settlement, philanthropic and community service organizations.

Since January 2014, Jehad has held the position of executive director with Laidlaw Foundation. For 10 years before that, Jehad was the executive director with Thorncliffe Neighbourhood Office, a multi-service agency in Toronto. Before that, he was regional director, Metro Region of Catholic Cross-Cultural Services. Jehad also worked with the Canadian Arab Federation for eight years, as race relations officer and, later, as executive director.

He has been a trustee of the Ontario Science Centre, a board member of Fred Victor Services, Canadian Council for Refugees and Ontario Council of Agencies Serving Immigrants (OCASI). In 2010 Jehad was the recipient of the Local Hero Award from the Canadian Urban Institute and the 2002 City of Toronto William P Hubbard Race Relations Award.

Annabelle Berthiaume

Annabelle Berthiaume is a doctoral candidate at the School of Social Work at McGill University. Her research focuses on community intervention, the fight against poverty and the increasing emphasis on early childhood in Quebec and Canadian social policies.

Myriam Bérubé

Myriam Bérubé is the director of experimental projects and learning at Centraide of Greater Montreal. One of the main projects she has led is the Collective Impact Project (CIP) since its launch in 2015. She has helped structure the project, and acts as the bridge between communities and the funding and strategic partners that support them.

Myriam is motivated by a deep interest in the development of communities. This interest has had an impact on her personal, academic and professional journey. Over the past 15 years, she has held various positions in management of development projects in Canada and abroad. She studied and worked in Colombia, Mexico, Spain and the Netherlands. She holds a master's degree in Migration and Ethnic Studies from the University of Amsterdam and a bachelor's degree in International Development Studies from McGill.

Tim Brodhead

Tim Brodhead was from 1995 to 2011 president and chief executive officer of the JW McConnell Family Foundation. He continued with the Foundation as a senior fellow of Social Innovation Generation (SIG) until 2013, and was appointed interim president of the Pierre Elliot Trudeau Foundation in 2013–14. In 2001, Tim was appointed an Officer of the Order of Canada.

Currently he is a board member of the Ottawa Community Foundation, the Jarislowsky, Shorefast, Inspirit, OMEGA Foundations, Reconciliation Canada and the Arctic Inspiration Prize Trust. He chairs the advisory board of the MaRS Solutions Lab and is on the advisory boards of Musagetes and the Turtle Island Institute.

François Brouard

François is a bilingual chartered professional accountant with a bachelor's degree in business administration (BAA) from HEC Montréal, a master's degree in accounting (MSc) from Université du Québec à Montréal (UQAM) and a doctorate in business administration (DBA) from Université du Québec à Trois-Rivières (UQTR). He is a full professor in the accounting group (taxation and financial accounting) at the Sprott School of Business, Carleton University and founding director of the Sprott Centre for Social Enterprises (SCSE)/Centre Sprott pour les entreprises sociales (CSES). Between 2009 and 2015, he was the founding co-editor in chief of the *Canadian Journal of Nonprofit and Social Economy Research/Revue canadienne de recherche sur les OBSL et l'économie sociale (ANSERJ),* official journal of ANSER/ARES. His research interests include social entrepreneurship, social enterprises, financial management, governance, foundations, nonprofits, strategic intelligence, SME, tax, business transfer, and the accounting profession.

Laurel Carlton

Laurel Carlton works with organizations and businesses as they bring their ambitious goals to life, through support related to project management and governance. Laurel was a member of the staff team at Community Foundations of Canada between 2014 and 2019, and as director, Strategic Initiatives, she developed and led pan-Canadian collaborations between community foundations, the government of Canada and the private sector. Those initiatives included the Community Fund for Canada's 150th as well as several subsequent grantmaking programs. Laurel was also a member of the team that incubated the Rideau Hall Foundation. Before her time at CFC, Laurel held roles related to research and project management in the charitable sector, working in both Canada and Guatemala. Laurel has a master's of Public Administration (MPA) from the School of Public Policy and Administration at Carleton University.

Stephen Couchman

Stephen Couchman has been committed to making a difference in the social sector for more than 25 years. For 18 of those years he was at the helm of a private foundation granting across Canada to a mission to enable low-income and challenged children, families and seniors to enrich and strengthen their lives through arts, education, health and entrepreneurial opportunities. He is a founding director and chair of the Circle on Philanthropy and Aboriginal Peoples in Canada, and advisor to Ashoka Canada and Futurpreneur (formerly Canadian Youth Business Foundation). Stephen has written regularly on sector issues and is currently working in Bhutan on the restoration of a historic trail combining his passion for history, the outdoors and learning about measures of gross national happiness.

Peter R. Elson

Peter is adjunct assistant professor, School of Public Administration, University of Victoria. In 2019, he completed a two-year graduate certificate in Indigenous Nationhood. He is co-lead with Jean-Marc of UQAM on the six-year SSHRC Partnership Project (2018–24), focusing on the impact of grantmaking foundations in Canada on environmental issues and social inequalities.

Between 2010 and 2015 Peter and co-author Peter Hall collaborated with provincial partners to conduct the first comprehensive survey of social enterprises across Canada (http://sess.ca/). Peter is author of *High Ideals and Noble Intentions: Voluntary Sector–Government Relations in Canada* (2011), and editor of *Funding Policies and the Nonprofit Sector in Western Canada* (2016), both published by the University of Toronto Press.

Peter acknowledges that he resides on the unceded territory of the Lekwungen peoples and the Songees, Xwsepsum (Esquimault), and WSÁNEĆ peoples, who continue to care for their homeland and waterways.

Jean-Marc Fontan

Jean-Marc Fontan, PhD, sociology and anthropology, teaches economic sociology at *Université du Québec à Montréal* (UQAM). Since 2000, he has been an active member in the *Centre de recherche sur les innovations sociales* (http://crises.uqam.ca/presentation-en), a world-leading francophone research organization on social innovation. From 2003 to 2010, he co-led, with Nancy Neamtan, previous director of *Chantier de l'économie sociale*, a *Social economy research consortium* financed by *Social Sciences and Humanities Research Council* of Canada (SSHRC). Since 2006, he has led a social innovation book collection at *Presses de l'Université du Québec* (https://www.puq.ca/catalogue/collections/liste-innovation-sociale-39.html). Since 2010, Jean-Marc has studied Canadian philanthropy. In 2013, with Peter Elson, from University of Victoria, he co-directed an important SSHRC research project on Canadian grantmaking foundations, and established, in 2018, with SSHRC grant support and in partnership with philanthropic organizations, the *Canadian Philanthropy Partnership Research Network*, a pan-Canadian research organization dedicated to knowledge mobilization on philanthropic foundations (https://philab.uqam.ca/?lang=en).

Carla Funk

Associate faculty at Royal Roads University, Carla Funk studied private aid in Tanzania, partially examining how donor decisions influence nonprofits. Funk works at Islands Trust Conservancy in BC, preserving and protecting the distinctive islands of the Salish Sea. A Mitacs scholar, she completed a partnership with Development Action Canada (2017) translating her doctoral research into leadership skills training workshops for nonprofits. These workshops have been conducted at a national level in Canada and used in the US and five African countries (2018). On behalf of the Canadian philanthropic sector she researched and authored *Doing Good for Business – The inclusion of philanthropy in the Canadian professional advisor business practice* (2018).

Nonprofit management and philanthropy are recurring themes throughout Funk's career, and she is increasingly focusing her attention on the value and complexities of creating learning organizations. In her spare time she manages the knowledge-sharing network Transform International Canada, working with community partners in eight countries.

Cathy Glover

Cathy Glover was the director of Community Investment and the Suncor Energy Foundation (SEF) for more than 16 years. It was a position she came to in 2001, following 20 years of experience working in the nonprofit and charitable sector in Calgary. By working both inside and outside the organization to help address questions about Suncor's role in Truth and Reconciliation, and by providing support for Indigenous youth, Cathy was gifted the name of Aahpii Pitahgii (White Eagle Woman) by Elder Casey Eagle Speaker, also known as Sorrel Horse of the Kainai Nation.

As Changemaker in Residence at Mount Royal University, Cathy has the space to act as a catalyst, mentor, facilitator, teacher and contributor. Cathy has a BSc in psychology and an MBA, both from the University of Calgary. She is currently completing an MFA in creative non-fiction at University of King's College in Halifax.

Roberta L Jamieson

A Mohawk from the Six Nations of the Grand River Territory in Ontario, Roberta Jamieson is the president and CEO of Indspire, one of Canada's premier charities. She spearheaded the creation of the K-12 Indspire Institute to support educators and ensure Indigenous students graduate and, under her leadership, Indspire has disbursed almost $100 million in bursaries to more than 32,000 Indigenous students.

Throughout her career, Roberta Jamieson has shown an ability to lead in a complex environment, as a lawyer, mediator, Chief of her community, board member and international thought-leader, forging partnerships between the public and private sectors to create and sustain change.

Jamieson served as the Ombudsman of Ontario between 1989 and 1999, is an Officer of the Order of Canada and recipient of numerous awards. In 2018 Roberta was appointed to the Gender Equality Advisory Council during Canada's Presidency of the G7 Summit.

Marcel Lauzière

For much of his career, Marcel Lauzière has led national umbrella organizations: the Canadian Federation for the Humanities & Social Sciences, the Canadian Council on Social Development, and Imagine Canada.

He has also been a senior civil servant in Canada and abroad as special advisor to the president at the Social Sciences and Humanities Research Council, and as assistant deputy minister in the New Zealand Ministry of Social Development. He is currently CEO of the Lawson Foundation.

Marcel's volunteer service on boards include: the International Council of Social Welfare, the Accounting Standards Oversight Council and the Public Policy Forum. He is currently chair of the board at YMCA Canada. Marcel was awarded the Queen Elizabeth Jubilee Medal (2012) and the Governor General's Cross for Meritorious Service (2016) for his contributions to the charitable sector.

He holds an MA in history from the University of Ottawa and an honorary degree from George Brown College.

Bruce Lawson

Bruce Lawson has been president of the Counselling Foundation of Canada since October 2008. He also serves as executive officer of CERIC, an organization that advances career development in Canada, and is an ex-officio member of the CERIC board of directors.

Bruce is a founder of Foundation House, a collaborative workspace housing three foundations and several charitable and nonprofit network organizations in Toronto. He was part of the steering committee that co-authored the Philanthropic Community's Declaration of Action presented at the closing event of the Truth & Reconciliation Commission in 2015. In 2019, he was appointed to the federal government's Advisory Committee on the Charitable Sector (ACCS). He is also a past chair of the board of Philanthropic Foundations Canada (PFC).

Before joining the Foundation, Bruce provided meeting planning, project management and communications services to a variety of corporations, associations and not-for-profit organizations.

Sylvain A. Lefèvre

Sylvain A. Lefèvre holds a doctorate in political science and is a tenured professor in the Département de stratégie, responsabilité sociale et environnementale at Université du Québec à Montréal. His research focuses on the transformations of collective action and the role of philanthropic foundations. He is currently a researcher at PhiLab, where he was scientific director from 2015 to 2018. He is also the director of CRISES (Centre de recherche sur les innovations sociales) and co-chairs TIESS (Territoires innovants en économie sociale et solidaire), an organization that bridges research and practice communities in Quebec.

Sara Lyons

Sara Lyons is vice-president, Strategic Initiatives for Community Foundations of Canada (CFC). Sara has been with Canada's community foundation movement for more than a decade. She has worked in local community foundations as well as at the national leadership organization. Over her years with CFC, Sara has played a leadership role in bringing foundations together for impact, often in partnership with the corporate sector and government, such as through the Community Foundations of Canada *Vital Signs*, the Youth Catalyst Fund and the Welcome Fund for Syrian Refugees programs.

A graduate of McGill and the University of Toronto, she is a frequent speaker on philanthropy, innovation, and social finance. Sara is currently the co-chair of the Circle on Philanthropy and Aboriginal Peoples in Canada, a charity that transforms philanthropy and contributes to positive change with Indigenous communities by creating spaces of learning, innovation, relationship-building, co-creation, and activation.

Natalie Ord

Natalie Ord has worked in philanthropy over eight years and was most recently the Manager of Learning and Evaluation at Vancouver Foundation. In that position she created space for relationship-building and learning around complex issues, ideas and feelings. Before that she was the grant administrator and then coordinator of the Fostering Change initiative. She holds a master's degree in urban studies and recently completed a Certificate in Social Innovation, both from Simon Fraser University. She was born and raised in Vancouver and is grateful to live and work on the unceded and occupied territories of the Musqueam, Squamish and Tsleil-Waututh peoples.

Hilary M Pearson

Hilary Pearson has had a 20-year career in the field of foundation philanthropy in Canada. She was the founding president of Philanthropic Foundations Canada, a position that she held for almost 18 years, and in which capacity she has worked with and been a strategic advisor to many of the largest private charitable foundations in the country.

Author of numerous articles and reviews on foundation philanthropy, Ms Pearson also speaks frequently at conferences and workshops in Canada and across the world. She currently serves as co-chair of the federal Advisory Committee on the Charitable Sector, advising the federal government on policy and regulatory issues for the charitable sector.

In July 2018, she was appointed to the Order of Canada for her contributions to building the field of philanthropy in Canada.

She has a BA and MA in political economy from the University of Toronto, and honorary doctorates from Carleton University and the University of New Brunswick.

Nancy Pole

Nancy Pole is an independent consultant (www.co-spire.ca) supporting evaluation, learning, strategy and operations across a variety of collaborative endeavours. In her work with foundations, nonprofits and public-sector organizations, she brings a particular focus on philanthropy and public policy and on place-based, cross-sector strategies for poverty reduction.

The chapter that she co-wrote for this book draws upon the findings of a commissioned action research project Nancy carried out with Jean-Marc Fontan of PhiLab. Through other research mandates with PhiLab, Nancy investigated foundation collaborations as well as other expressions of place-based philanthropy.

Nancy holds a master's degree in philanthropy and nonprofit leadership (Carleton University), and completed graduate programs in social innovation (University of Waterloo) and community economic development (Concordia University).

Marc Pilon

Marc obtained his PhD from the Sprott School of Business, Carleton University. He is an assistant professor in the Department of Accounting, Faculty of Management at Laurentian University, teaching financial accounting and assurance courses in English and French. He obtained his Chartered Professional Accountant designation in 2009 and previously worked as a manager in public accounting. He is a member of the Sprott Centre for Social Enterprises (SCSE)/Centre Sprott pour les entreprises sociales (CSES). His research interests include accountability and governance in nonprofits, social enterprises and the health care sector.

Diane Roussin

Diane Roussin is a dedicated community leader and a proud member of the Skownan First Nation. Diane has worked tirelessly for over two decades, primarily in Winnipeg's inner city, with organizations and projects that respect the ability and the right of Indigenous families, children and individuals to care for themselves and thrive. Diane is the project director for The Winnipeg

Boldness Project, a research and development project focusing on improving outcomes for children in the North End of Winnipeg, through social innovation and social lab processes. Diane holds bachelor of arts and bachelor of social work degrees. In January 2018, Diane received the Governor General's Award for Outstanding Indigenous Leadership. Also in 2018, Diane presented at TEDx Winnipeg on the topic of Indigenous social innovation. She is a cherished member of a large extended family and a loving mother of two daughters whom she adores.

Gladys Rowe

Gladys Rowe, MSW, PhD candidate is a Muskego Inninew Iskwe (Swampy Cree woman) of mixed ancestry with membership in Fox Lake Cree Nation in Northern Manitoba. Her research interests and experiences include identity development, personal and ancestral stories and cultural practices as mechanisms for healing and decolonization, and wellbeing across the lifespan. Gladys has worked for more than 12 years in community-driven, Indigenous-grounded and Indigenist-founded research projects. From these experiences she has been able to build her knowledge and skills to work as the lead with several projects and organizations in the design and implementation of evaluation and research based on Indigenous ways of knowing, being, feeling and doing. These projects have graciously invited her to be a part of important community building that leaves a trail for others to build their own work upon. These are experiences based on respect, trust, love, courage, humility, reciprocity, and responsibility.

Kelli Stevens

Kelli Stevens first came to know her co-author Cathy Glover at Suncor Energy, where Kelli worked in corporate communications – she and Cathy worked together on files related to corporate social responsibility. Kelli eventually left Suncor to pursue a master's of social work focused on community development, and to manage a multi-stakeholder youth gang-prevention project. She also gained experience with the Institute for Community Prosperity and the Trico Changemakers Studio at Mount Royal University, and by volunteering with several organizations in both "frontline" and governance-related positions.

Marilyn Struthers

Marilyn Struthers is a long-time writer, researcher and organizer in the nonprofit sector. She worked as a funder for the Ontario Trillium Foundation's (OTF) province-wide program for many years and through this work she became alert to inequities in funding Indigenous communities. With support from OTF, she helped to establish the Circle on Philanthropy and Aboriginal Peoples in Canada, becoming a founding member of the Governing Circle. She continued this engagement as the Eaton Chair of Social Innovation at Ryerson University, and continues now as a volunteer in the Circle's research program. Marilyn lives a stone's throw from Georgian Bay on the traditional territories of the Saugeen Ojibway Nation and currently works in her freelance practice.

Justin Wiebe

Justin Wiebe is Michif (Métis) from Saskatoon in Treaty 6 and Métis Territory, and currently lives in Toronto in territories covered by the Dish with One Spoon Wampum Belt Covenant. Justin is passionate about rethinking philanthropy, youth leadership, and building movements of solidarity across different communities. He currently works at Mastercard Foundation co-developing and delivering the EleV program, which focuses on improving Indigenous youth education and employment outcomes in pursuit of living the good life. Justin formerly worked at Ontario Trillium Foundation, is a current member of the governing circle of the Circle on Philanthropy and Aboriginal Peoples, and a co-founder of the Mamawi Project.

Contributors

Jehad Aliweiwi
Annabelle Berthiaume
Myriam Bérubé
Tim Brodhead
François Brouard
Laurel Carlton
Steven Couchman
Peter R. Elson
Jean-Marc Fontan
Carla Funk
Cathy Glover
Roberta L Jamieson
Marcel Lauzière
Bruce Lawson
Sylvain A. Lefèvre
Sara Lyons
Natalie Ord
Hilary M Pearson
Nancy Pole
Marc Pilon
Diane Roussin
Gladys Rowe
Kelli Stevens
Marilyn Struthers
Justin Wiebe

Edited by
Peter R. Elson
Sylvain A. Lefèvre
Jean-Marc Fontan

Manufactured by Amazon.ca
Bolton, ON